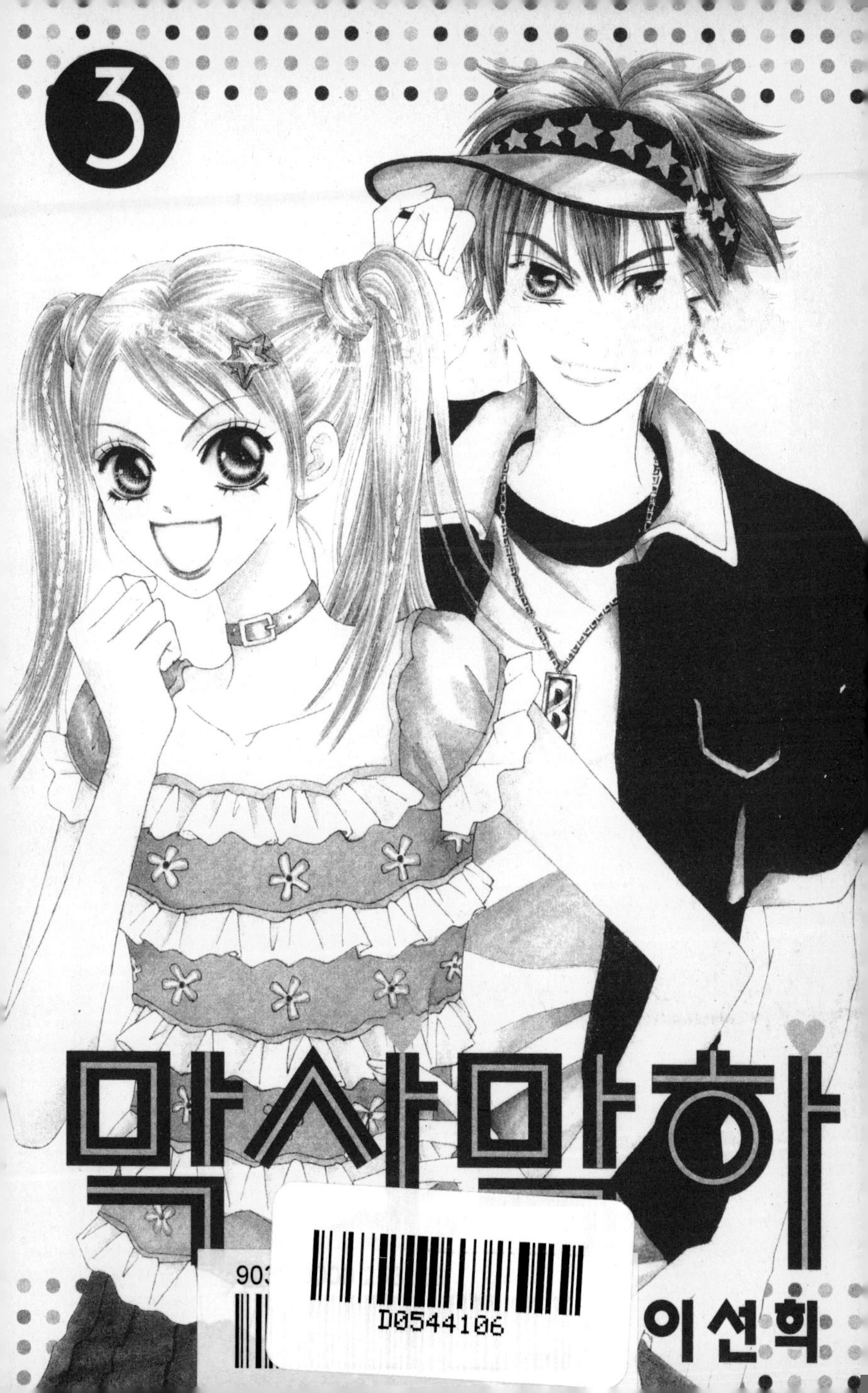
3
막상막하
이선희

Neck and Neck

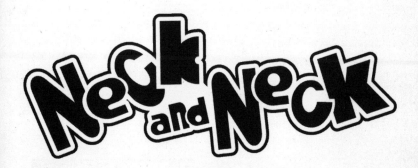

Neck and Neck Vol. 3
Created by Lee Sun-Hee

Translation - Sunah Kim Schultz
English Adaptation - Tim Beedle
Copy Editor - Suzanne Waldman
Retouch and Lettering - Eva Han
Production Artist - James Lee
Cover Design - Anna Kernbaum

Editor - Tim Beedle
Digital Imaging Manager - Chris Buford
Pre-Press Manager - Antonio DePietro
Production Managers - Jennifer Miller and Mutsumi Miyazaki
Art Director - Matt Alford
Managing Editor - Jill Freshney
VP of Production - Ron Klamert
Editor-in-Chief - Mike Kiley
President and C.O.O. - John Parker
Publisher and C.E.O. - Stuart Levy

A **TOKYOPOP**® Manga

TOKYOPOP Inc.
5900 Wilshire Blvd. Suite 2000
Los Angeles, CA 90036

E-mail: info@TOKYOPOP.com
Come visit us online at www.TOKYOPOP.com

ISBN: 1-59532-255-8

First TOKYOPOP printing: June 2005
10 9 8 7 6 5 4 3 2 1
Printed in the USA

Vol. 3

**by
Lee Sun-Hee**

HAMBURG // LONDON // LOS ANGELES // TOKYO

My name is Dabin Choi, and I'm 15 years old. All my life, I've lived with my father, and I can't imagine things any other way. Now, if you didn't know, my dad is kind of... special. He's the boss of one of the largest and most powerful organized crime families in Korea. He's really a sweetheart, though! Seriously!

Why doesn't anyone ever believe me about this?

Oh well, back to the matter at hand. My father has a lot of people working for him. So many, in fact, that I can hardly even remember all their names...with one big, glaring, oh-so-beautiful exception. Eugene Sung's father and my father were good friends when they were younger. The two of us pretty much grew up together. When he became a teenager, Daddy gave Eugene a job helping him handle some of his more legitimate business deals. This meant that I got to see Eugene a lot more, but it still wasn't enough for me. You see, if it's not obvious by now, I have the world's biggest crush on Eugene, and I won't be satisfied until he's fallen completely head over heels for me.

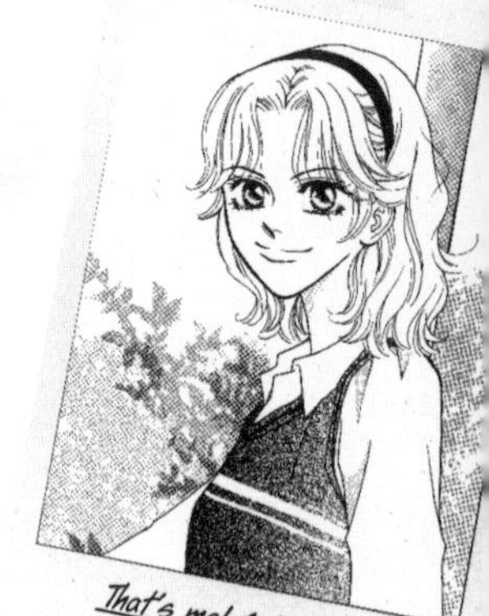

That's me! Cute, eh?

The problem is that Eugene views me as a little sister rather than a potential prom date. To change this, I convinced my father to allow me to transfer to Eugene's high school (when you're Daddy's ONLY little girl, these sort of requests come easily). However, this hasn't proven to be the thrill that I thought it would be. Yes, Eugene and I have gotten a lot closer, and yes, I've made some great new friends. However, I've also made an enemy—Shihu Myoung.

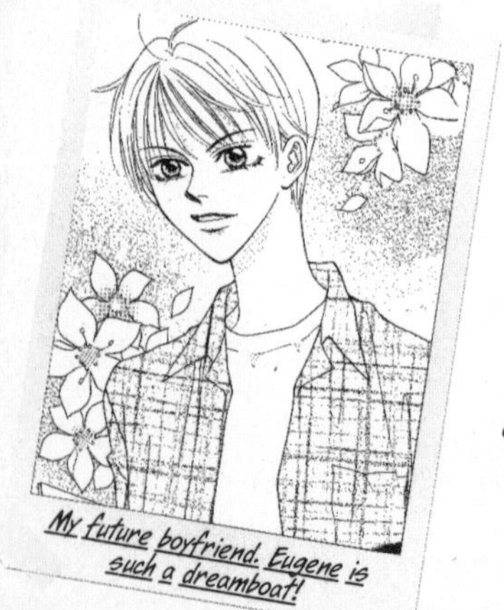

My future boyfriend. Eugene is such a dreamboat!

You see, Shihu's father and my father used to be partners. Daddy doesn't like to talk about it, but several years ago, they had some sort of falling out and now they're enemies. My dad would kill me if he knew I was in his son's class! Even worse, Shihu seems intent on making my life a living hell.

Neck and Neck

Story So Far

He's not the only one, either. A problem from my past has reemerged—a nasty little nightmare who calls herself Black Rose.

I think it's time for a little history lesson. Before I transferred to Eugene's school, the only drama in my life came from Black Rose. Personally, I think she's jealous of me, but whatever the reason, never a day went by when Rose didn't put gum in my hair or start some nasty rumor about me. (Except for Thursdays. Rose always seemed to leave me alone on Thursdays. I don't know why. Maybe Thursday was her Prozac day or something.)

Anyhow, she's been running rampant at my new school, and that spells trouble. Particularly since she's been spotted with Minhyuk Kwon. Minhyuk is the Captain of the Senior Class, but he's a real jerk. (He scared people into voting for him.) I really don't want to think of what Minhyuk and Rose are capable of when they put their filthy minds together, but lately, it seems I have no choice.

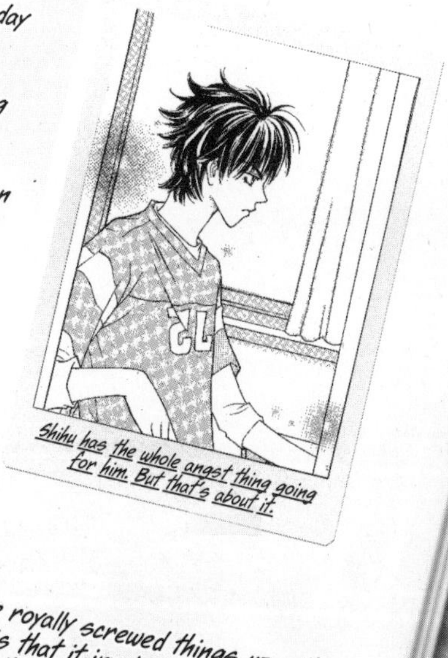

Shihu has the whole angst thing going for him. But that's about it.

And to top everything off, I've royally screwed things up with Eugene. All you need to know is that it involved a Kendo stick and Eugene's butt. Trust me, the less said about it the better. However, Eugene's angry with me, and it seems like I can't even talk to him these days without embarrassing myself.

Yeah, I know. So what else is new, right?

C·O·N·T·E·N·T·S

Neck and Neck

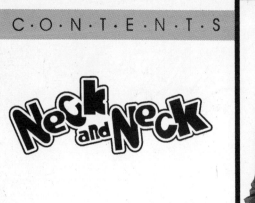

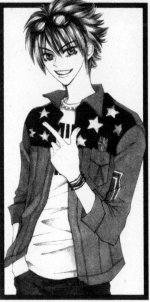

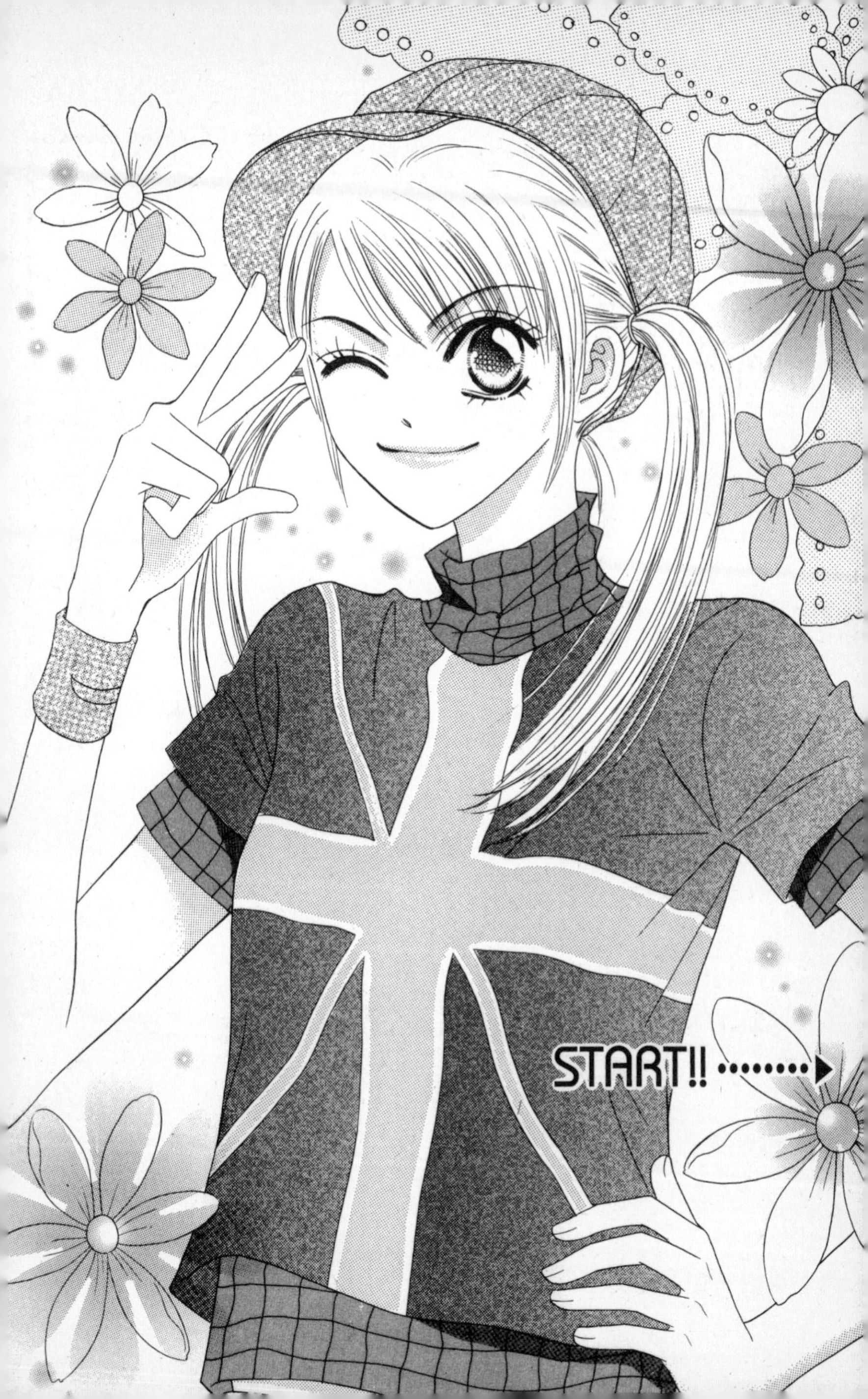
START!! ....▸

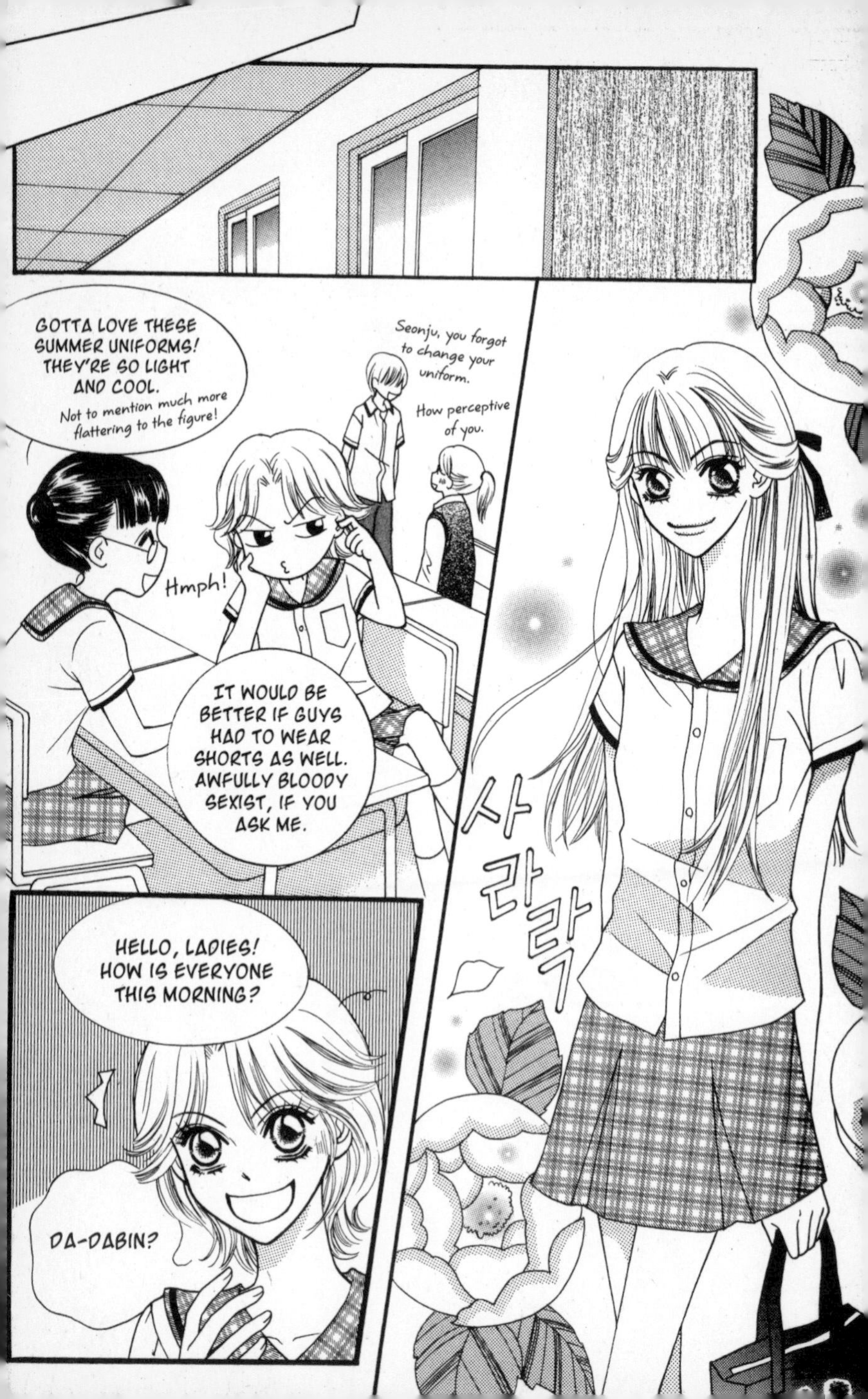
GOTTA LOVE THESE SUMMER UNIFORMS! THEY'RE SO LIGHT AND COOL.
Not to mention much more flattering to the figure!
Seonju, you forgot to change your uniform.
How perceptive of you.
Hmph!
IT WOULD BE BETTER IF GUYS HAD TO WEAR SHORTS AS WELL. AWFULLY BLOODY SEXIST, IF YOU ASK ME.
HELLO, LADIES! HOW IS EVERYONE THIS MORNING?
DA-DABIN?
사라락

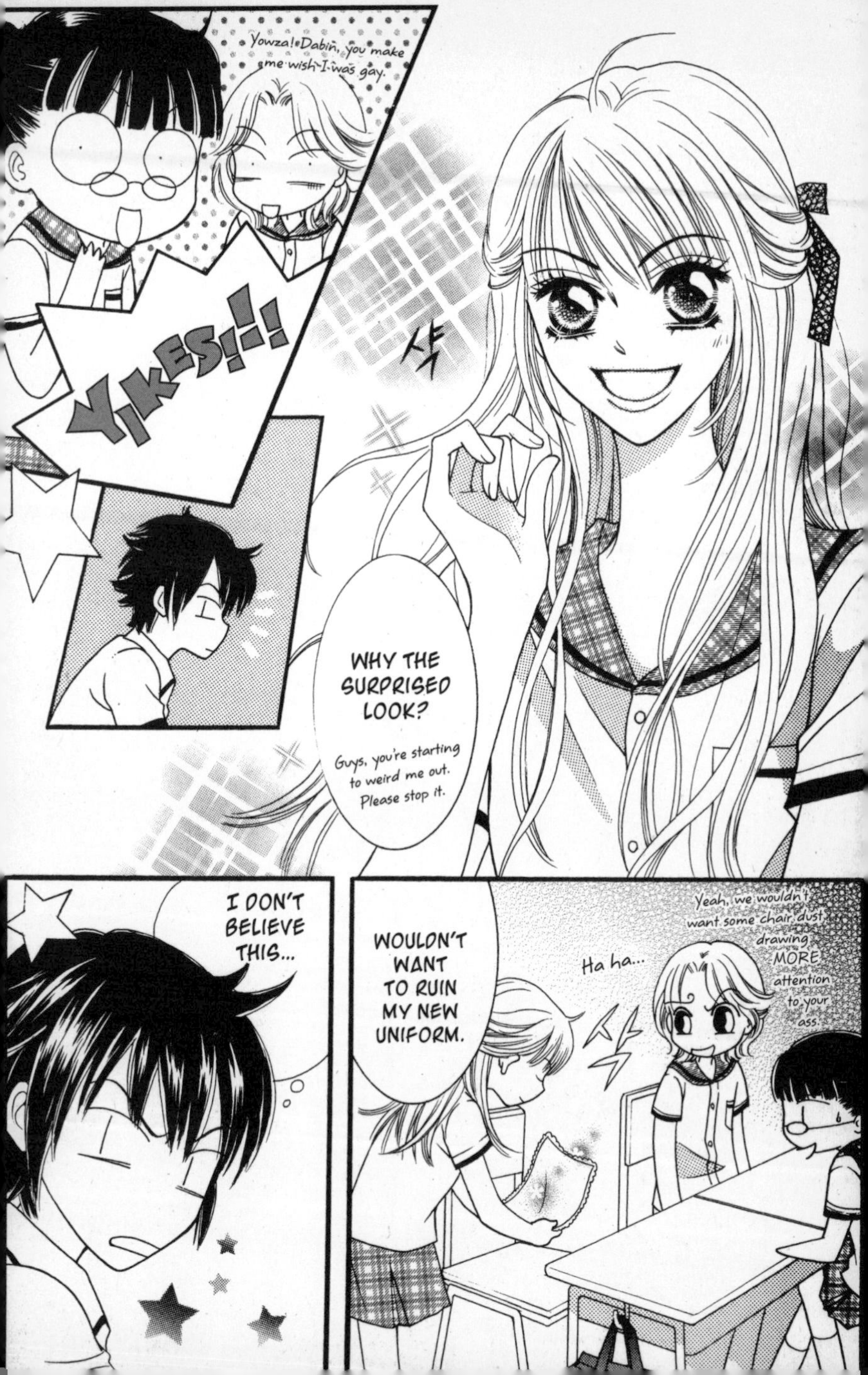
Yowza! Dabin, you make me wish I was gay.
YIKES!!!
WHY THE SURPRISED LOOK?
Guys, you're starting to weird me out. Please stop it.
I DON'T BELIEVE THIS...
WOULDN'T WANT TO RUIN MY NEW UNIFORM.
Ha ha...
Yeah, we wouldn't want some chair dust drawing MORE attention to your ass.

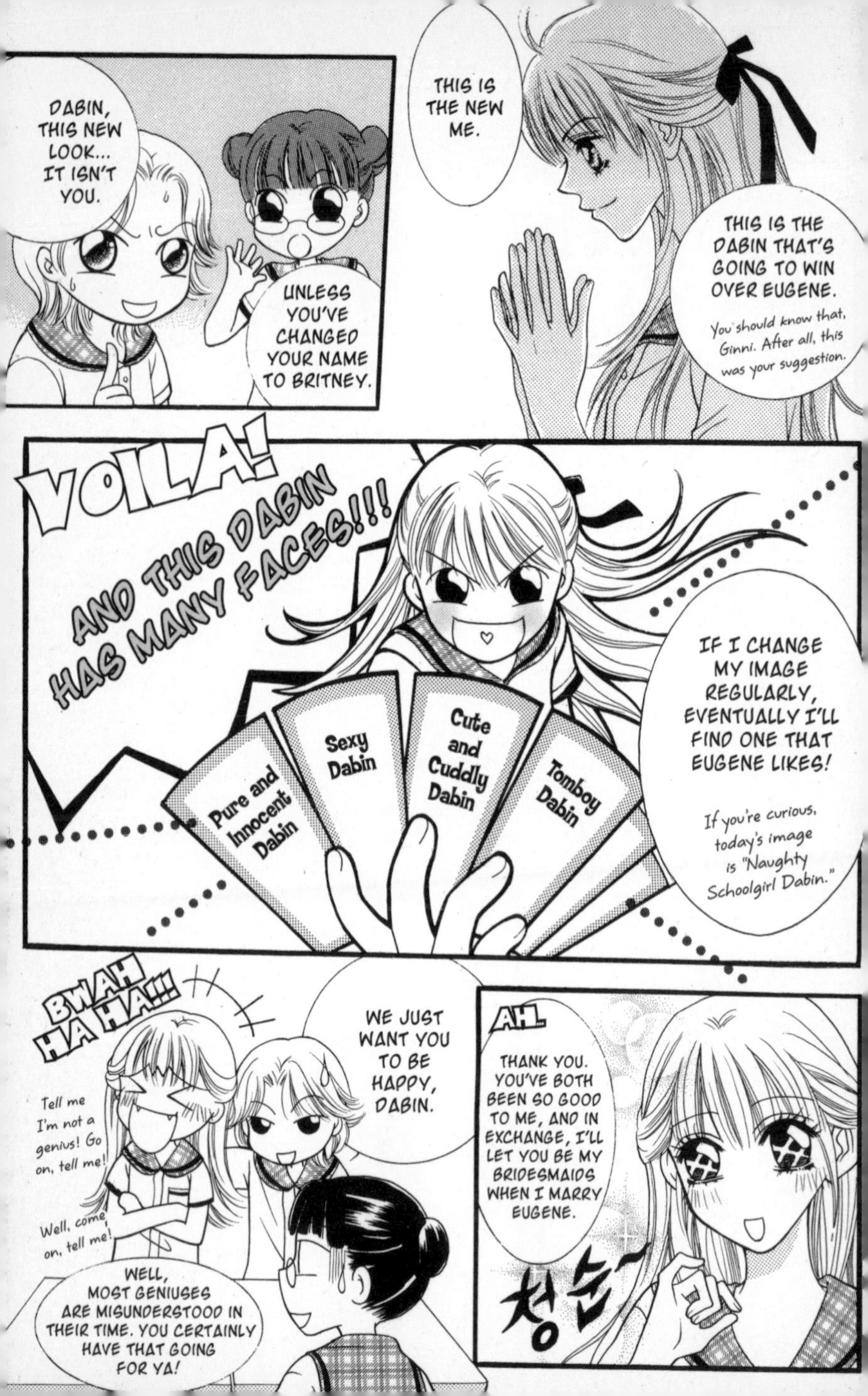
DABIN, THIS NEW LOOK... IT ISN'T YOU.
UNLESS YOU'VE CHANGED YOUR NAME TO BRITNEY.
THIS IS THE NEW ME.
THIS IS THE DABIN THAT'S GOING TO WIN OVER EUGENE.
You should know that, Ginni. After all, this was your suggestion.
VOILA!
AND THIS DABIN HAS MANY FACES!!!
Pure and Innocent Dabin
Sexy Dabin
Cute and Cuddly Dabin
Tomboy Dabin
IF I CHANGE MY IMAGE REGULARLY, EVENTUALLY I'LL FIND ONE THAT EUGENE LIKES!
If you're curious, today's image is "Naughty Schoolgirl Dabin."
BWAH HA HA!!!
Tell me I'm not a genius! Go on, tell me!
Well, come on, tell me!
WE JUST WANT YOU TO BE HAPPY, DABIN.
WELL, MOST GENIUSES ARE MISUNDERSTOOD IN THEIR TIME. YOU CERTAINLY HAVE THAT GOING FOR YA!
AH.
THANK YOU. YOU'VE BOTH BEEN SO GOOD TO ME, AND IN EXCHANGE, I'LL LET YOU BE MY BRIDESMAIDS WHEN I MARRY EUGENE.
청순~

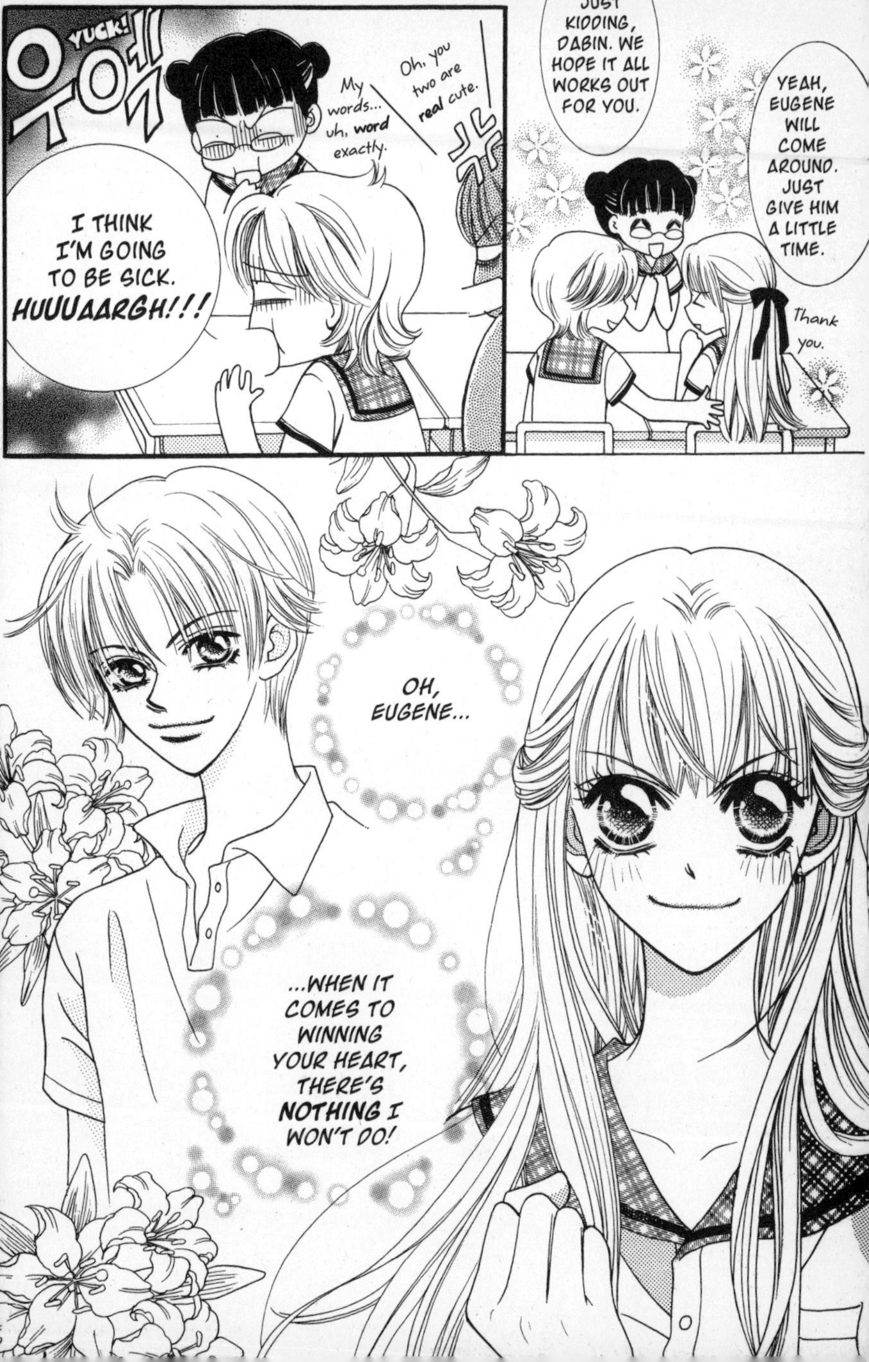
YUCK!
I THINK I'M GOING TO BE SICK. **HUUUAARGH!!!**
My words... uh, **word** exactly.
Oh, you two are **real** cute.
JUST KIDDING, DABIN. WE HOPE IT ALL WORKS OUT FOR YOU.
YEAH, EUGENE WILL COME AROUND. JUST GIVE HIM A LITTLE TIME.
Thank you.
OH, EUGENE...
...WHEN IT COMES TO WINNING YOUR HEART, THERE'S **NOTHING** I WON'T DO!

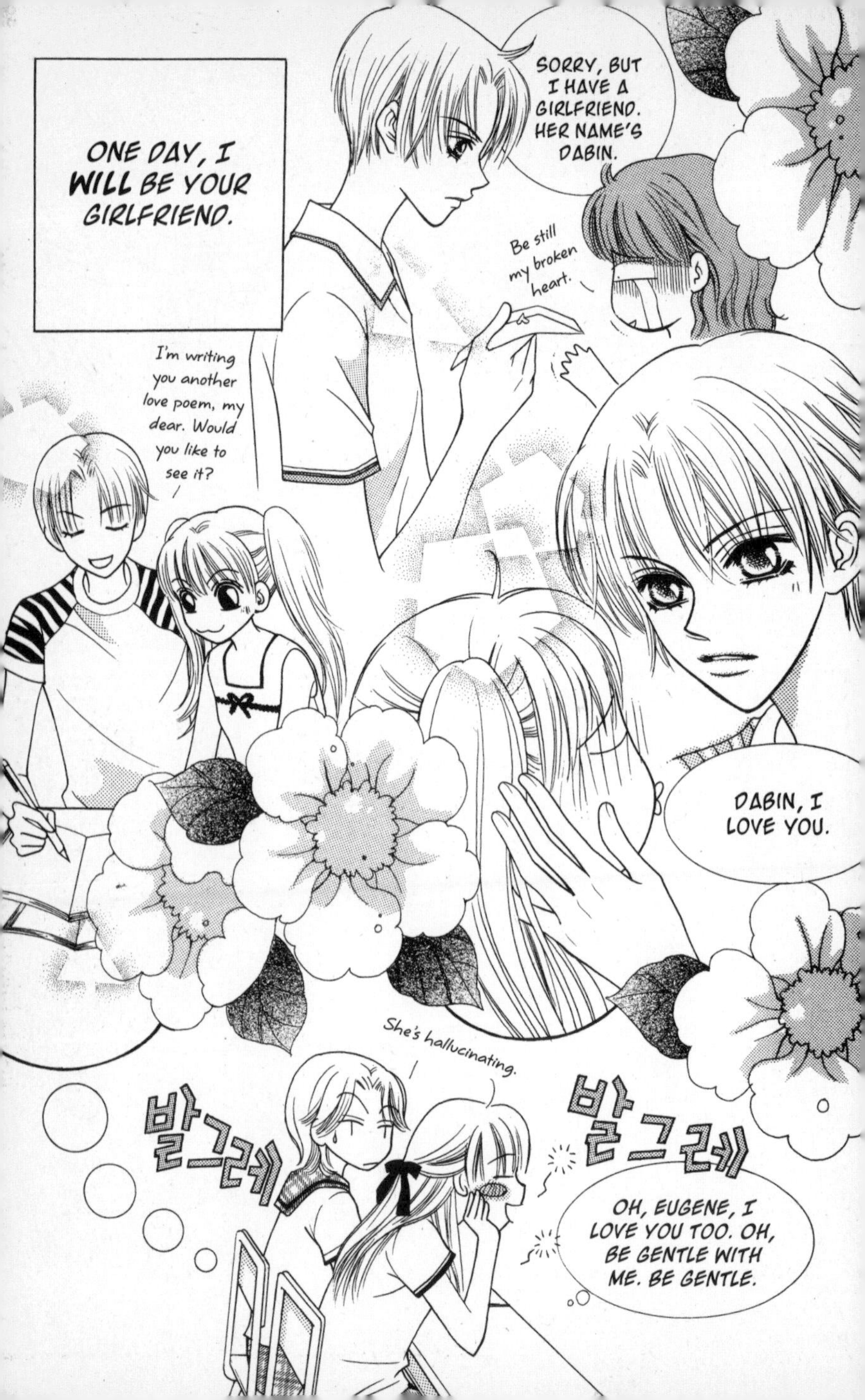
ONE DAY, I **WILL** BE YOUR GIRLFRIEND.
SORRY, BUT I HAVE A GIRLFRIEND. HER NAME'S DABIN.
Be still my broken heart.
I'm writing you another love poem, my dear. Would you like to see it?
DABIN, I LOVE YOU.
She's hallucinating.
발그레
발그레
OH, EUGENE, I LOVE YOU TOO. OH, BE GENTLE WITH ME. BE GENTLE.

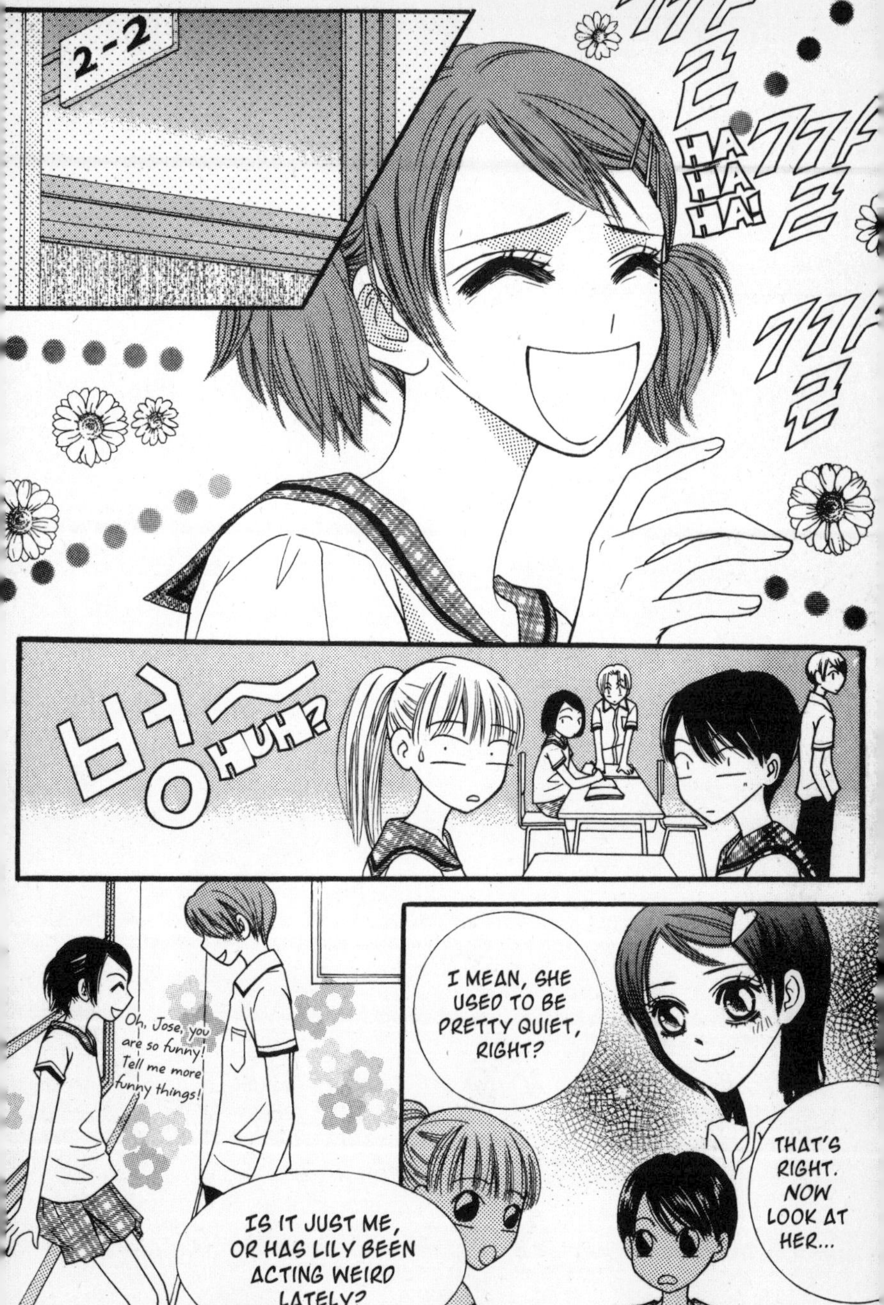
2-2
HA HA HA!
벙~
HUH?
Oh, Jose, you are so funny! Tell me more funny things!
IS IT JUST ME, OR HAS LILY BEEN ACTING WEIRD LATELY?
I MEAN, SHE USED TO BE PRETTY QUIET, RIGHT?
THAT'S RIGHT. NOW LOOK AT HER...

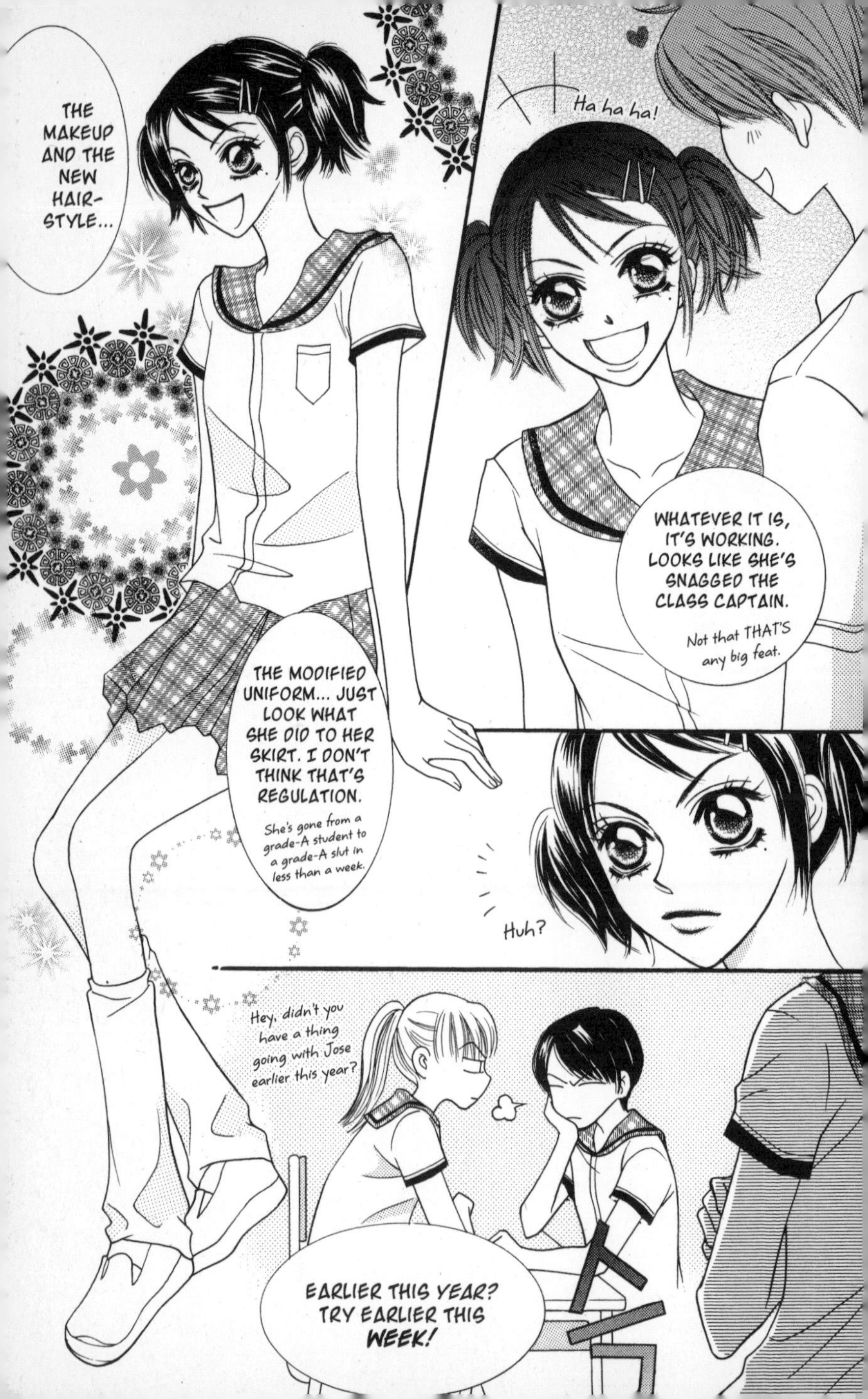
THE MAKEUP AND THE NEW HAIR-STYLE...
THE MODIFIED UNIFORM... JUST LOOK WHAT SHE DID TO HER SKIRT. I DON'T THINK THAT'S REGULATION.
She's gone from a grade-A student to a grade-A slut in less than a week.
Ha ha ha!
WHATEVER IT IS, IT'S WORKING. LOOKS LIKE SHE'S SNAGGED THE CLASS CAPTAIN.
Not that THAT'S any big feat.
Huh?
Hey, didn't you have a thing going with Jose earlier this year?
EARLIER THIS YEAR? TRY EARLIER THIS WEEK!

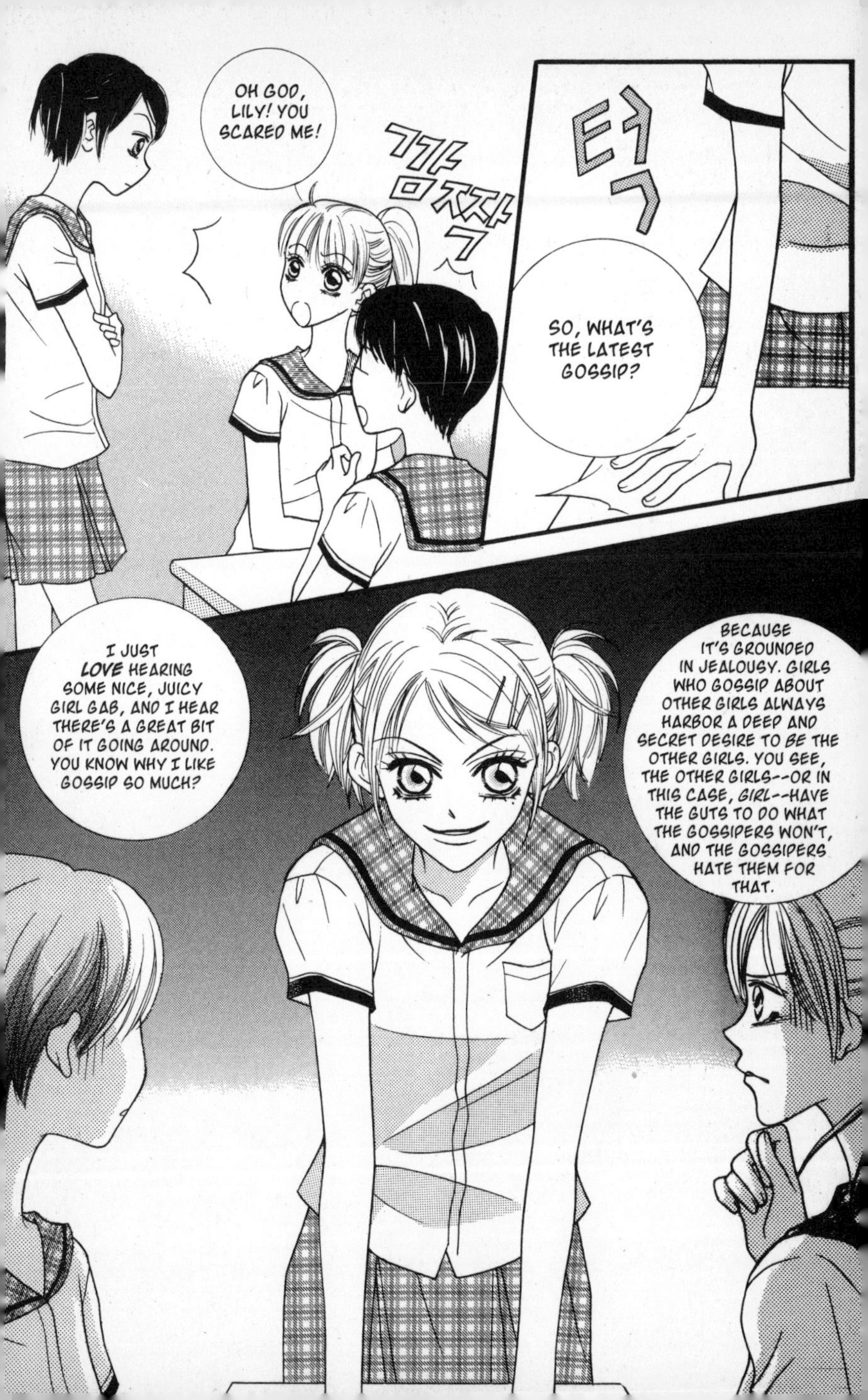
OH GOD, LILY! YOU SCARED ME!
깜짝
턱
SO, WHAT'S THE LATEST GOSSIP?
I JUST *LOVE* HEARING SOME NICE, JUICY GIRL GAB, AND I HEAR THERE'S A GREAT BIT OF IT GOING AROUND. YOU KNOW WHY I LIKE GOSSIP SO MUCH?
BECAUSE IT'S GROUNDED IN JEALOUSY. GIRLS WHO GOSSIP ABOUT OTHER GIRLS ALWAYS HARBOR A DEEP AND SECRET DESIRE TO BE THE OTHER GIRLS. YOU SEE, THE OTHER GIRLS--OR IN THIS CASE, *GIRL*--HAVE THE GUTS TO DO WHAT THE GOSSIPERS WON'T, AND THE GOSSIPERS HATE THEM FOR THAT.

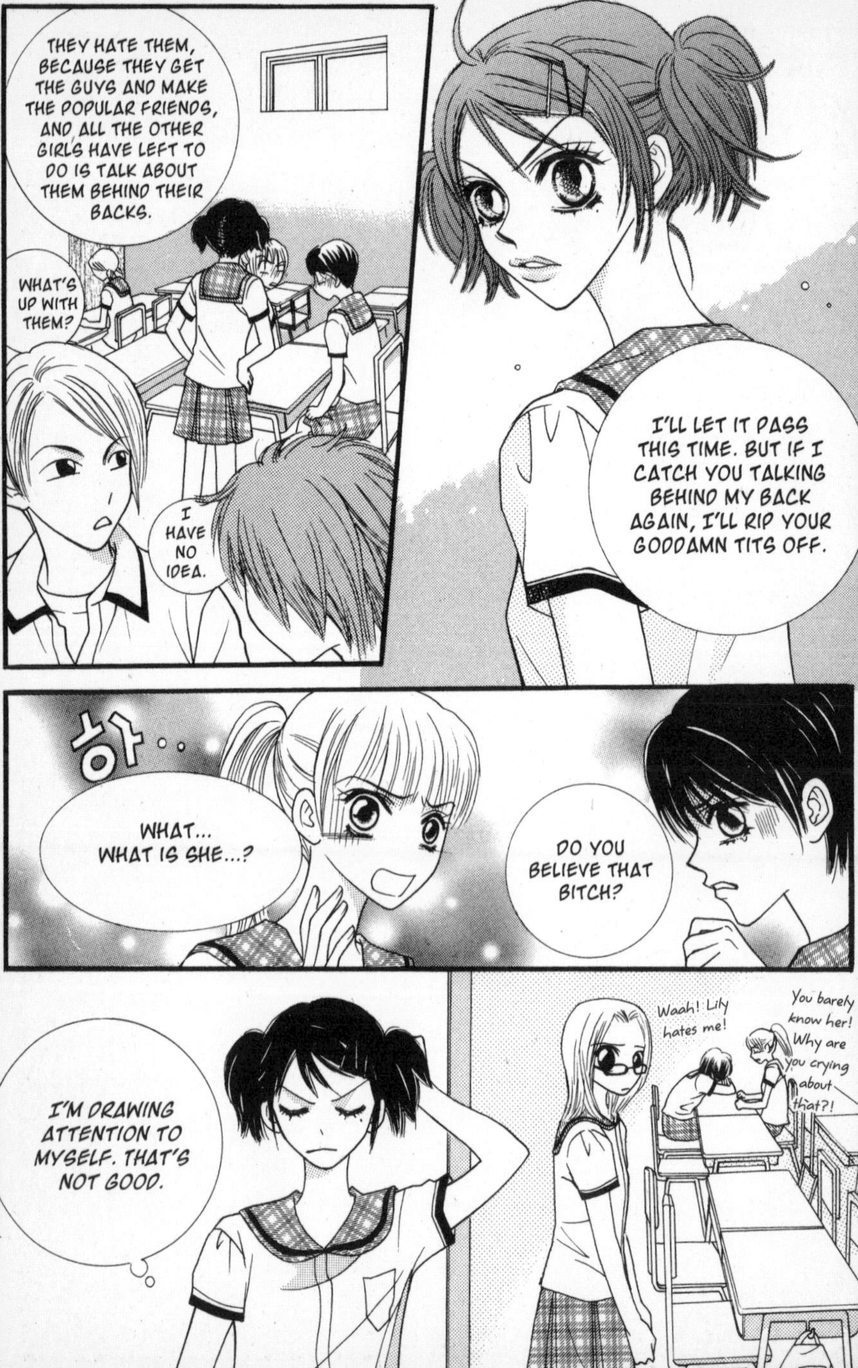
THEY HATE THEM, BECAUSE THEY GET THE GUYS AND MAKE THE POPULAR FRIENDS, AND ALL THE OTHER GIRLS HAVE LEFT TO DO IS TALK ABOUT THEM BEHIND THEIR BACKS.
WHAT'S UP WITH THEM?
I HAVE NO IDEA.
I'LL LET IT PASS THIS TIME. BUT IF I CATCH YOU TALKING BEHIND MY BACK AGAIN, I'LL RIP YOUR GODDAMN TITS OFF.
하..
WHAT... WHAT IS SHE...?
DO YOU BELIEVE THAT BITCH?
I'M DRAWING ATTENTION TO MYSELF. THAT'S NOT GOOD.
Waah! Lily hates me!
You barely know her! Why are you crying about that?!

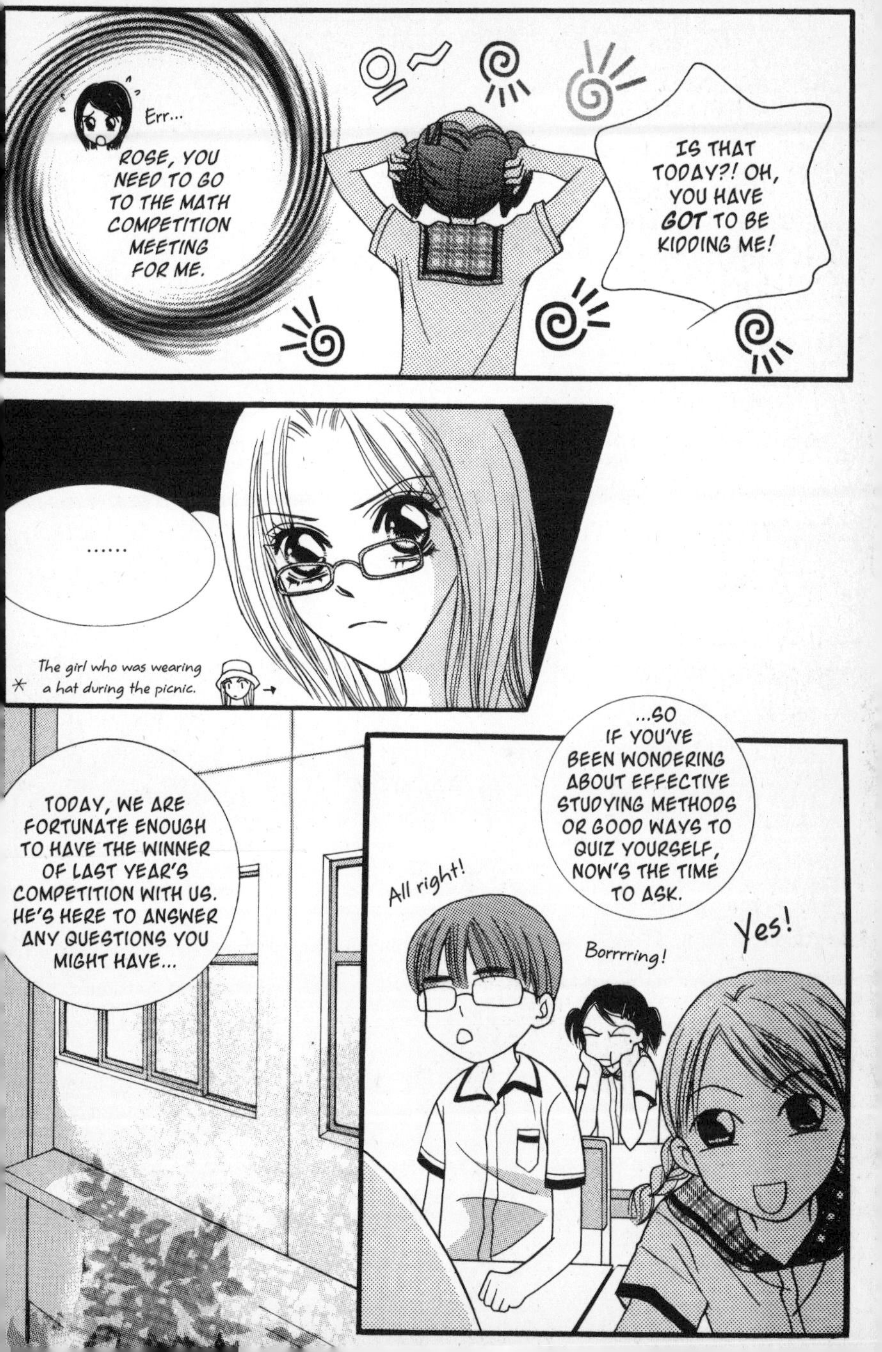
Err...
ROSE, YOU NEED TO GO TO THE MATH COMPETITION MEETING FOR ME.
IS THAT TODAY?! OH, YOU HAVE GOT TO BE KIDDING ME!
......
* The girl who was wearing a hat during the picnic.
TODAY, WE ARE FORTUNATE ENOUGH TO HAVE THE WINNER OF LAST YEAR'S COMPETITION WITH US. HE'S HERE TO ANSWER ANY QUESTIONS YOU MIGHT HAVE...
...SO IF YOU'VE BEEN WONDERING ABOUT EFFECTIVE STUDYING METHODS OR GOOD WAYS TO QUIZ YOURSELF, NOW'S THE TIME TO ASK.
All right!
Borrrring!
Yes!

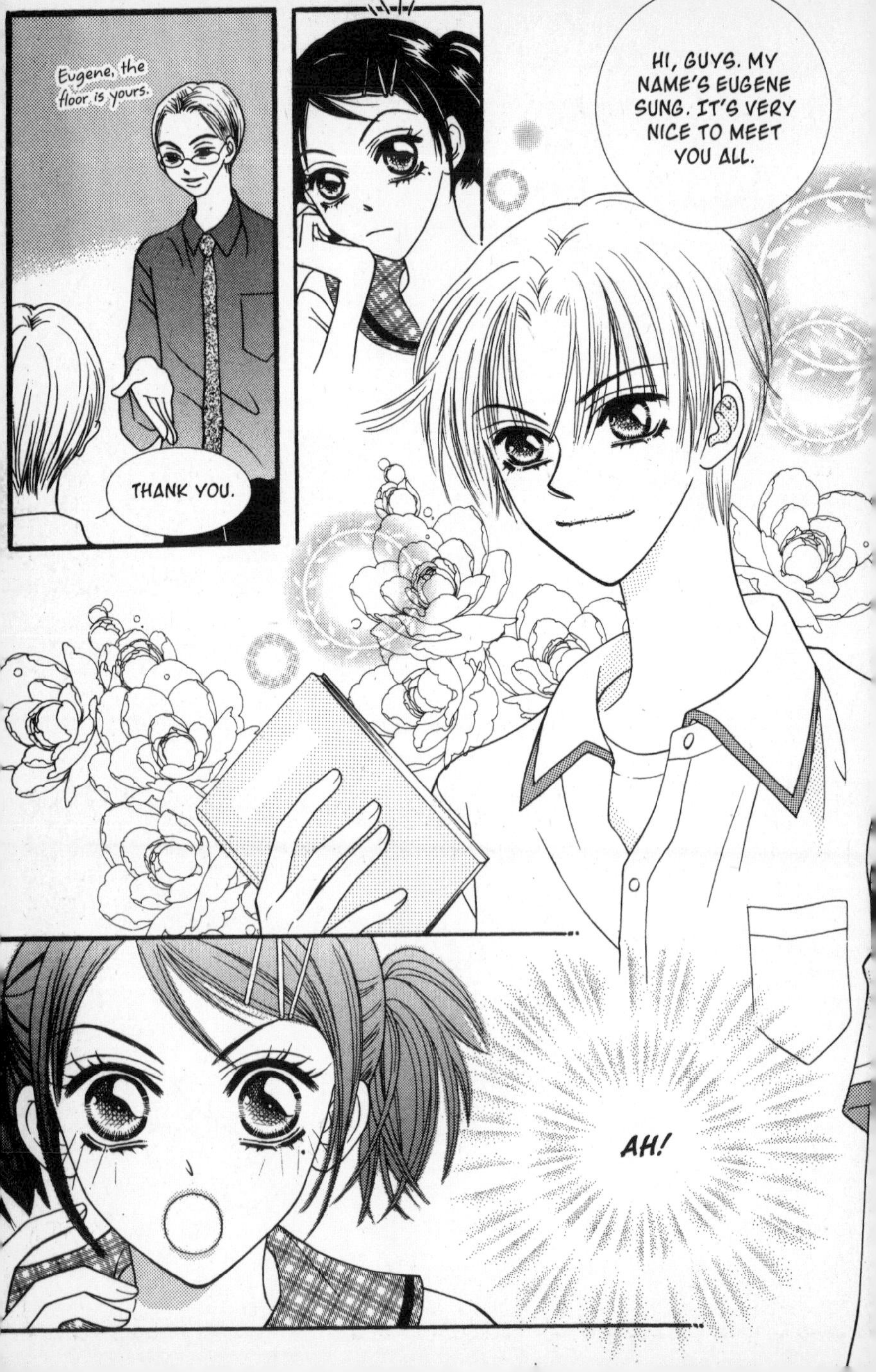

Eugene, the floor is yours.
THANK YOU.
HI, GUYS. MY NAME'S EUGENE SUNG. IT'S VERY NICE TO MEET YOU ALL.
AH!

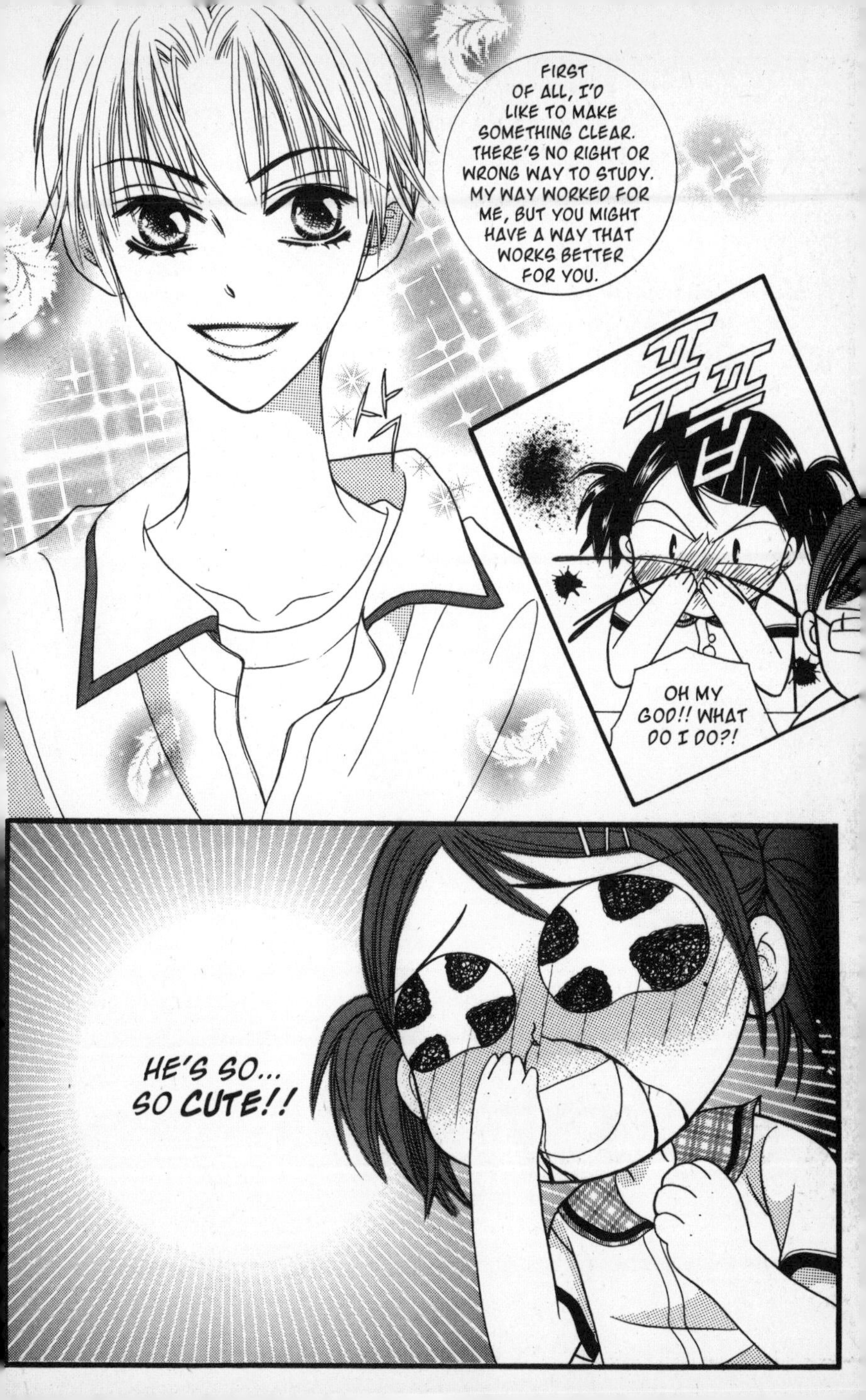
FIRST OF ALL, I'D LIKE TO MAKE SOMETHING CLEAR. THERE'S NO RIGHT OR WRONG WAY TO STUDY. MY WAY WORKED FOR ME, BUT YOU MIGHT HAVE A WAY THAT WORKS BETTER FOR YOU.
OH MY GOD!! WHAT DO I DO?!
HE'S SO... SO CUTE!!

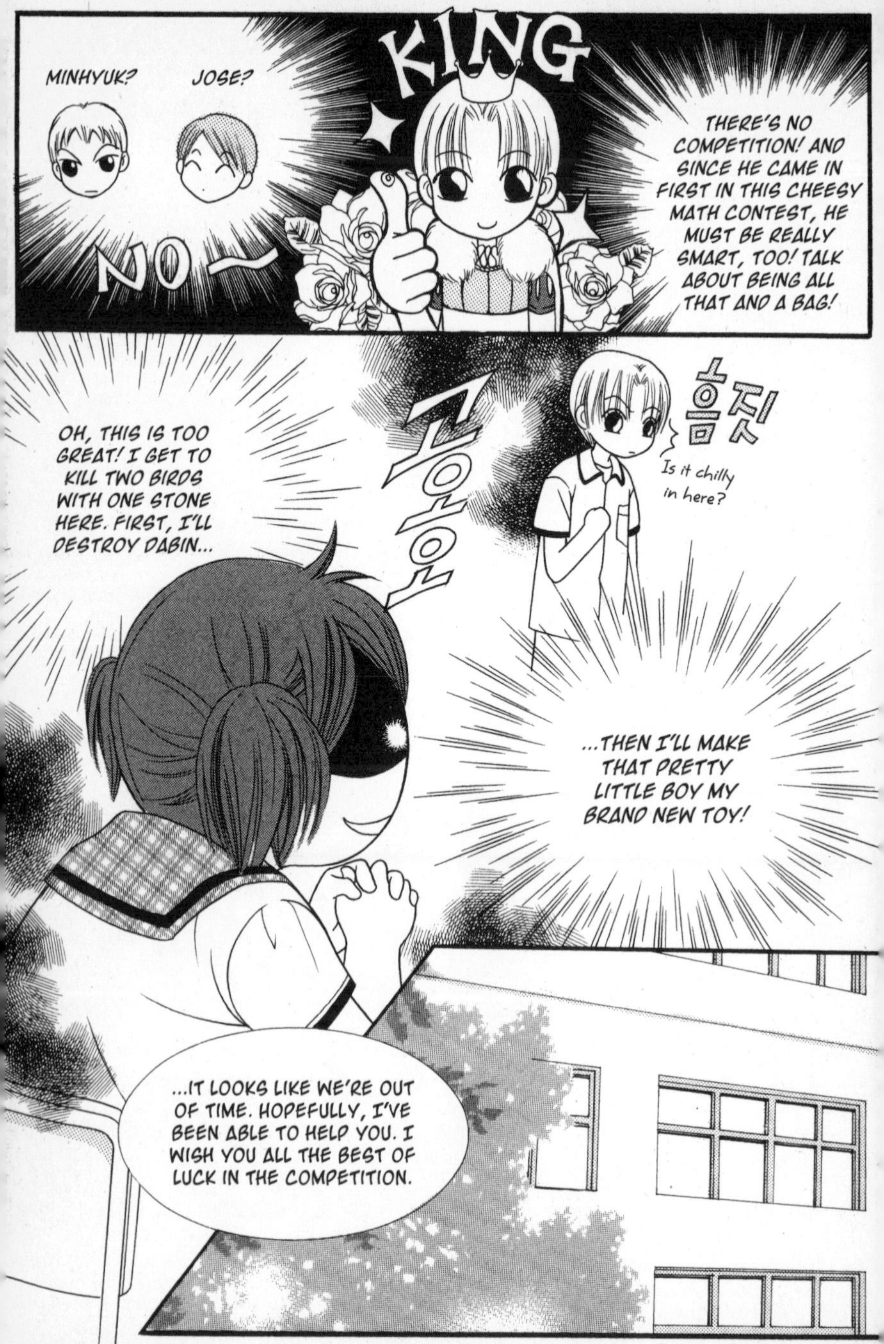
KING
MINHYUK?
JOSE?
NO~
THERE'S NO COMPETITION! AND SINCE HE CAME IN FIRST IN THIS CHEESY MATH CONTEST, HE MUST BE REALLY SMART, TOO! TALK ABOUT BEING ALL THAT AND A BAG!
OH, THIS IS TOO GREAT! I GET TO KILL TWO BIRDS WITH ONE STONE HERE. FIRST, I'LL DESTROY DABIN...
흠짓
Is it chilly in here?
...THEN I'LL MAKE THAT PRETTY LITTLE BOY MY BRAND NEW TOY!
...IT LOOKS LIKE WE'RE OUT OF TIME. HOPEFULLY, I'VE BEEN ABLE TO HELP YOU. I WISH YOU ALL THE BEST OF LUCK IN THE COMPETITION.

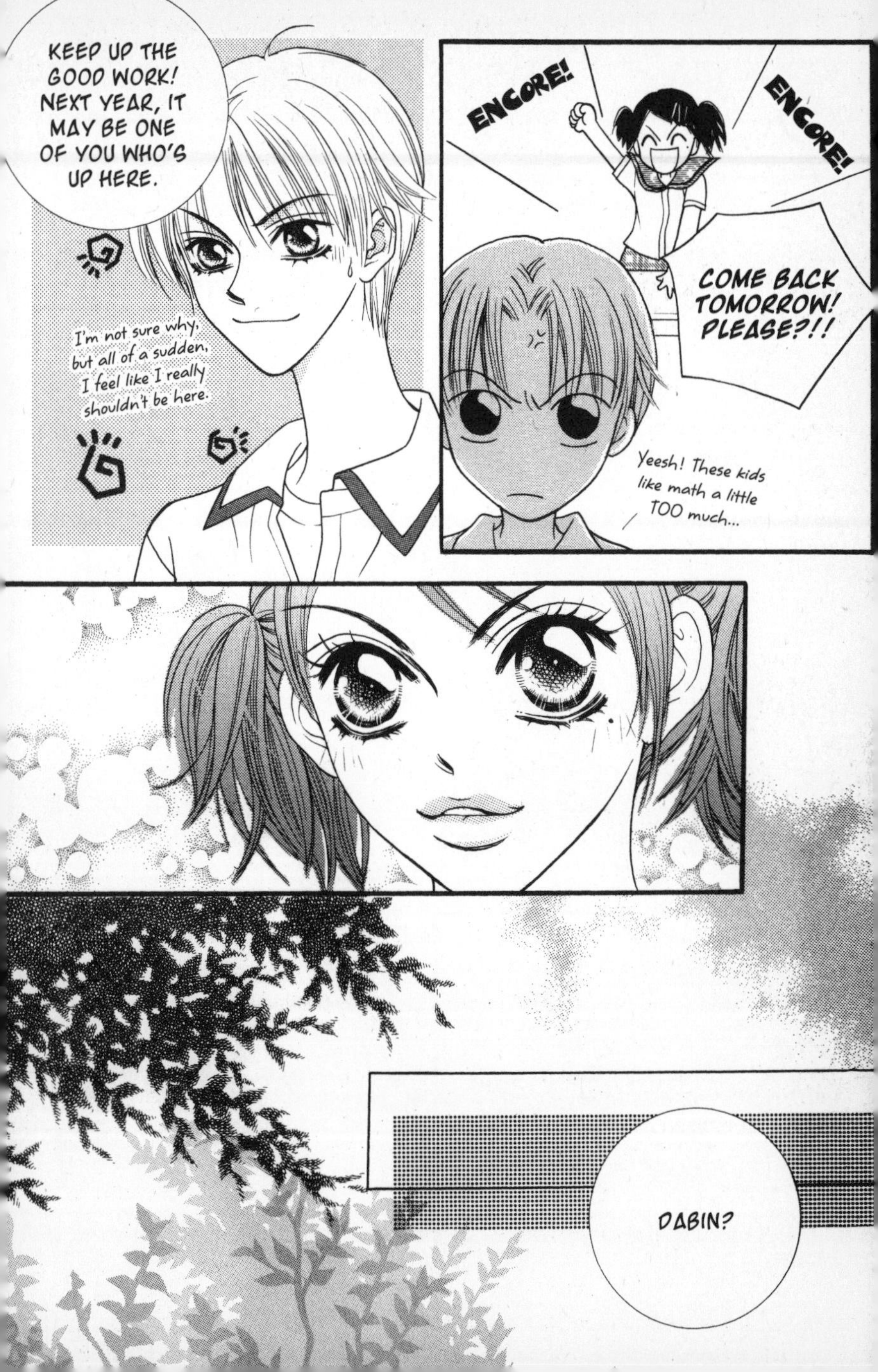
KEEP UP THE GOOD WORK! NEXT YEAR, IT MAY BE ONE OF YOU WHO'S UP HERE.
I'm not sure why, but all of a sudden, I feel like I really shouldn't be here.
ENCORE!
ENCORE!
COME BACK TOMORROW! PLEASE?!!
Yeesh! These kids like math a little TOO much...
DABIN?

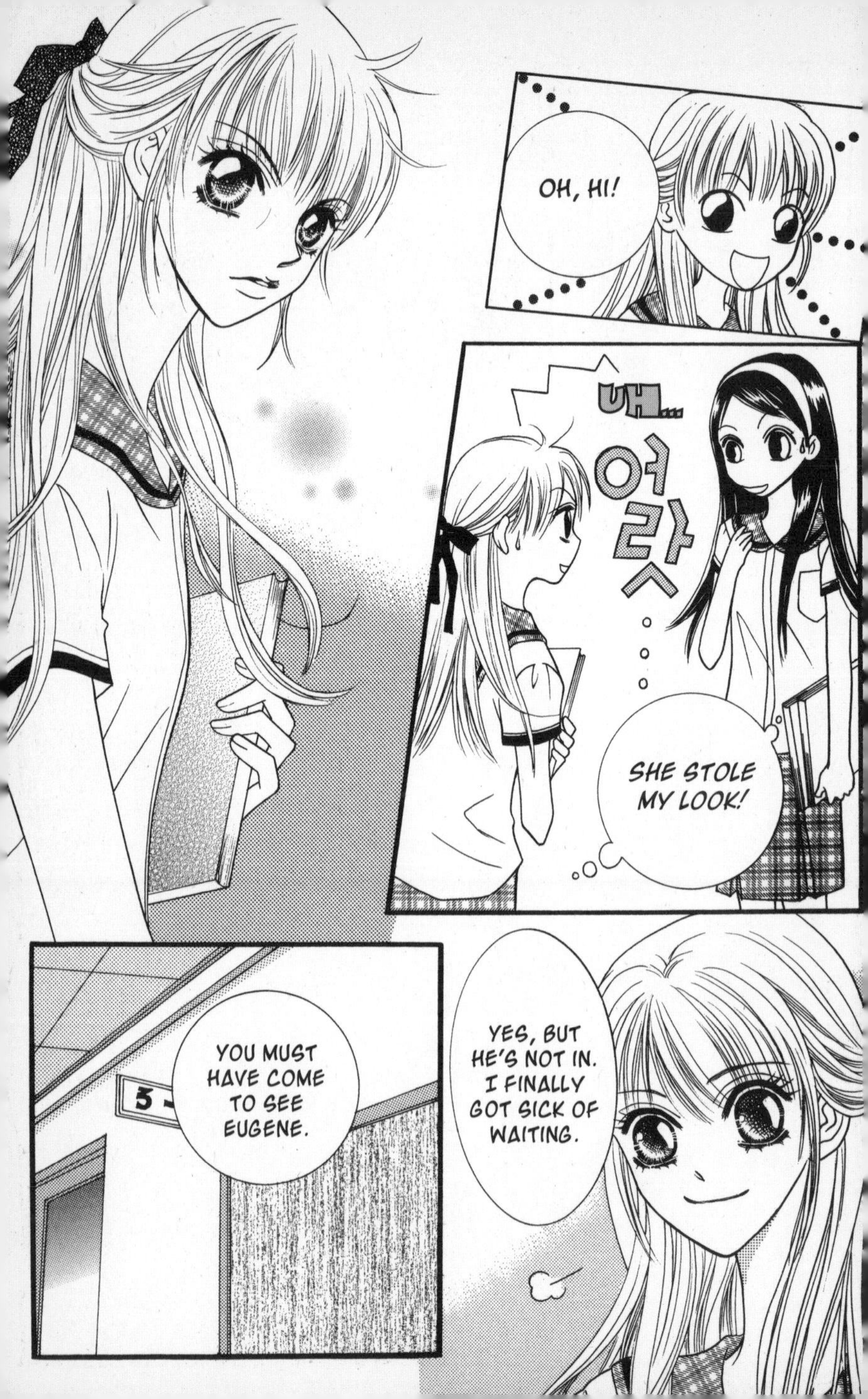
OH, HI!
UH...
어랏
SHE STOLE MY LOOK!
3 -
YOU MUST HAVE COME TO SEE EUGENE.
YES, BUT HE'S NOT IN. I FINALLY GOT SICK OF WAITING.

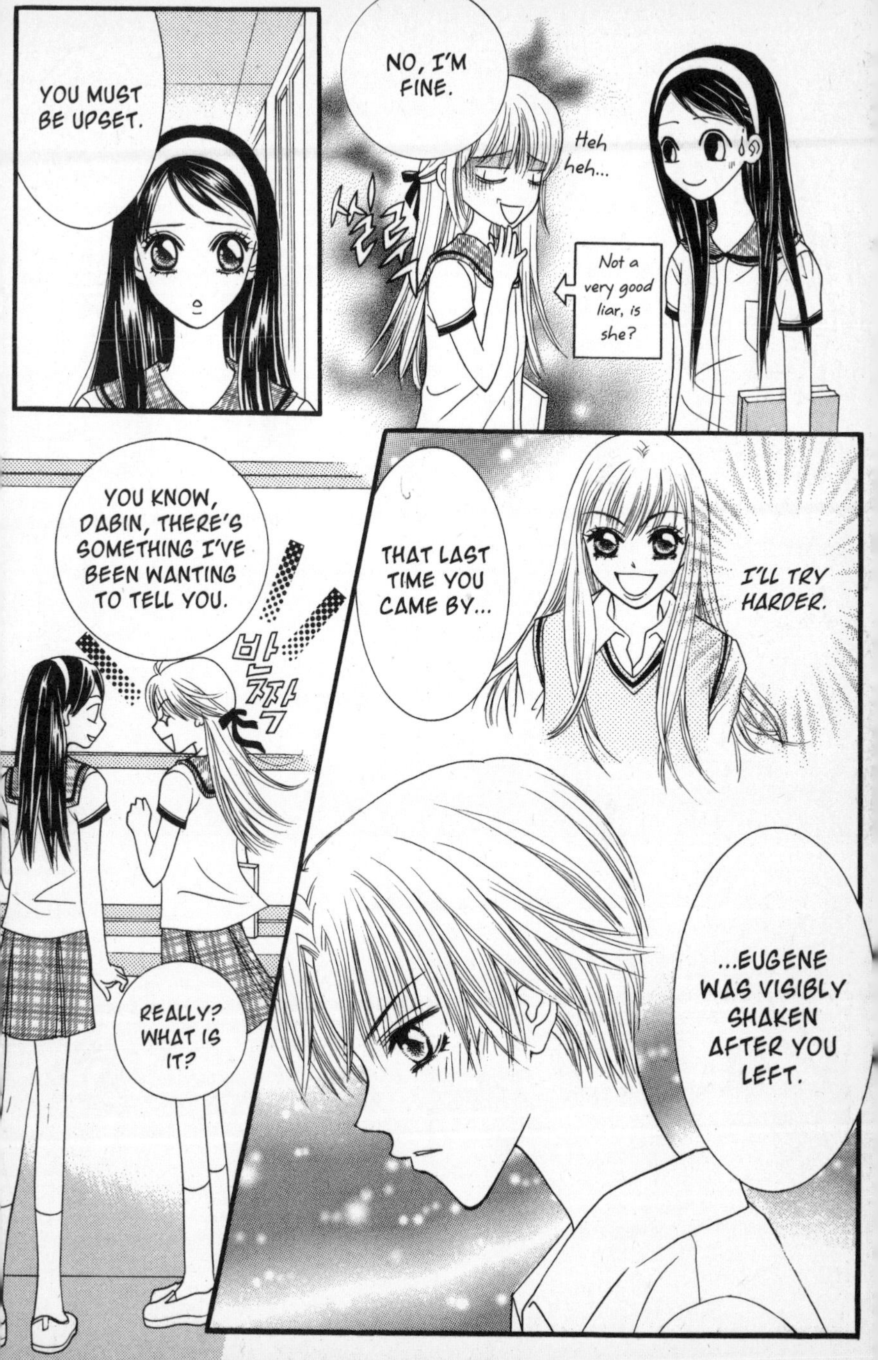
YOU MUST BE UPSET.
NO, I'M FINE.
Heh heh...
Not a very good liar, is she?
YOU KNOW, DABIN, THERE'S SOMETHING I'VE BEEN WANTING TO TELL YOU.
REALLY? WHAT IS IT?
THAT LAST TIME YOU CAME BY...
I'LL TRY HARDER.
...EUGENE WAS VISIBLY SHAKEN AFTER YOU LEFT.

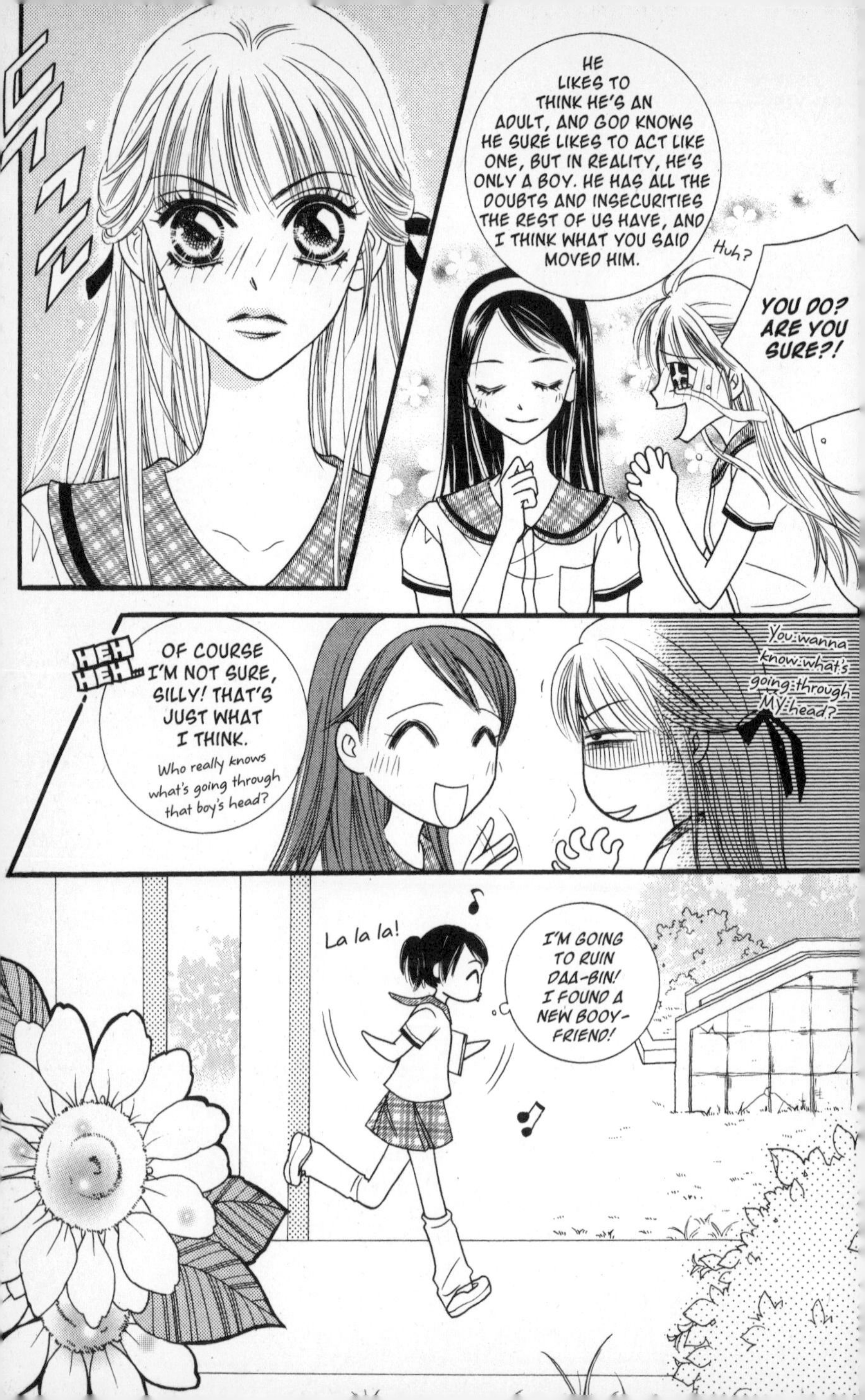
HE LIKES TO THINK HE'S AN ADULT, AND GOD KNOWS HE SURE LIKES TO ACT LIKE ONE, BUT IN REALITY, HE'S ONLY A BOY. HE HAS ALL THE DOUBTS AND INSECURITIES THE REST OF US HAVE, AND I THINK WHAT YOU SAID MOVED HIM.
Huh?
YOU DO? ARE YOU SURE?!
HEH HEH...
OF COURSE I'M NOT SURE, SILLY! THAT'S JUST WHAT I THINK.
Who really knows what's going through that boy's head?
You wanna know what's going through MY head?
La la la!
I'M GOING TO RUIN DAA-BIN! I FOUND A NEW BOOY-FRIEND!

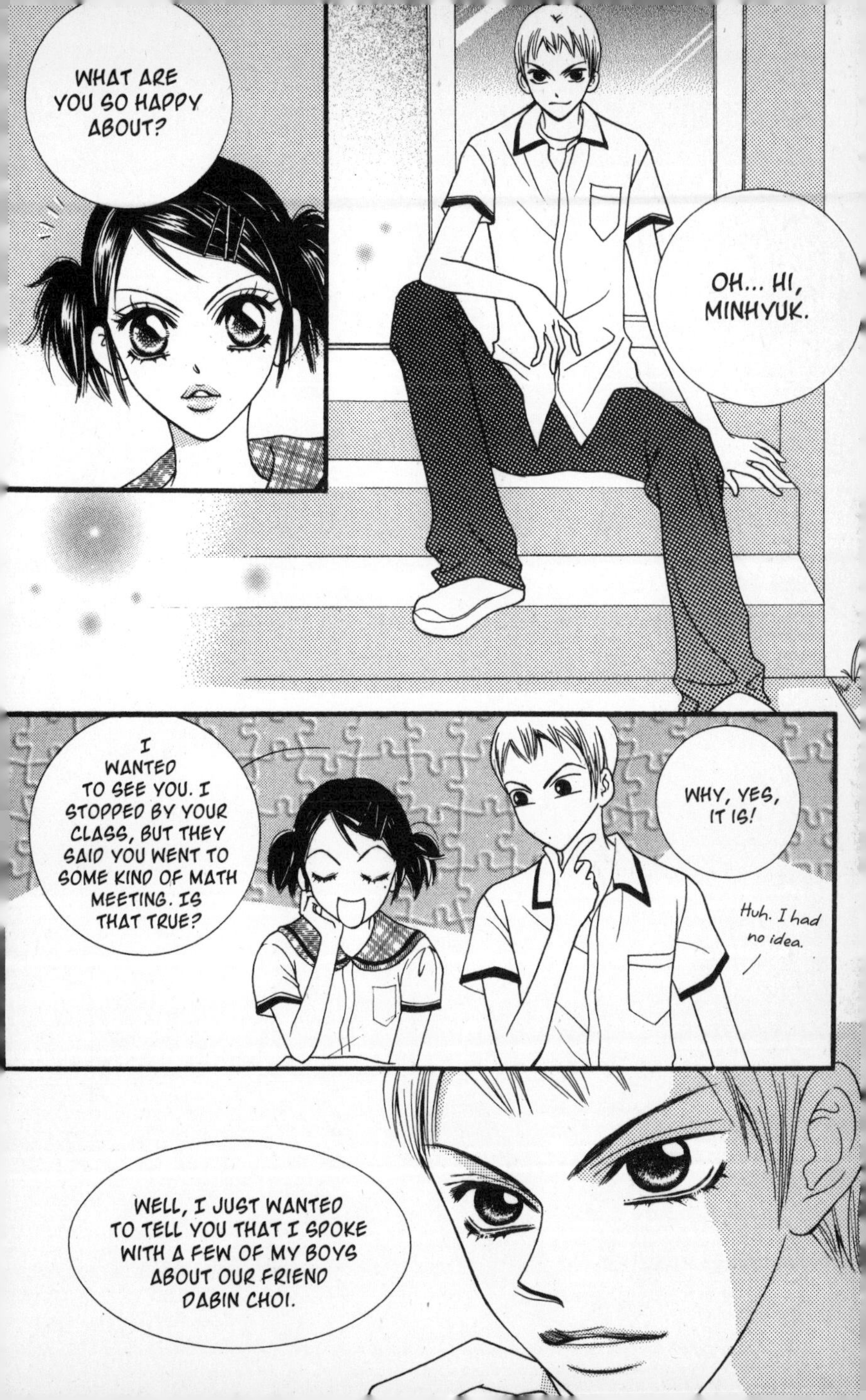
WHAT ARE YOU SO HAPPY ABOUT?
OH... HI, MINHYUK.
I WANTED TO SEE YOU. I STOPPED BY YOUR CLASS, BUT THEY SAID YOU WENT TO SOME KIND OF MATH MEETING. IS THAT TRUE?
WHY, YES, IT IS!
Huh. I had no idea.
WELL, I JUST WANTED TO TELL YOU THAT I SPOKE WITH A FEW OF MY BOYS ABOUT OUR FRIEND DABIN CHOI.

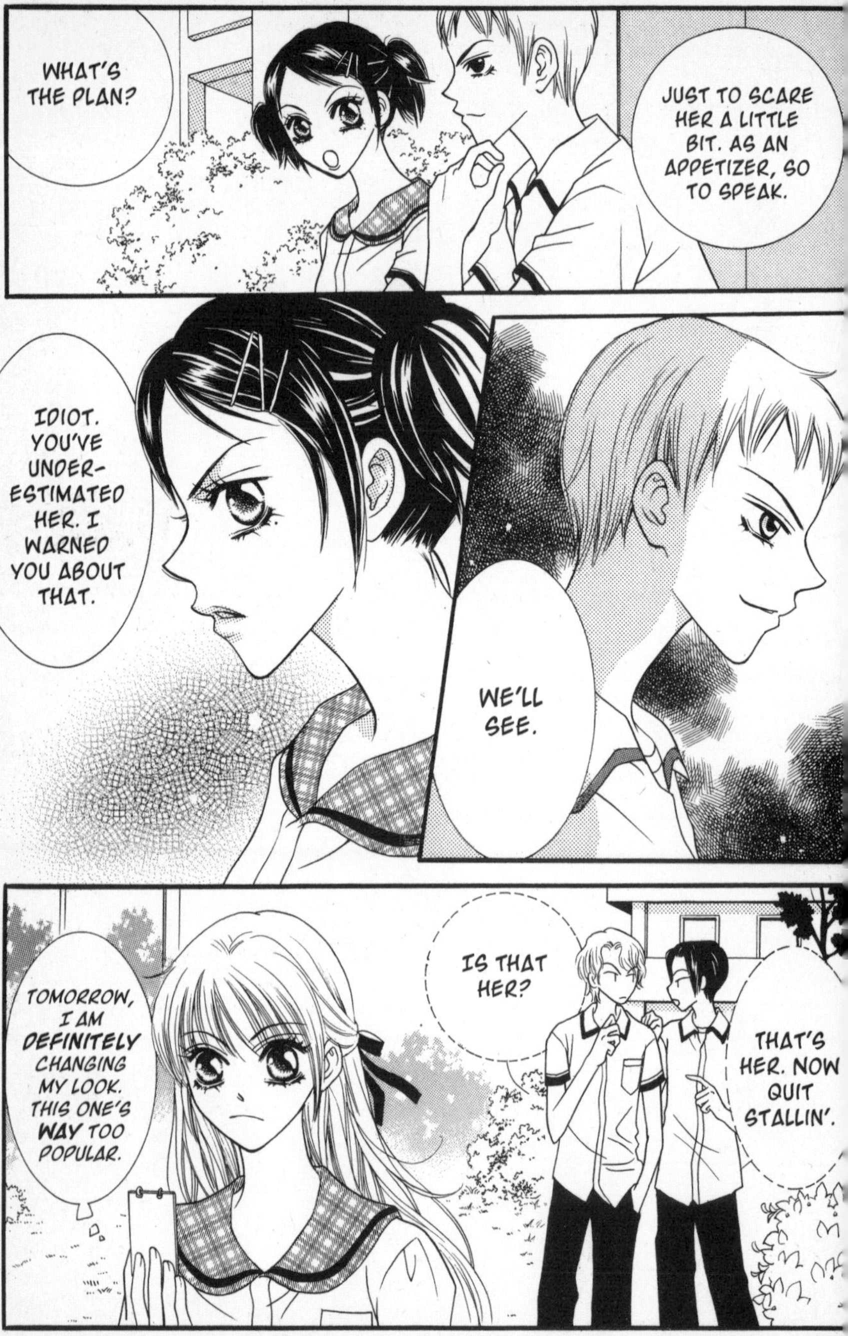
WHAT'S THE PLAN?
JUST TO SCARE HER A LITTLE BIT. AS AN APPETIZER, SO TO SPEAK.
IDIOT. YOU'VE UNDER-ESTIMATED HER. I WARNED YOU ABOUT THAT.
WE'LL SEE.
TOMORROW, I AM **DEFINITELY** CHANGING MY LOOK. THIS ONE'S **WAY** TOO POPULAR.
IS THAT HER?
THAT'S HER. NOW QUIT STALLIN'.

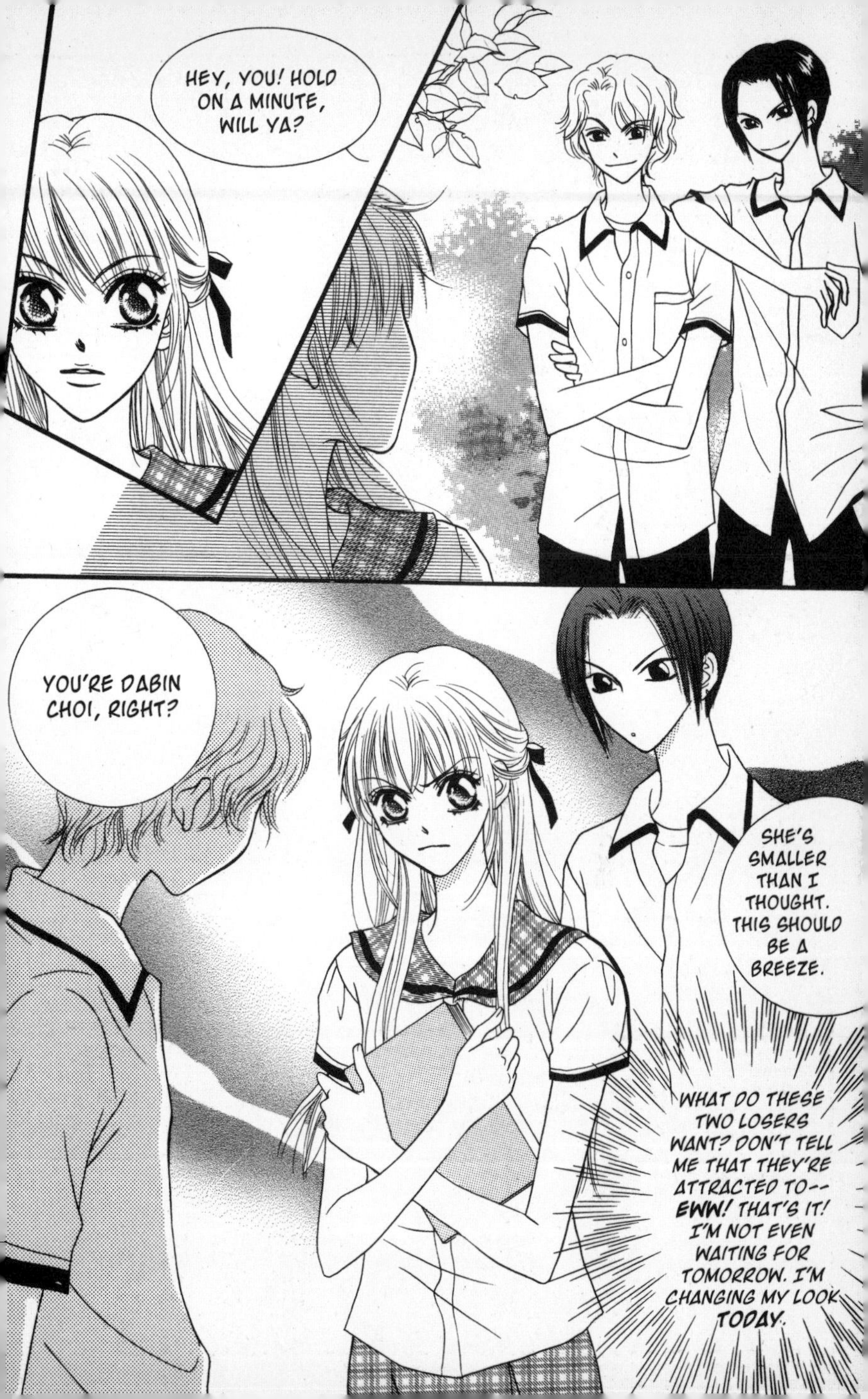
HEY, YOU! HOLD ON A MINUTE, WILL YA?
YOU'RE DABIN CHOI, RIGHT?
SHE'S SMALLER THAN I THOUGHT. THIS SHOULD BE A BREEZE.
WHAT DO THESE TWO LOSERS WANT? DON'T TELL ME THAT THEY'RE ATTRACTED TO-- EWW! THAT'S IT! I'M NOT EVEN WAITING FOR TOMORROW. I'M CHANGING MY LOOK TODAY.

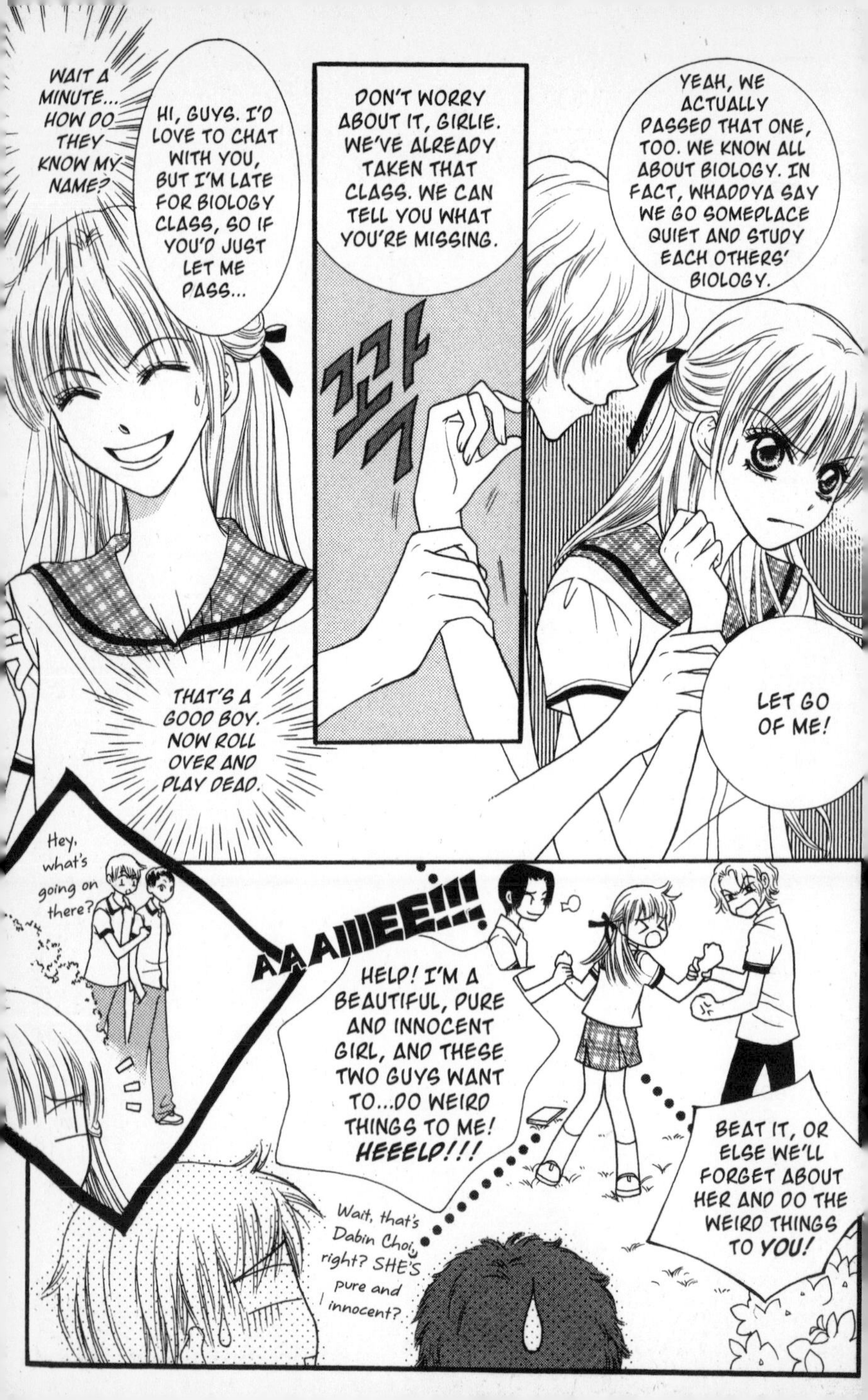
WAIT A MINUTE... HOW DO THEY KNOW MY NAME?
HI, GUYS. I'D LOVE TO CHAT WITH YOU, BUT I'M LATE FOR BIOLOGY CLASS, SO IF YOU'D JUST LET ME PASS...
THAT'S A GOOD BOY. NOW ROLL OVER AND PLAY DEAD.
DON'T WORRY ABOUT IT, GIRLIE. WE'VE ALREADY TAKEN THAT CLASS. WE CAN TELL YOU WHAT YOU'RE MISSING.
꽉
YEAH, WE ACTUALLY PASSED THAT ONE, TOO. WE KNOW ALL ABOUT BIOLOGY. IN FACT, WHADDYA SAY WE GO SOMEPLACE QUIET AND STUDY EACH OTHERS' BIOLOGY.
LET GO OF ME!
Hey, what's going on there?
AAAIIIEE!!!
HELP! I'M A BEAUTIFUL, PURE AND INNOCENT GIRL, AND THESE TWO GUYS WANT TO...DO WEIRD THINGS TO ME! HEEELP!!!
BEAT IT, OR ELSE WE'LL FORGET ABOUT HER AND DO THE WEIRD THINGS TO YOU!
Wait, that's Dabin Choi, right? SHE'S pure and innocent?

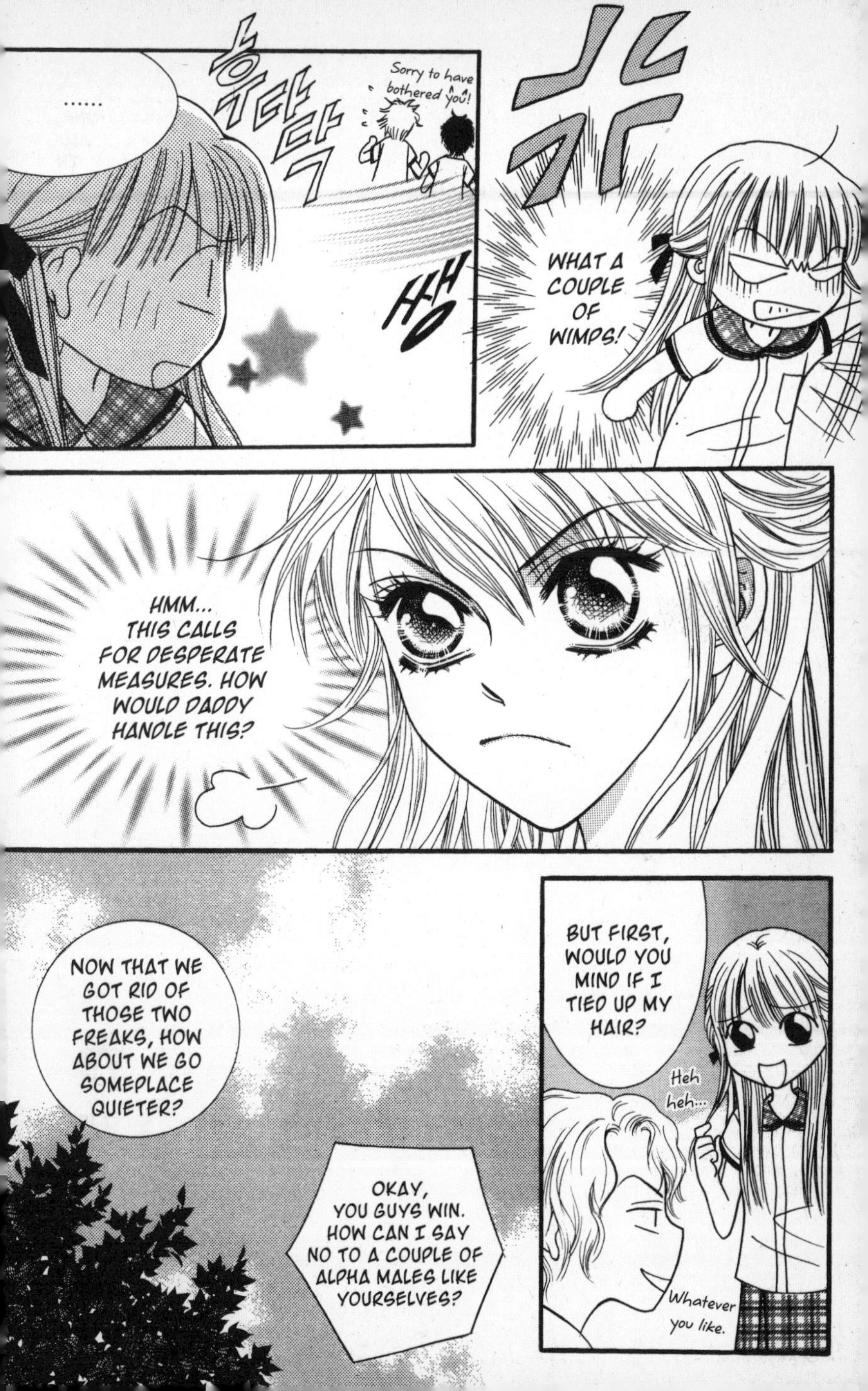
......
Sorry to have bothered you!
WHAT A COUPLE OF WIMPS!
HMM... THIS CALLS FOR DESPERATE MEASURES. HOW WOULD DADDY HANDLE THIS?
NOW THAT WE GOT RID OF THOSE TWO FREAKS, HOW ABOUT WE GO SOMEPLACE QUIETER?
OKAY, YOU GUYS WIN. HOW CAN I SAY NO TO A COUPLE OF ALPHA MALES LIKE YOURSELVES?
BUT FIRST, WOULD YOU MIND IF I TIED UP MY HAIR?
Heh heh...
Whatever you like.

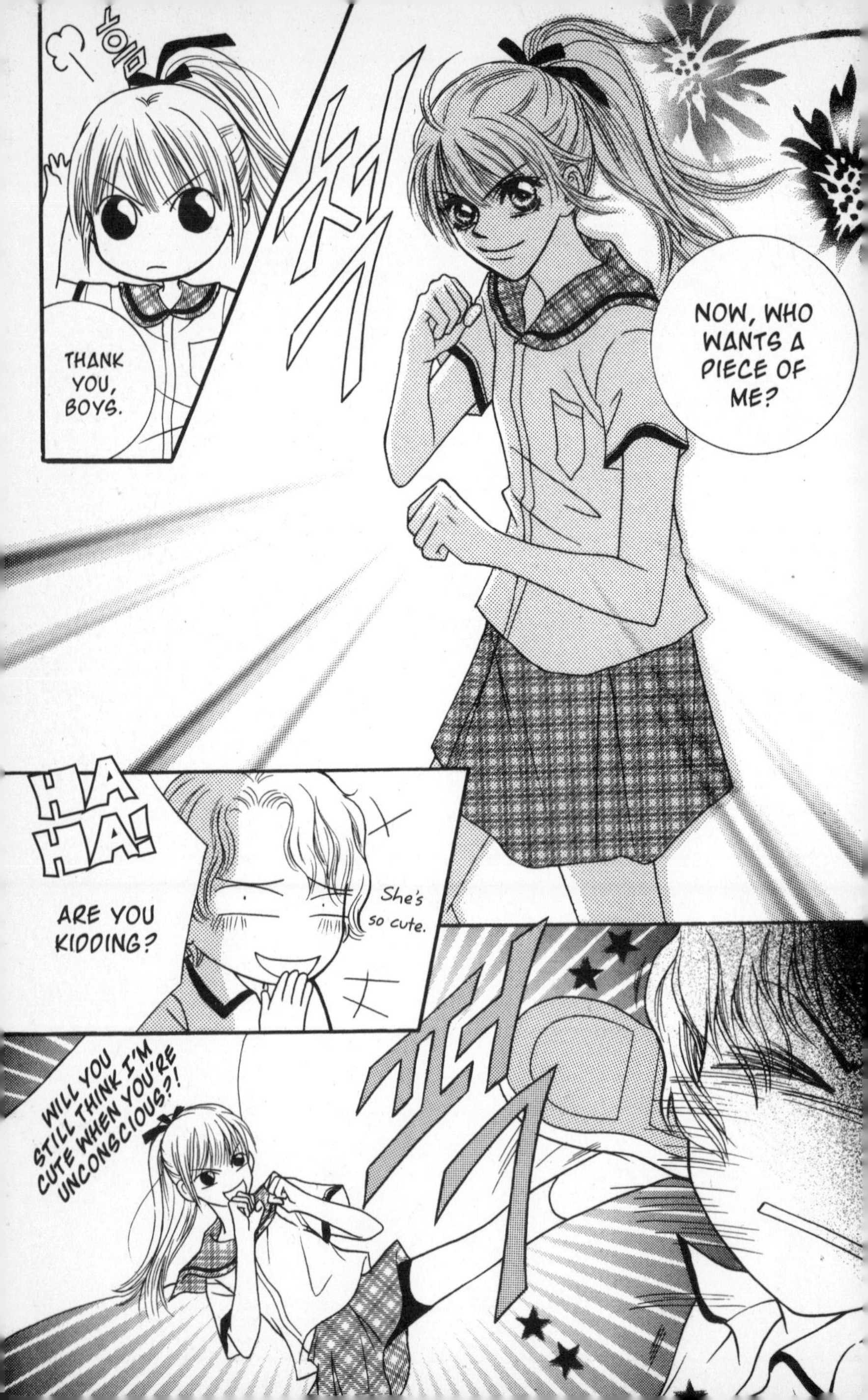
THANK YOU, BOYS.
NOW, WHO WANTS A PIECE OF ME?
HA HA!
ARE YOU KIDDING?
She's so cute.
WILL YOU STILL THINK I'M CUTE WHEN YOU'RE UNCONSCIOUS?!

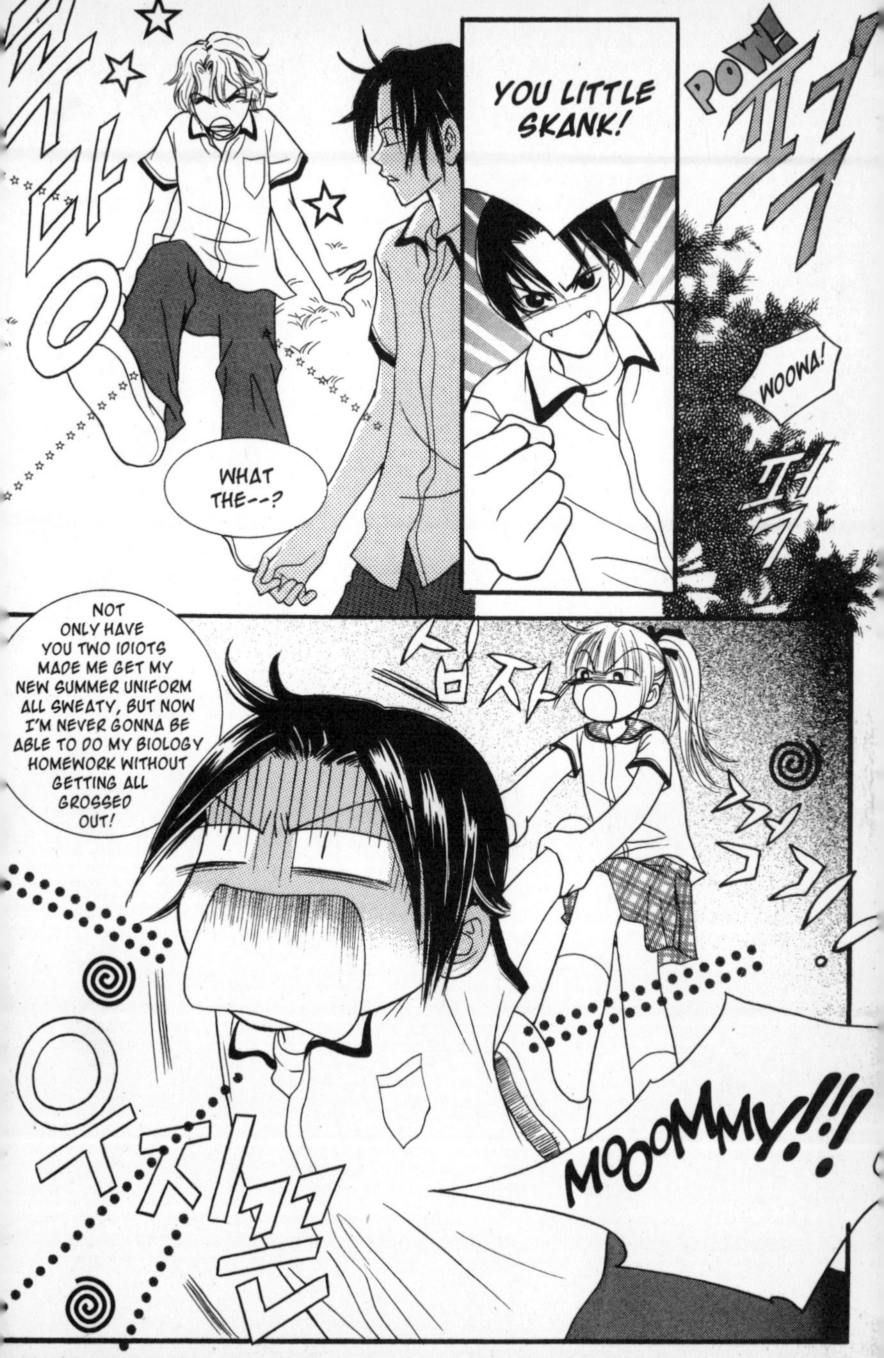
WHAT THE--?
YOU LITTLE SKANK!
POW!
WOOWA!
NOT ONLY HAVE YOU TWO IDIOTS MADE ME GET MY NEW SUMMER UNIFORM ALL SWEATY, BUT NOW I'M NEVER GONNA BE ABLE TO DO MY BIOLOGY HOMEWORK WITHOUT GETTING ALL GROSSED OUT!
MOOOMMY!!!

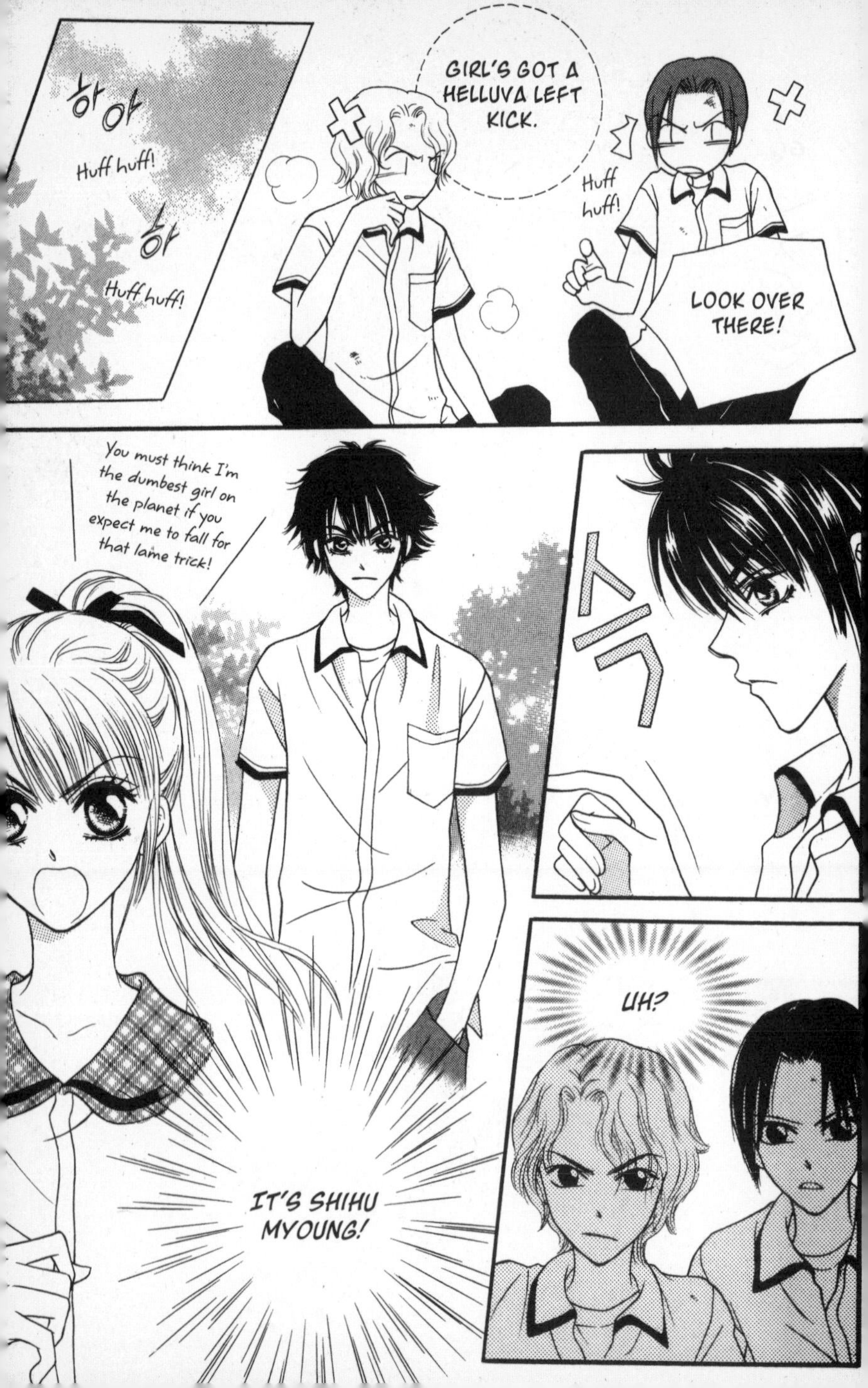
하아
Huff huff!
하
Huff huff!
GIRL'S GOT A HELLUVA LEFT KICK.
Huff huff!
LOOK OVER THERE!
You must think I'm the dumbest girl on the planet if you expect me to fall for that lame trick!
IT'S SHIHU MYOUNG!
UH?

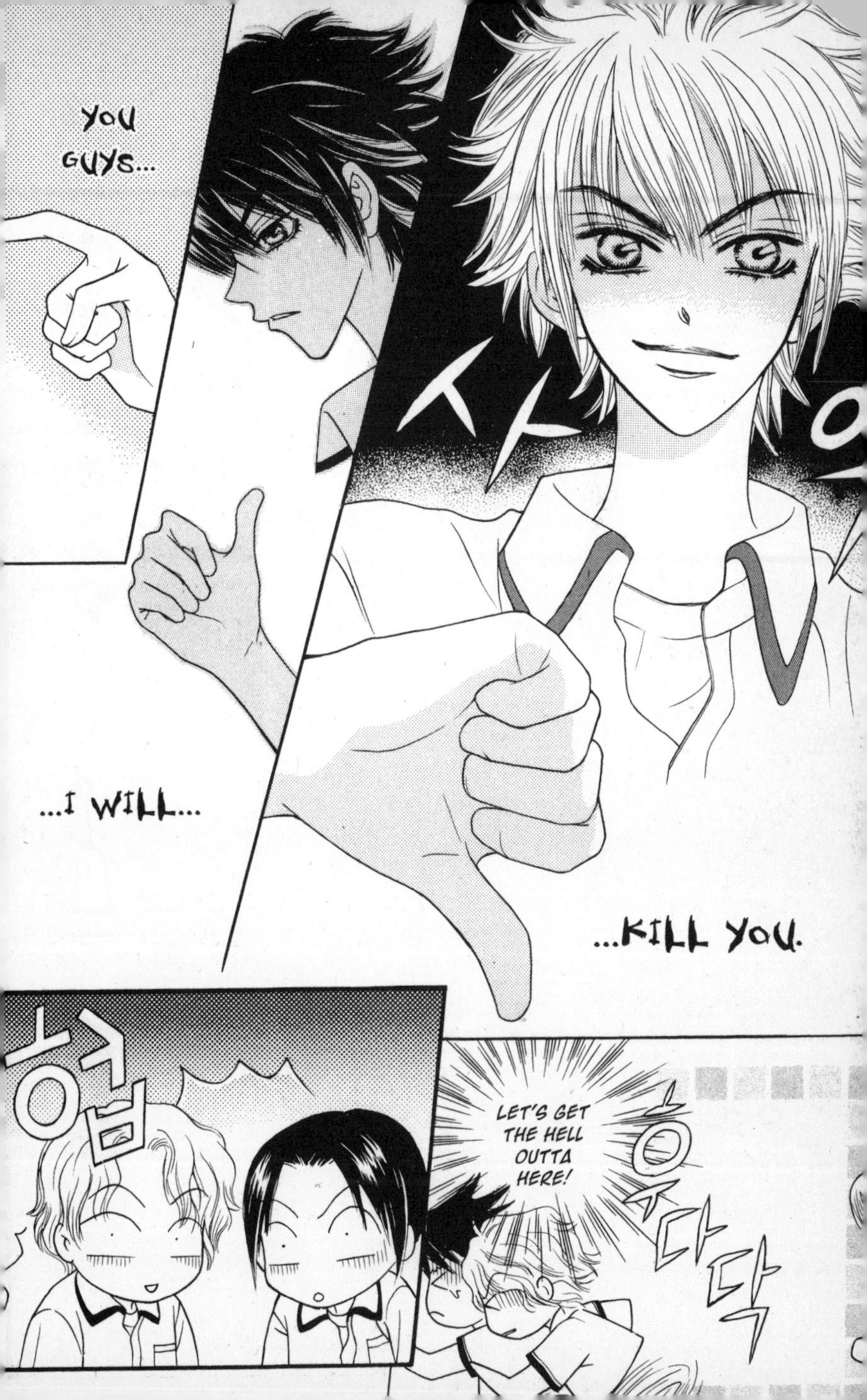
YOU GUYS...
...I WILL...
...KILL YOU.
LET'S GET THE HELL OUTTA HERE!

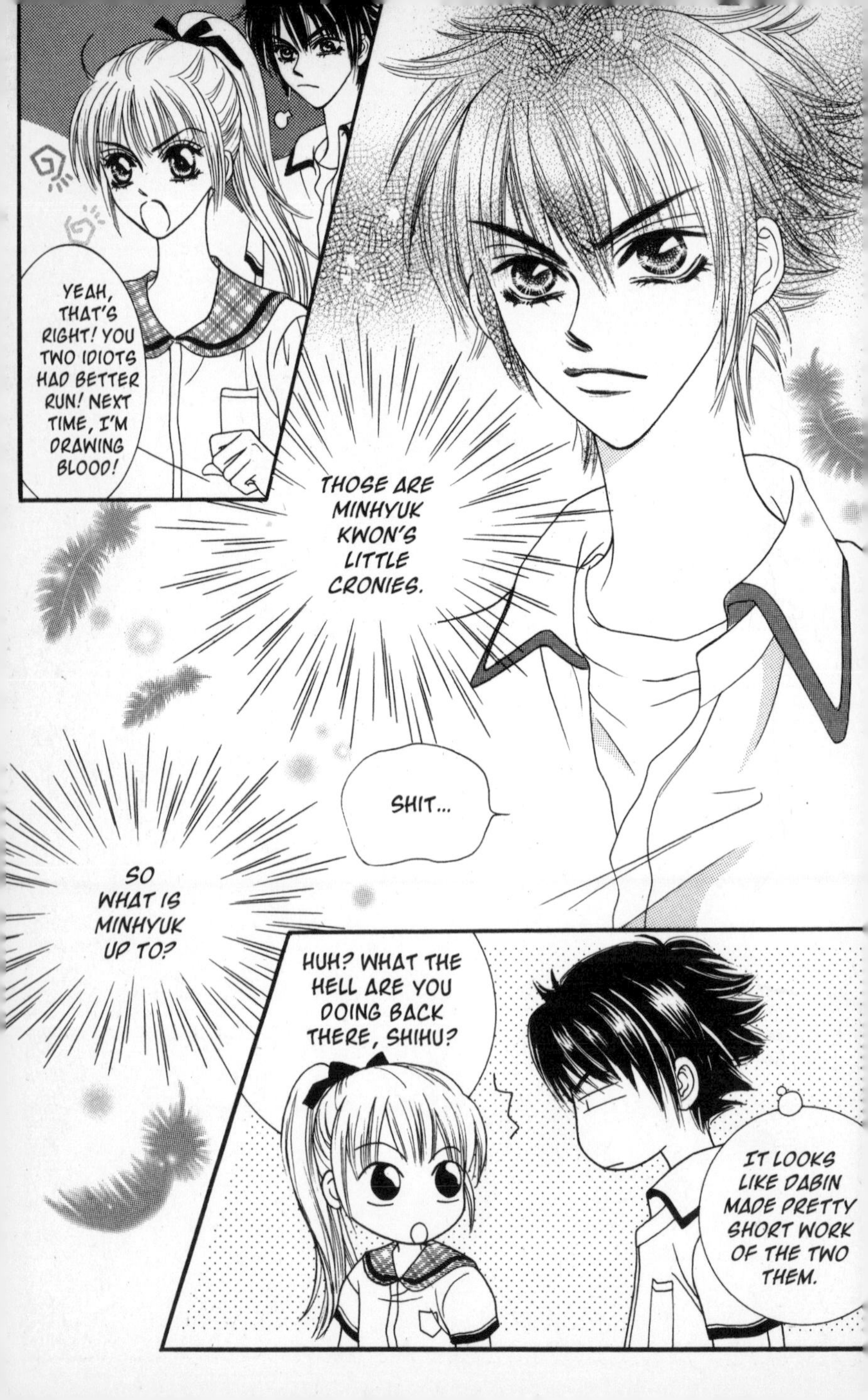
YEAH, THAT'S RIGHT! YOU TWO IDIOTS HAD BETTER RUN! NEXT TIME, I'M DRAWING BLOOD!
THOSE ARE MINHYUK KWON'S LITTLE CRONIES.
SHIT...
SO WHAT IS MINHYUK UP TO?
HUH? WHAT THE HELL ARE YOU DOING BACK THERE, SHIHU?
IT LOOKS LIKE DABIN MADE PRETTY SHORT WORK OF THE TWO THEM.

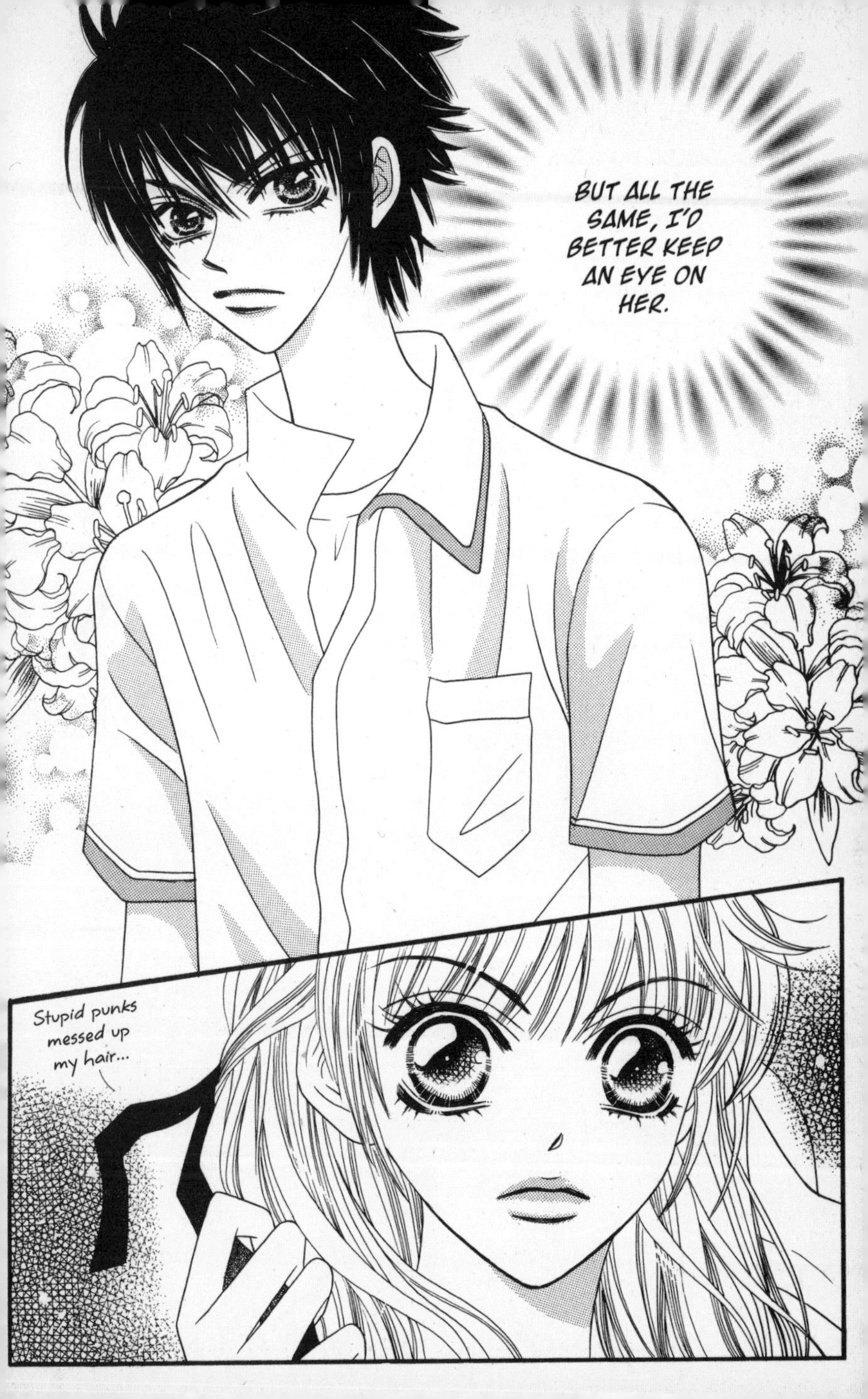
BUT ALL THE SAME, I'D BETTER KEEP AN EYE ON HER.
Stupid punks messed up my hair...

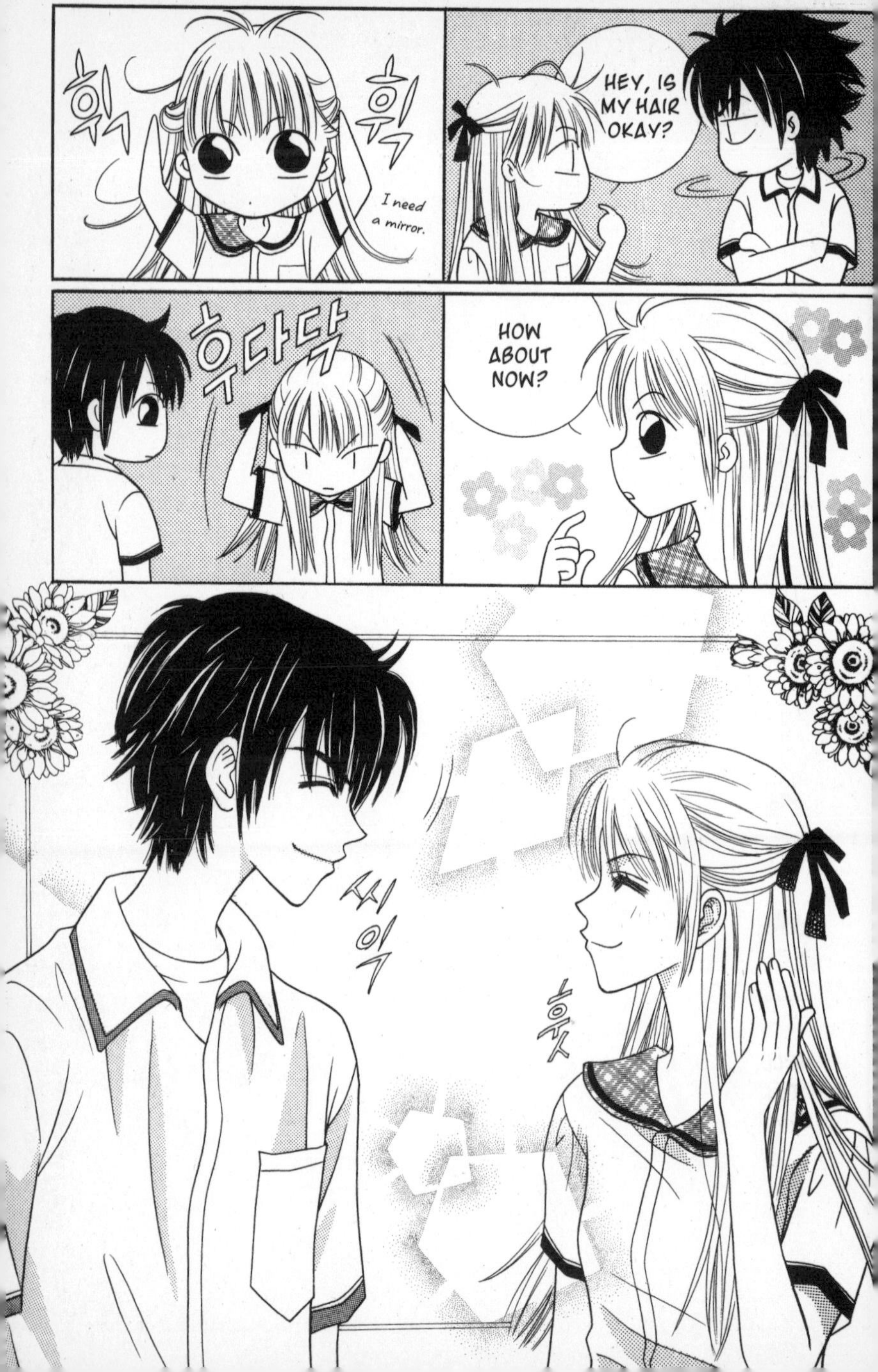
휙
휙
I need a mirror.
HEY, IS MY HAIR OKAY?
후다닥
HOW ABOUT NOW?
씨익
훗

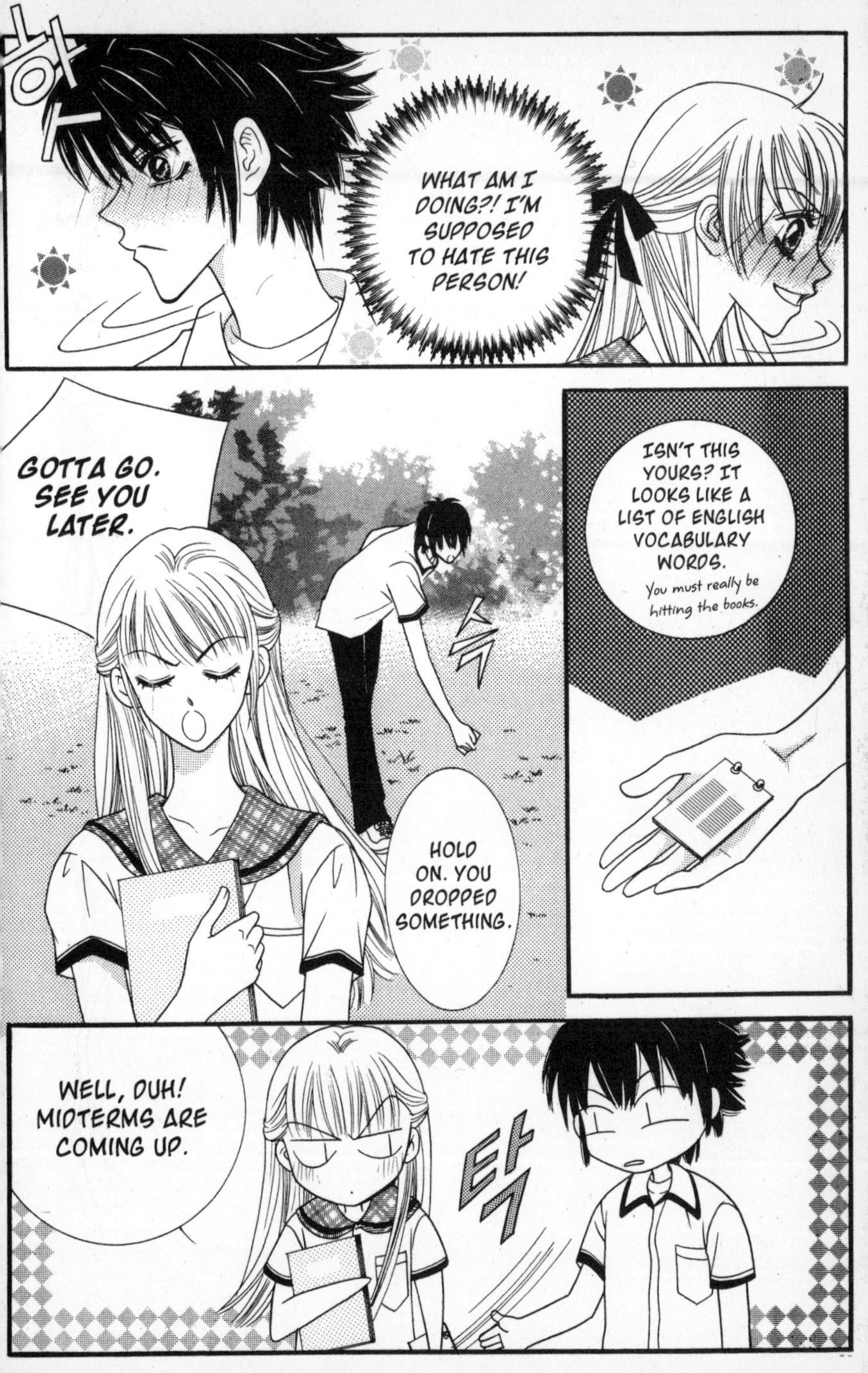
WHAT AM I DOING?! I'M SUPPOSED TO HATE THIS PERSON!
GOTTA GO. SEE YOU LATER.
HOLD ON. YOU DROPPED SOMETHING.
ISN'T THIS YOURS? IT LOOKS LIKE A LIST OF ENGLISH VOCABULARY WORDS.
You must really be hitting the books.
WELL, DUH! MIDTERMS ARE COMING UP.

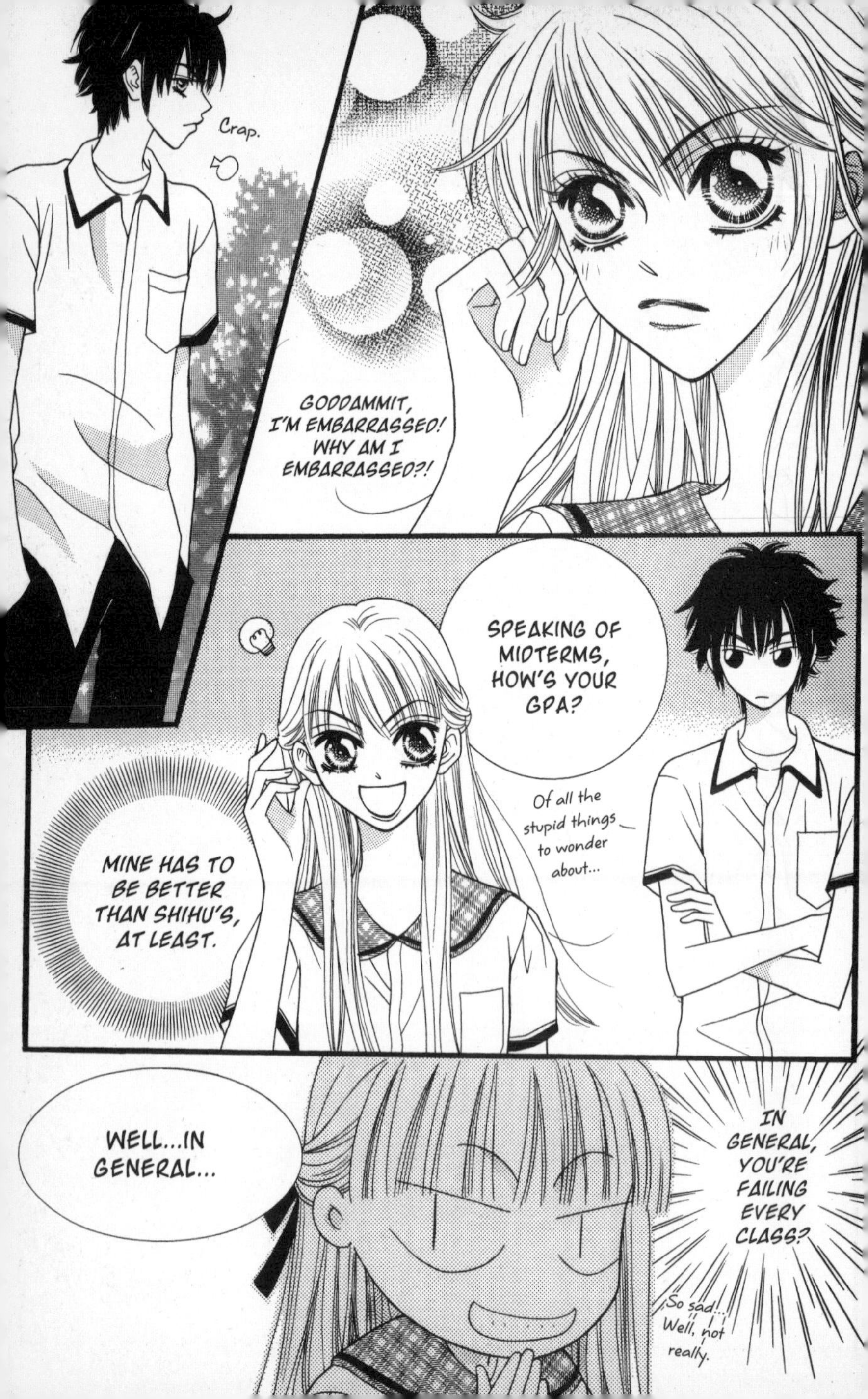
Crap.
GODDAMMIT, I'M EMBARRASSED! WHY AM I EMBARRASSED?!
SPEAKING OF MIDTERMS, HOW'S YOUR GPA?
MINE HAS TO BE BETTER THAN SHIHU'S, AT LEAST.
Of all the stupid things to wonder about...
WELL...IN GENERAL...
IN GENERAL, YOU'RE FAILING EVERY CLASS?
So sad... Well, not really.

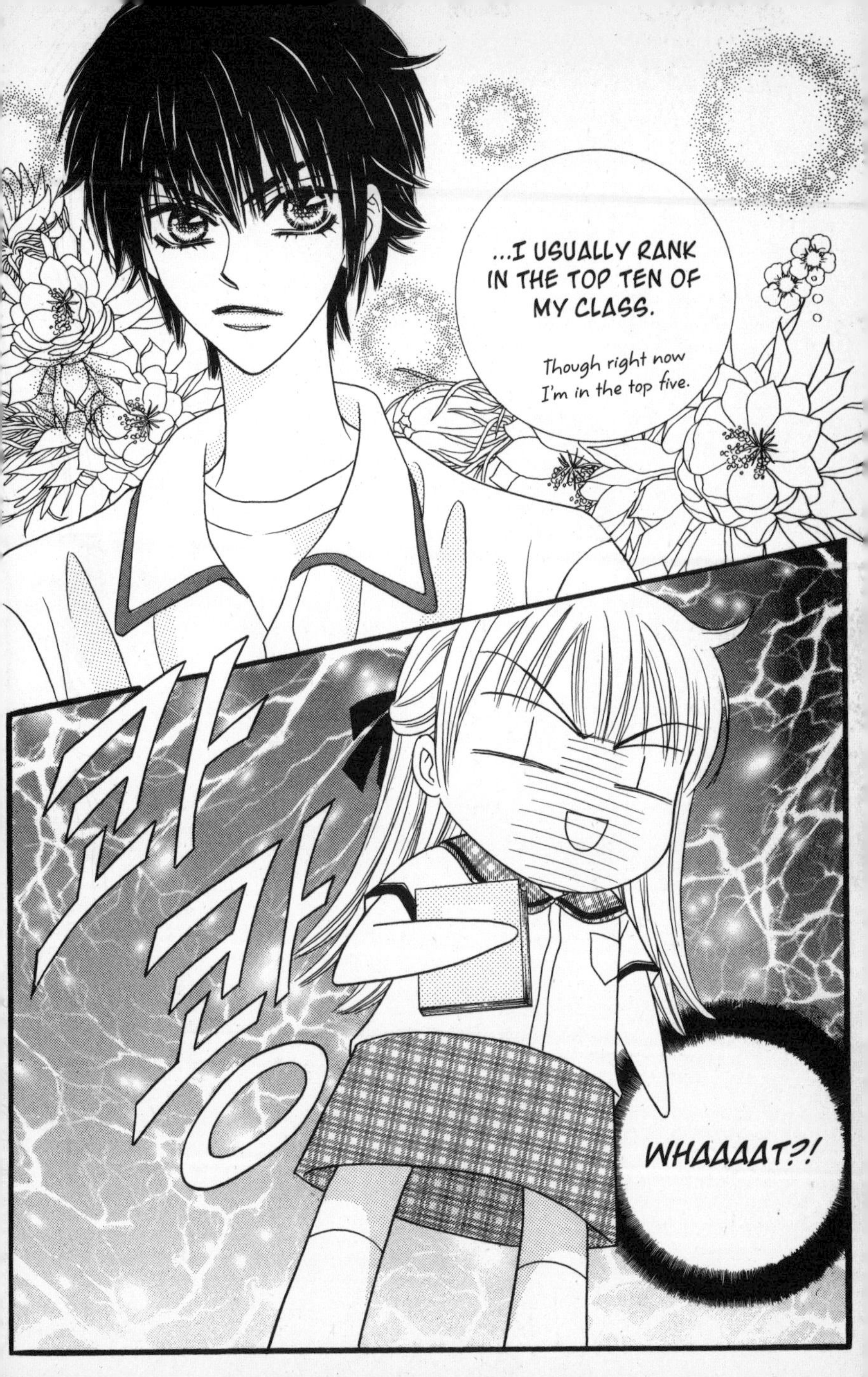
...I USUALLY RANK IN THE TOP TEN OF MY CLASS.
Though right now I'm in the top five.
WHAAAAT?!

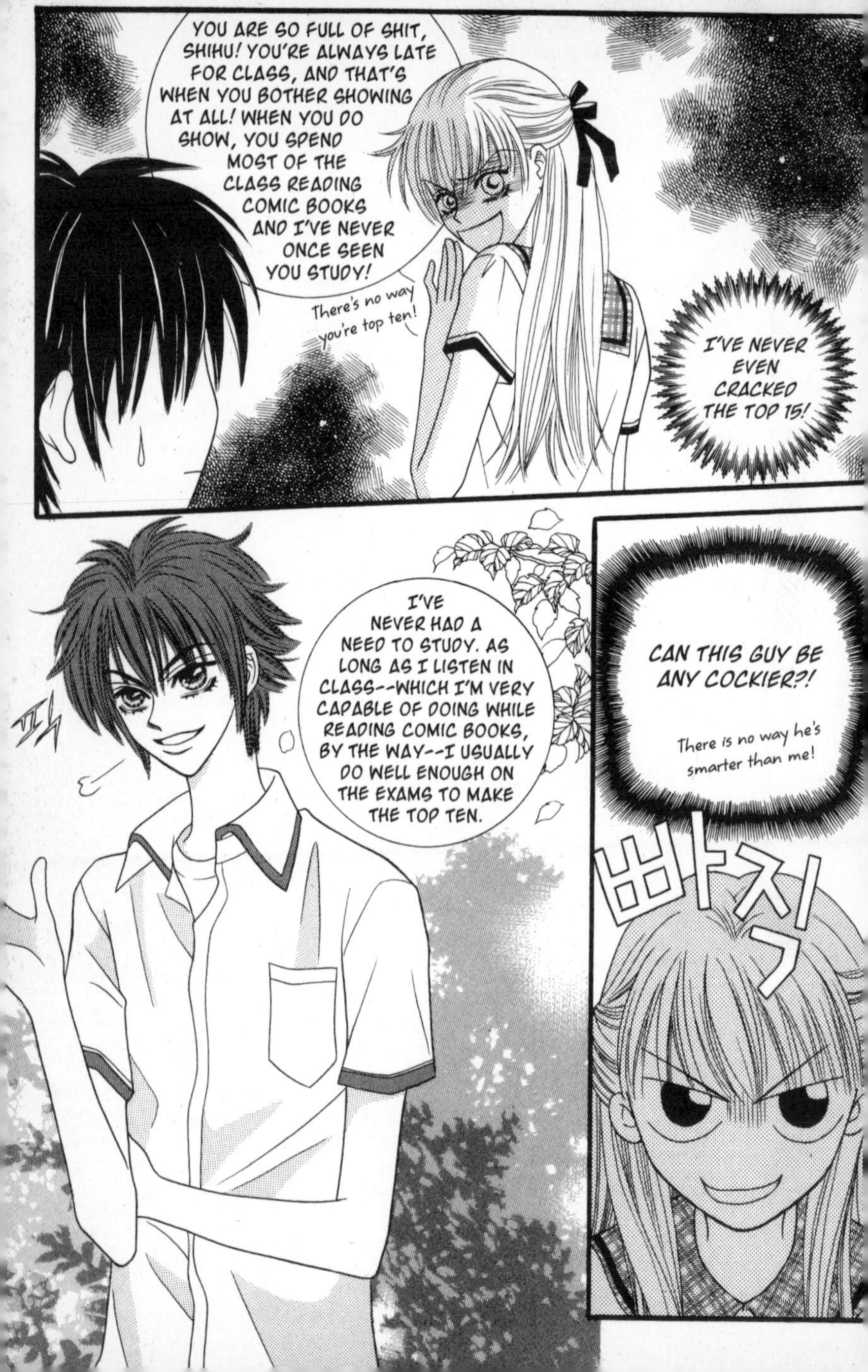
YOU ARE SO FULL OF SHIT, SHIHU! YOU'RE ALWAYS LATE FOR CLASS, AND THAT'S WHEN YOU BOTHER SHOWING AT ALL! WHEN YOU DO SHOW, YOU SPEND MOST OF THE CLASS READING COMIC BOOKS AND I'VE NEVER ONCE SEEN YOU STUDY!
There's no way you're top ten!
I'VE NEVER EVEN CRACKED THE TOP 15!
I'VE NEVER HAD A NEED TO STUDY. AS LONG AS I LISTEN IN CLASS--WHICH I'M VERY CAPABLE OF DOING WHILE READING COMIC BOOKS, BY THE WAY--I USUALLY DO WELL ENOUGH ON THE EXAMS TO MAKE THE TOP TEN.
CAN THIS GUY BE ANY COCKIER?!
There is no way he's smarter than me!
빠직

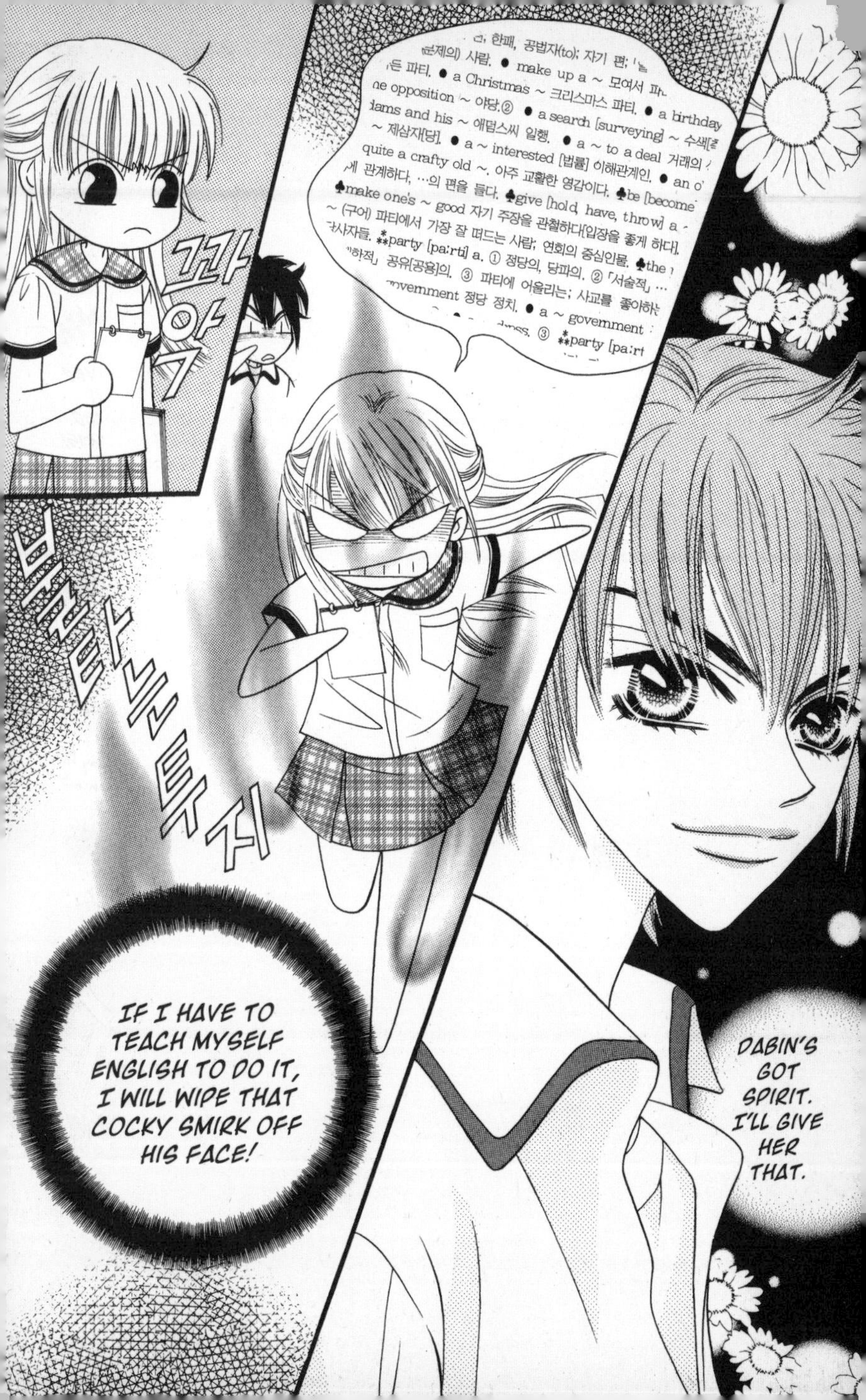

(문제의) 사람. ● make up a ~ 모여서 파
든 파티. ● a Christmas ~ 크리스마스 파티. ● a birthday
ne opposition ~ 야당.② ● a search [surveying] ~ 수색[
dams and his ~ 애덤스씨 일행. ● a ~ to a deal 거래의
~ 제삼자[당]. ● a ~ interested [법률] 이해관계인. ● an o
quite a crafty old ~. 아주 교활한 영감이다. ♣be [become
에 관계하다, …의 편을 들다. ♣give [hold, have, throw] a
♣make one's ~ good 자기 주장을 관철하다[입장을 좋게 하다].
~ (구어) 파티에서 가장 잘 떠드는 사람; 연회의 중심인물. ♣the
사자들. **party [pa:rti] a. ① 정당의, 당파의. ② 「서술적」…
「하학적」 공유[공용]의. ③ 파티에 어울리는; 사교를 좋아하는
overnment 정당 정치. ● a ~ government
IF I HAVE TO TEACH MYSELF ENGLISH TO DO IT, I WILL WIPE THAT COCKY SMIRK OFF HIS FACE!
DABIN'S GOT SPIRIT. I'LL GIVE HER THAT.

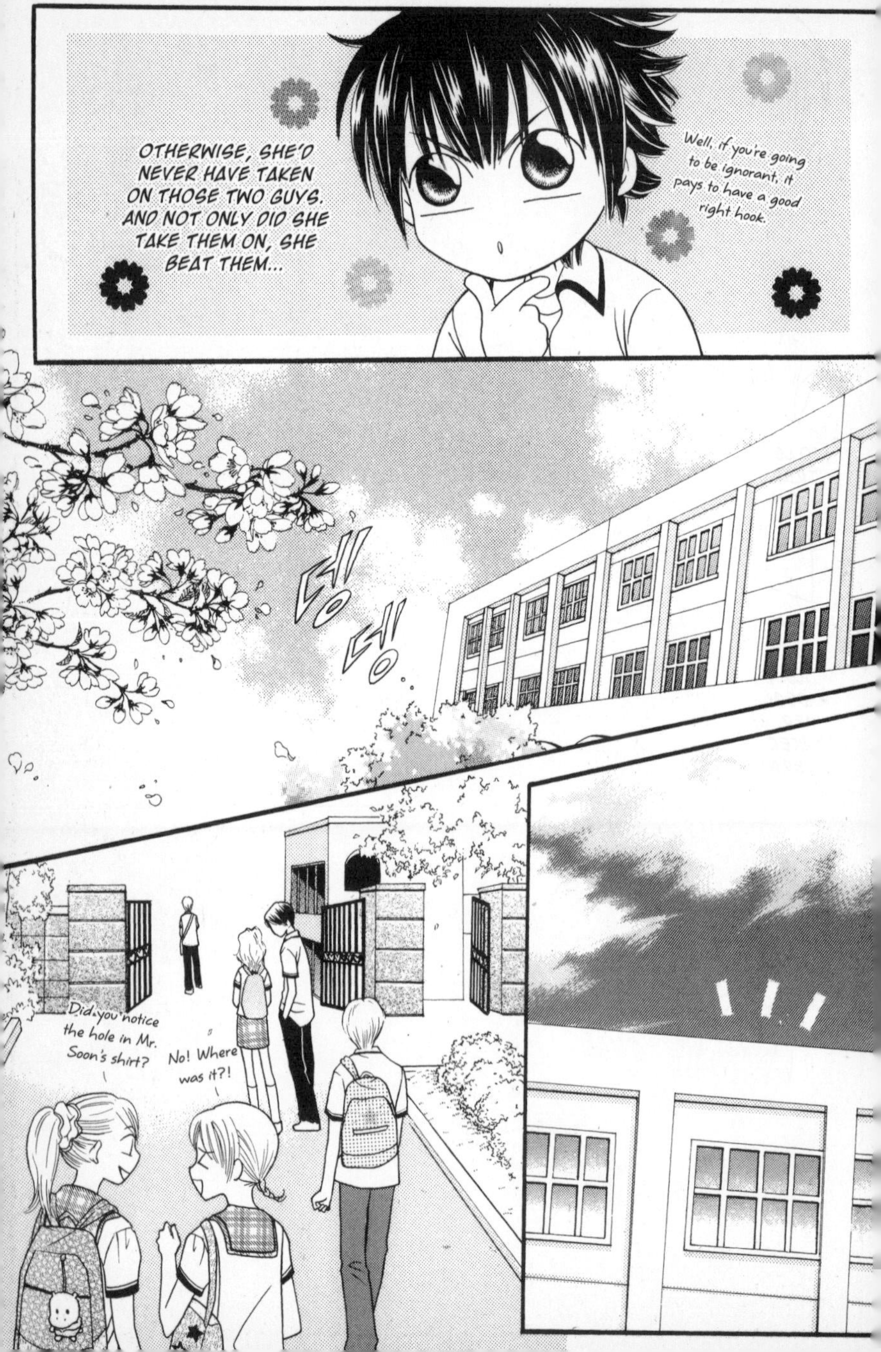
OTHERWISE, SHE'D NEVER HAVE TAKEN ON THOSE TWO GUYS. AND NOT ONLY DID SHE TAKE THEM ON, SHE BEAT THEM...
Well, if you're going to be ignorant, it pays to have a good right hook.
뎅 뎅
Did you notice the hole in Mr. Soon's shirt?
No! Where was it?!

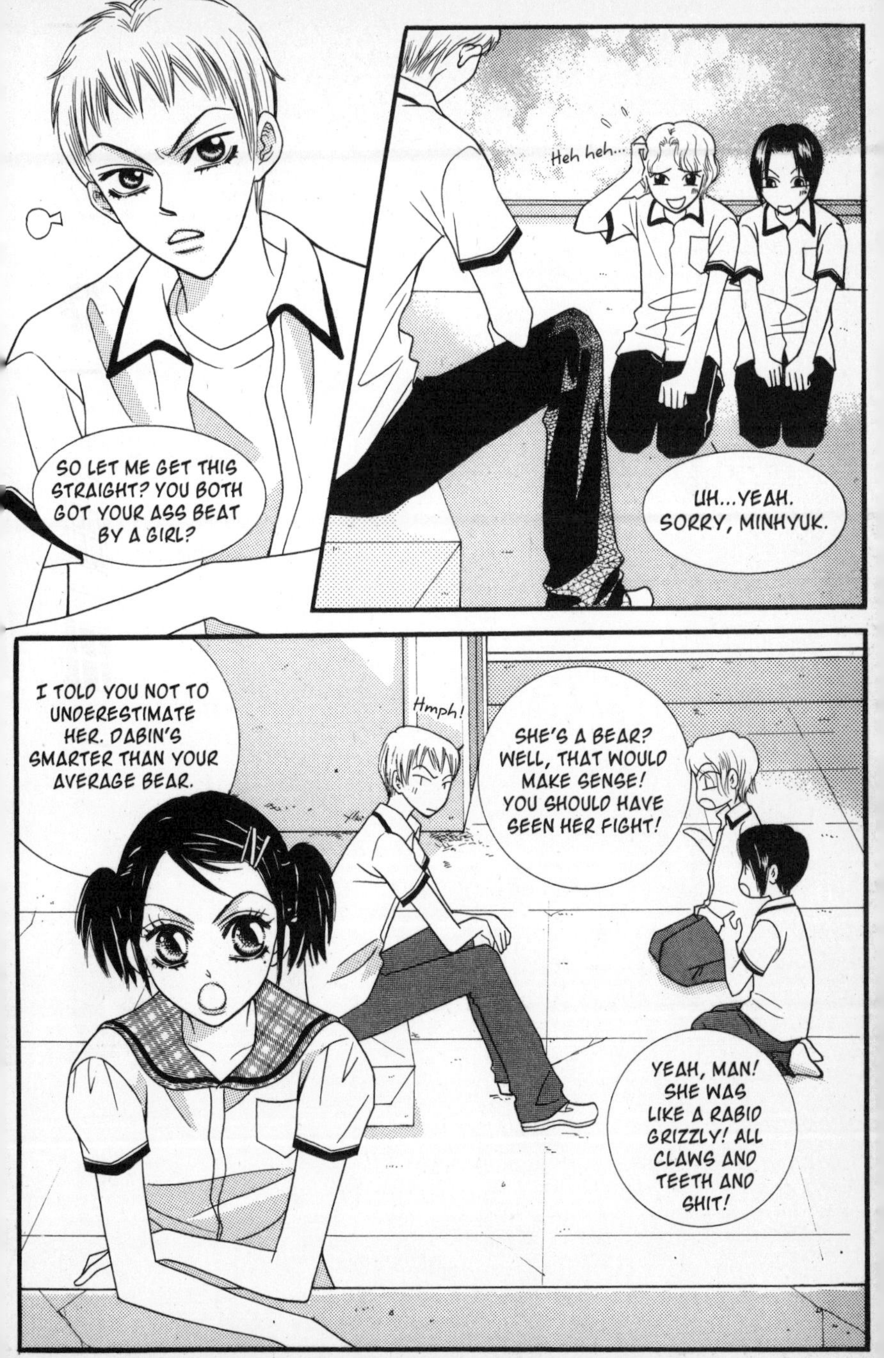
SO LET ME GET THIS STRAIGHT? YOU BOTH GOT YOUR ASS BEAT BY A GIRL?
Heh heh...
UH...YEAH. SORRY, MINHYUK.
I TOLD YOU NOT TO UNDERESTIMATE HER. DABIN'S SMARTER THAN YOUR AVERAGE BEAR.
Hmph!
SHE'S A BEAR? WELL, THAT WOULD MAKE SENSE! YOU SHOULD HAVE SEEN HER FIGHT!
YEAH, MAN! SHE WAS LIKE A RABID GRIZZLY! ALL CLAWS AND TEETH AND SHIT!

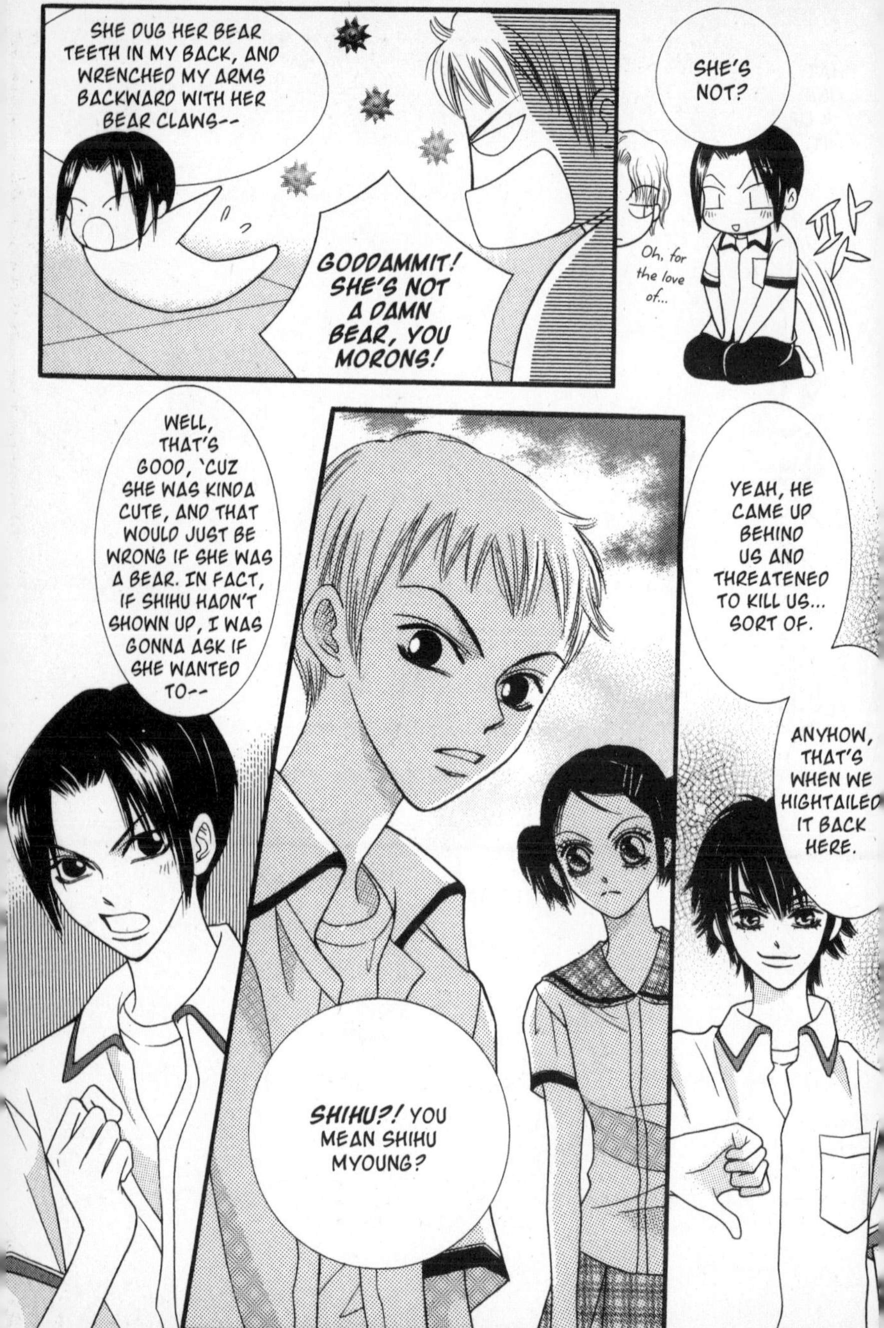
SHE DUG HER BEAR TEETH IN MY BACK, AND WRENCHED MY ARMS BACKWARD WITH HER BEAR CLAWS--
GODDAMMIT! SHE'S NOT A DAMN BEAR, YOU MORONS!
SHE'S NOT?
Oh, for the love of...
WELL, THAT'S GOOD, 'CUZ SHE WAS KINDA CUTE, AND THAT WOULD JUST BE WRONG IF SHE WAS A BEAR. IN FACT, IF SHIHU HADN'T SHOWN UP, I WAS GONNA ASK IF SHE WANTED TO--
SHIHU?! YOU MEAN SHIHU MYOUNG?
YEAH, HE CAME UP BEHIND US AND THREATENED TO KILL US... SORT OF.
ANYHOW, THAT'S WHEN WE HIGHTAILED IT BACK HERE.

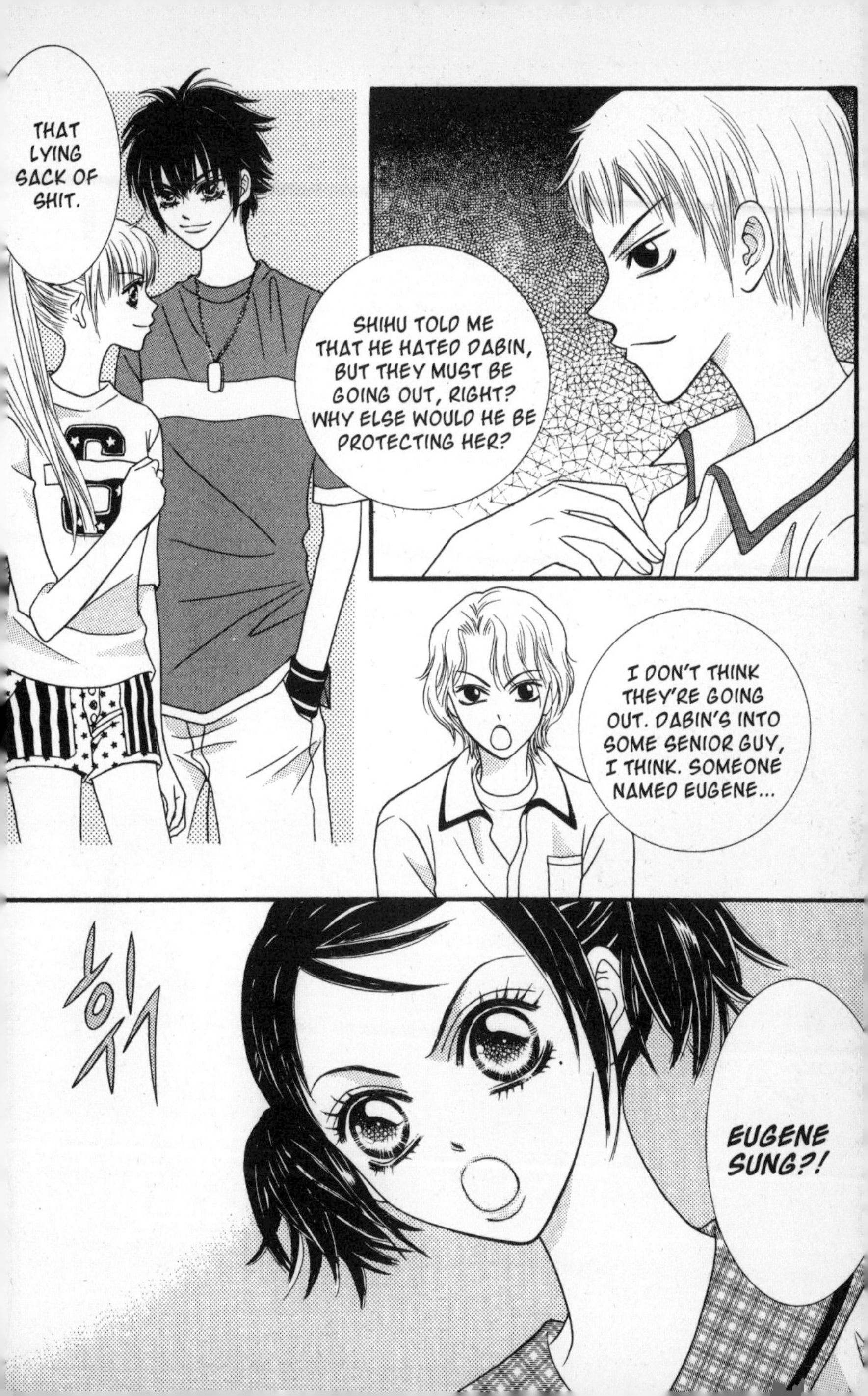
THAT LYING SACK OF SHIT.
SHIHU TOLD ME THAT HE HATED DABIN, BUT THEY MUST BE GOING OUT, RIGHT? WHY ELSE WOULD HE BE PROTECTING HER?
I DON'T THINK THEY'RE GOING OUT. DABIN'S INTO SOME SENIOR GUY, I THINK. SOMEONE NAMED EUGENE...
EUGENE SUNG?!

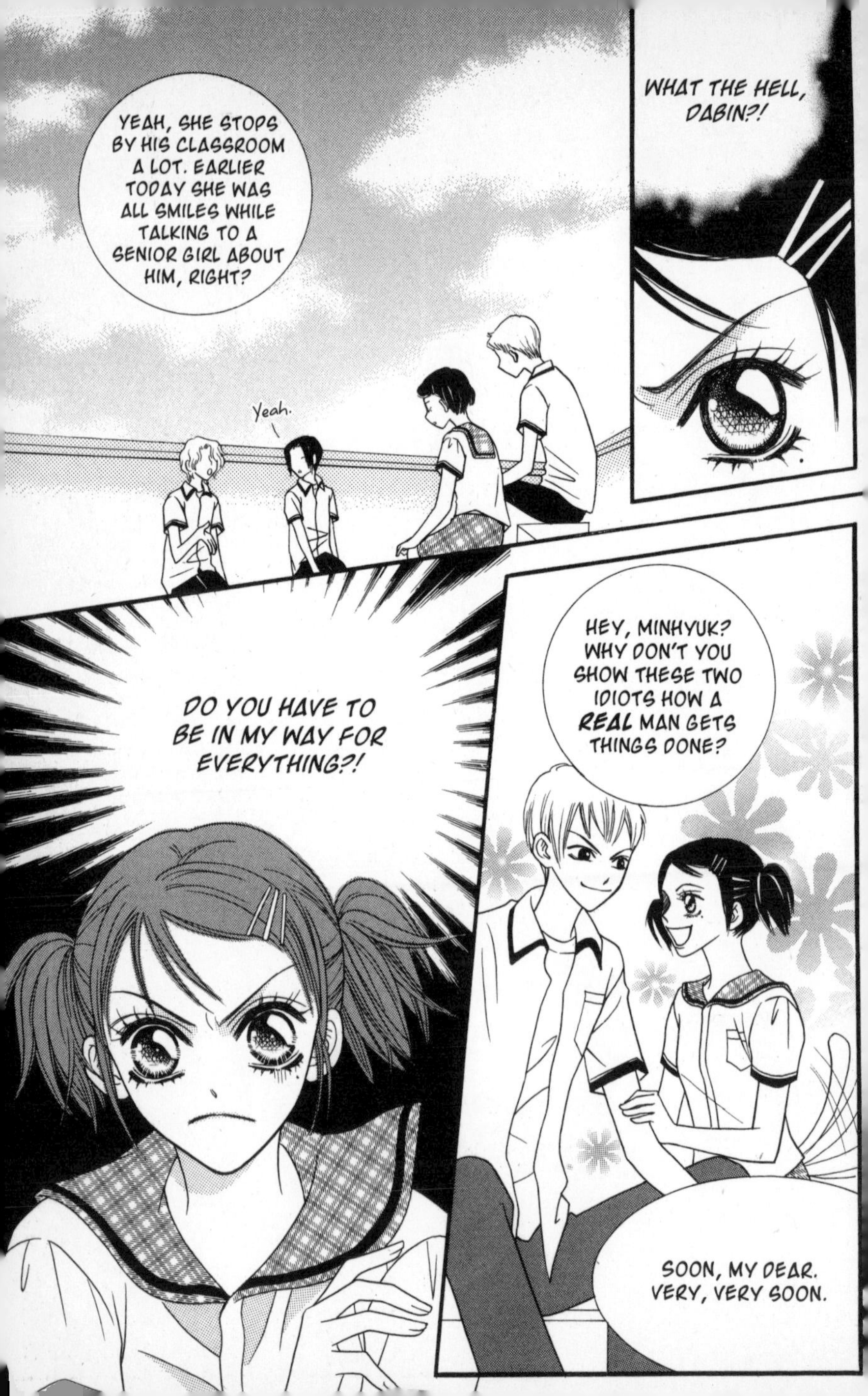
YEAH, SHE STOPS BY HIS CLASSROOM A LOT. EARLIER TODAY SHE WAS ALL SMILES WHILE TALKING TO A SENIOR GIRL ABOUT HIM, RIGHT?
Yeah.
WHAT THE HELL, DABIN?!
DO YOU HAVE TO BE IN MY WAY FOR EVERYTHING?!
HEY, MINHYUK? WHY DON'T YOU SHOW THESE TWO IDIOTS HOW A REAL MAN GETS THINGS DONE?
SOON, MY DEAR. VERY, VERY SOON.

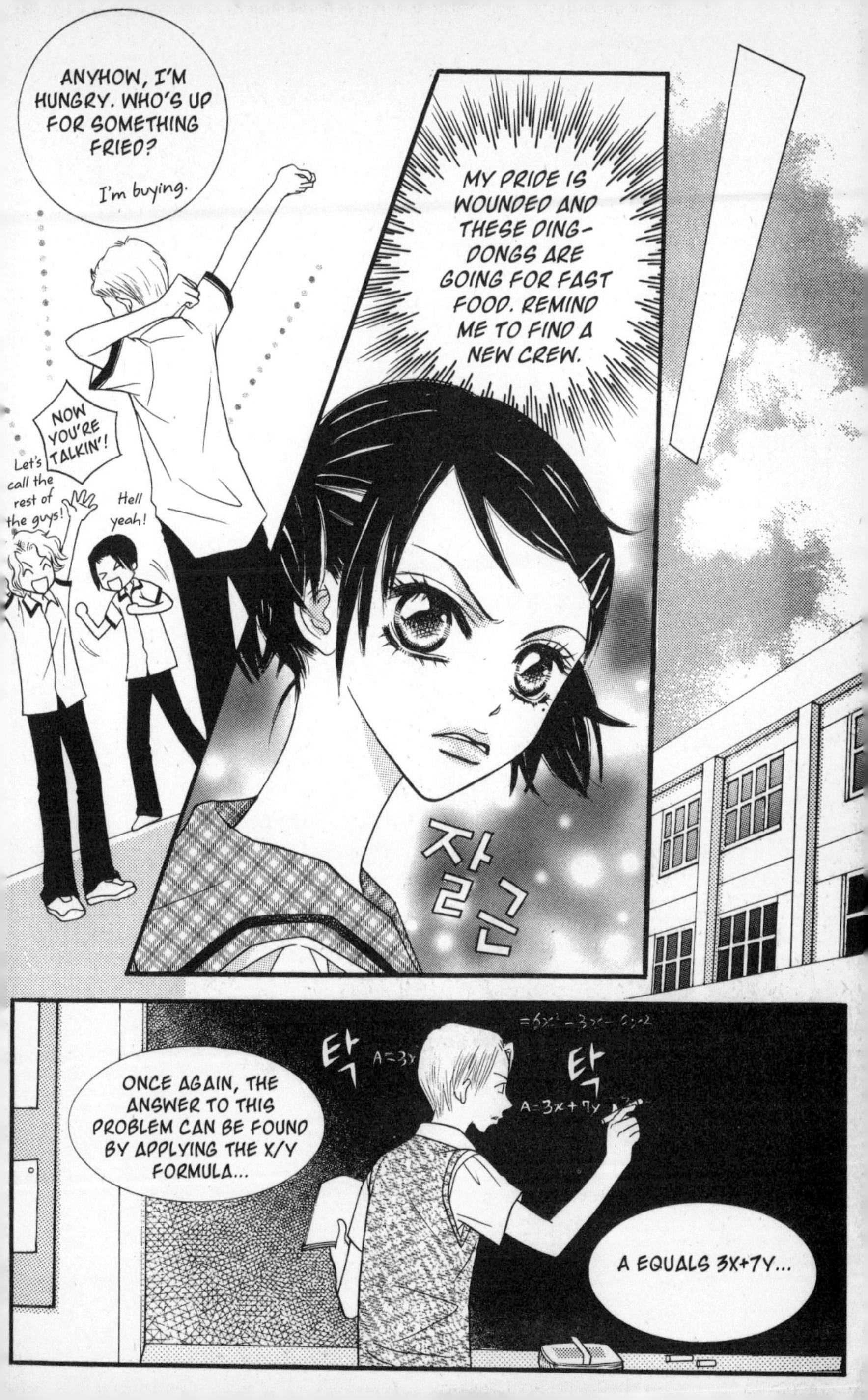
ANYHOW, I'M HUNGRY. WHO'S UP FOR SOMETHING FRIED?
I'm buying.
NOW YOU'RE TALKIN'!
Let's call the rest of the guys!
Hell yeah!
MY PRIDE IS WOUNDED AND THESE DING-DONGS ARE GOING FOR FAST FOOD. REMIND ME TO FIND A NEW CREW.
잘근
탁
A=3y
탁
A=3x+7y
ONCE AGAIN, THE ANSWER TO THIS PROBLEM CAN BE FOUND BY APPLYING THE X/Y FORMULA...
A EQUALS 3X+7Y...

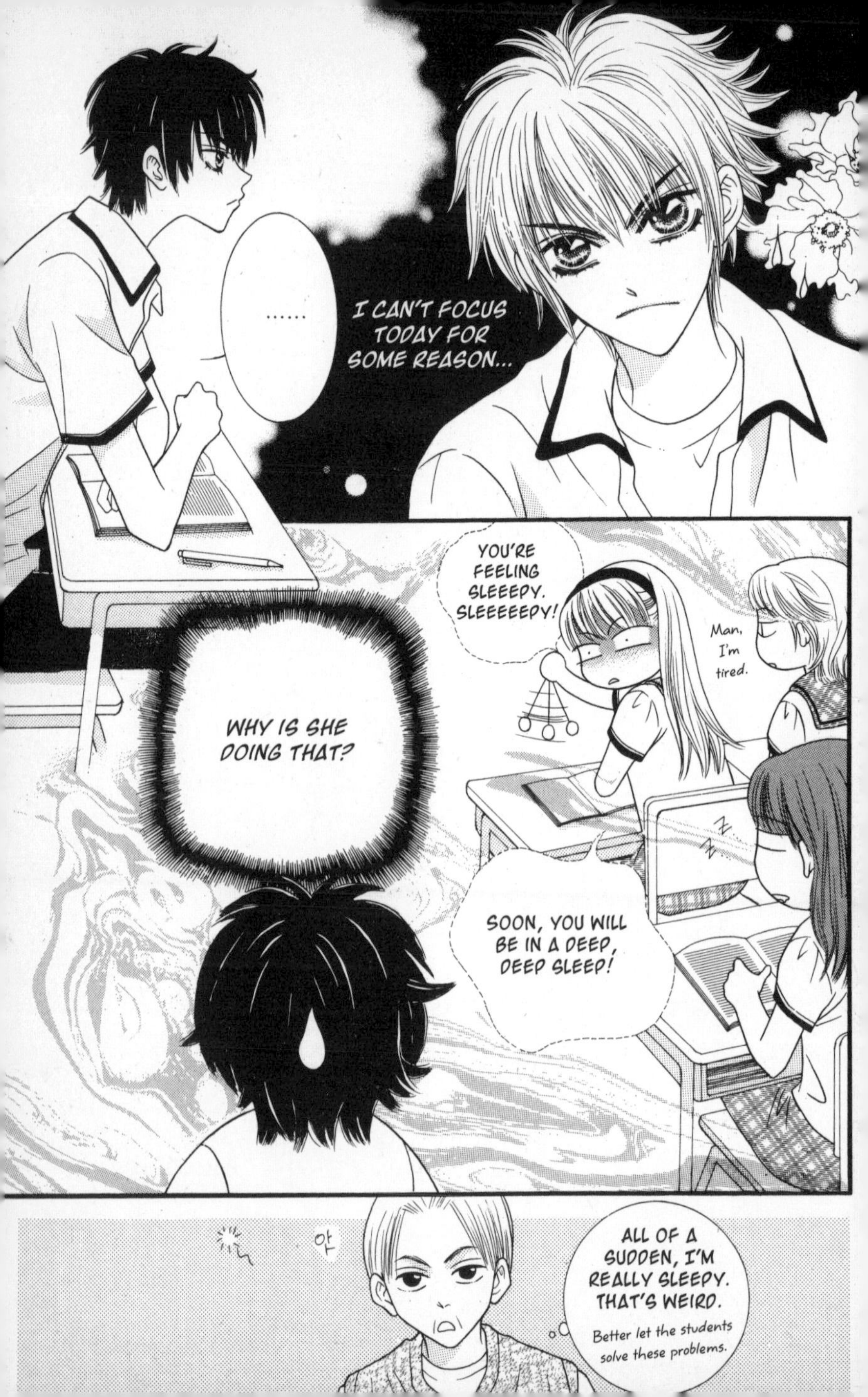
......
I CAN'T FOCUS TODAY FOR SOME REASON...
YOU'RE FEELING SLEEEPY. SLEEEEEPY!
Man, I'm tired.
WHY IS SHE DOING THAT?
Z Z
SOON, YOU WILL BE IN A DEEP, DEEP SLEEP!
약
ALL OF A SUDDEN, I'M REALLY SLEEPY. THAT'S WEIRD.
Better let the students solve these problems.

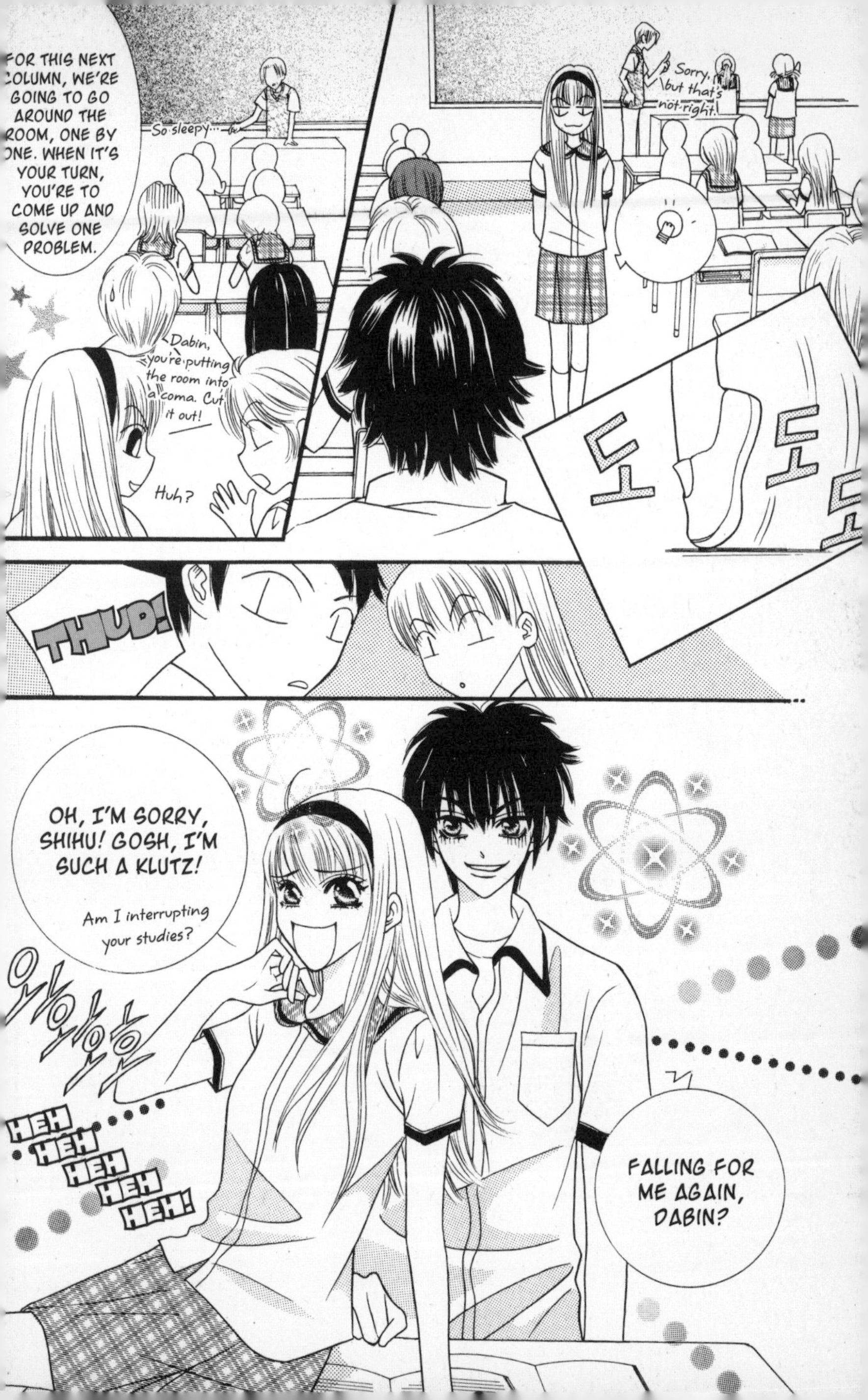

FOR THIS NEXT COLUMN, WE'RE GOING TO GO AROUND THE ROOM, ONE BY ONE. WHEN IT'S YOUR TURN, YOU'RE TO COME UP AND SOLVE ONE PROBLEM.
So sleepy...
Dabin, you're putting the room into a coma. Cut it out!
Huh?
Sorry, but that's not right.
도 도 도
THUD!
OH, I'M SORRY, SHIHU! GOSH, I'M SUCH A KLUTZ!
Am I interrupting your studies?
HEH HEH HEH HEH HEH!
FALLING FOR ME AGAIN, DABIN?

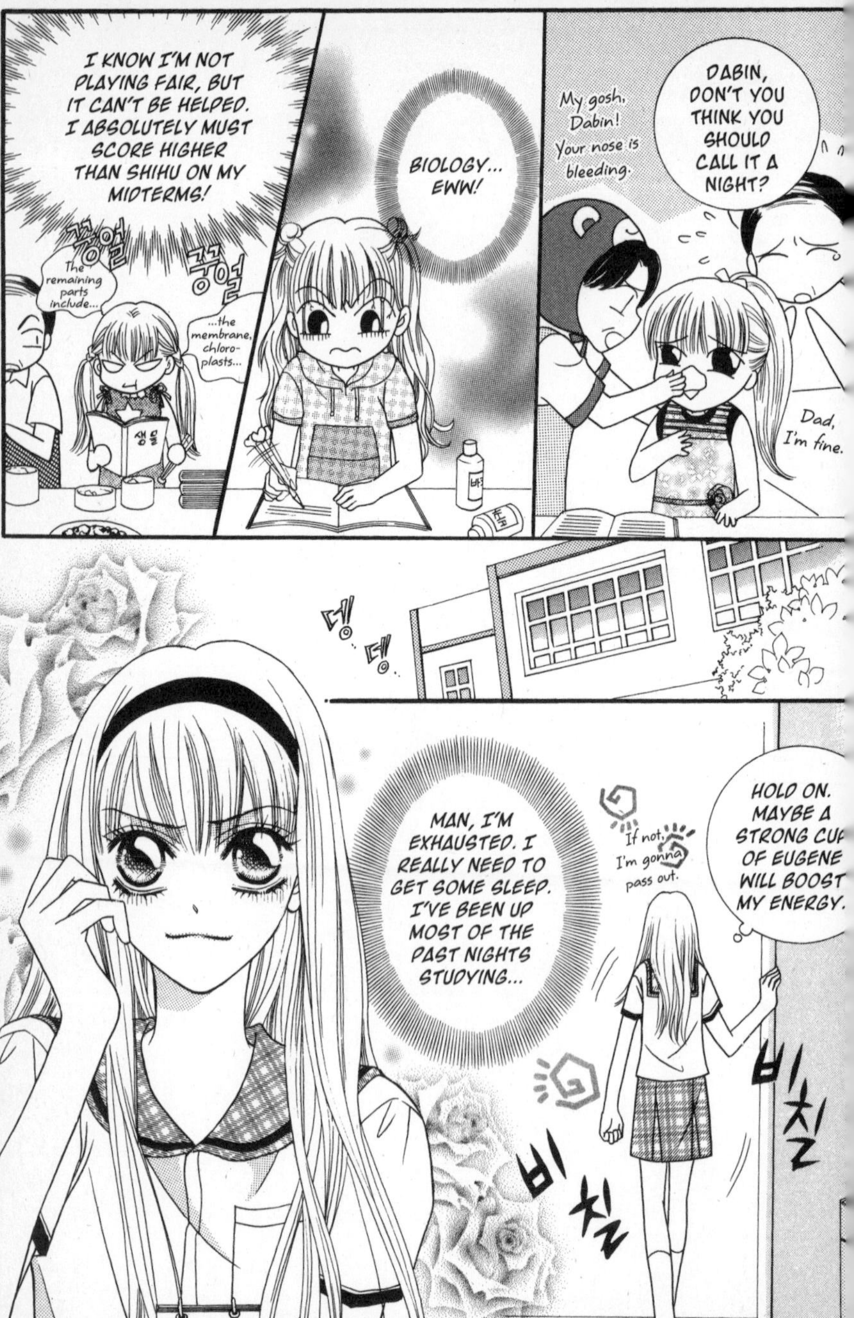
I KNOW I'M NOT PLAYING FAIR, BUT IT CAN'T BE HELPED. I ABSOLUTELY MUST SCORE HIGHER THAN SHIHU ON MY MIDTERMS!
중얼
중얼
The remaining parts include...
...the membrane, chloroplasts...
생물
BIOLOGY... EWW!
My gosh, Dabin! Your nose is bleeding.
DABIN, DON'T YOU THINK YOU SHOULD CALL IT A NIGHT?
Dad, I'm fine.
뎅..
뎅..
MAN, I'M EXHAUSTED. I REALLY NEED TO GET SOME SLEEP. I'VE BEEN UP MOST OF THE PAST NIGHTS STUDYING...
If not, I'm gonna pass out.
HOLD ON. MAYBE A STRONG CUP OF EUGENE WILL BOOST MY ENERGY.
비칠
비칠

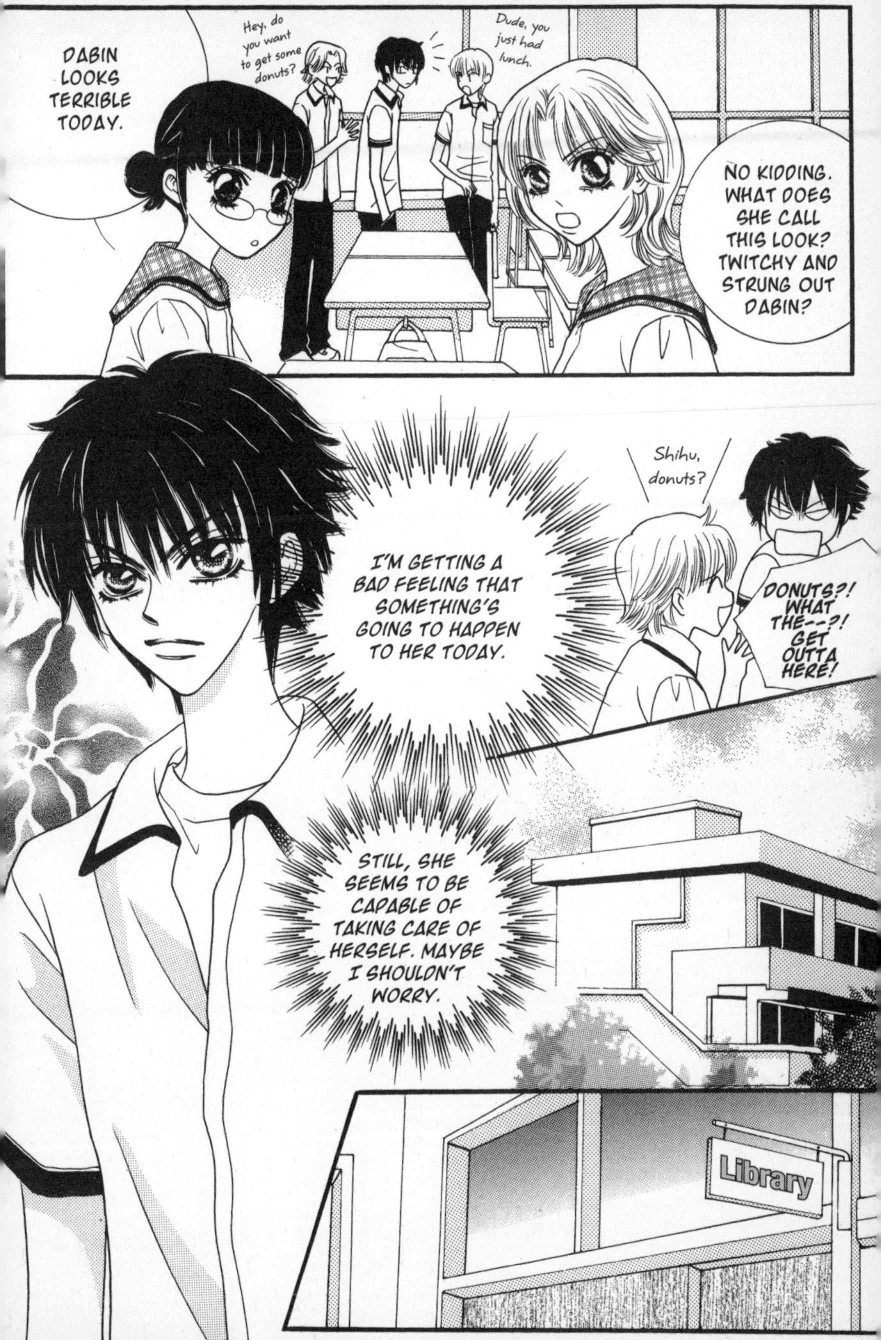
DABIN LOOKS TERRIBLE TODAY.
Hey, do you want to get some donuts?
Dude, you just had lunch.
NO KIDDING. WHAT DOES SHE CALL THIS LOOK? TWITCHY AND STRUNG OUT DABIN?
I'M GETTING A BAD FEELING THAT SOMETHING'S GOING TO HAPPEN TO HER TODAY.
Shihu, donuts?
DONUTS?! WHAT THE--?! GET OUTTA HERE!
STILL, SHE SEEMS TO BE CAPABLE OF TAKING CARE OF HERSELF. MAYBE I SHOULDN'T WORRY.
Library

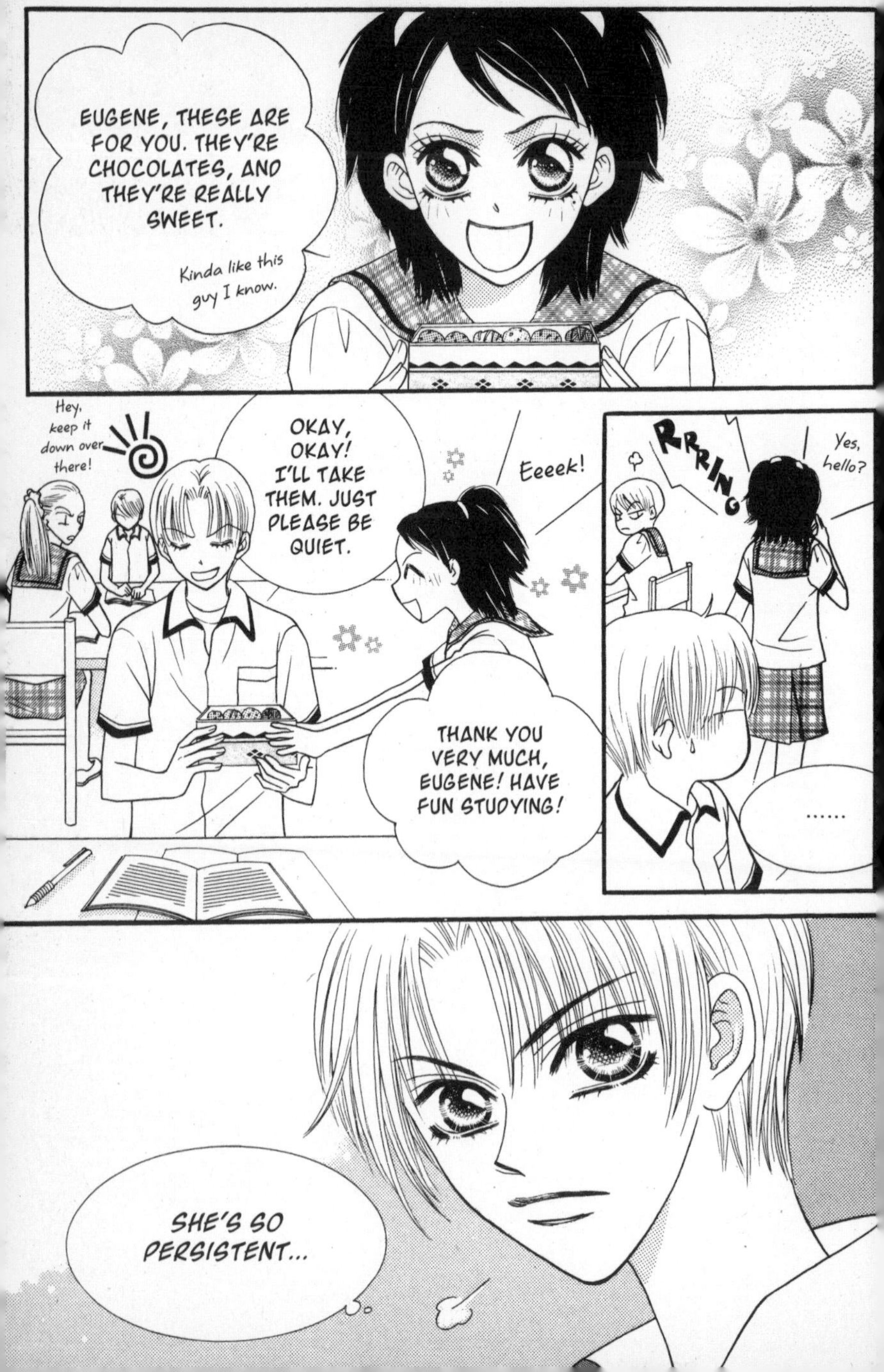
EUGENE, THESE ARE FOR YOU. THEY'RE CHOCOLATES, AND THEY'RE REALLY SWEET.
Kinda like this guy I know.
Hey, keep it down over there!
OKAY, OKAY! I'LL TAKE THEM. JUST PLEASE BE QUIET.
Eeeek!
THANK YOU VERY MUCH, EUGENE! HAVE FUN STUDYING!
RRRING
Yes, hello?
......
SHE'S SO PERSISTENT...

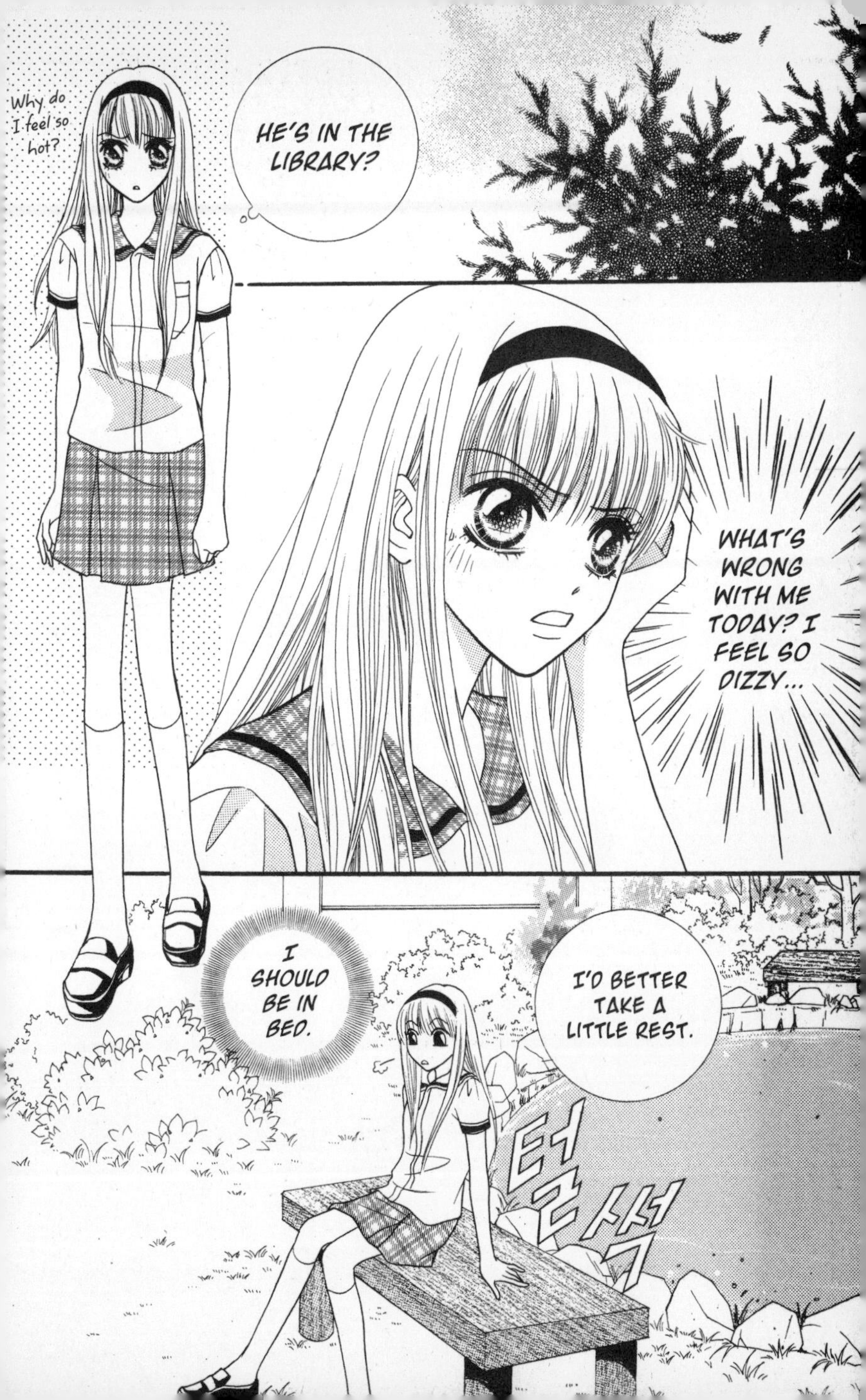
Why do I feel so hot?
HE'S IN THE LIBRARY?
WHAT'S WRONG WITH ME TODAY? I FEEL SO DIZZY...
I SHOULD BE IN BED.
I'D BETTER TAKE A LITTLE REST.
털썩

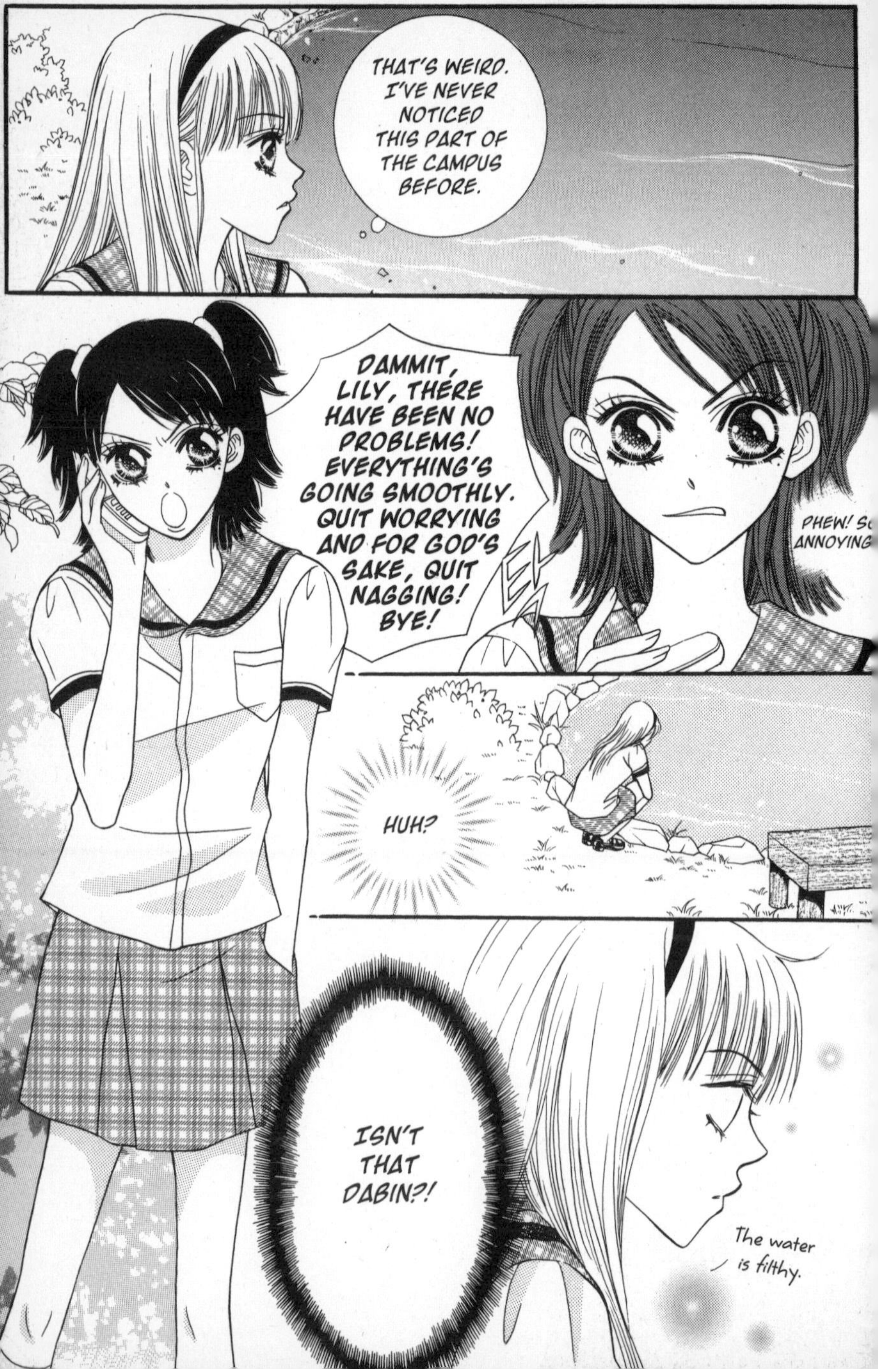
THAT'S WEIRD. I'VE NEVER NOTICED THIS PART OF THE CAMPUS BEFORE.
DAMMIT, LILY, THERE HAVE BEEN NO PROBLEMS! EVERYTHING'S GOING SMOOTHLY. QUIT WORRYING AND FOR GOD'S SAKE, QUIT NAGGING! BYE!
PHEW! S ANNOYING
HUH?
ISN'T THAT DABIN?!
The water is filthy.

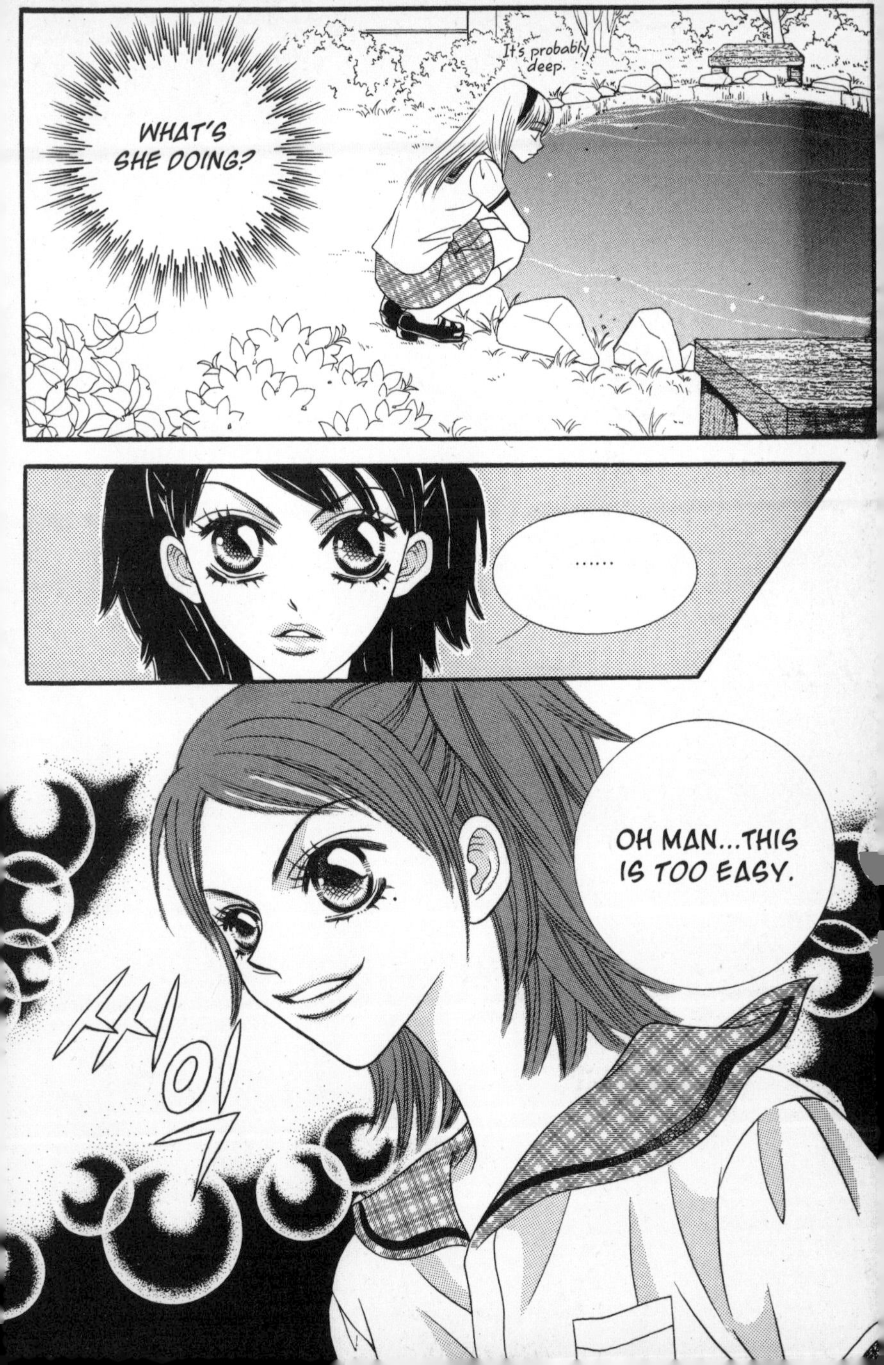
WHAT'S SHE DOING?
It's probably deep.
......
OH MAN...THIS IS TOO EASY.

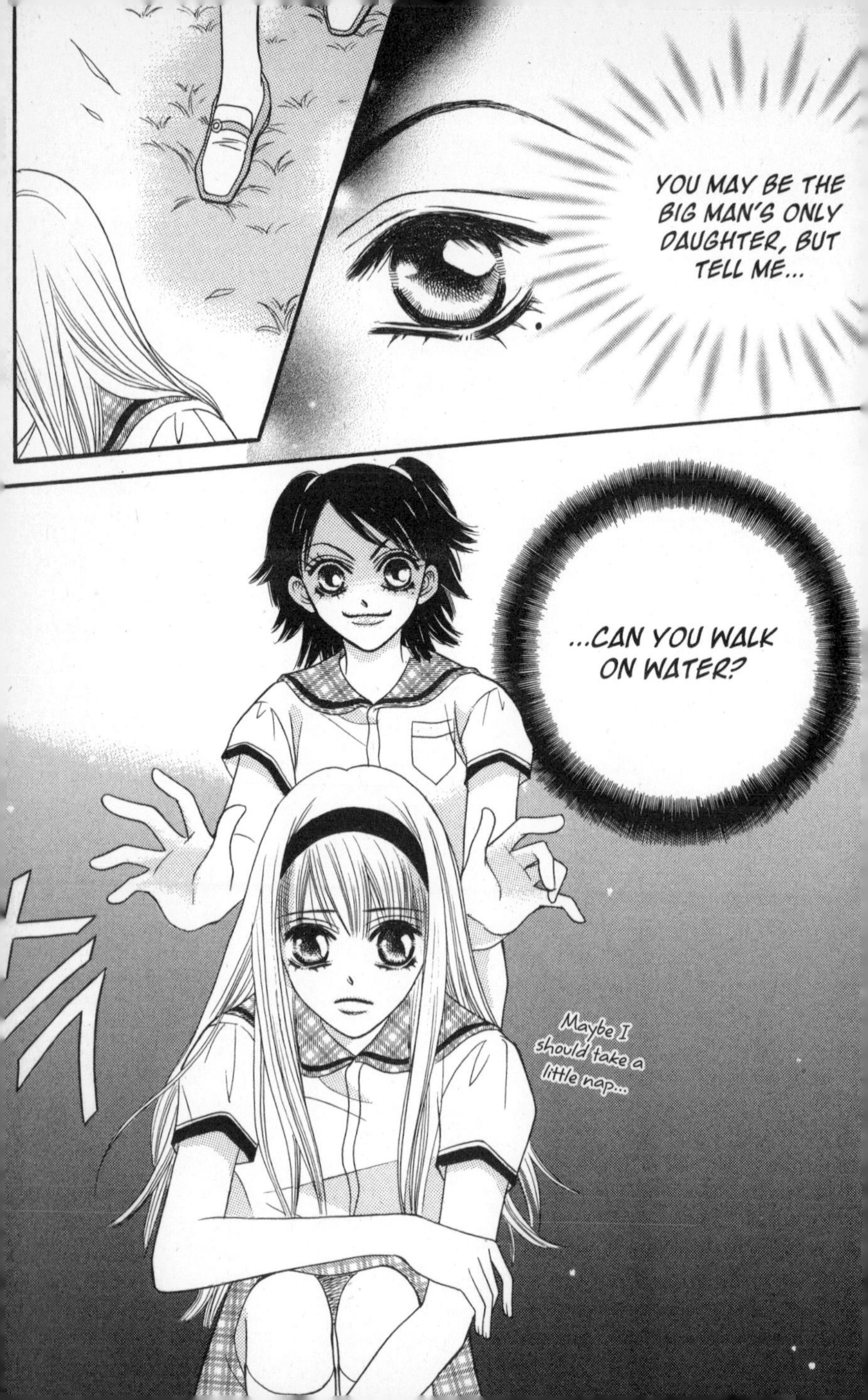
YOU MAY BE THE BIG MAN'S ONLY DAUGHTER, BUT TELL ME...
...CAN YOU WALK ON WATER?
Maybe I should take a little nap...

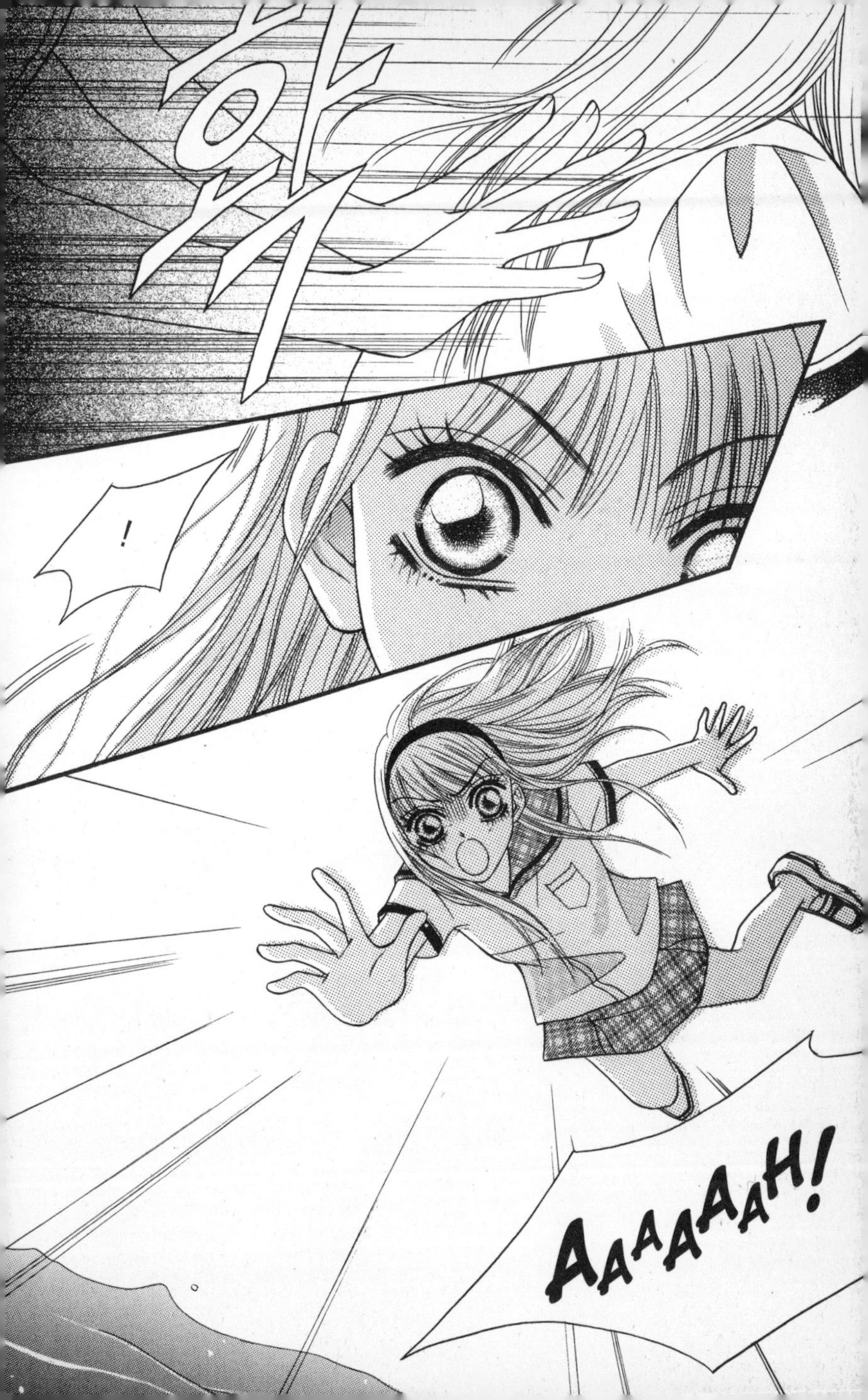
!
AAAAAAH!

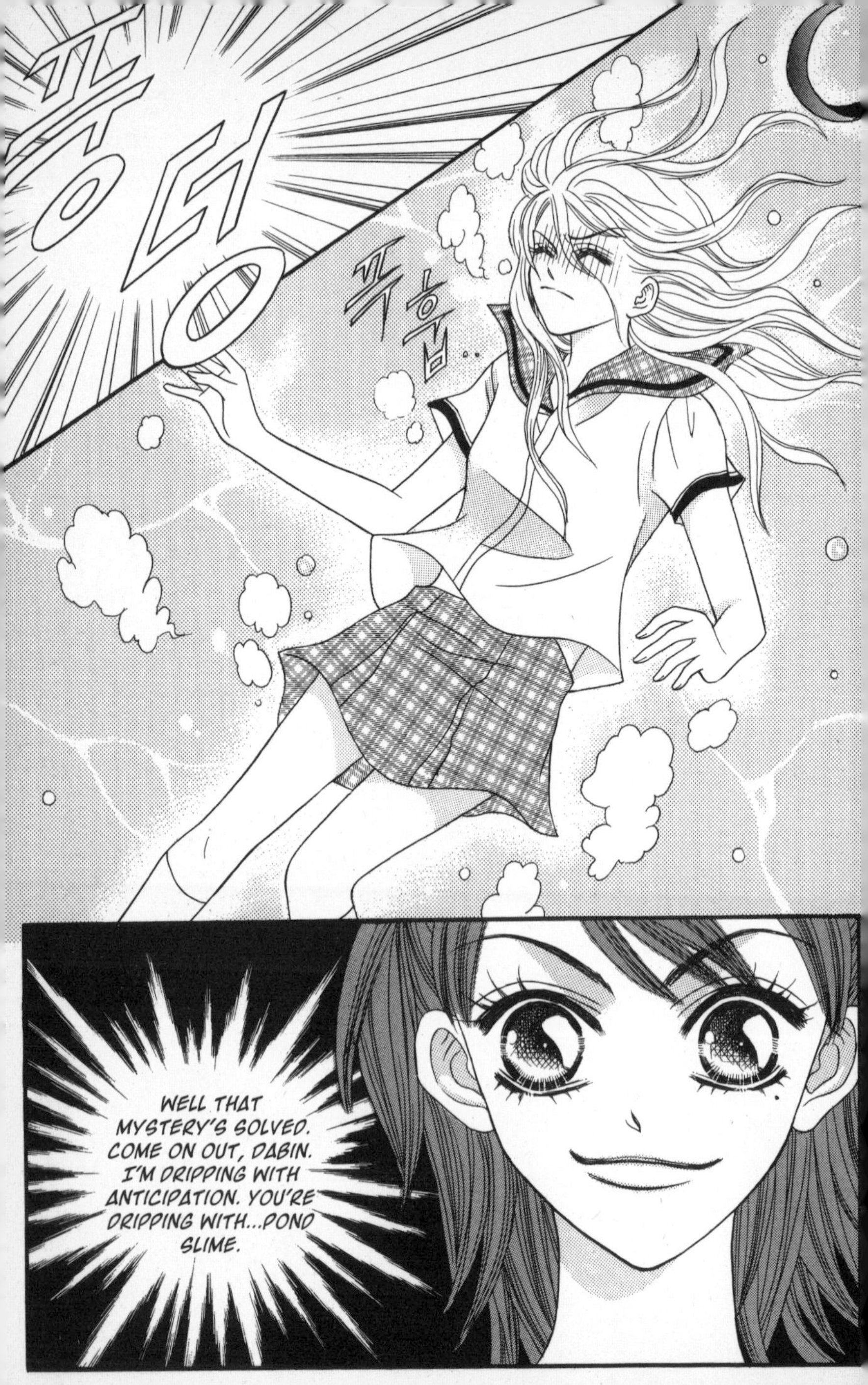

풍덩
푸흡..
WELL THAT MYSTERY'S SOLVED. COME ON OUT, DABIN. I'M DRIPPING WITH ANTICIPATION. YOU'RE DRIPPING WITH...POND SLIME.

| Cute | Sweet | Bright | Fresh |

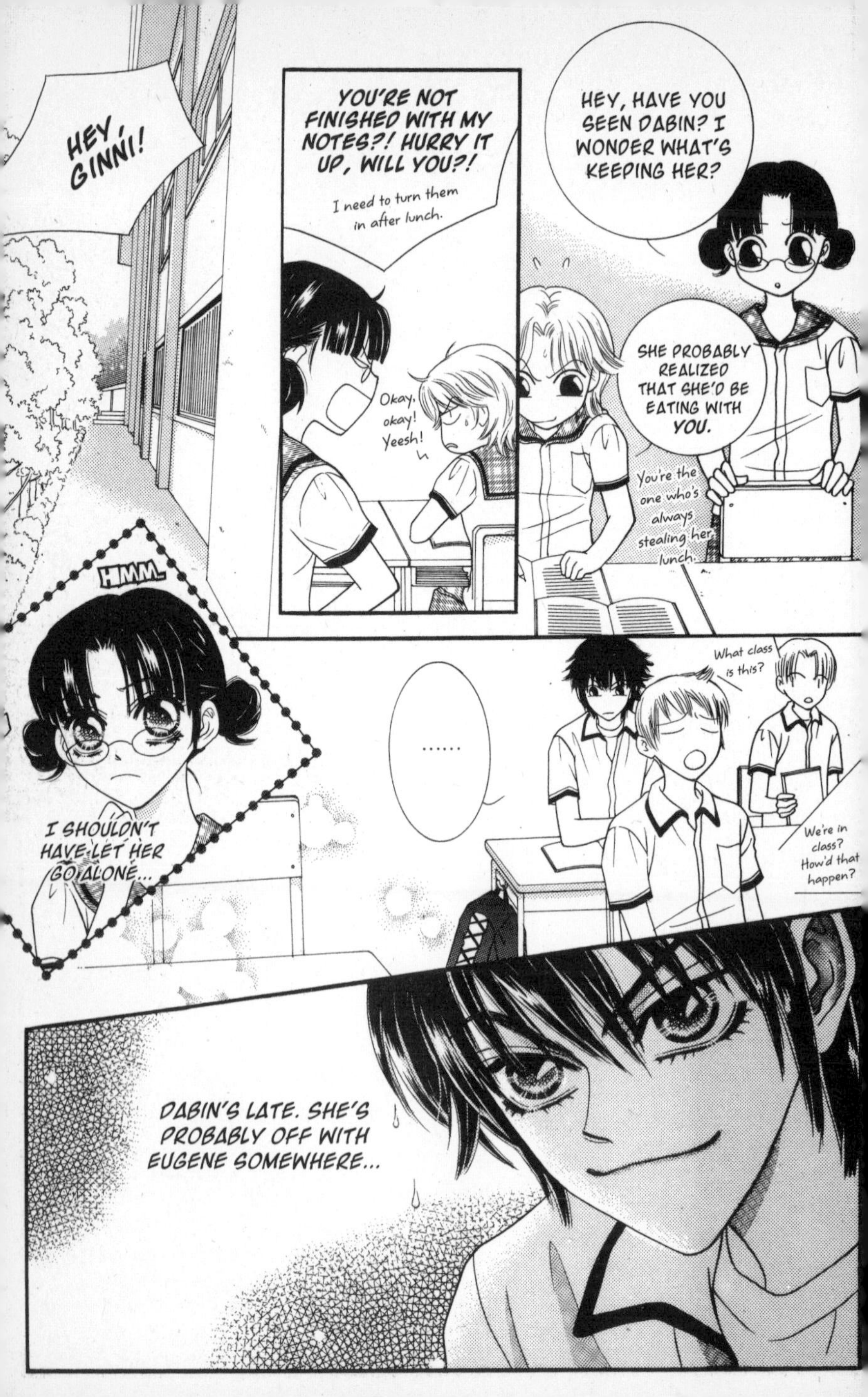
HEY, GINNI!
YOU'RE NOT FINISHED WITH MY NOTES?! HURRY IT UP, WILL YOU?!
I need to turn them in after lunch.
Okay, okay! Yeesh!
HEY, HAVE YOU SEEN DABIN? I WONDER WHAT'S KEEPING HER?
SHE PROBABLY REALIZED THAT SHE'D BE EATING WITH YOU.
You're the one who's always stealing her lunch.
HMM..
I SHOULDN'T HAVE LET HER GO ALONE...
......
What class is this?
We're in class? How'd that happen?
DABIN'S LATE. SHE'S PROBABLY OFF WITH EUGENE SOMEWHERE...

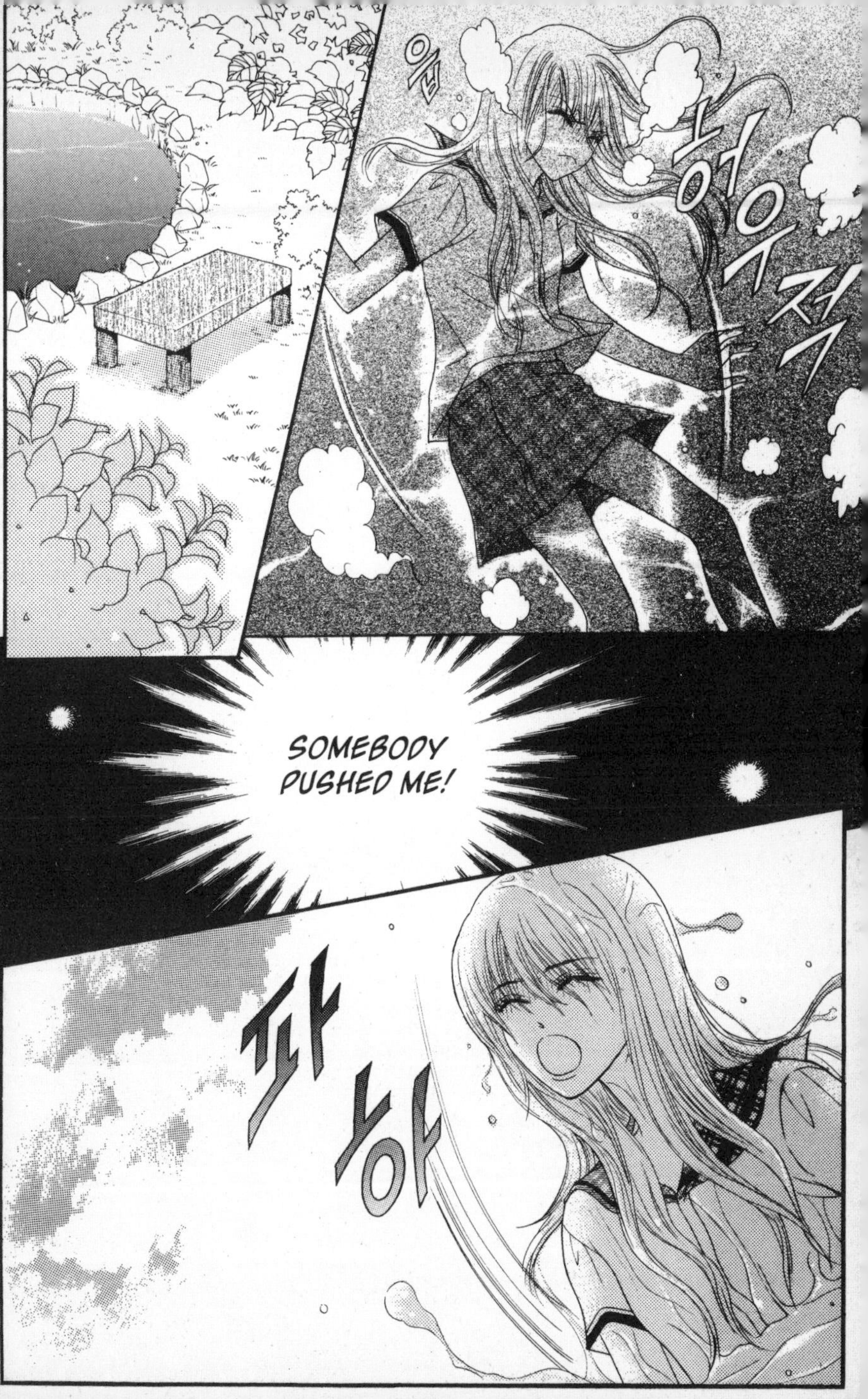
SOMEBODY
PUSHED ME!

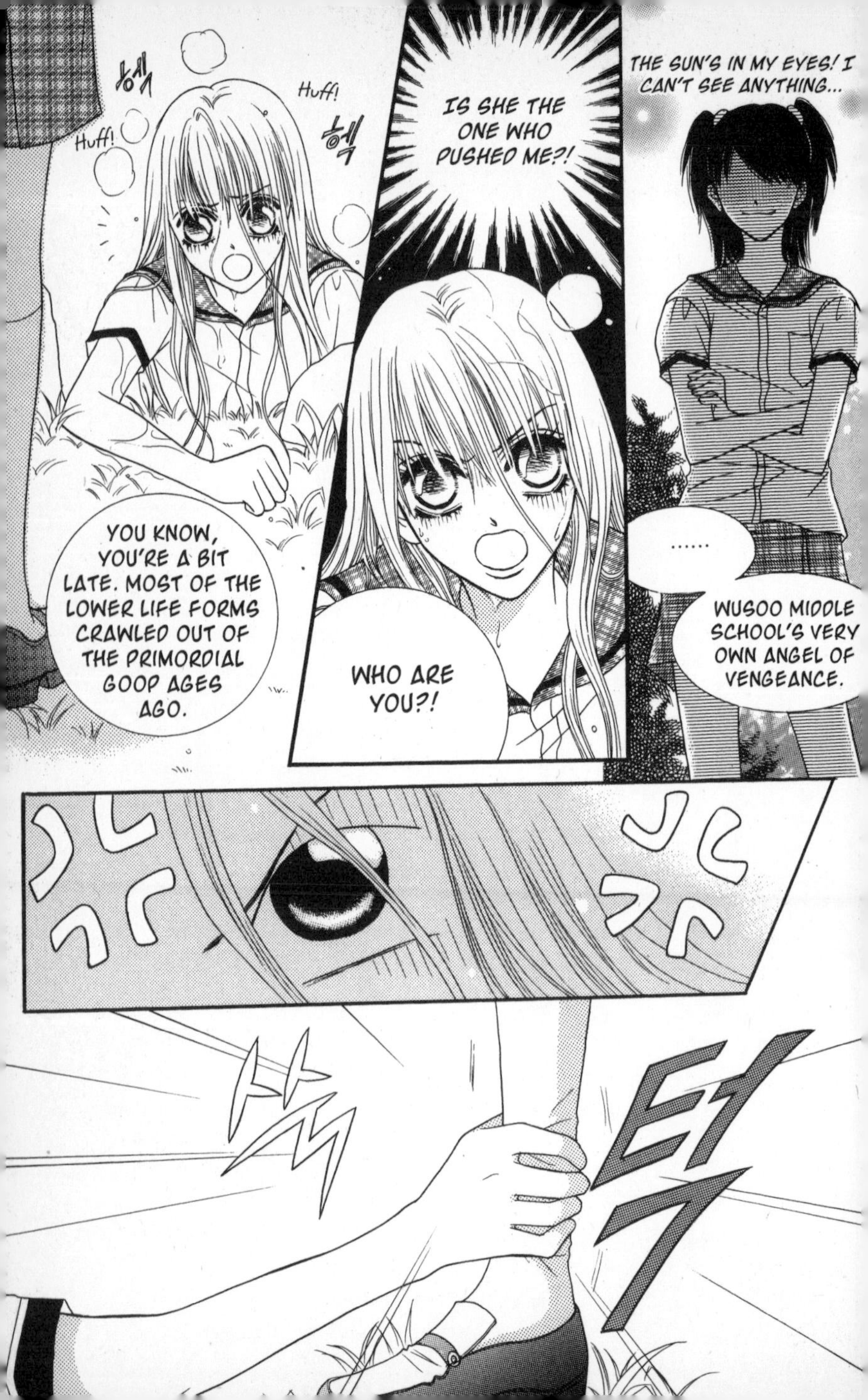
Huff!
Huff!
YOU KNOW, YOU'RE A BIT LATE. MOST OF THE LOWER LIFE FORMS CRAWLED OUT OF THE PRIMORDIAL GOOP AGES AGO.
IS SHE THE ONE WHO PUSHED ME?!
WHO ARE YOU?!
THE SUN'S IN MY EYES! I CAN'T SEE ANYTHING...
......
WUSOO MIDDLE SCHOOL'S VERY OWN ANGEL OF VENGEANCE.

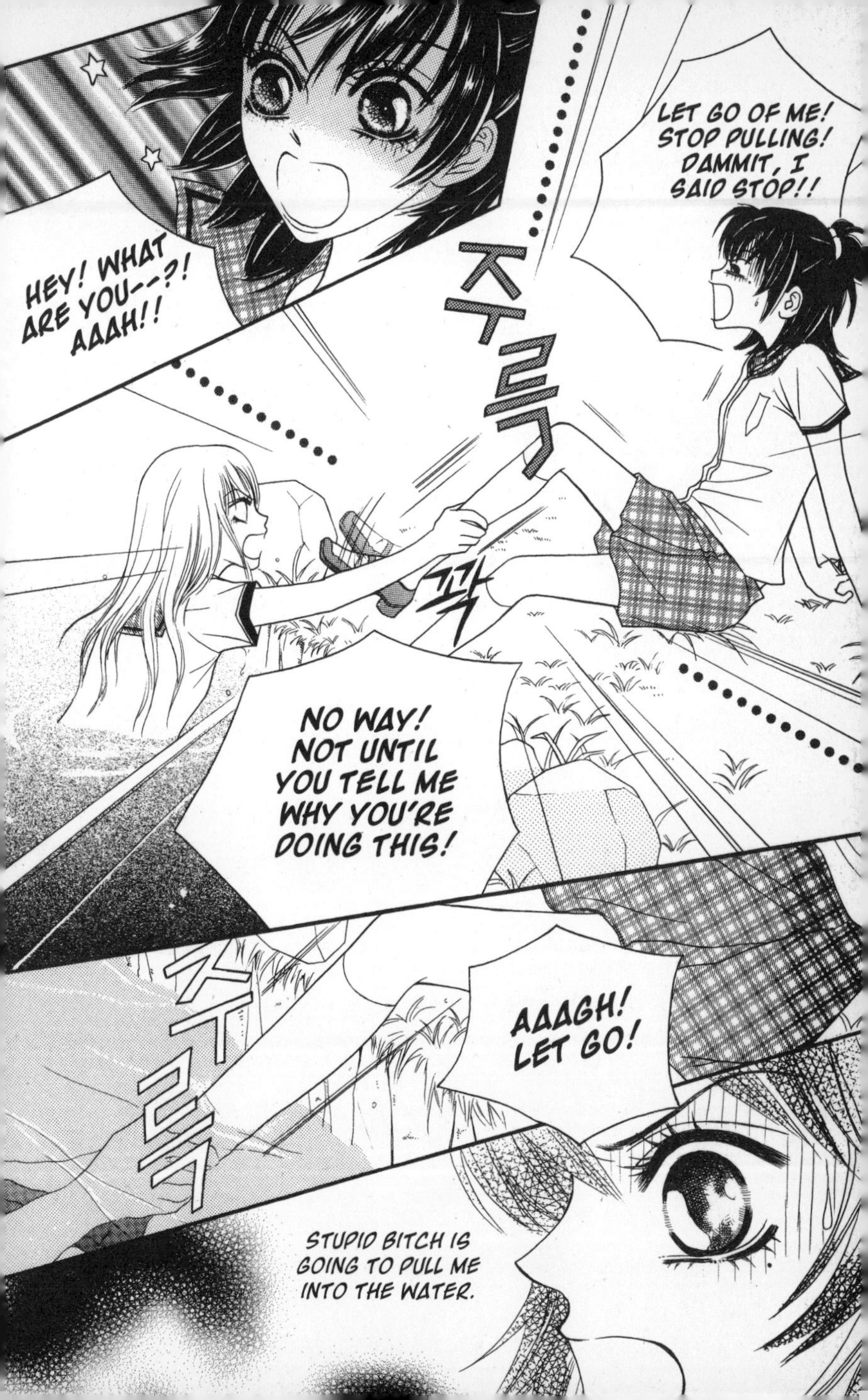
HEY! WHAT ARE YOU--?! AAAH!!
LET GO OF ME! STOP PULLING! DAMMIT, I SAID STOP!!
꽉
NO WAY! NOT UNTIL YOU TELL ME WHY YOU'RE DOING THIS!
AAAGH! LET GO!
STUPID BITCH IS GOING TO PULL ME INTO THE WATER.

ㅍ ㅏ � ㅏ

ㅓ ㅏ ㄱ

CUT IT OUT!

Hmph!

I'VE GOT TO GET GOING, BUT I'LL BE SEEING YOU. TRUST ME ON THAT ONE.

OH, ONE MORE THING--YOU REEK!

YOU'RE DAMN LUCKY I DIDN'T FALL IN.

You got my shoe wet, though. I'll add that to the list of things I'm pissed at you about.

What?!

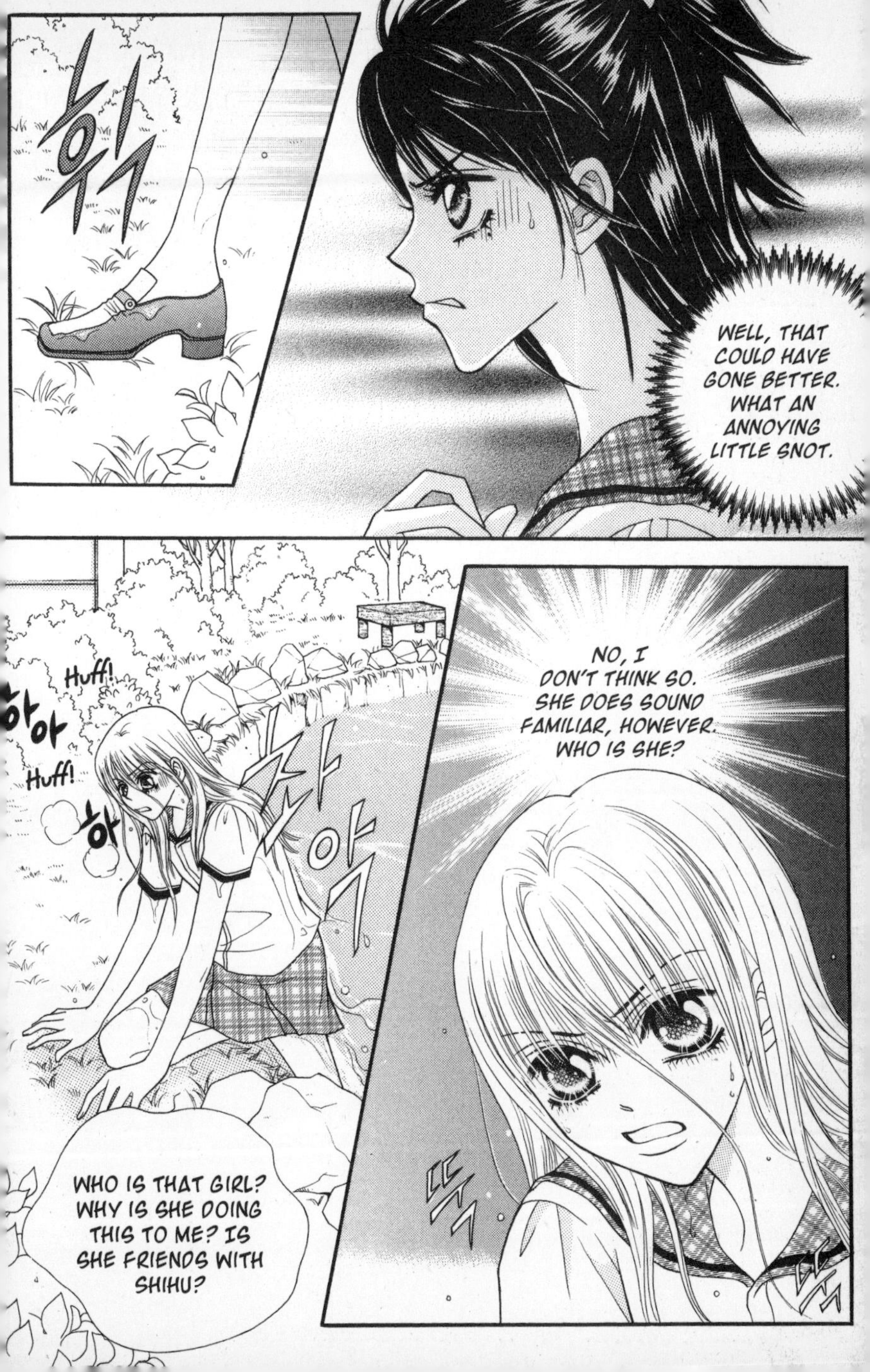
WELL, THAT COULD HAVE GONE BETTER. WHAT AN ANNOYING LITTLE SNOT.
Huff!
Huff!
WHO IS THAT GIRL? WHY IS SHE DOING THIS TO ME? IS SHE FRIENDS WITH SHIHU?
NO, I DON'T THINK SO. SHE DOES SOUND FAMILIAR, HOWEVER. WHO IS SHE?

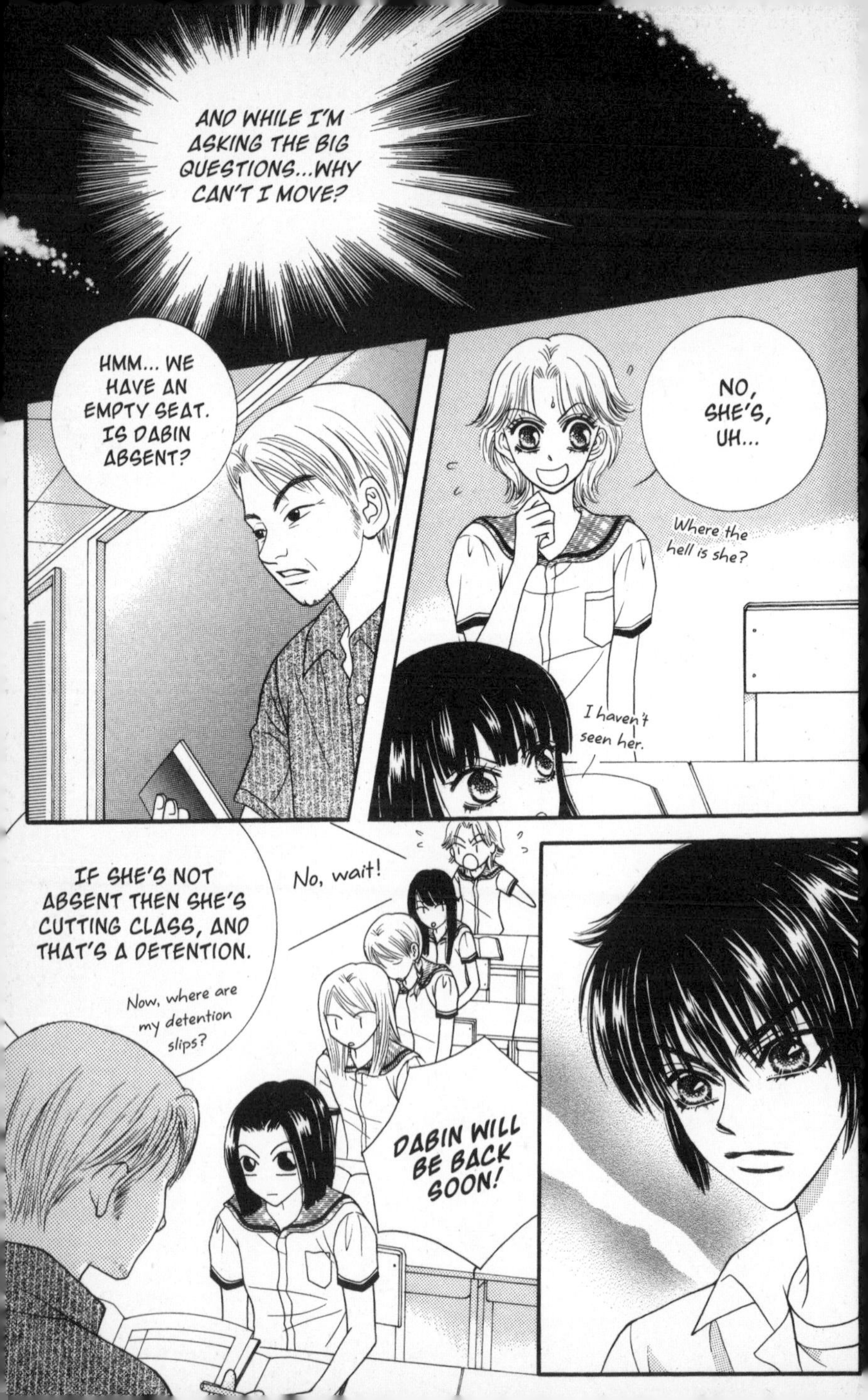
AND WHILE I'M ASKING THE BIG QUESTIONS...WHY CAN'T I MOVE?
HMM... WE HAVE AN EMPTY SEAT. IS DABIN ABSENT?
NO, SHE'S, UH...
Where the hell is she?
I haven't seen her.
IF SHE'S NOT ABSENT THEN SHE'S CUTTING CLASS, AND THAT'S A DETENTION.
Now, where are my detention slips?
No, wait!
DABIN WILL BE BACK SOON!

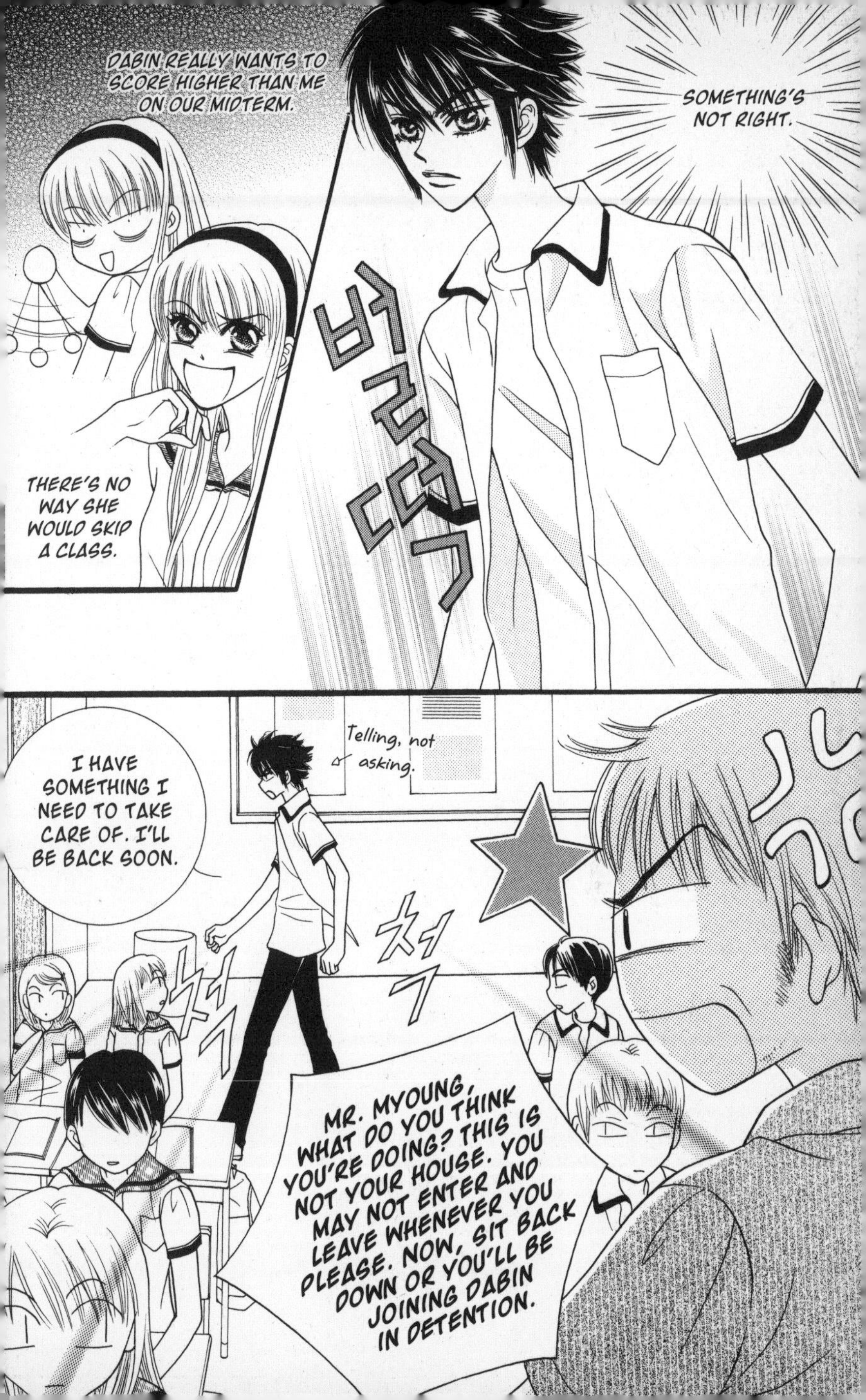
DABIN REALLY WANTS TO SCORE HIGHER THAN ME ON OUR MIDTERM.
THERE'S NO WAY SHE WOULD SKIP A CLASS.
SOMETHING'S NOT RIGHT.
I HAVE SOMETHING I NEED TO TAKE CARE OF. I'LL BE BACK SOON.
Telling, not asking.
MR. MYOUNG, WHAT DO YOU THINK YOU'RE DOING? THIS IS NOT YOUR HOUSE. YOU MAY NOT ENTER AND LEAVE WHENEVER YOU PLEASE. NOW, SIT BACK DOWN OR YOU'LL BE JOINING DABIN IN DETENTION.

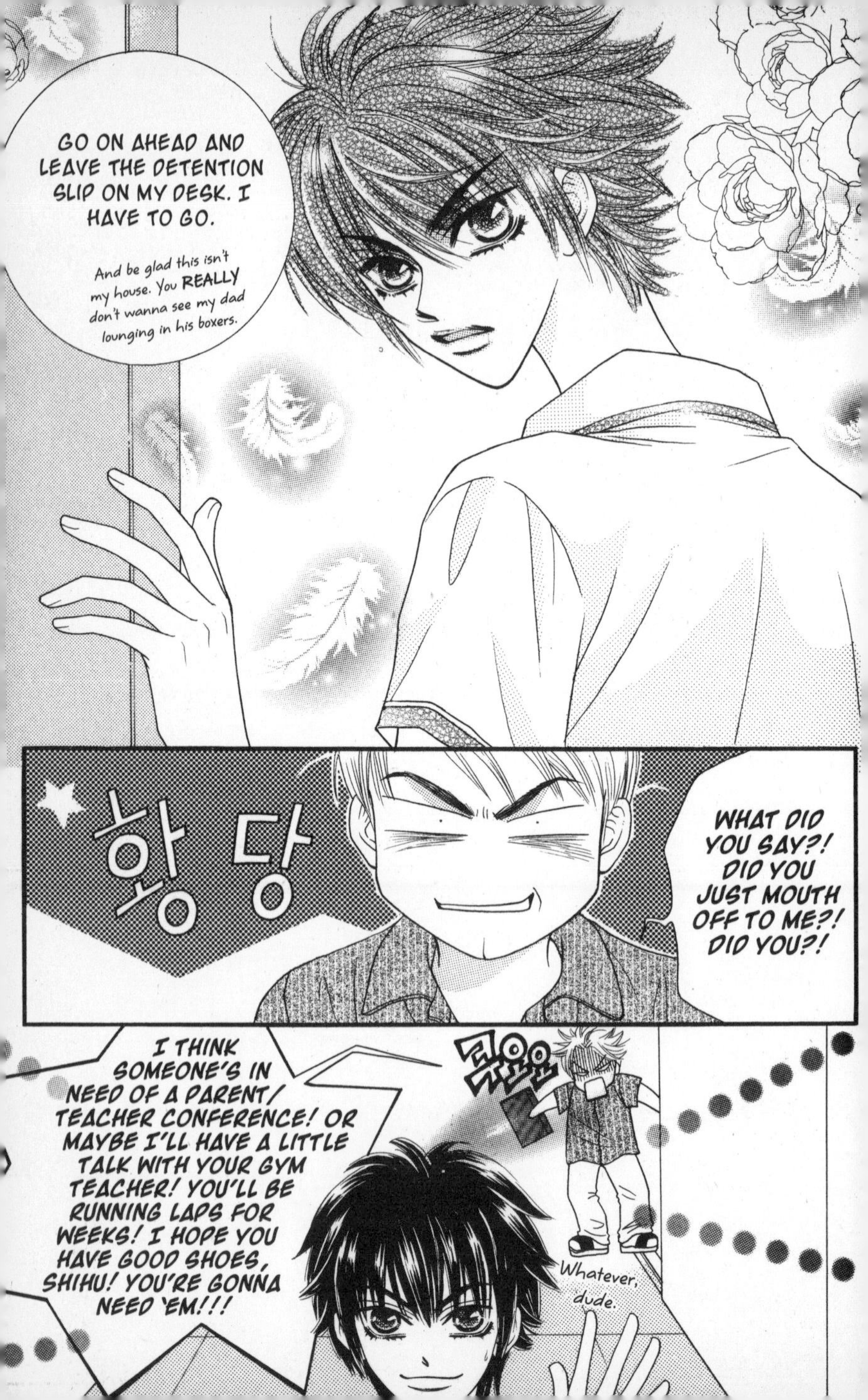
GO ON AHEAD AND LEAVE THE DETENTION SLIP ON MY DESK. I HAVE TO GO.
And be glad this isn't my house. You **REALLY** don't wanna see my dad lounging in his boxers.
황 당
WHAT DID YOU SAY?! DID YOU JUST MOUTH OFF TO ME?! DID YOU?!
I THINK SOMEONE'S IN NEED OF A PARENT/ TEACHER CONFERENCE! OR MAYBE I'LL HAVE A LITTLE TALK WITH YOUR GYM TEACHER! YOU'LL BE RUNNING LAPS FOR WEEKS! I HOPE YOU HAVE GOOD SHOES, SHIHU! YOU'RE GONNA NEED 'EM!!!
Whatever, dude.

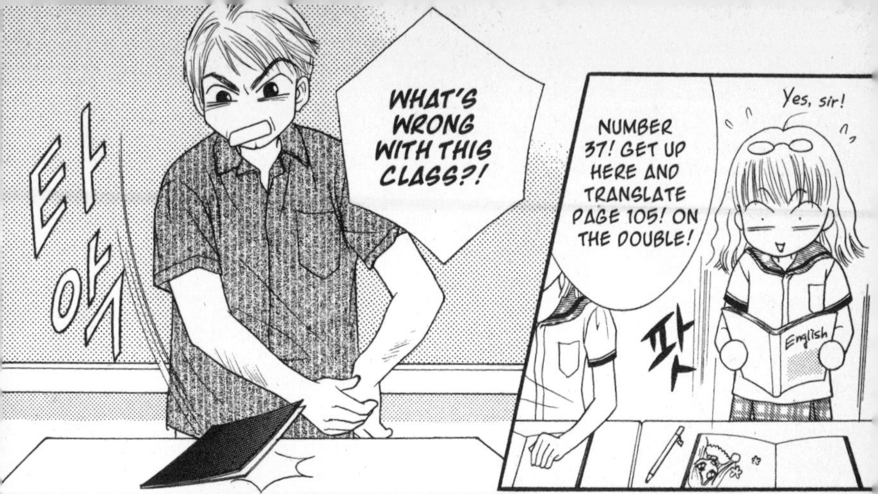
타악
WHAT'S WRONG WITH THIS CLASS?!
NUMBER 37! GET UP HERE AND TRANSLATE PAGE 105! ON THE DOUBLE!
팍
Yes, sir!
English

NOTE: Korean students are assigned numbers to be used in their classes.

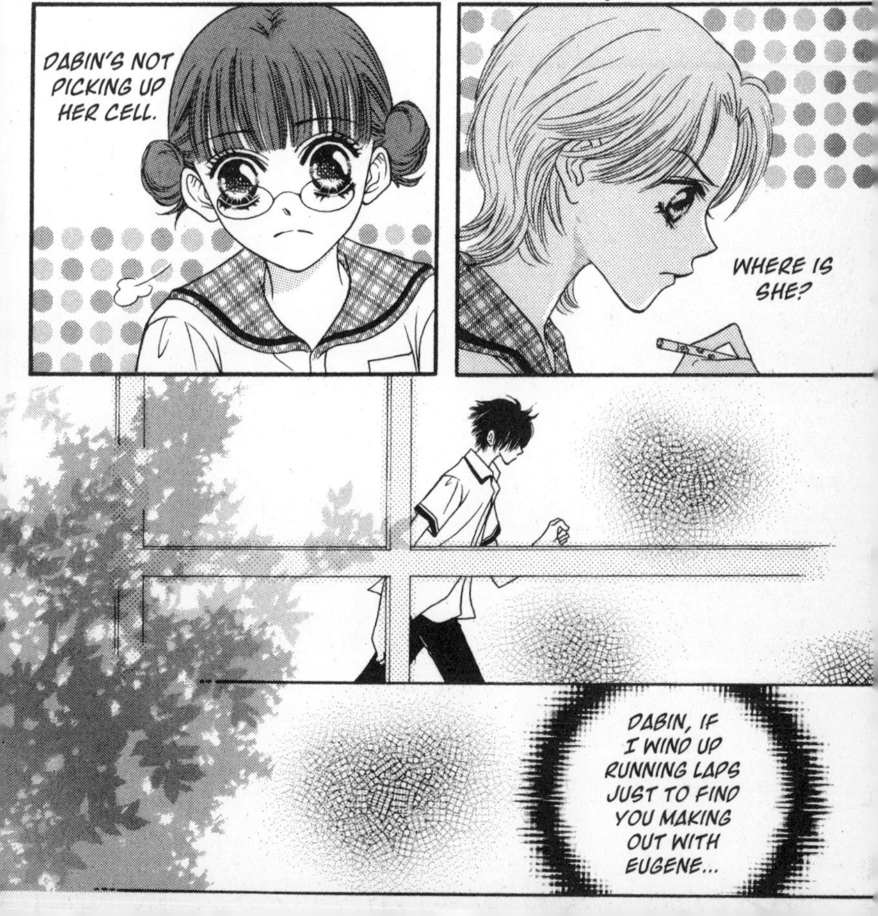
DABIN'S NOT PICKING UP HER CELL.
WHERE IS SHE?
DABIN, IF I WIND UP RUNNING LAPS JUST TO FIND YOU MAKING OUT WITH EUGENE...

...I'M GOING TO BE SERIOUSLY PISSED OFF.
I REALLY DON'T KNOW WHY I'M BOTHERING. GOD KNOWS YOU WOULDN'T DO THIS FOR ME.
WELL, YOU WOULD... BUT YOU'D COME LOOKING FOR ME **HOPING** THAT I WAS IN TROUBLE.
SHIHU, MY BOY, YOU HAVE SOME SERIOUS ISSUES...

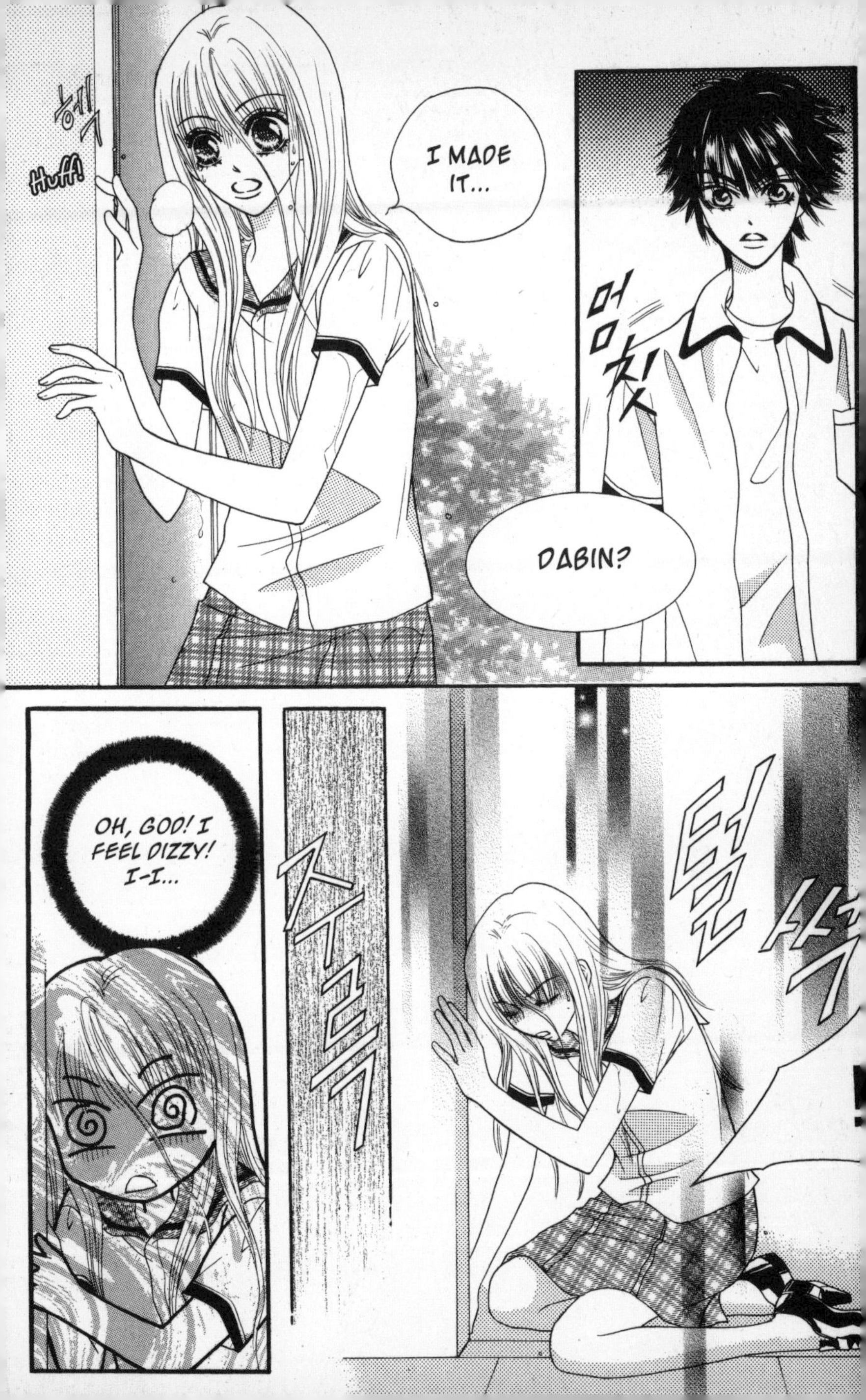

Huff!
I MADE IT...
멈칫
DABIN?
OH, GOD! I FEEL DIZZY! I-I...

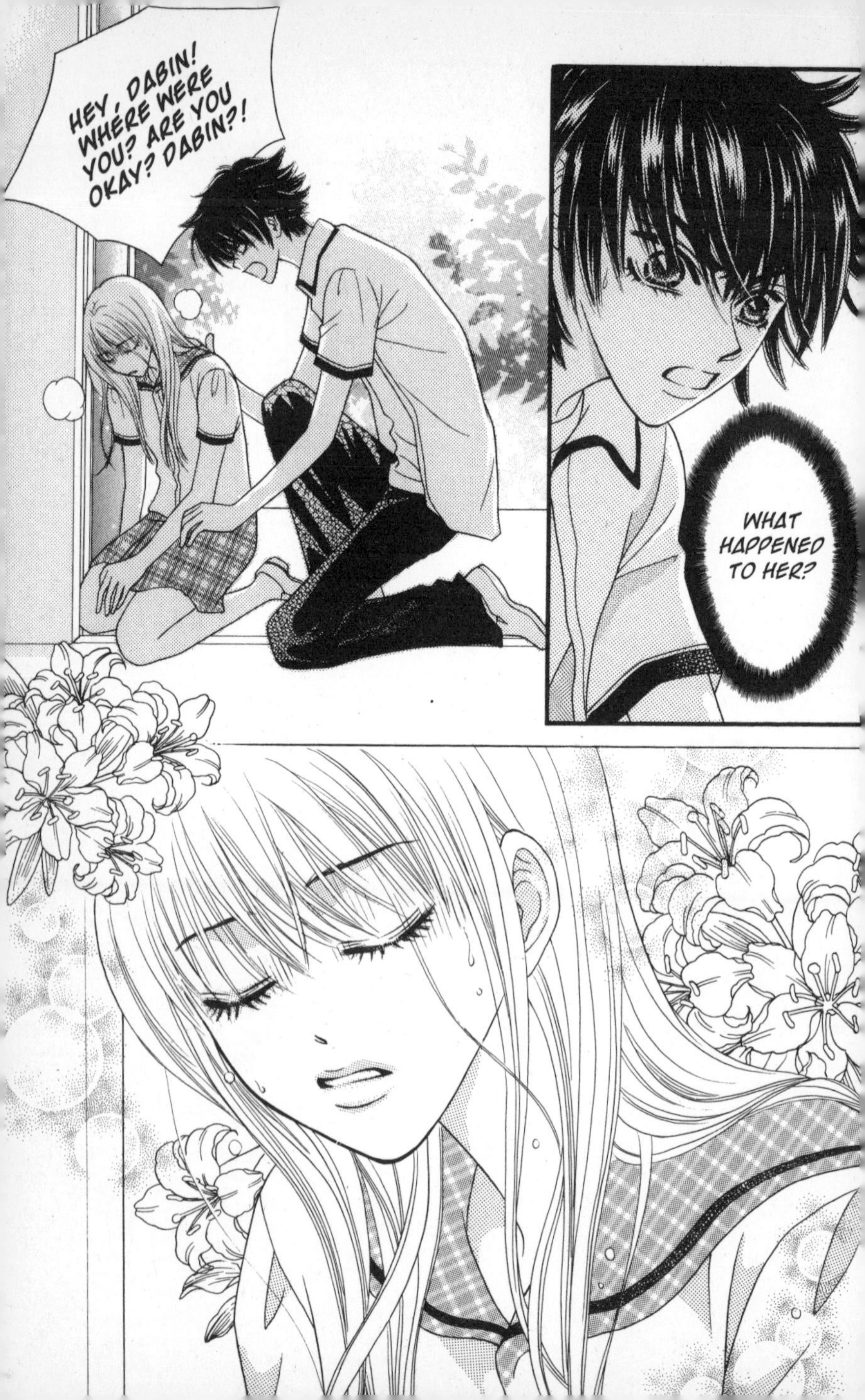
HEY, DABIN! WHERE WERE YOU? ARE YOU OKAY? DABIN?!
WHAT HAPPENED TO HER?

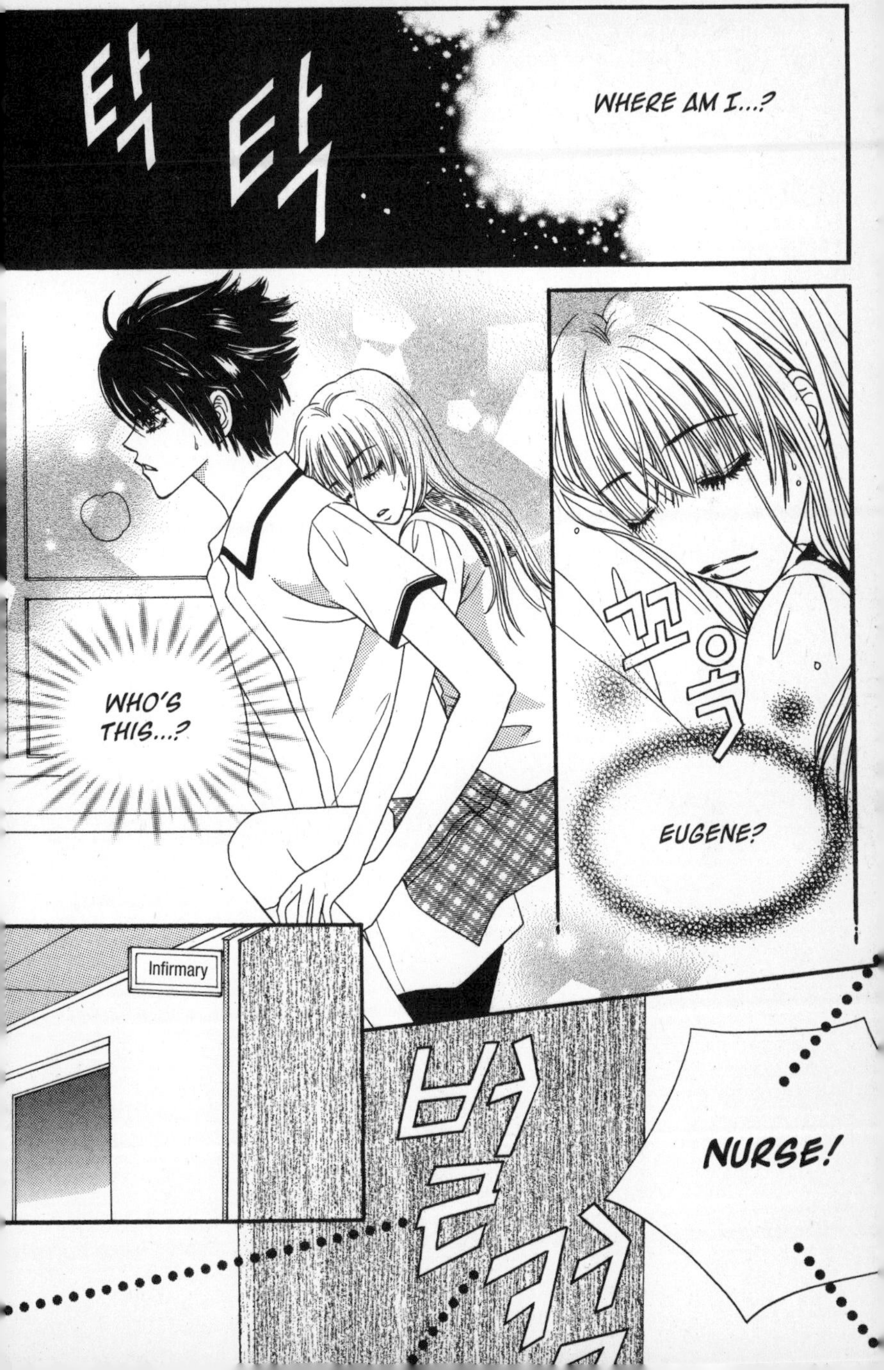
탁 탁
WHERE AM I...?
WHO'S THIS...?
EUGENE?
Infirmary
NURSE!

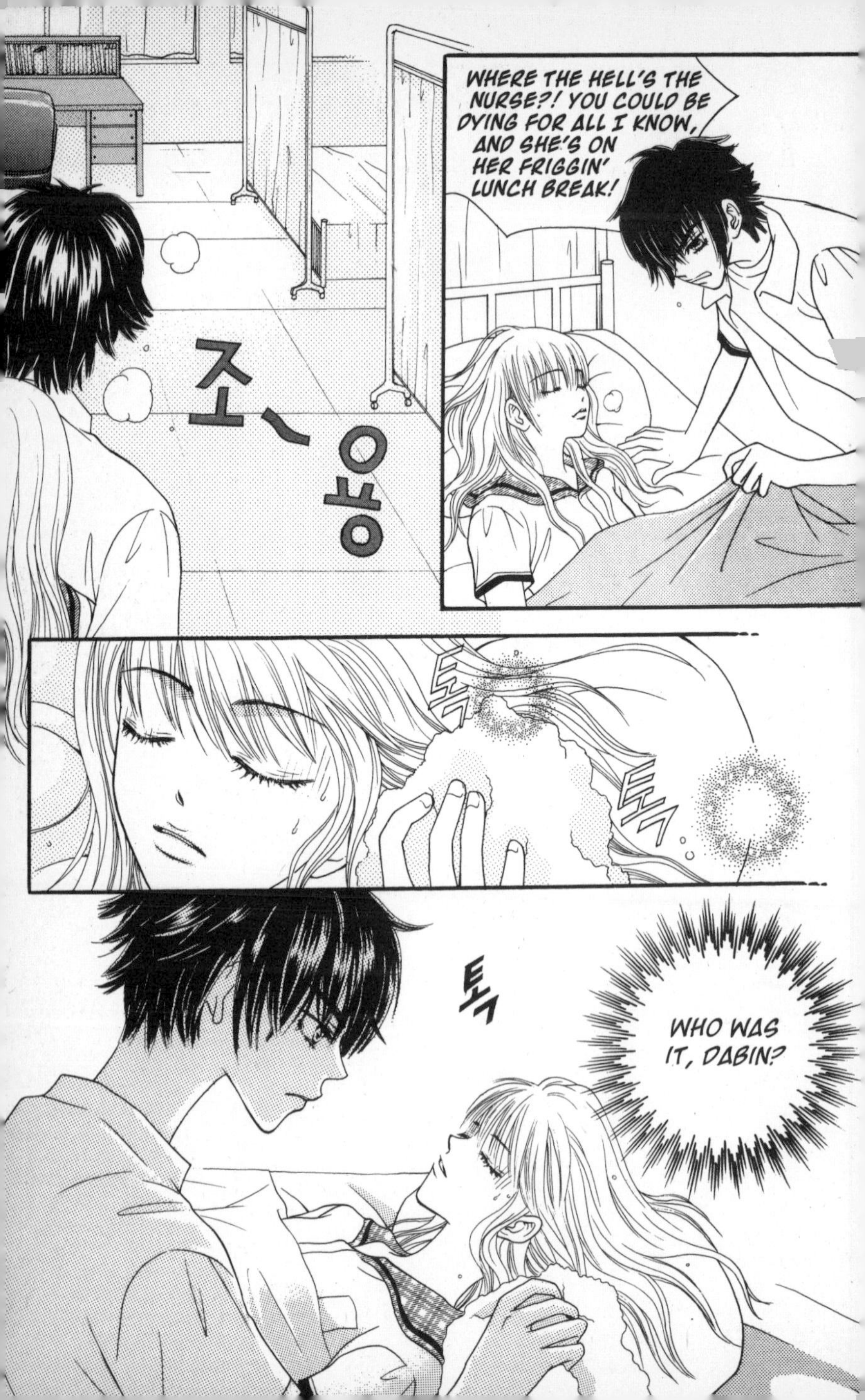
WHERE THE HELL'S THE NURSE?! YOU COULD BE DYING FOR ALL I KNOW, AND SHE'S ON HER FRIGGIN' LUNCH BREAK!
WHO WAS IT, DABIN?

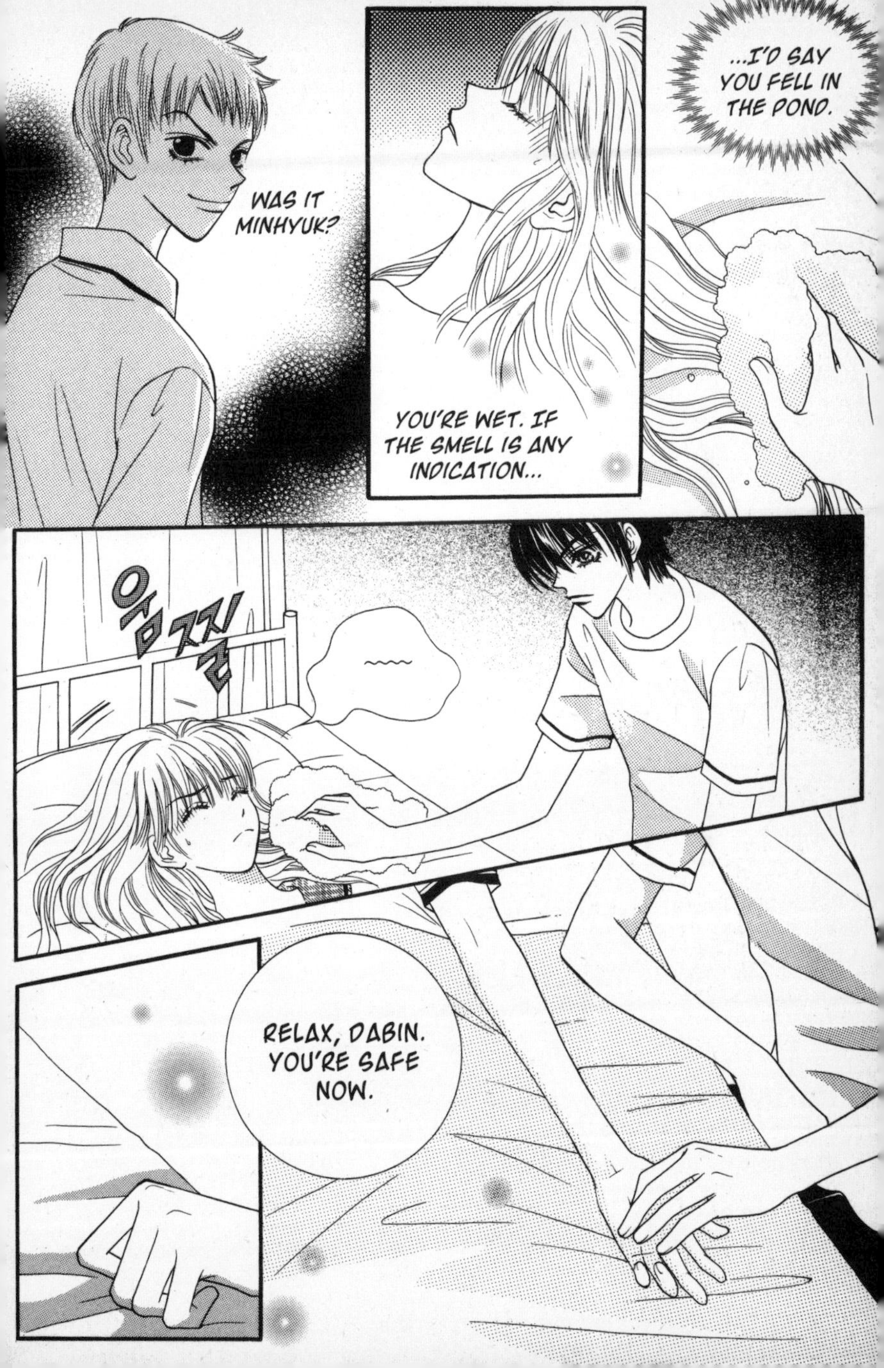
WAS IT MINHYUK?
YOU'RE WET. IF THE SMELL IS ANY INDICATION...
...I'D SAY YOU FELL IN THE POND.
움찔
~~~
RELAX, DABIN. YOU'RE SAFE NOW.
~~~

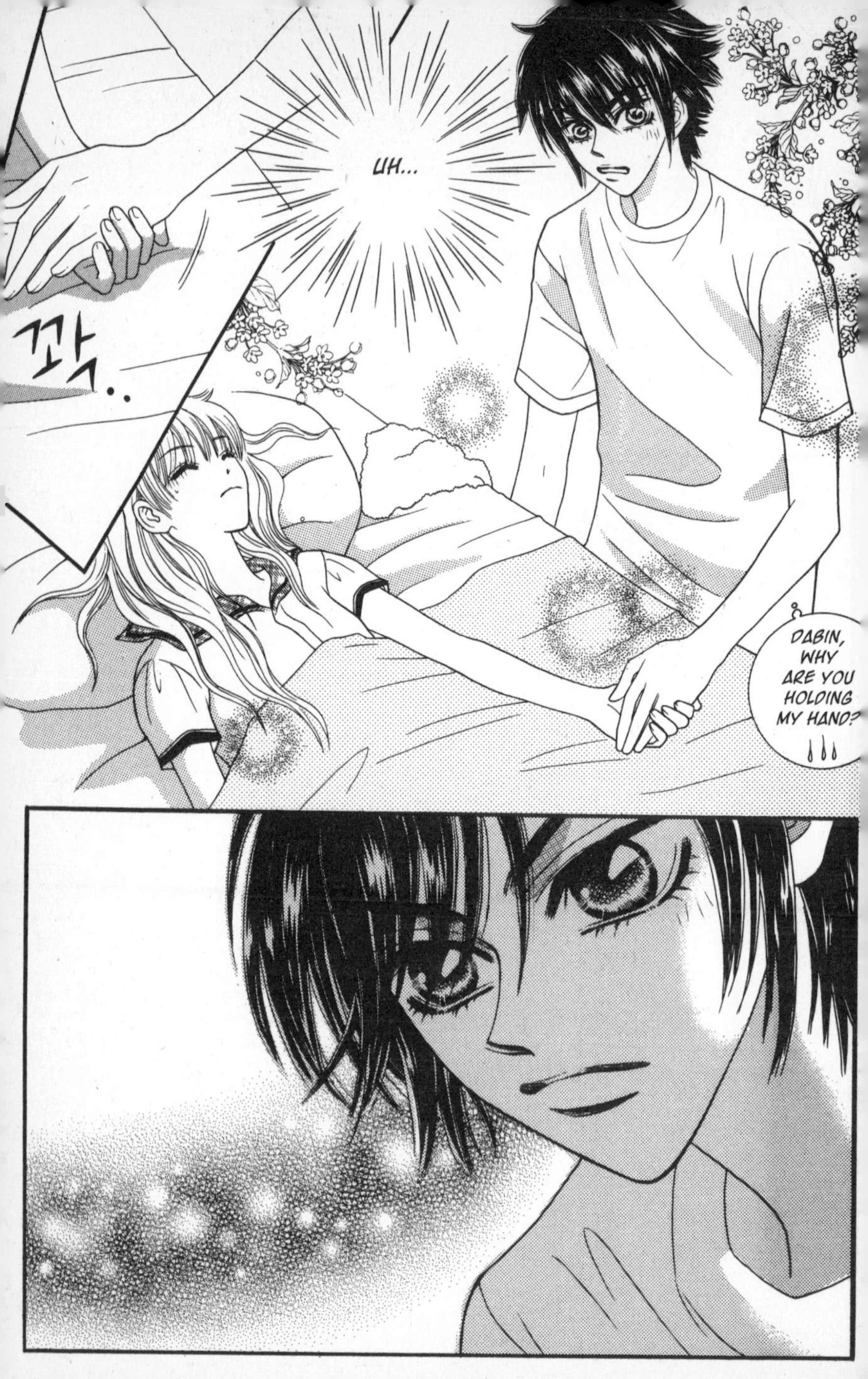
UH...
꽉..
DABIN, WHY ARE YOU HOLDING MY HAND?

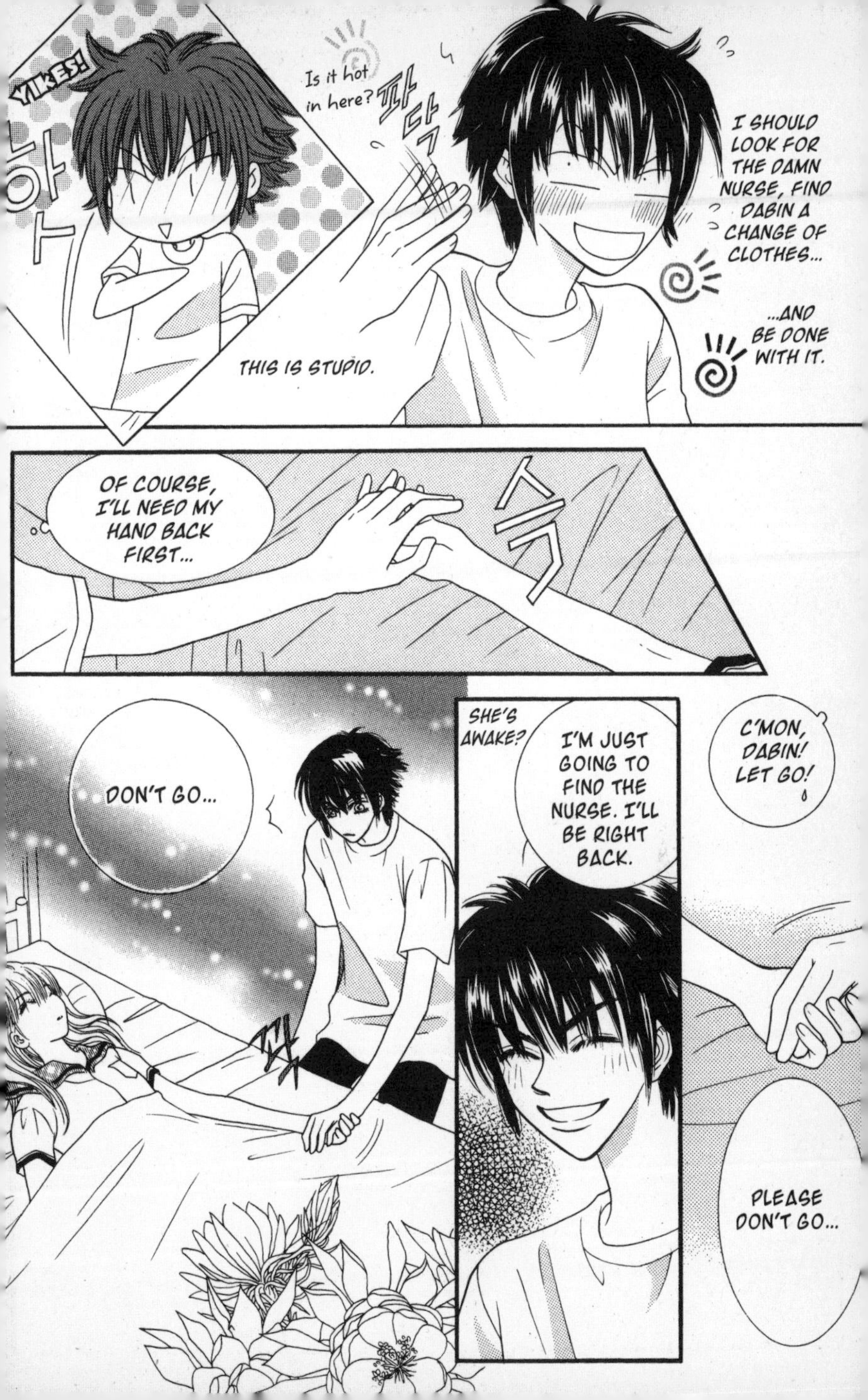
YIKES!
Is it hot in here?
THIS IS STUPID.
I SHOULD LOOK FOR THE DAMN NURSE, FIND DABIN A CHANGE OF CLOTHES...
...AND BE DONE WITH IT.
OF COURSE, I'LL NEED MY HAND BACK FIRST...
DON'T GO...
SHE'S AWAKE?
I'M JUST GOING TO FIND THE NURSE. I'LL BE RIGHT BACK.
C'MON, DABIN! LET GO!
PLEASE DON'T GO...

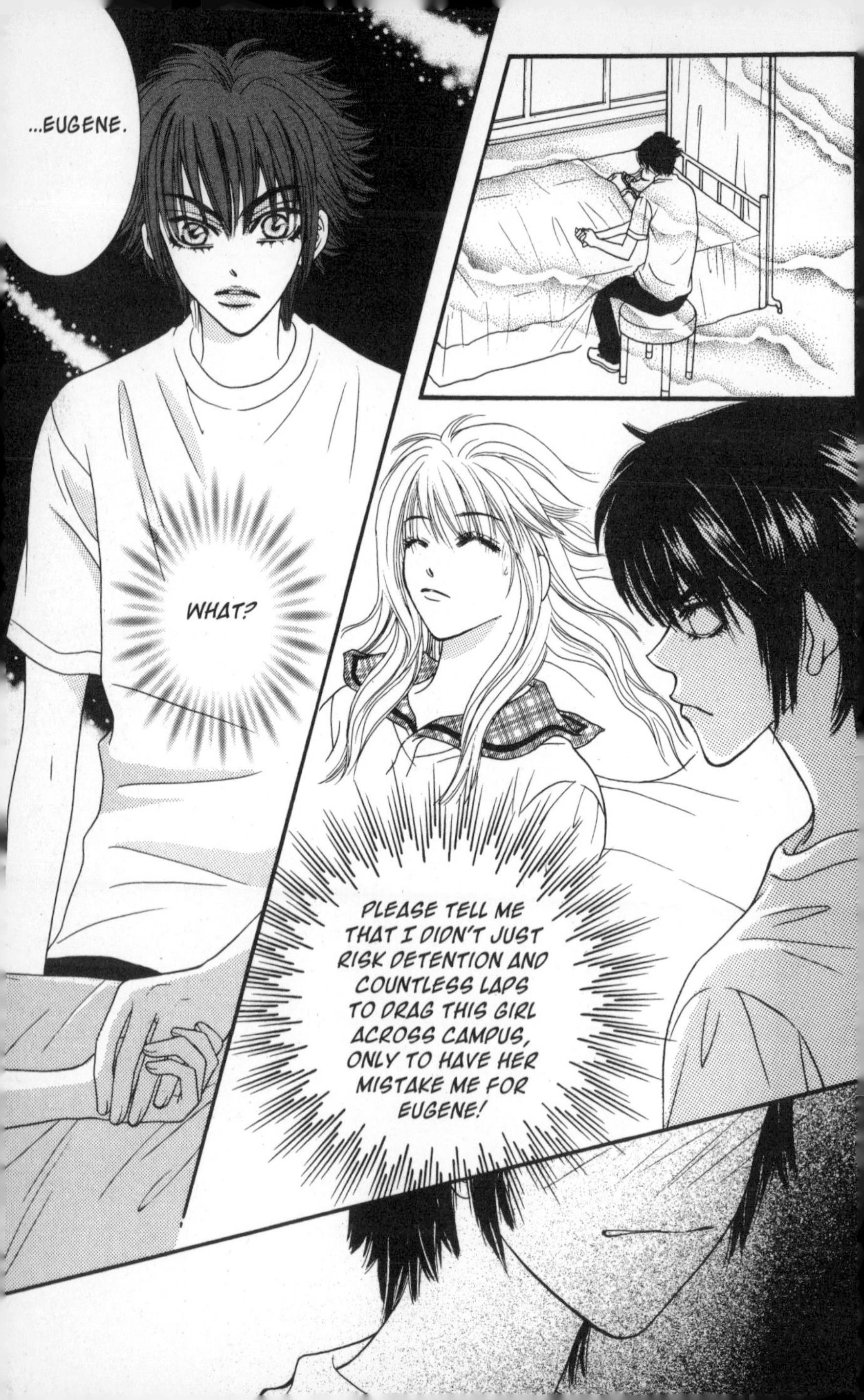
...EUGENE.
WHAT?
PLEASE TELL ME THAT I DIDN'T JUST RISK DETENTION AND COUNTLESS LAPS TO DRAG THIS GIRL ACROSS CAMPUS, ONLY TO HAVE HER MISTAKE ME FOR EUGENE!

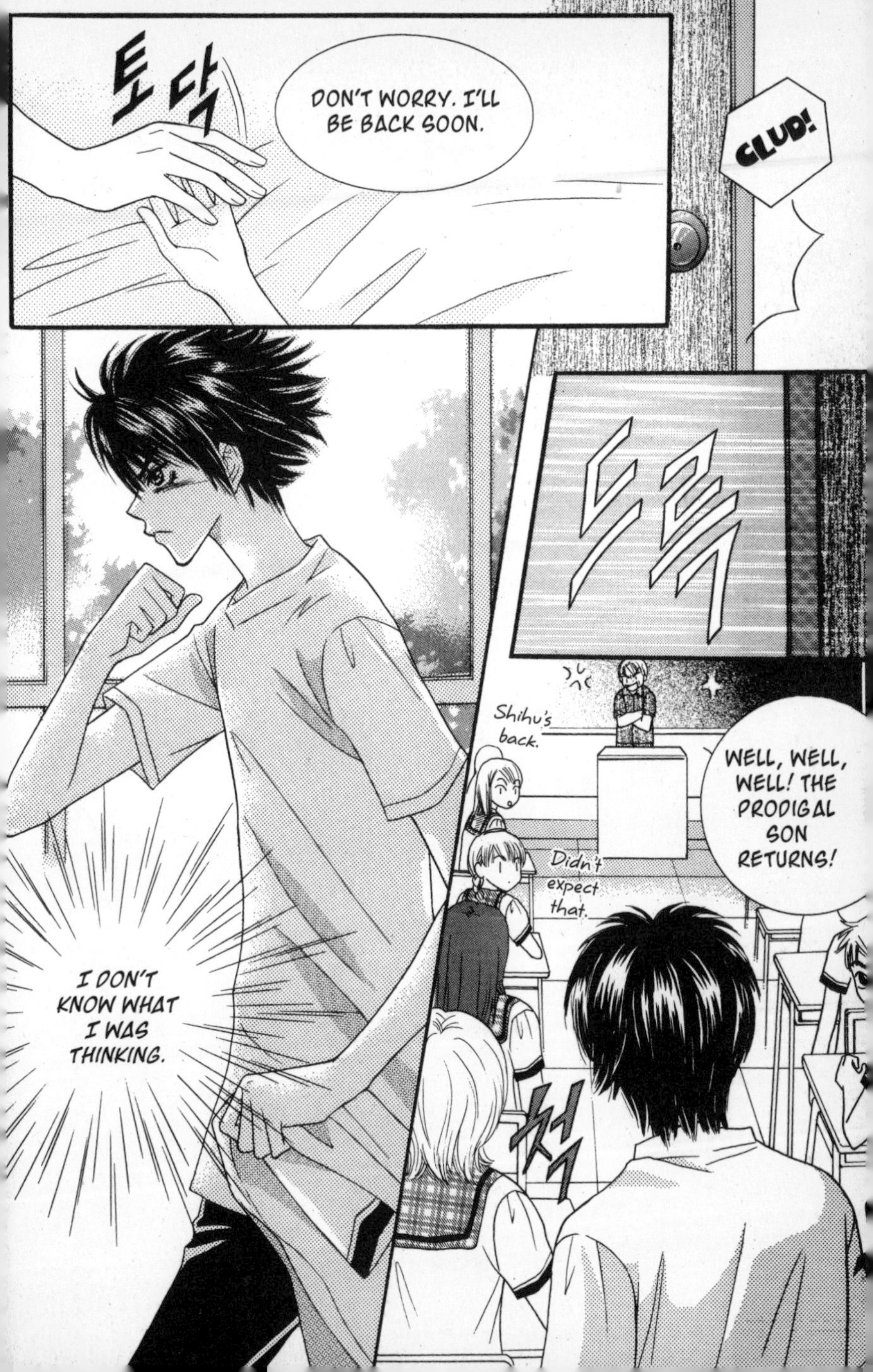
토닥
DON'T WORRY. I'LL BE BACK SOON.
CLUD!
I DON'T KNOW WHAT I WAS THINKING.
드르륵
Shihu's back.
Didn't expect that.
WELL, WELL, WELL! THE PRODIGAL SON RETURNS!
척

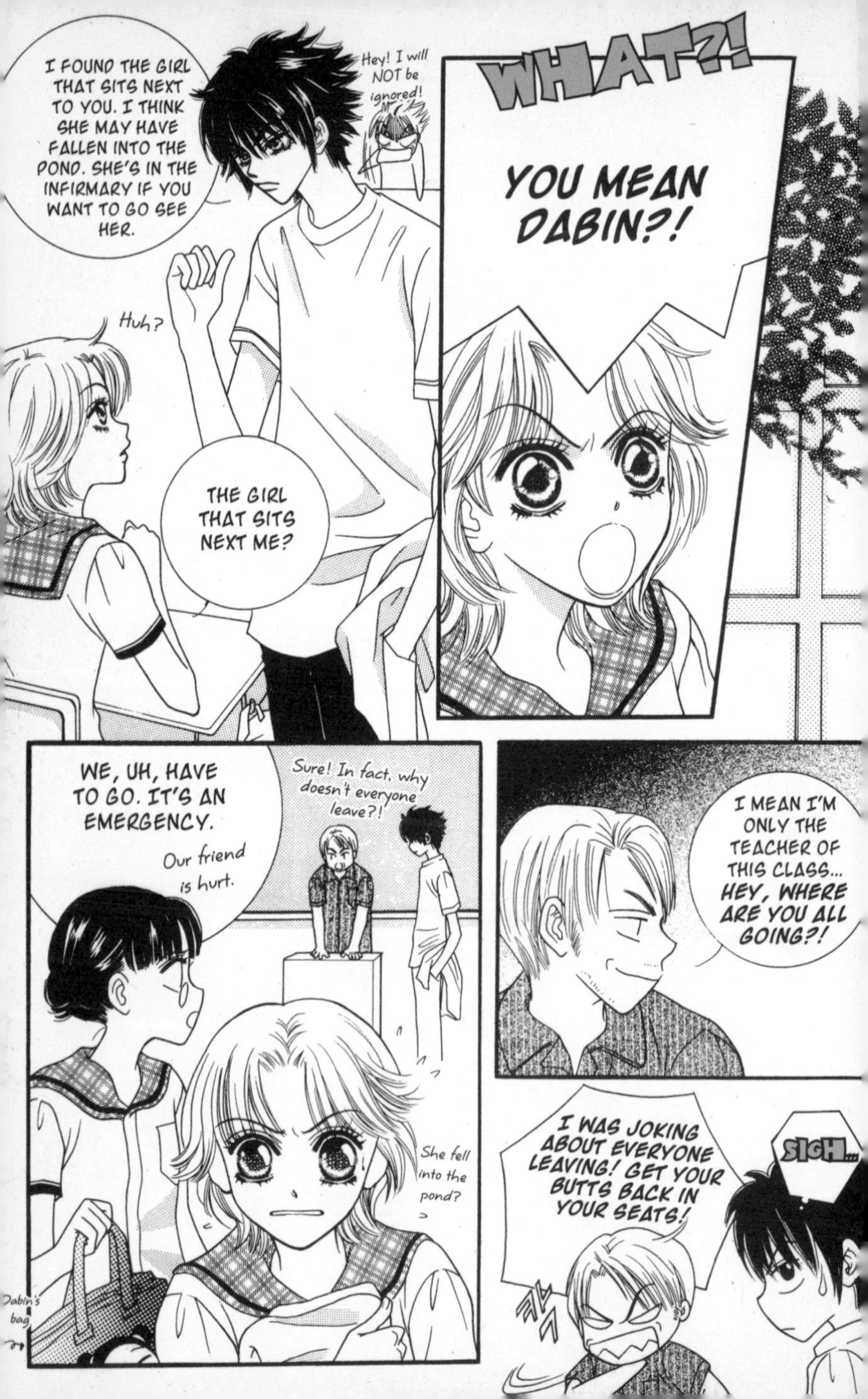
I FOUND THE GIRL THAT SITS NEXT TO YOU. I THINK SHE MAY HAVE FALLEN INTO THE POND. SHE'S IN THE INFIRMARY IF YOU WANT TO GO SEE HER.
Hey! I will NOT be ignored!
Huh?
THE GIRL THAT SITS NEXT ME?
WHAT?!
YOU MEAN DABIN?!
WE, UH, HAVE TO GO. IT'S AN EMERGENCY.
Our friend is hurt.
Sure! In fact, why doesn't everyone leave?!
She fell into the pond?
Dabin's bag
I MEAN I'M ONLY THE TEACHER OF THIS CLASS... HEY, WHERE ARE YOU ALL GOING?!
I WAS JOKING ABOUT EVERYONE LEAVING! GET YOUR BUTTS BACK IN YOUR SEATS!
SIGH...

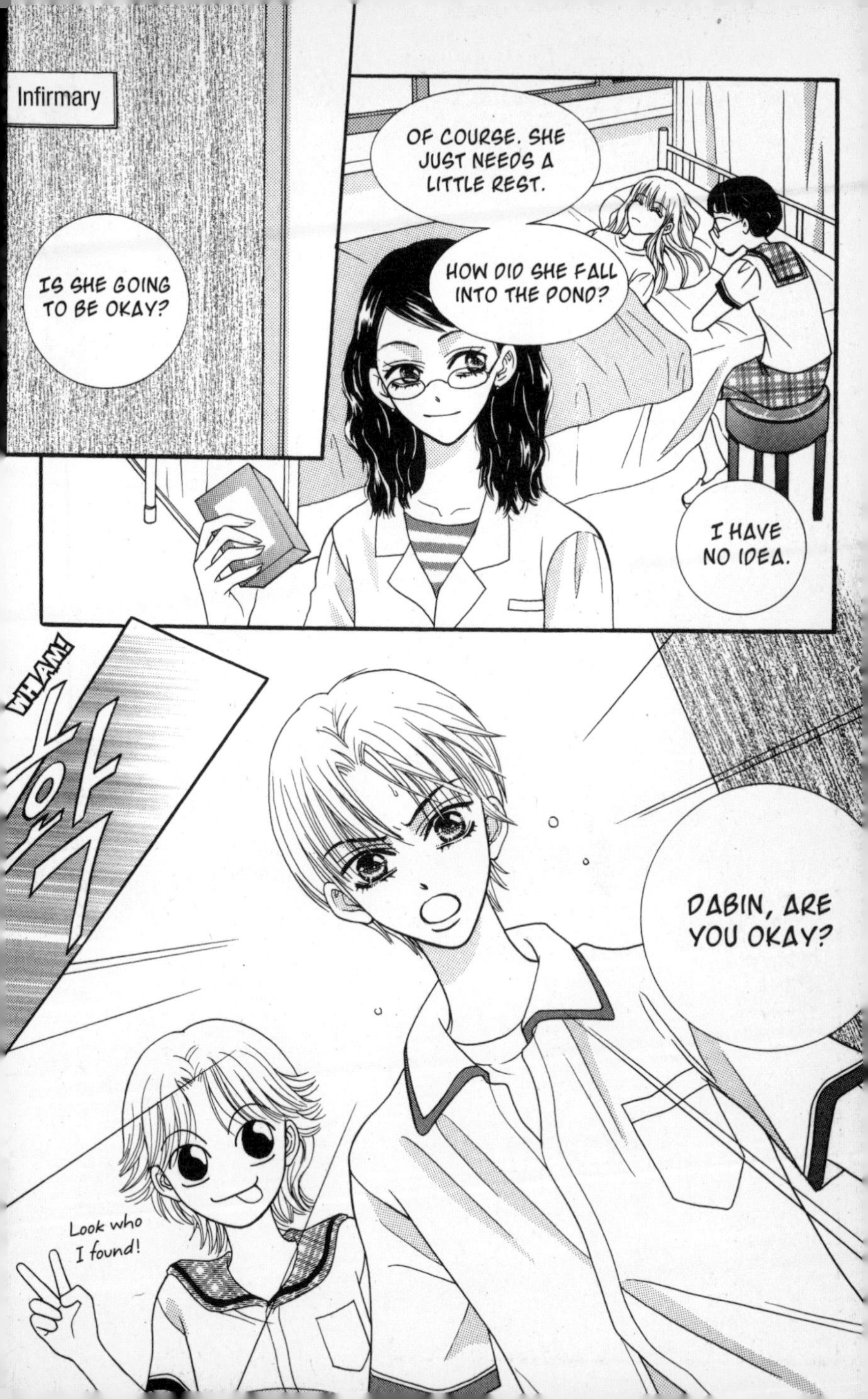
Infirmary
IS SHE GOING TO BE OKAY?
OF COURSE. SHE JUST NEEDS A LITTLE REST.
HOW DID SHE FALL INTO THE POND?
I HAVE NO IDEA.
WHAM!
DABIN, ARE YOU OKAY?
Look who I found!

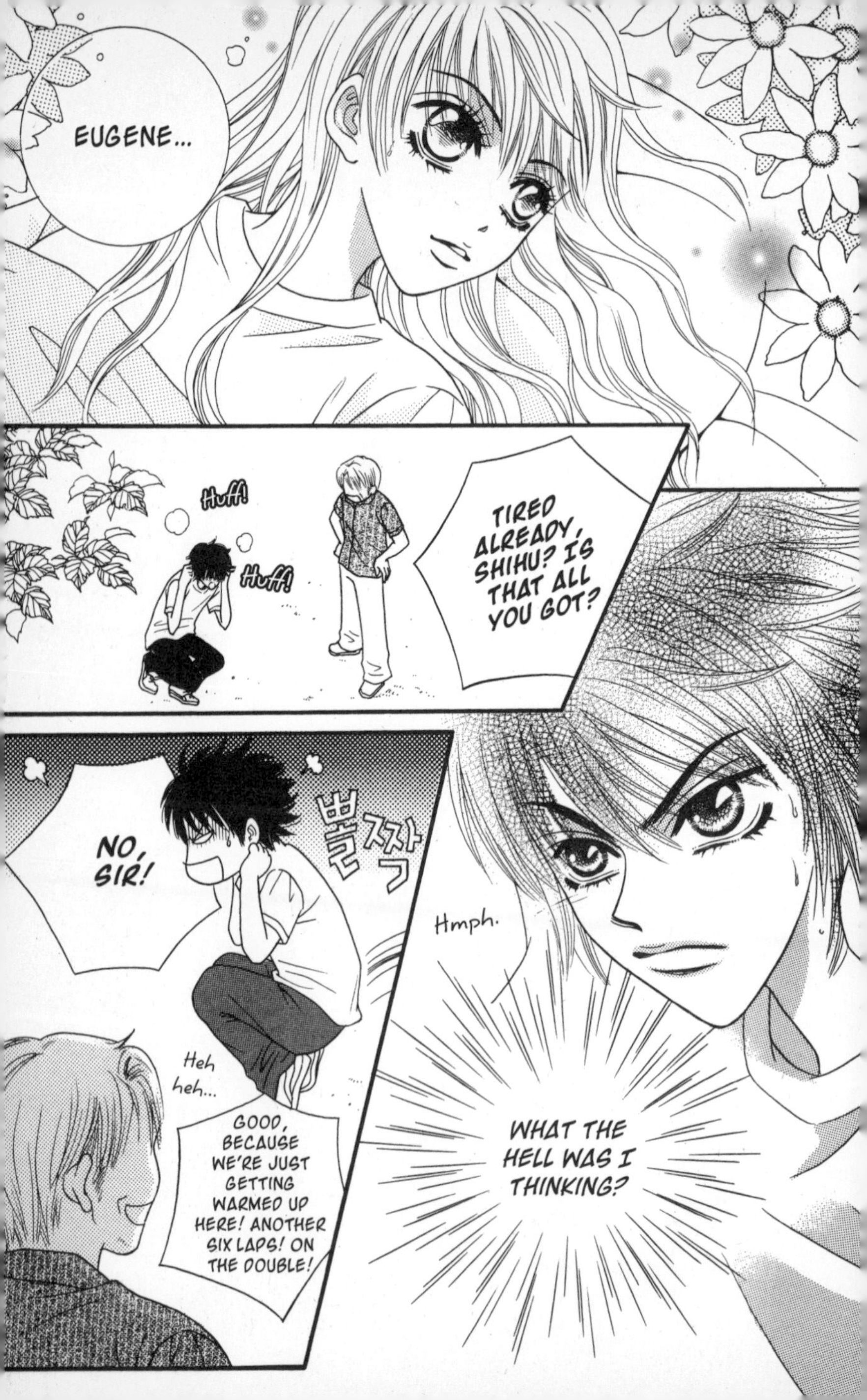
EUGENE...
Huff!
Huff!
TIRED ALREADY, SHIHU? IS THAT ALL YOU GOT?
NO, SIR!
Heh heh...
GOOD, BECAUSE WE'RE JUST GETTING WARMED UP HERE! ANOTHER SIX LAPS! ON THE DOUBLE!
Hmph.
WHAT THE HELL WAS I THINKING?

| Cute | Sweet | Bright | Fresh |

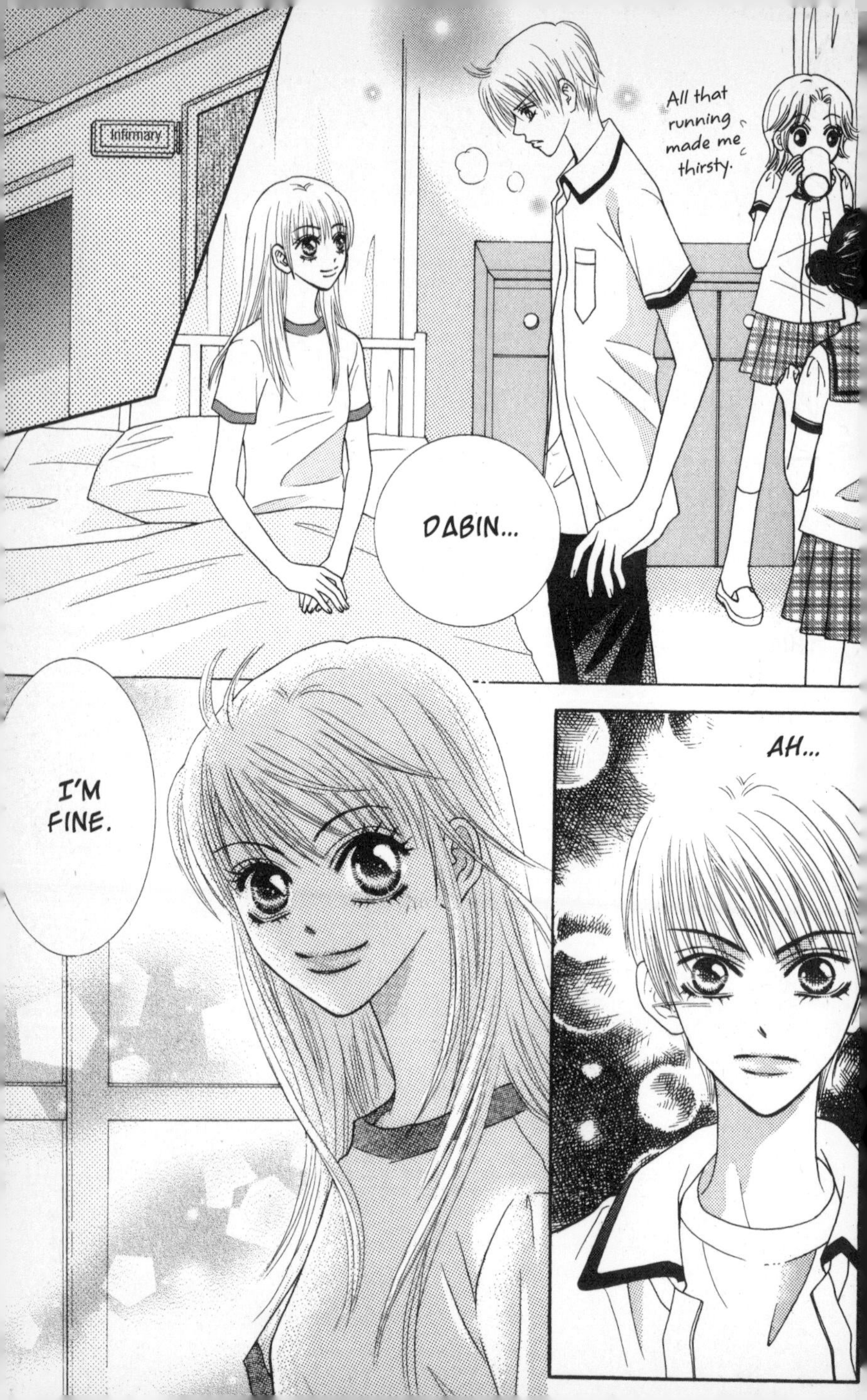
Infirmary
All that running made me thirsty.
DABIN...
I'M FINE.
AH...

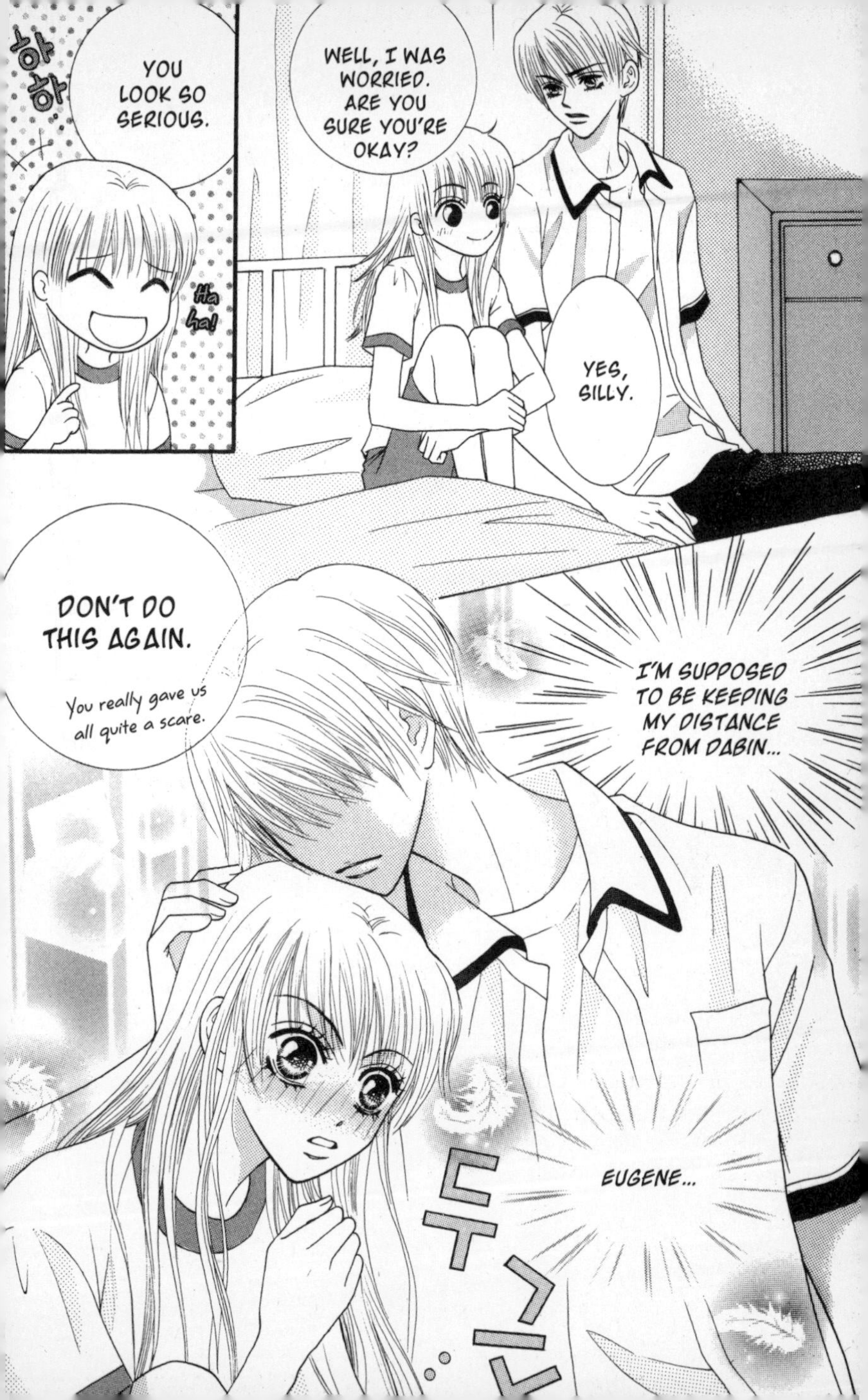

하하
YOU LOOK SO SERIOUS.
Ha ha!
WELL, I WAS WORRIED. ARE YOU SURE YOU'RE OKAY?
YES, SILLY.
DON'T DO THIS AGAIN.
You really gave us all quite a scare.
I'M SUPPOSED TO BE KEEPING MY DISTANCE FROM DABIN...
EUGENE...

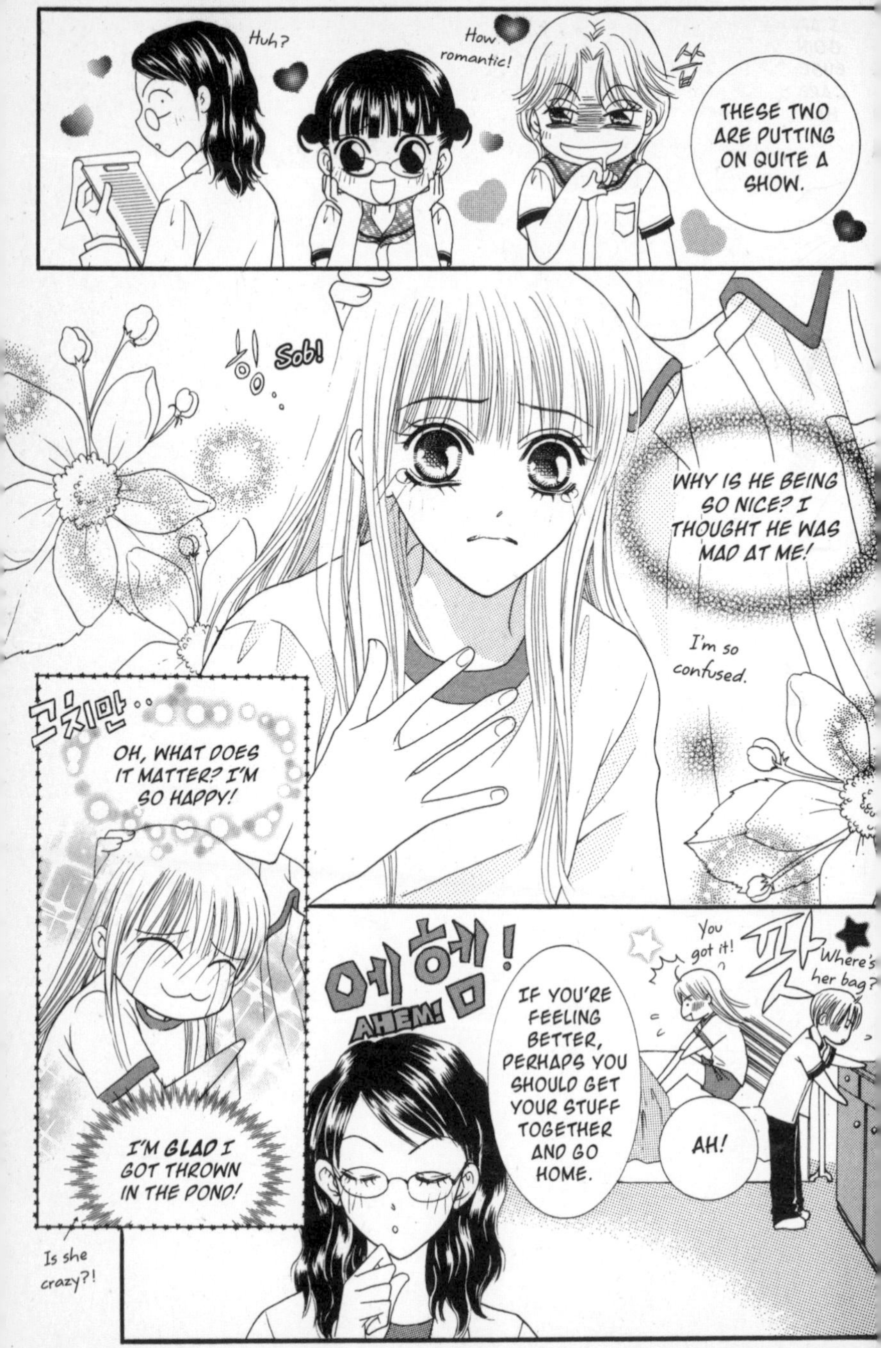

Huh?
How romantic!
THESE TWO ARE PUTTING ON QUITE A SHOW.
Sob!
WHY IS HE BEING SO NICE? I THOUGHT HE WAS MAD AT ME!
I'm so confused.
OH, WHAT DOES IT MATTER? I'M SO HAPPY!
I'M GLAD I GOT THROWN IN THE POND!
Is she crazy?!
에헴!
AHEM!
IF YOU'RE FEELING BETTER, PERHAPS YOU SHOULD GET YOUR STUFF TOGETHER AND GO HOME.
You got it!
Where's her bag?
AH!

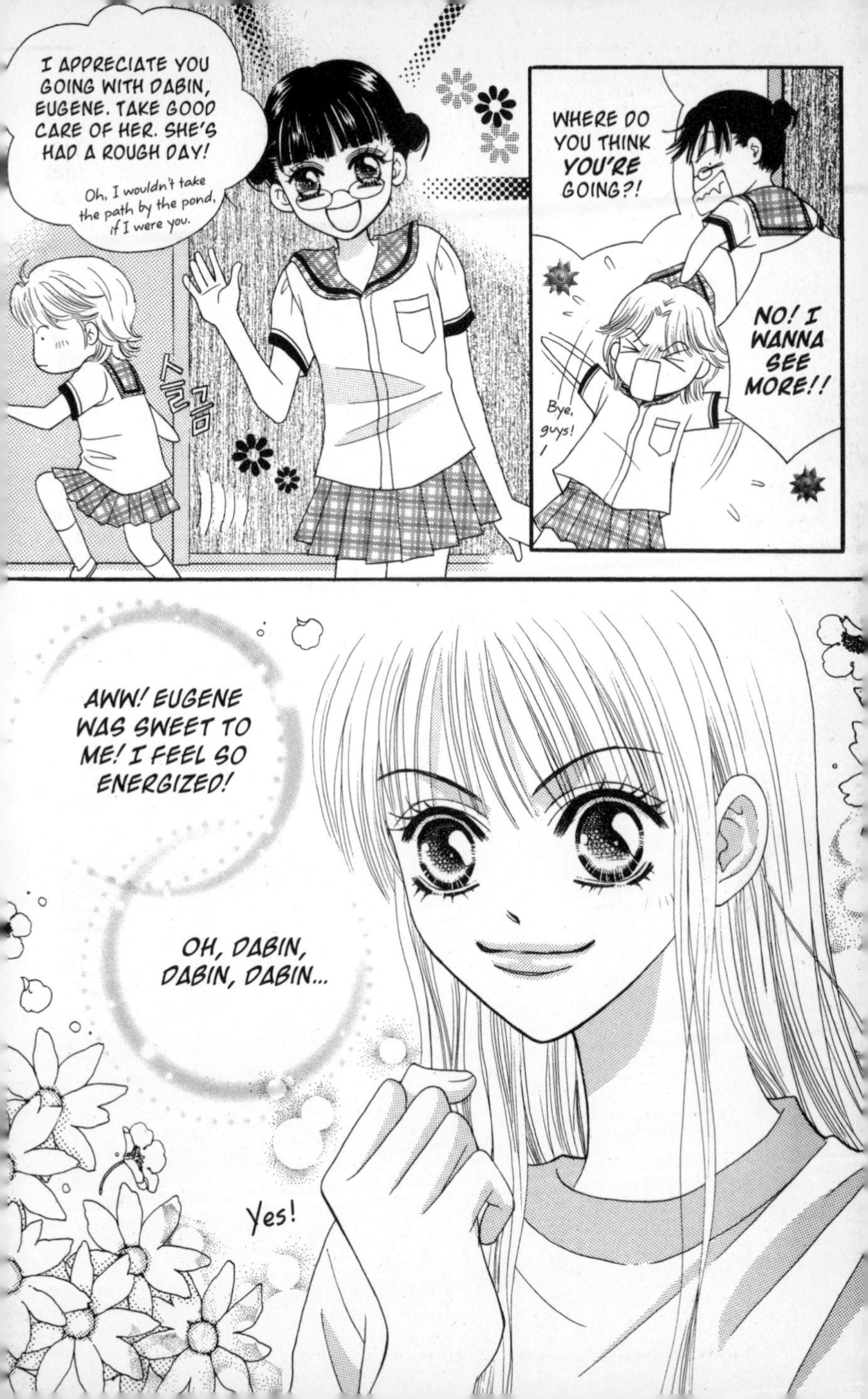
I APPRECIATE YOU GOING WITH DABIN, EUGENE. TAKE GOOD CARE OF HER. SHE'S HAD A ROUGH DAY!
Oh, I wouldn't take the path by the pond, if I were you.
WHERE DO YOU THINK YOU'RE GOING?!
NO! I WANNA SEE MORE!!
Bye, guys!
AWW! EUGENE WAS SWEET TO ME! I FEEL SO ENERGIZED!
OH, DABIN, DABIN, DABIN...
Yes!

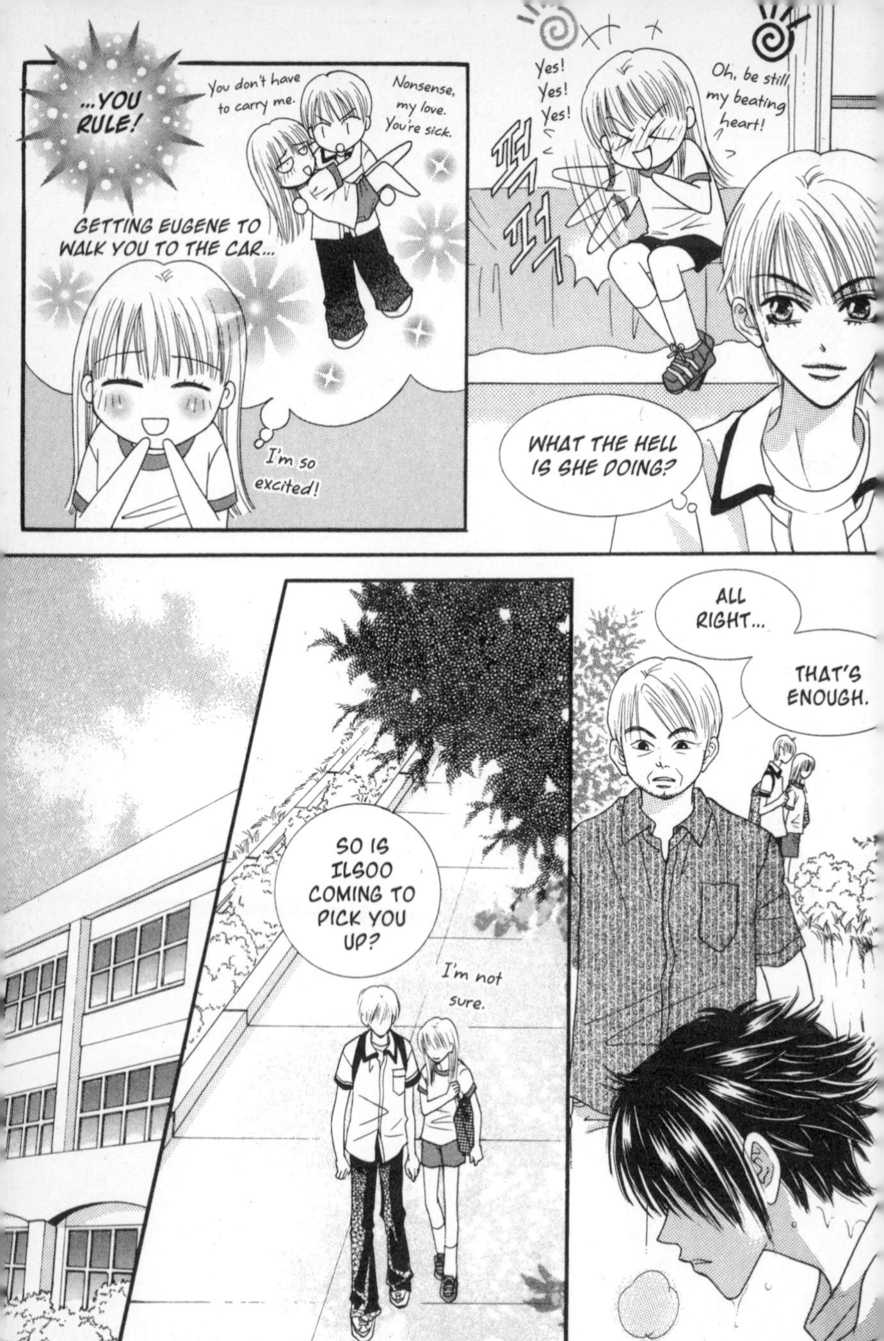
...YOU RULE!
You don't have to carry me.
Nonsense, my love. You're sick.
GETTING EUGENE TO WALK YOU TO THE CAR...
I'm so excited!
Yes! Yes! Yes!
Oh, be still my beating heart!
WHAT THE HELL IS SHE DOING?
SO IS ILSOO COMING TO PICK YOU UP?
I'm not sure.
ALL RIGHT...
THAT'S ENOUGH.

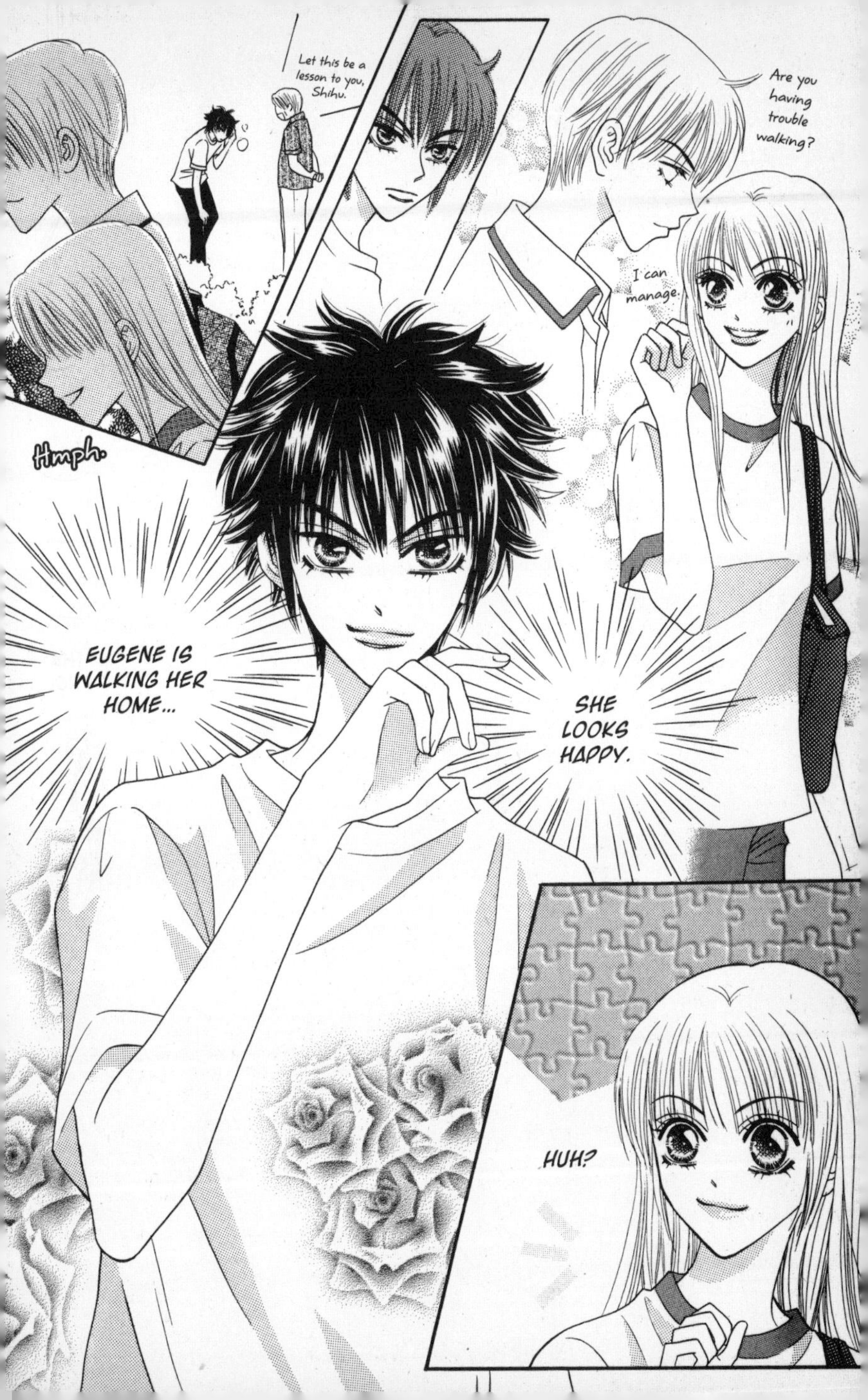
Let this be a lesson to you, Shihu.
Hmph.
Are you having trouble walking?
I can manage.
EUGENE IS WALKING HER HOME...
SHE LOOKS HAPPY.
HUH?

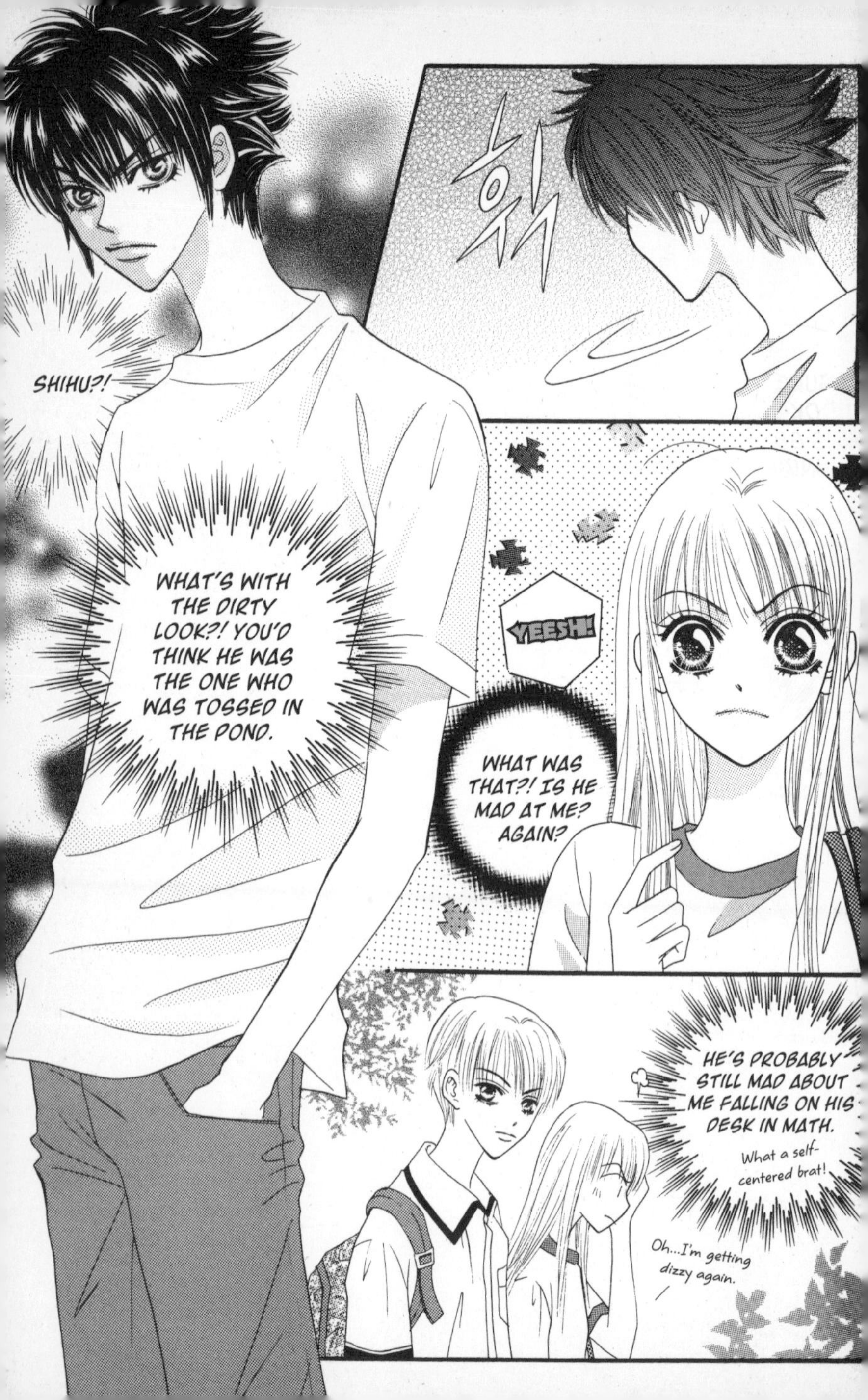
SHIHU?!
WHAT'S WITH THE DIRTY LOOK?! YOU'D THINK HE WAS THE ONE WHO WAS TOSSED IN THE POND.
YEESH!
WHAT WAS THAT?! IS HE MAD AT ME? AGAIN?
HE'S PROBABLY STILL MAD ABOUT ME FALLING ON HIS DESK IN MATH.
What a self-centered brat!
Oh...I'm getting dizzy again.

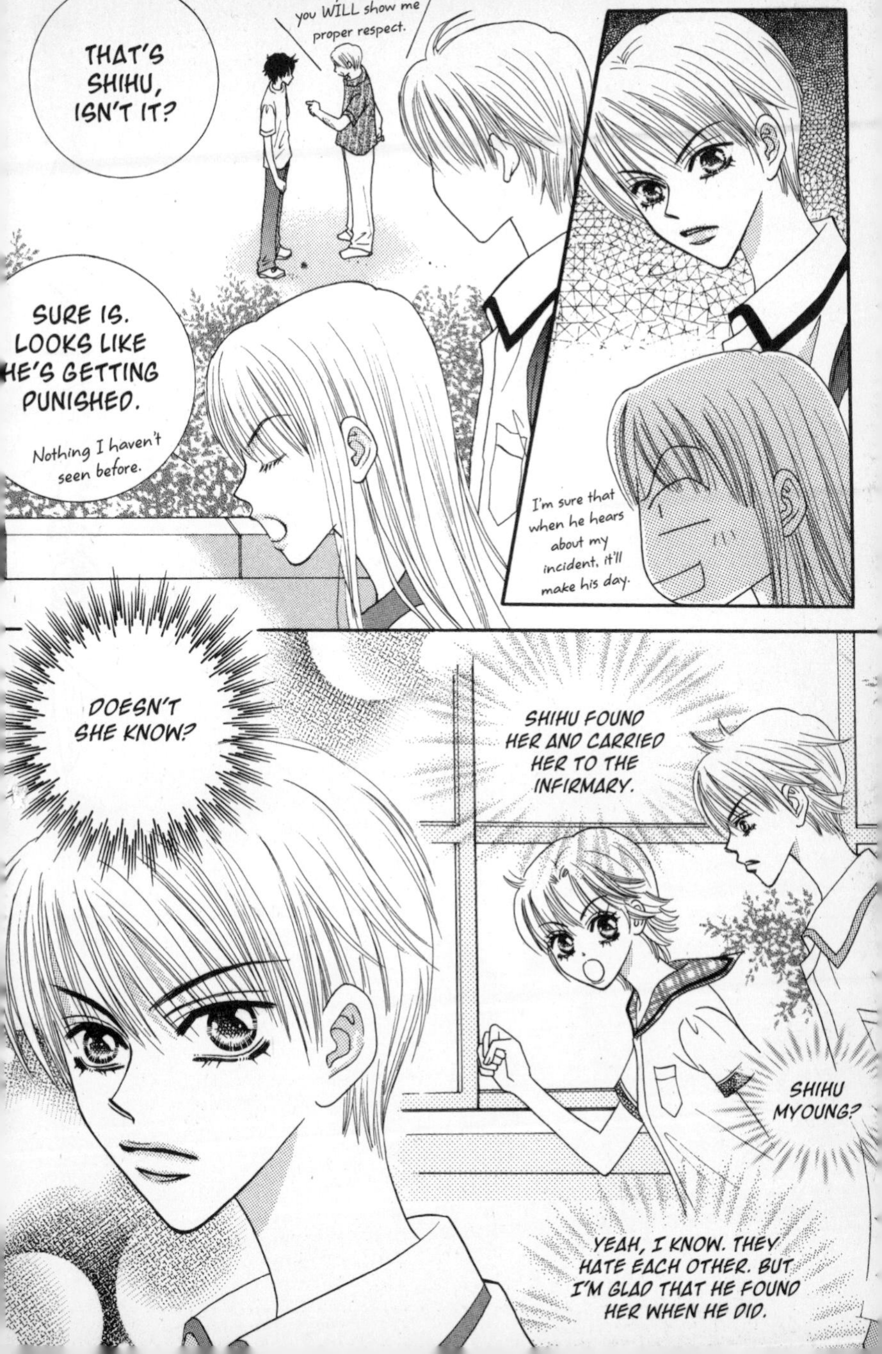

THAT'S SHIHU, ISN'T IT?
In my classroom, you WILL show me proper respect.
SURE IS. LOOKS LIKE HE'S GETTING PUNISHED.
Nothing I haven't seen before.
I'm sure that when he hears about my incident, it'll make his day.
DOESN'T SHE KNOW?
SHIHU FOUND HER AND CARRIED HER TO THE INFIRMARY.
SHIHU MYOUNG?
YEAH, I KNOW. THEY HATE EACH OTHER. BUT I'M GLAD THAT HE FOUND HER WHEN HE DID.

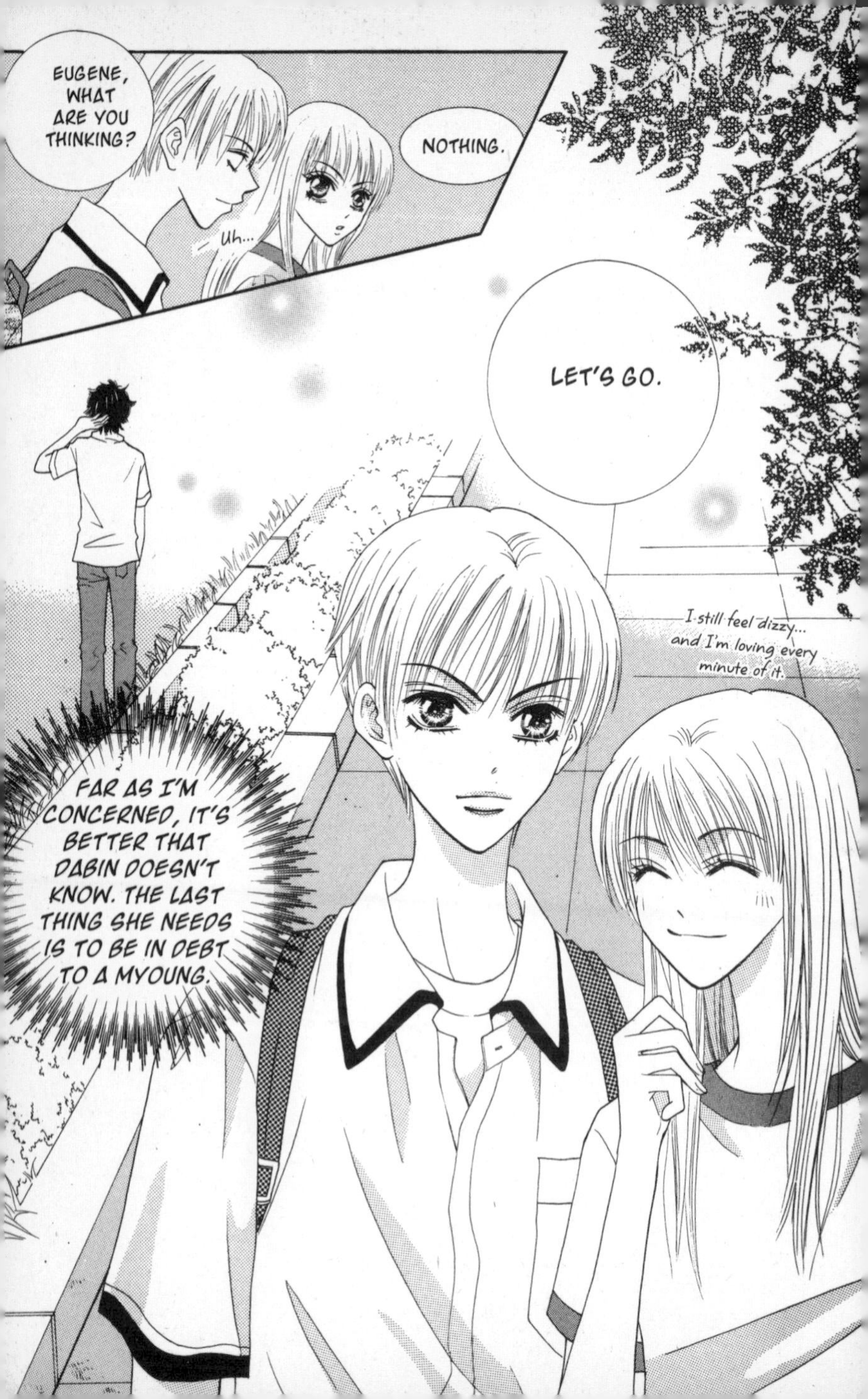
EUGENE, WHAT ARE YOU THINKING?
Uh...
NOTHING.
LET'S GO.
FAR AS I'M CONCERNED, IT'S BETTER THAT DABIN DOESN'T KNOW. THE LAST THING SHE NEEDS IS TO BE IN DEBT TO A MYOUNG.
I still feel dizzy... and I'm loving every minute of it.

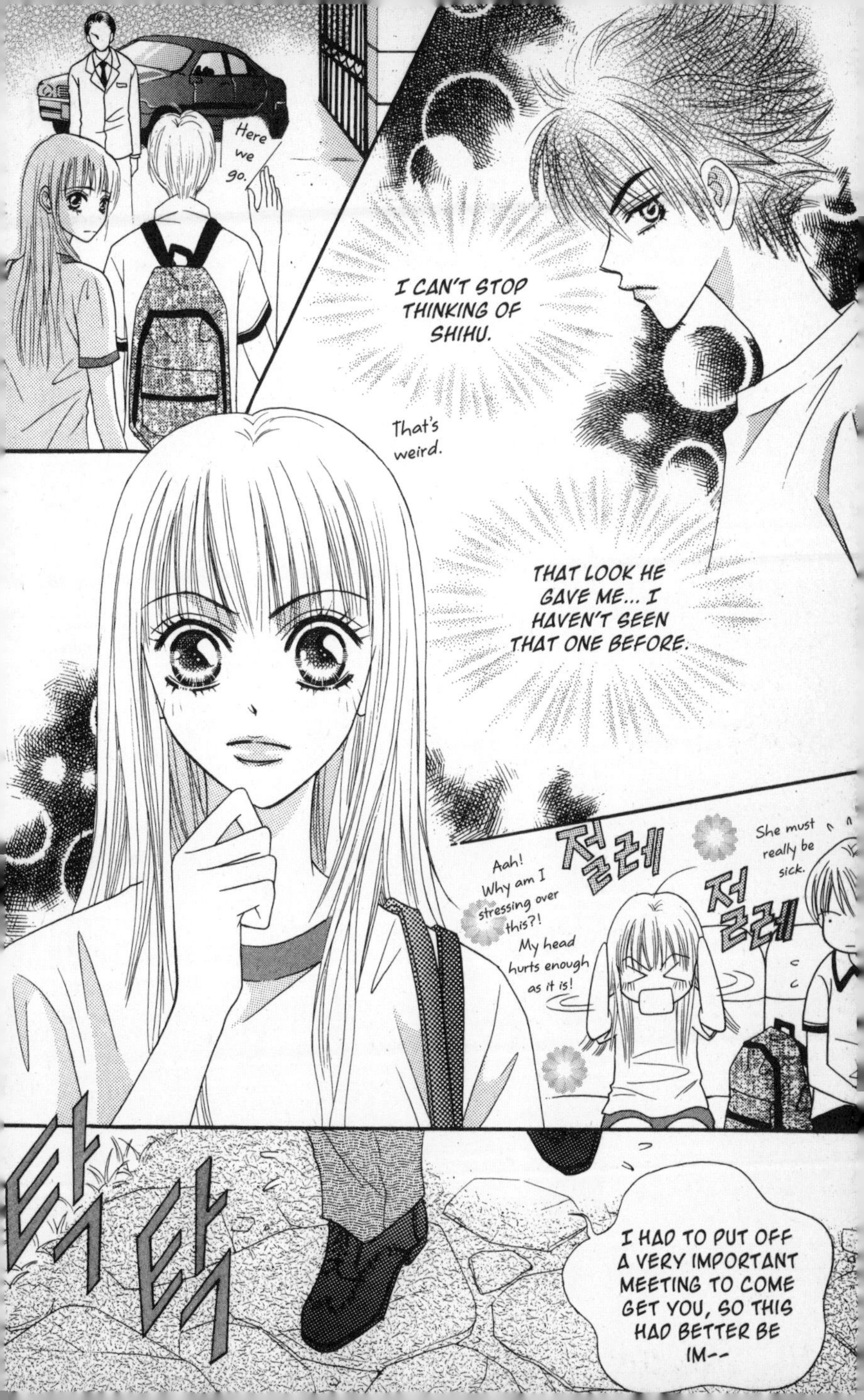

Here we go.
I CAN'T STOP THINKING OF SHIHU.
That's weird.
THAT LOOK HE GAVE ME... I HAVEN'T SEEN THAT ONE BEFORE.
Aah! Why am I stressing over this?! My head hurts enough as it is!
절레
She must really be sick.
절레
I HAD TO PUT OFF A VERY IMPORTANT MEETING TO COME GET YOU, SO THIS HAD BETTER BE IM--

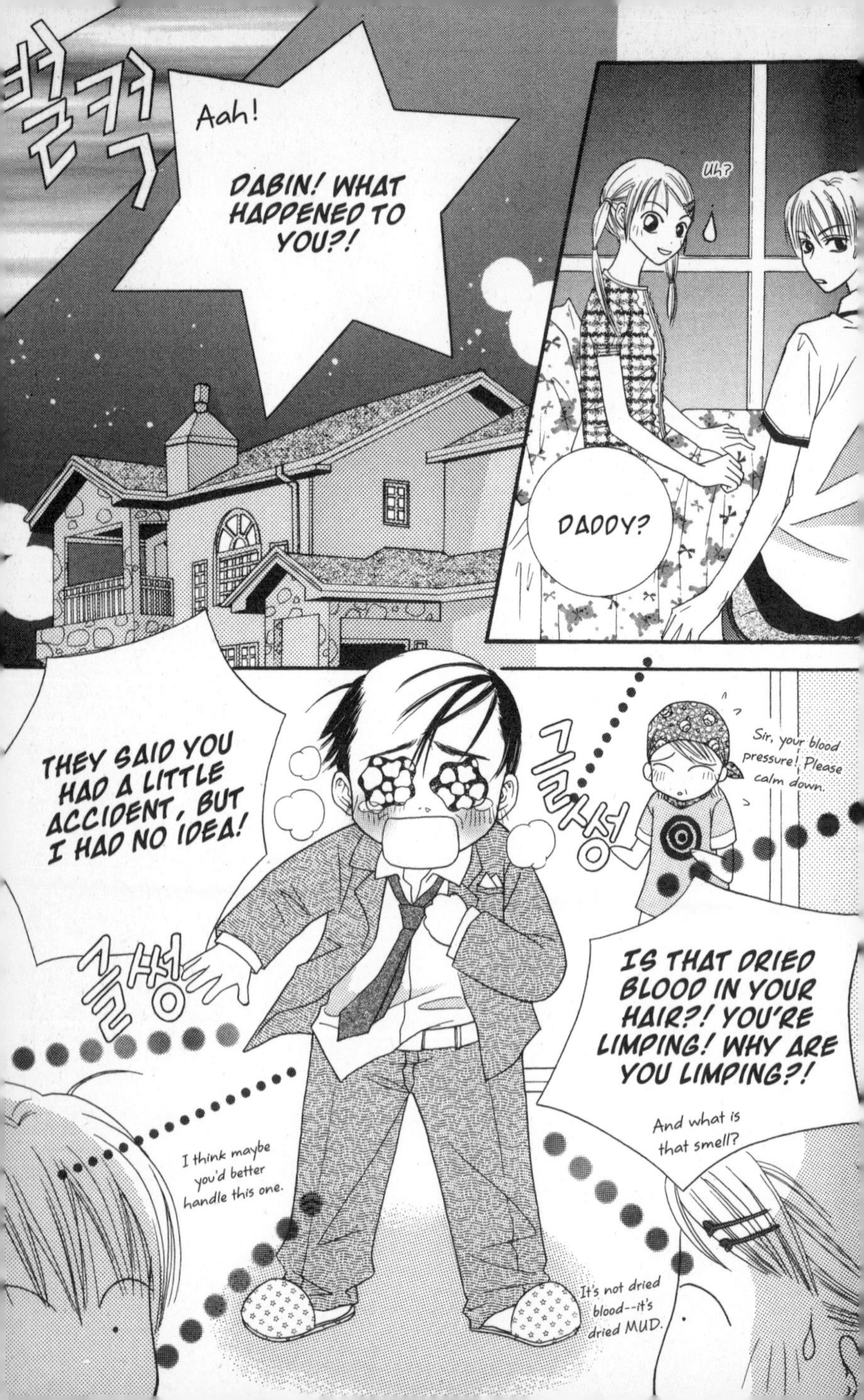
벌컥
Aah!
DABIN! WHAT HAPPENED TO YOU?!
Uh?
DADDY?
THEY SAID YOU HAD A LITTLE ACCIDENT, BUT I HAD NO IDEA!
글썽
글썽
Sir, your blood pressure! Please calm down.
IS THAT DRIED BLOOD IN YOUR HAIR?! YOU'RE LIMPING! WHY ARE YOU LIMPING?!
And what is that smell?
I think maybe you'd better handle this one.
It's not dried blood--it's dried MUD.

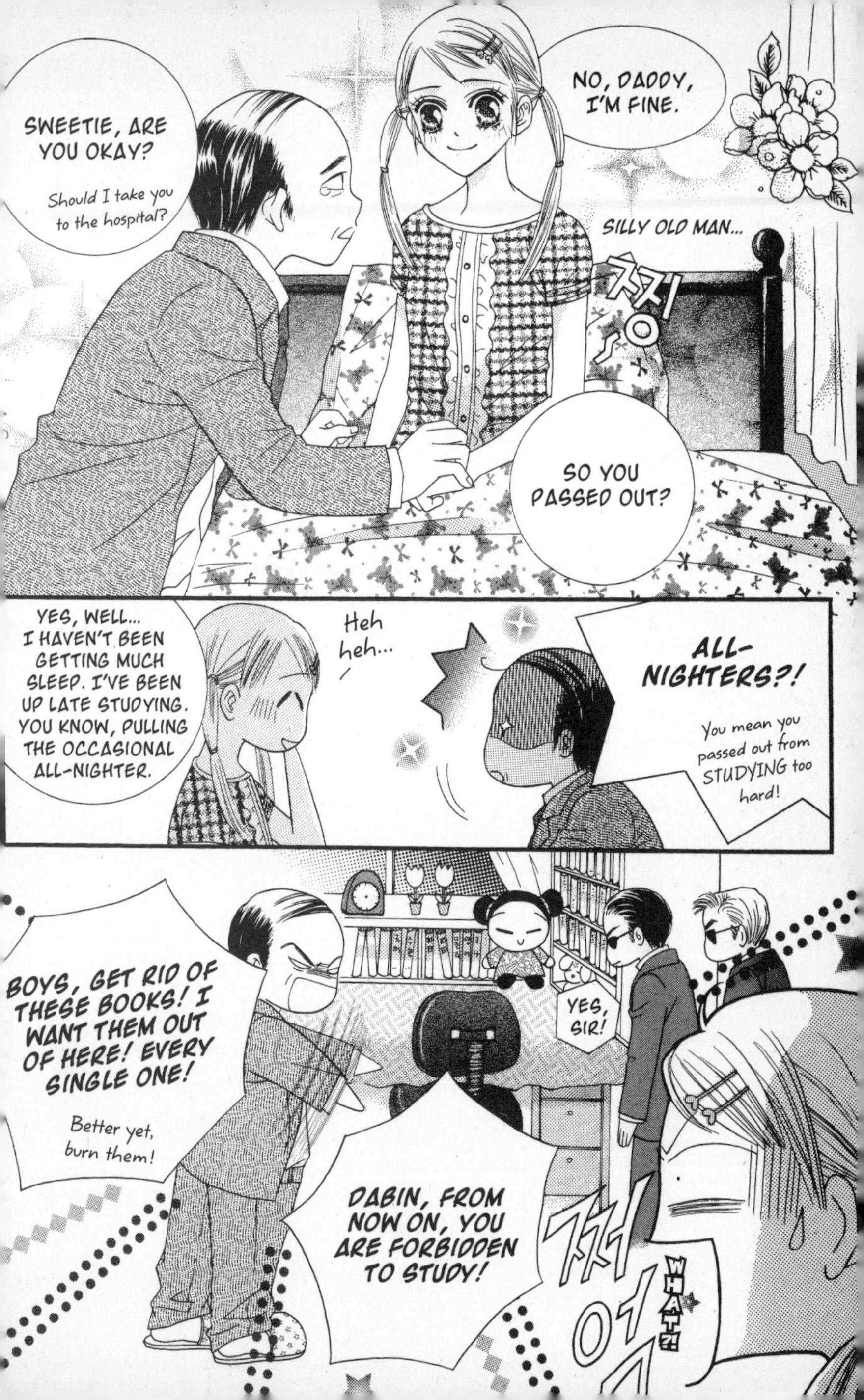
SWEETIE, ARE YOU OKAY?
Should I take you to the hospital?
NO, DADDY, I'M FINE.
SILLY OLD MAN...
SO YOU PASSED OUT?
YES, WELL... I HAVEN'T BEEN GETTING MUCH SLEEP. I'VE BEEN UP LATE STUDYING. YOU KNOW, PULLING THE OCCASIONAL ALL-NIGHTER.
Heh heh...
ALL-NIGHTERS?!
You mean you passed out from STUDYING too hard!
BOYS, GET RID OF THESE BOOKS! I WANT THEM OUT OF HERE! EVERY SINGLE ONE!
Better yet, burn them!
YES, SIR!
DABIN, FROM NOW ON, YOU ARE FORBIDDEN TO STUDY!
WHAT?!

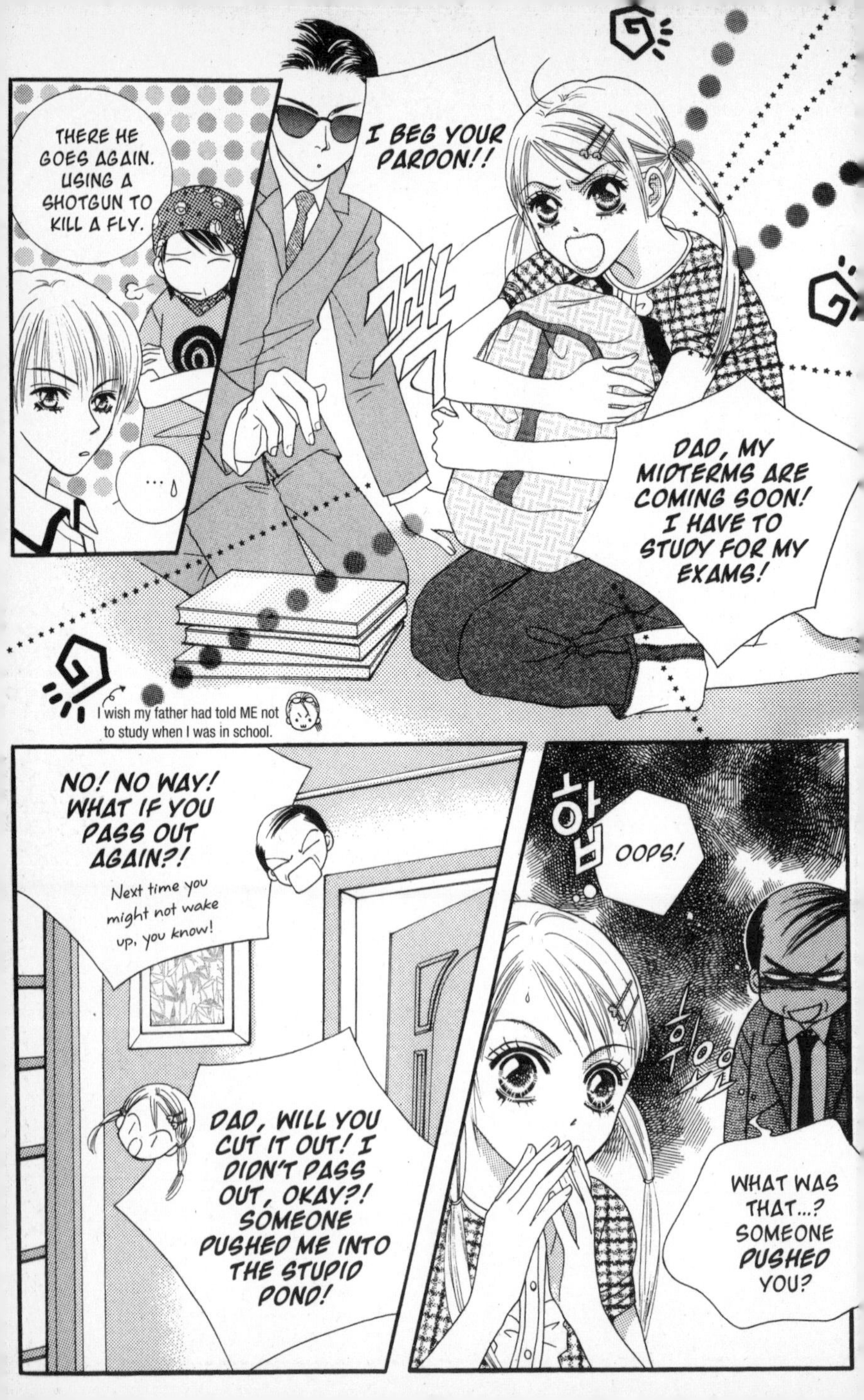
THERE HE GOES AGAIN. USING A SHOTGUN TO KILL A FLY.
...
I BEG YOUR PARDON!!
DAD, MY MIDTERMS ARE COMING SOON! I HAVE TO STUDY FOR MY EXAMS!
I wish my father had told ME not to study when I was in school.
NO! NO WAY! WHAT IF YOU PASS OUT AGAIN?!
Next time you might not wake up, you know!
DAD, WILL YOU CUT IT OUT! I DIDN'T PASS OUT, OKAY?! SOMEONE PUSHED ME INTO THE STUPID POND!
OOPS!
WHAT WAS THAT...? SOMEONE PUSHED YOU?

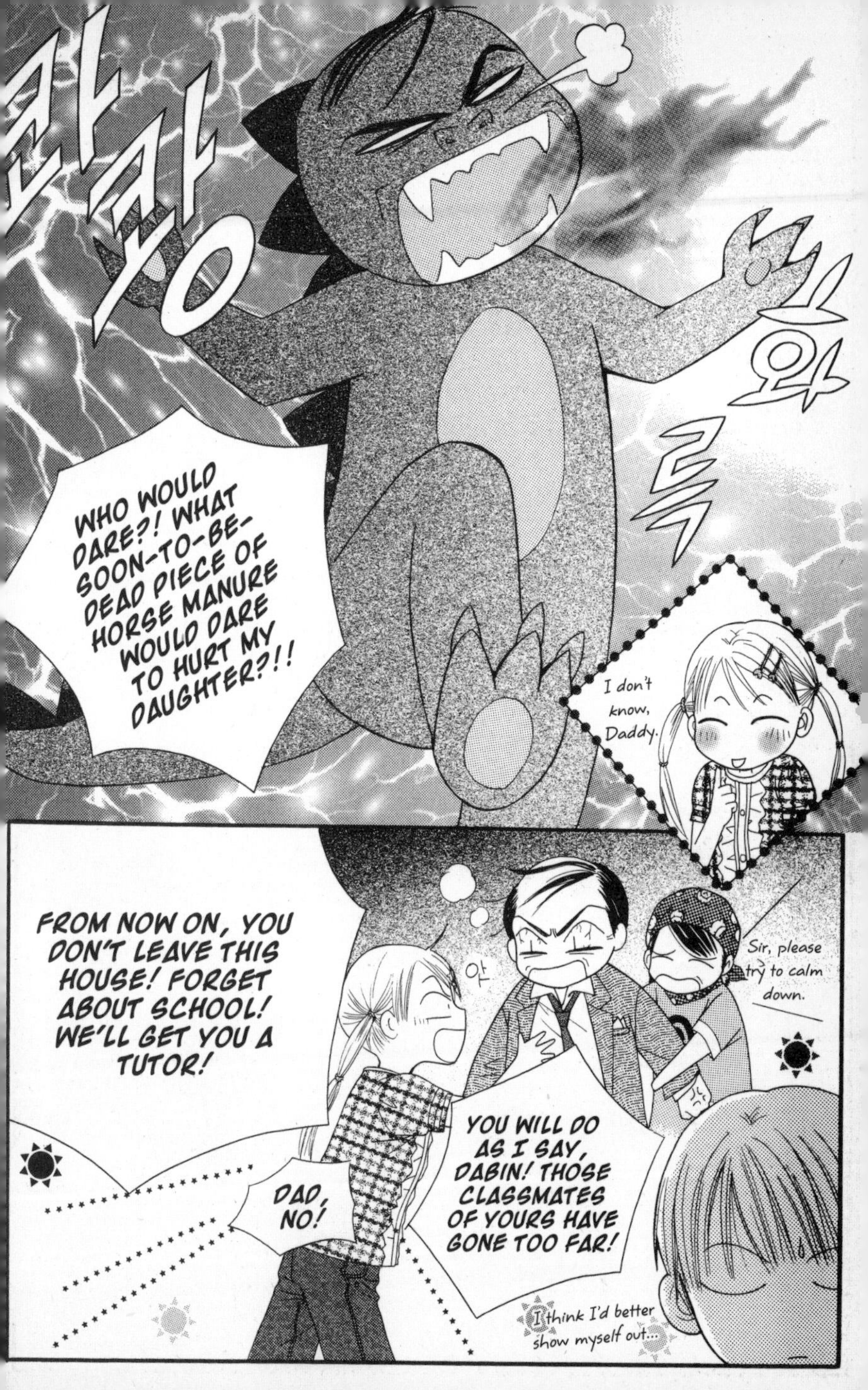

WHO WOULD DARE?! WHAT SOON-TO-BE-DEAD PIECE OF HORSE MANURE WOULD DARE TO HURT MY DAUGHTER?!!
I don't know, Daddy.
FROM NOW ON, YOU DON'T LEAVE THIS HOUSE! FORGET ABOUT SCHOOL! WE'LL GET YOU A TUTOR!
악
Sir, please try to calm down.
DAD, NO!
YOU WILL DO AS I SAY, DABIN! THOSE CLASSMATES OF YOURS HAVE GONE TOO FAR!
I think I'd better show myself out...

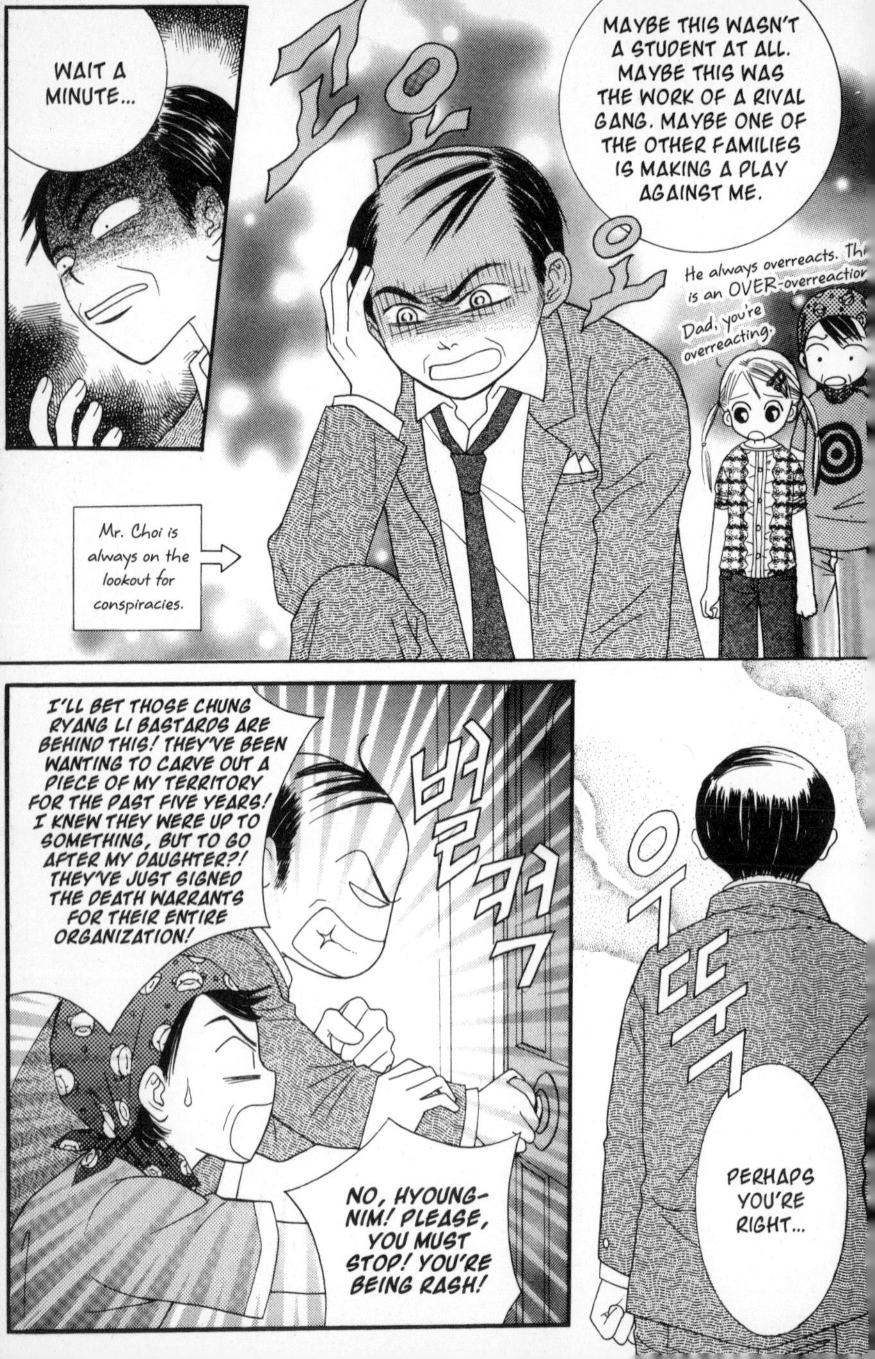
WAIT A MINUTE...
MAYBE THIS WASN'T A STUDENT AT ALL. MAYBE THIS WAS THE WORK OF A RIVAL GANG. MAYBE ONE OF THE OTHER FAMILIES IS MAKING A PLAY AGAINST ME.
He always overreacts. Th
is an OVER-overreactio
Dad, you're overreacting.
Mr. Choi is always on the lookout for conspiracies.
I'LL BET THOSE CHUNG RYANG LI BASTARDS ARE BEHIND THIS! THEY'VE BEEN WANTING TO CARVE OUT A PIECE OF MY TERRITORY FOR THE PAST FIVE YEARS! I KNEW THEY WERE UP TO SOMETHING, BUT TO GO AFTER MY DAUGHTER?! THEY'VE JUST SIGNED THE DEATH WARRANTS FOR THEIR ENTIRE ORGANIZATION!
NO, HYOUNG-NIM! PLEASE, YOU MUST STOP! YOU'RE BEING RASH!
PERHAPS YOU'RE RIGHT...

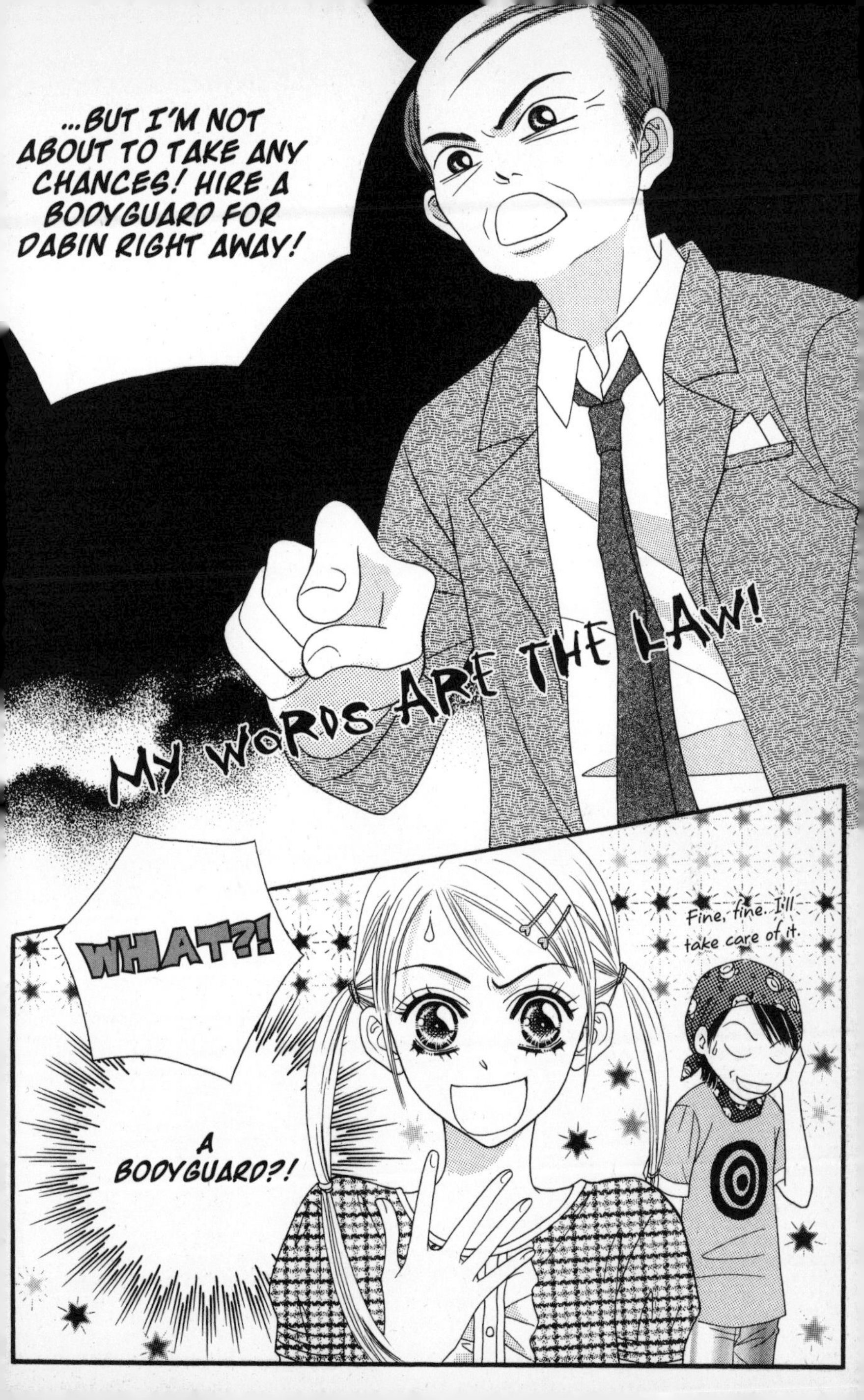
...BUT I'M NOT ABOUT TO TAKE ANY CHANCES! HIRE A BODYGUARD FOR DABIN RIGHT AWAY!
MY WORDS ARE THE LAW!
WHAT?!
A BODYGUARD?!
Fine, fine. I'll take care of it.

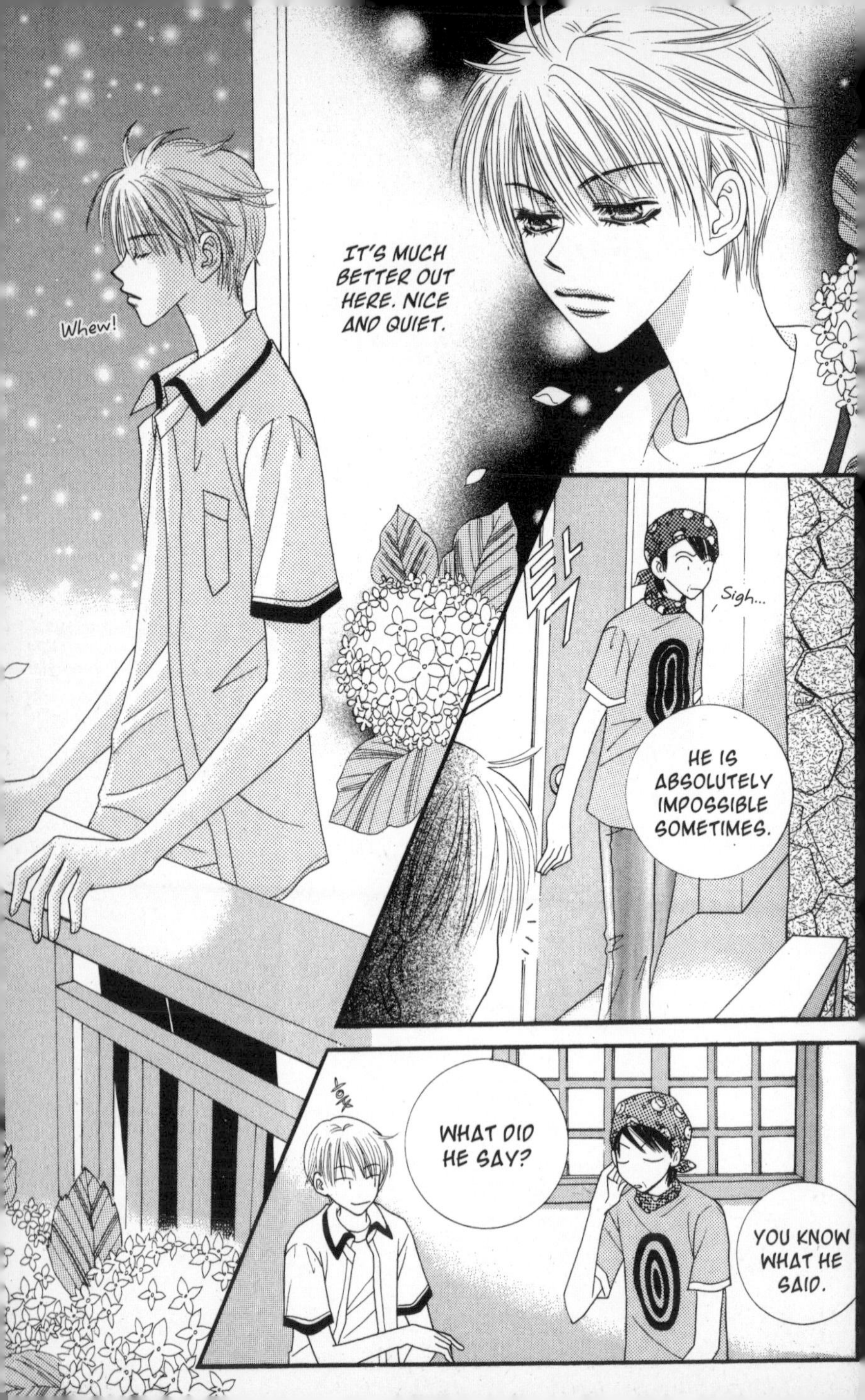
Whew!
IT'S MUCH BETTER OUT HERE. NICE AND QUIET.
탁
Sigh...
HE IS ABSOLUTELY IMPOSSIBLE SOMETIMES.
WHAT DID HE SAY?
YOU KNOW WHAT HE SAID.

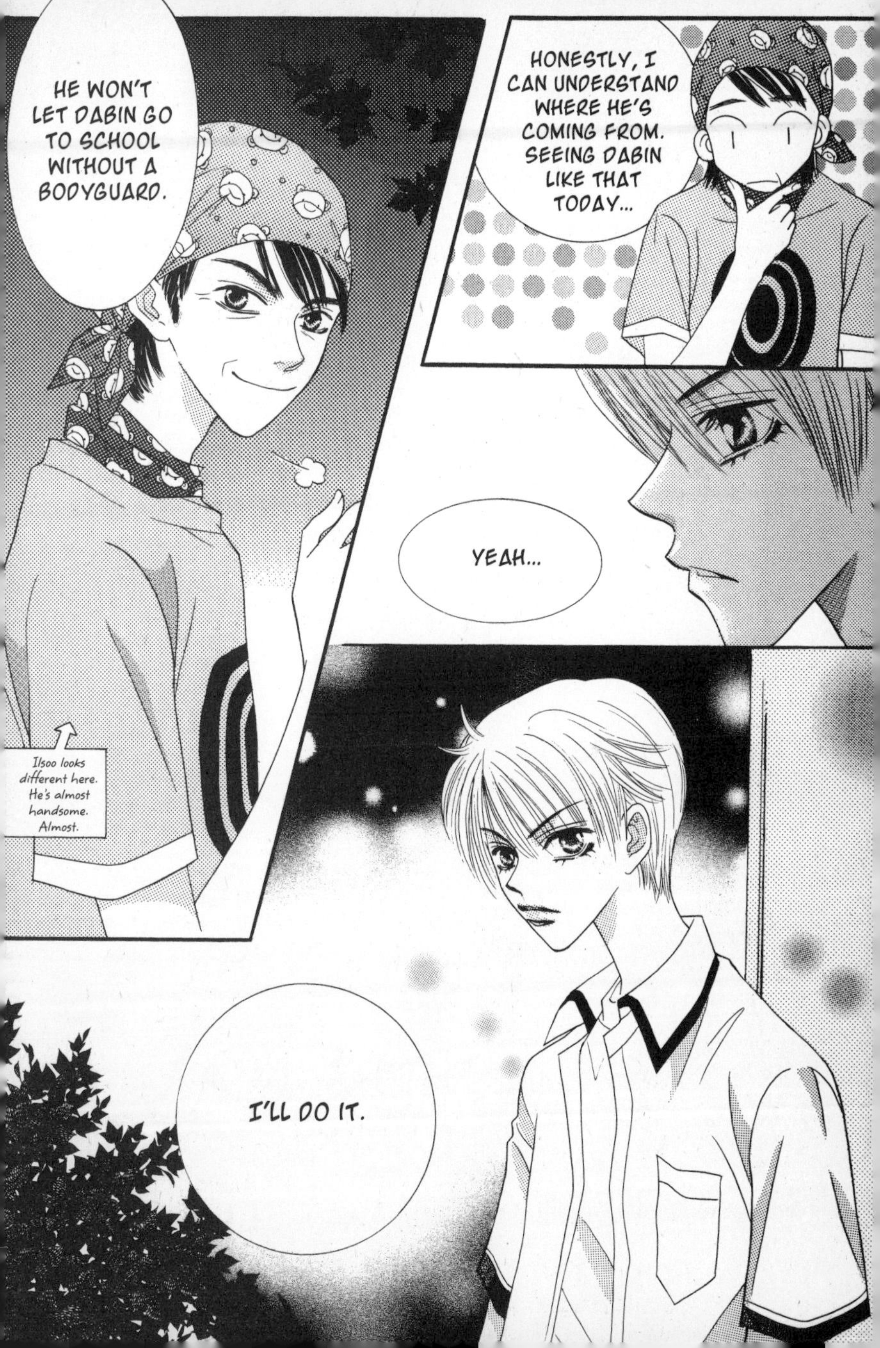
HE WON'T LET DABIN GO TO SCHOOL WITHOUT A BODYGUARD.
Ilsoo looks different here. He's almost handsome. Almost.
HONESTLY, I CAN UNDERSTAND WHERE HE'S COMING FROM. SEEING DABIN LIKE THAT TODAY...
YEAH...
I'LL DO IT.

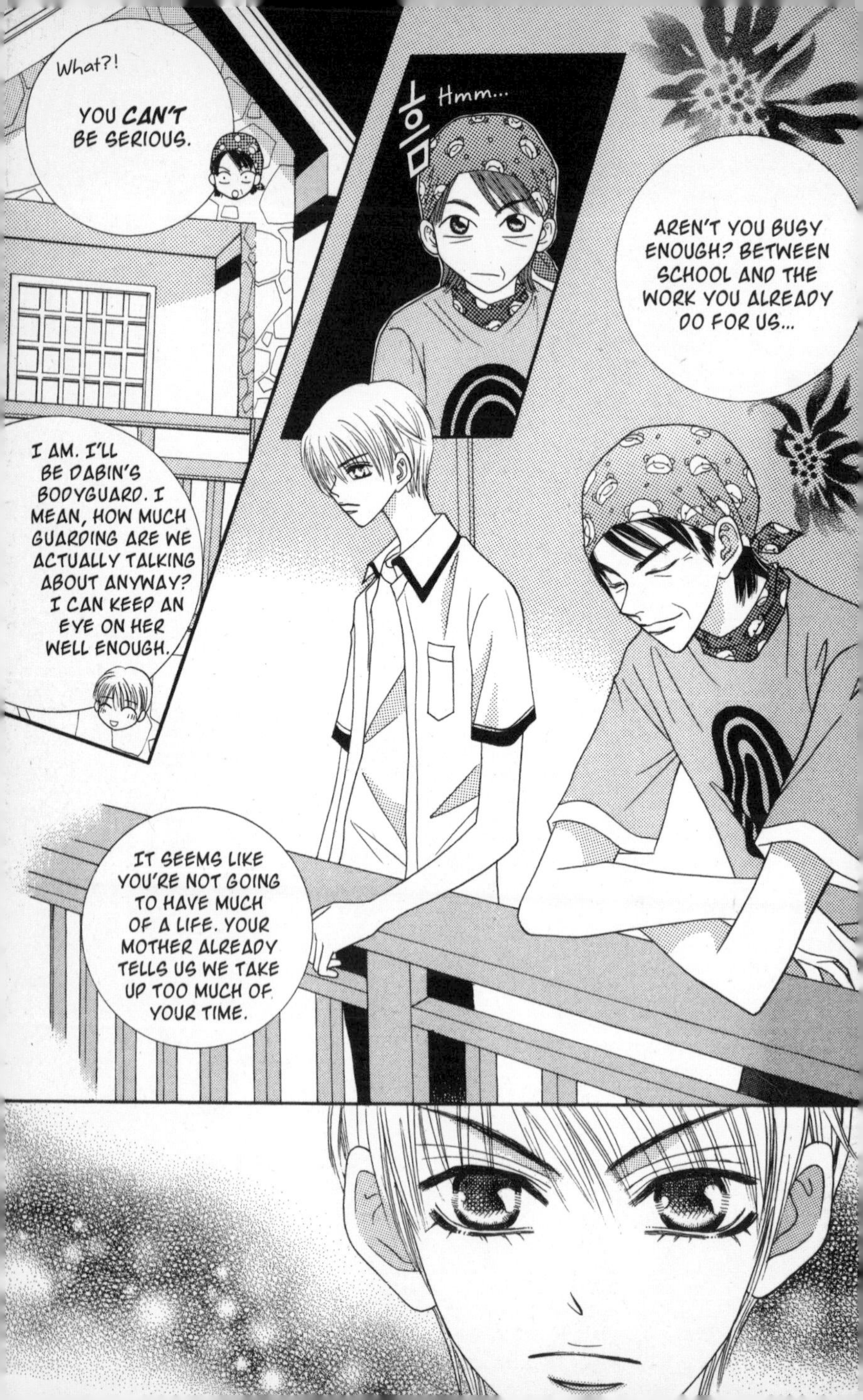
What?!
YOU CAN'T BE SERIOUS.
I AM. I'LL BE DABIN'S BODYGUARD. I MEAN, HOW MUCH GUARDING ARE WE ACTUALLY TALKING ABOUT ANYWAY? I CAN KEEP AN EYE ON HER WELL ENOUGH.
흠
Hmm...
AREN'T YOU BUSY ENOUGH? BETWEEN SCHOOL AND THE WORK YOU ALREADY DO FOR US...
IT SEEMS LIKE YOU'RE NOT GOING TO HAVE MUCH OF A LIFE. YOUR MOTHER ALREADY TELLS US WE TAKE UP TOO MUCH OF YOUR TIME.

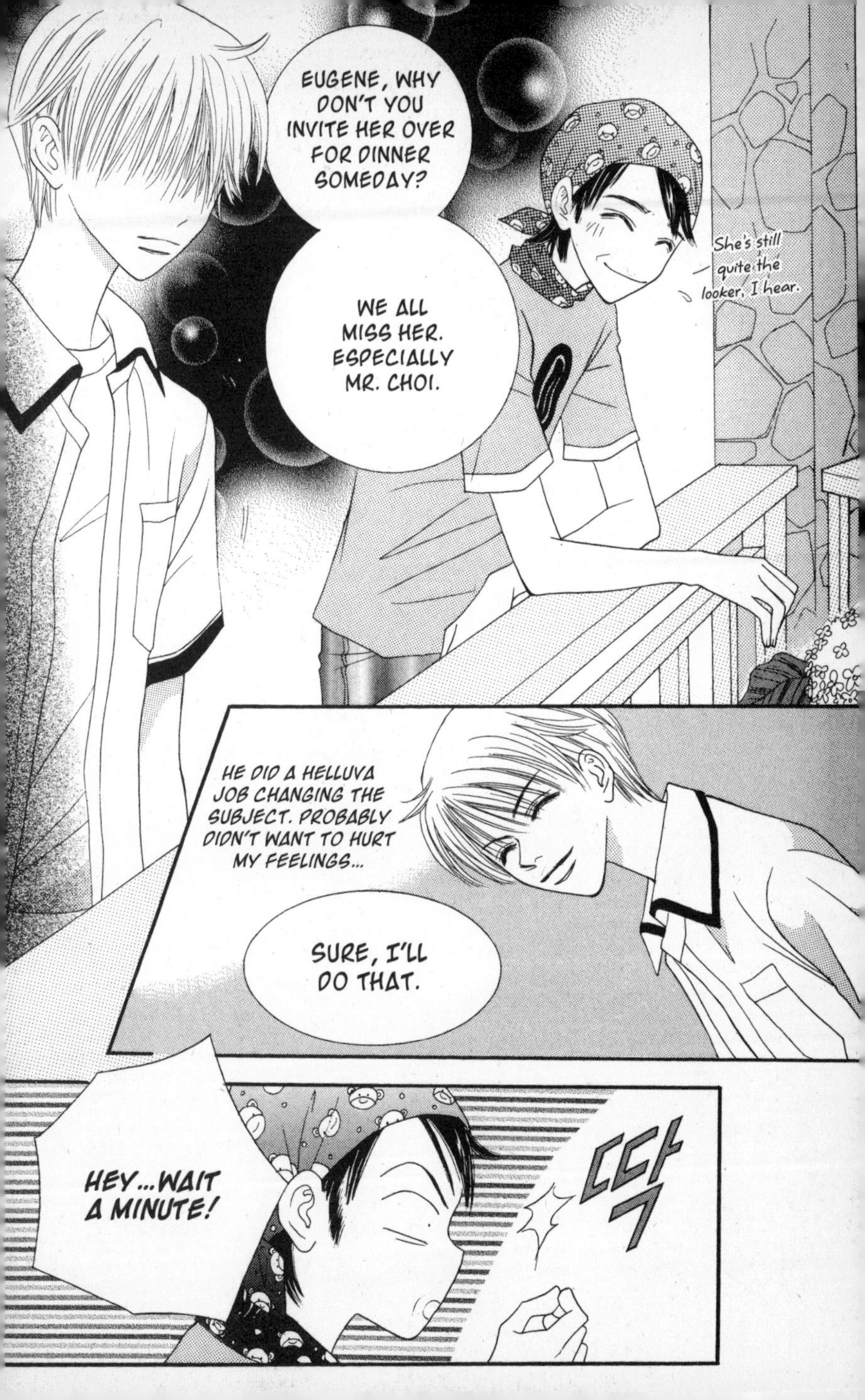
EUGENE, WHY DON'T YOU INVITE HER OVER FOR DINNER SOMEDAY?
WE ALL MISS HER. ESPECIALLY MR. CHOI.
She's still quite the looker, I hear.
HE DID A HELLUVA JOB CHANGING THE SUBJECT. PROBABLY DIDN'T WANT TO HURT MY FEELINGS...
SURE, I'LL DO THAT.
HEY...WAIT A MINUTE!

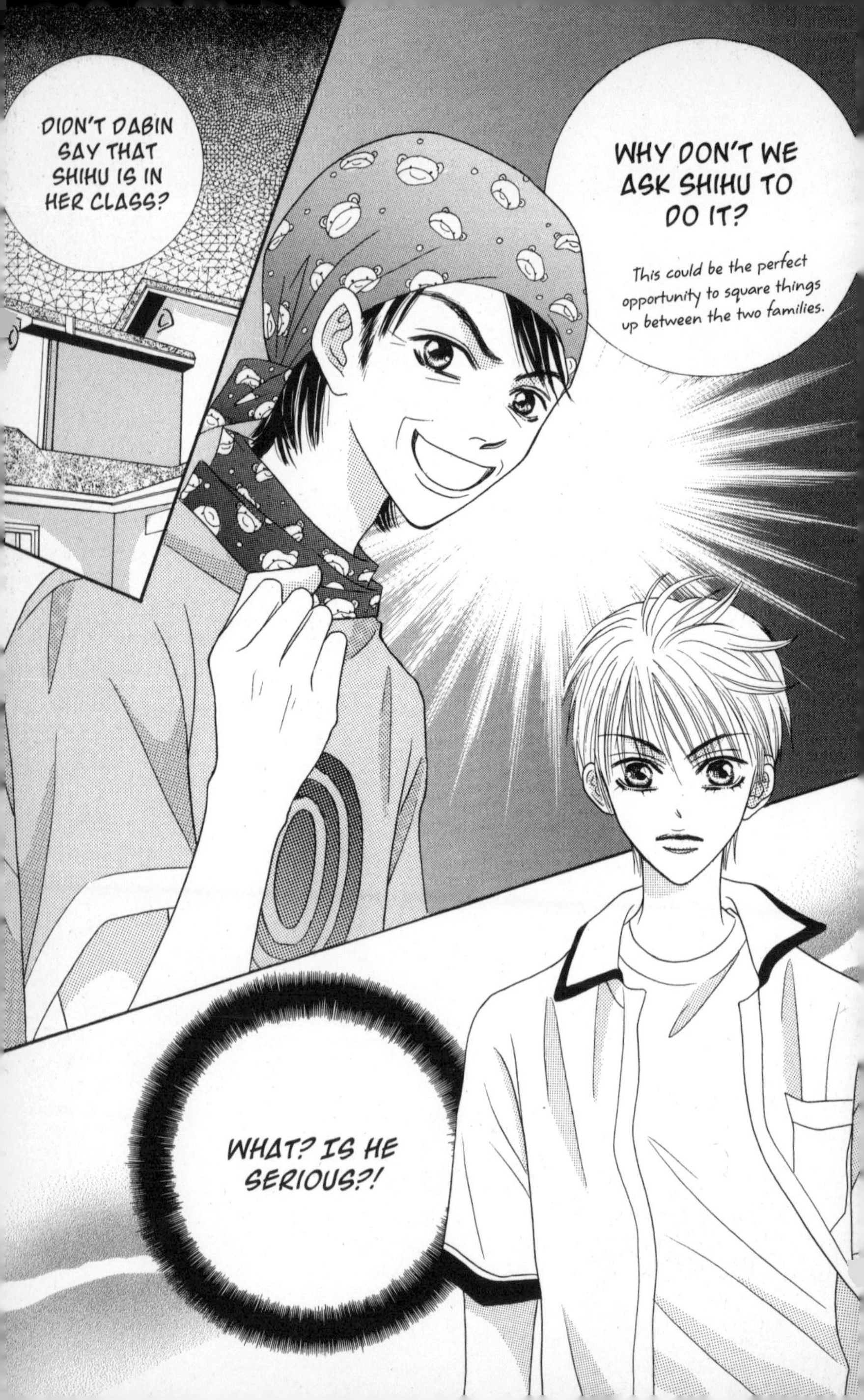
DIDN'T DABIN SAY THAT SHIHU IS IN HER CLASS?
WHY DON'T WE ASK SHIHU TO DO IT?
This could be the perfect opportunity to square things up between the two families.
WHAT? IS HE SERIOUS?!

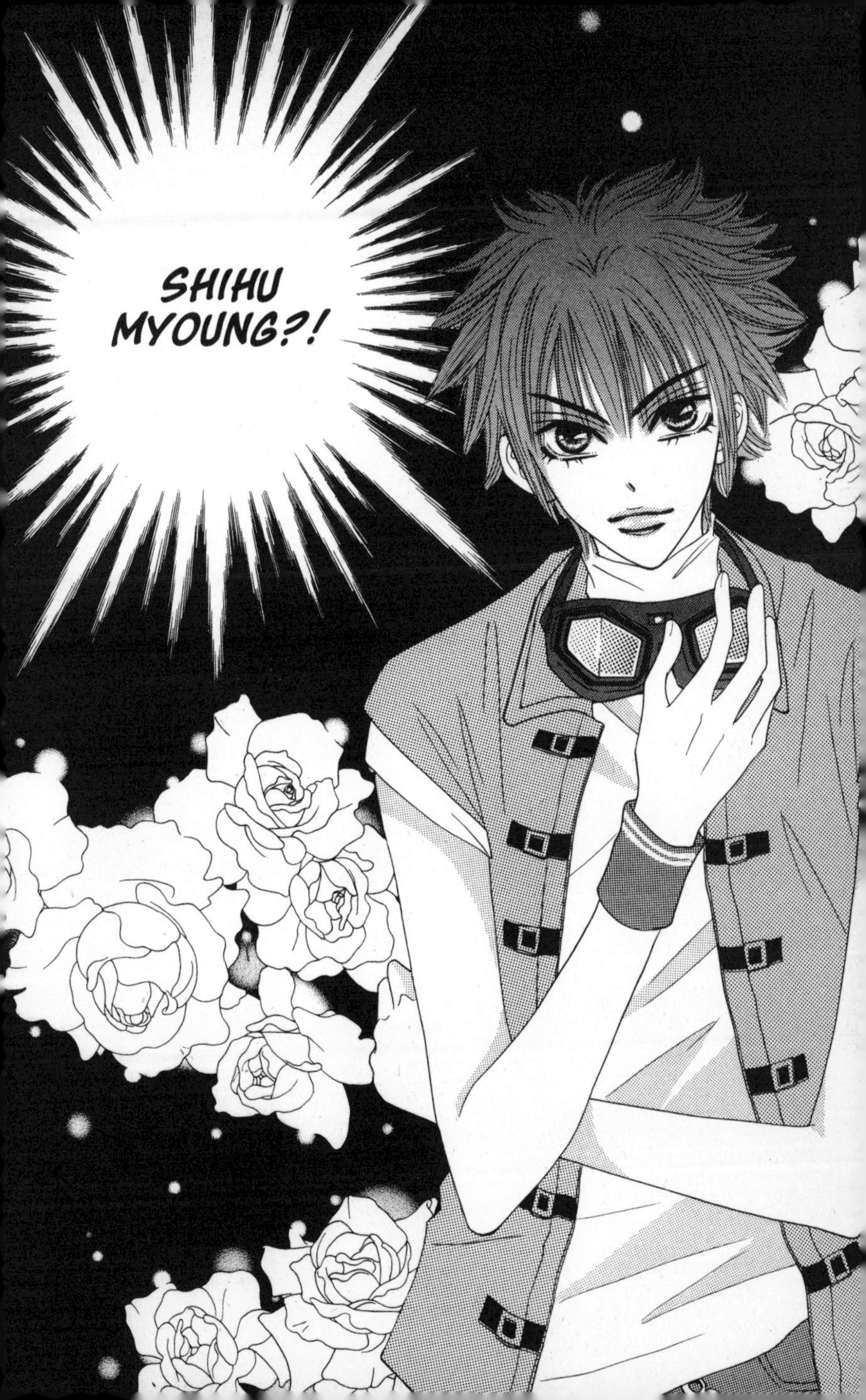
SHIHU MYOUNG?!

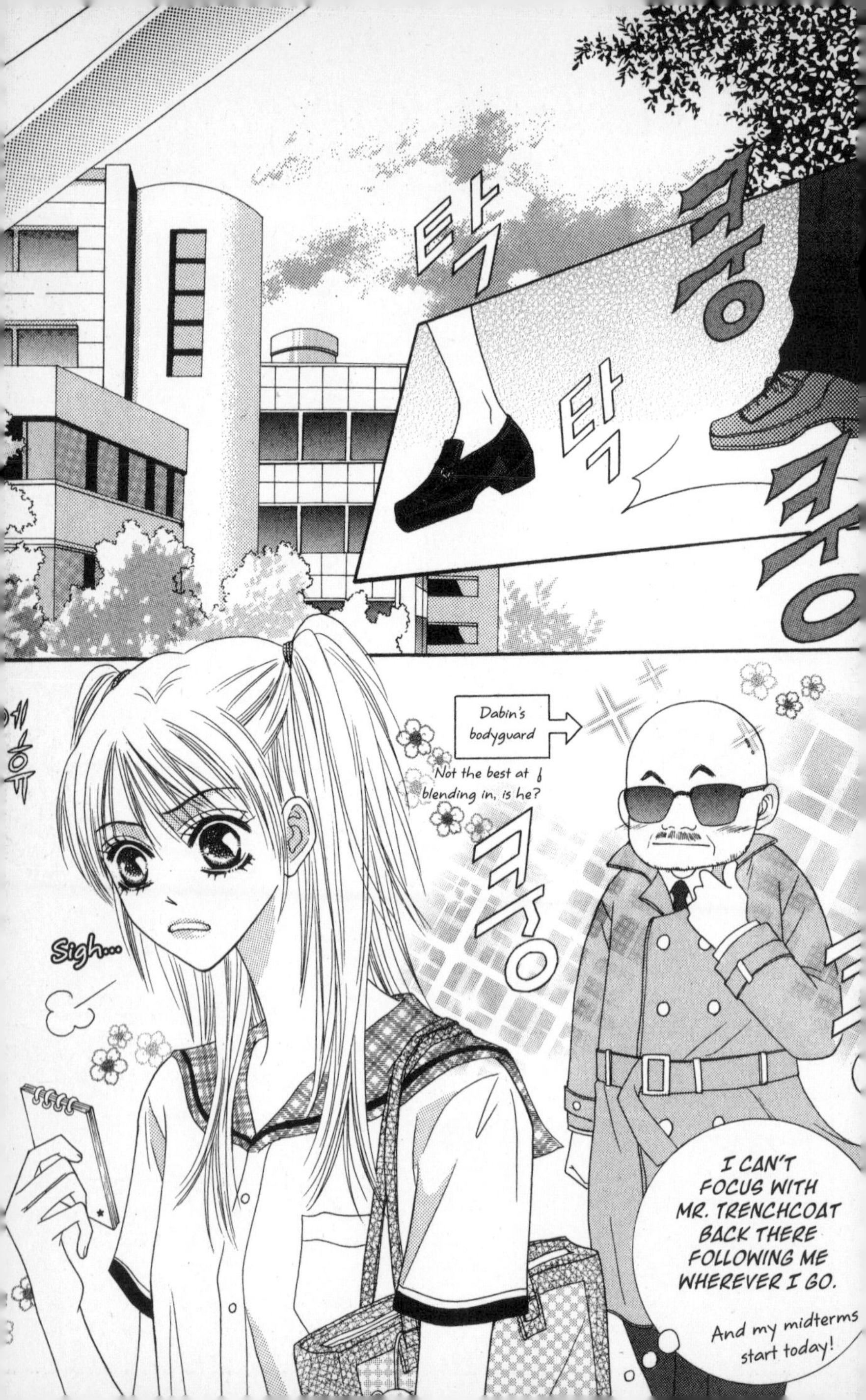

Sigh...
Dabin's bodyguard
Not the best at blending in, is he?
I CAN'T FOCUS WITH MR. TRENCHCOAT BACK THERE FOLLOWING ME WHEREVER I GO.
And my midterms start today!

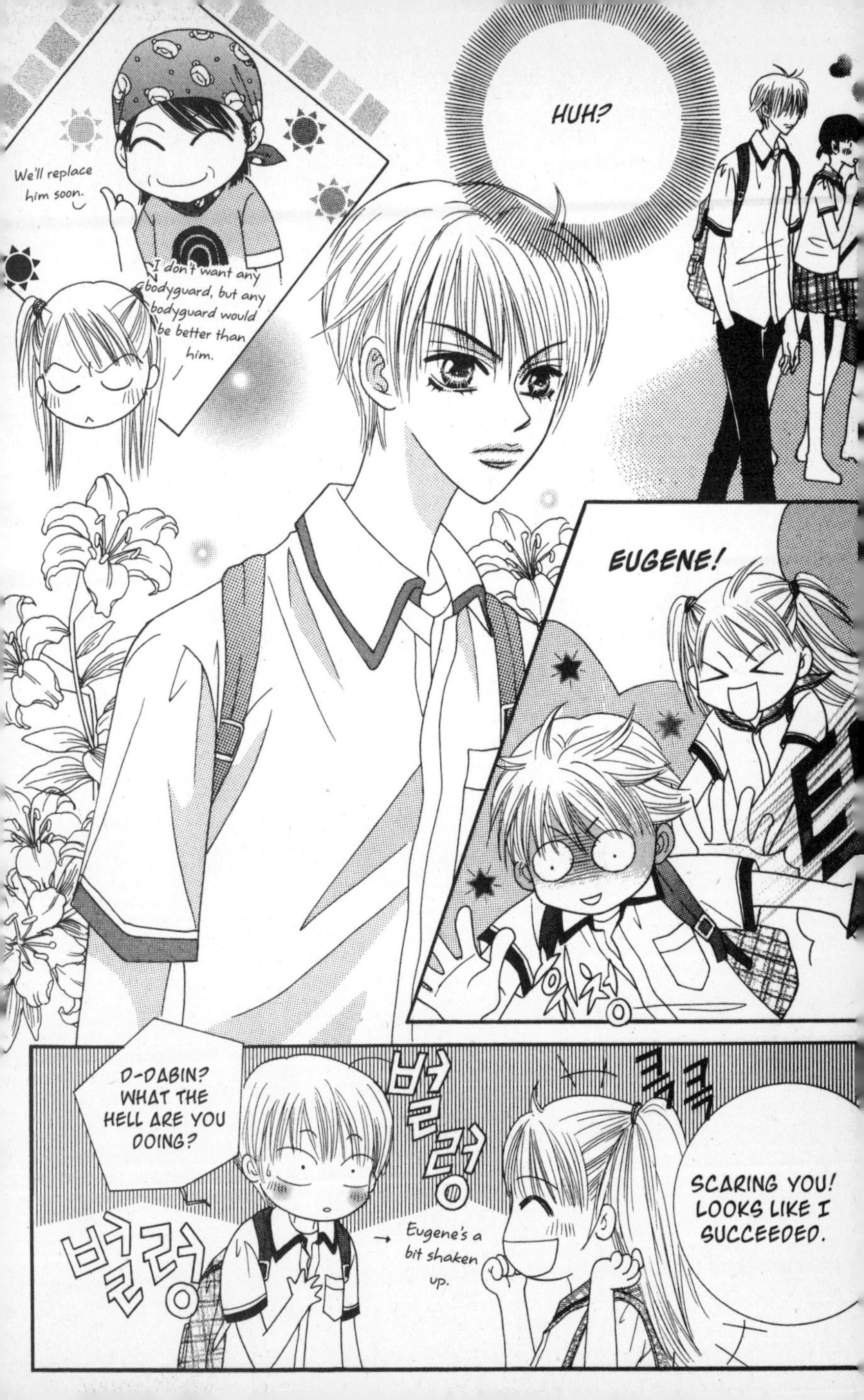

We'll replace him soon.
I don't want any bodyguard, but any bodyguard would be better than him.
HUH?
EUGENE!
D-DABIN? WHAT THE HELL ARE YOU DOING?
벌렁
벌렁
Eugene's a bit shaken up.
크크
SCARING YOU! LOOKS LIKE I SUCCEEDED.

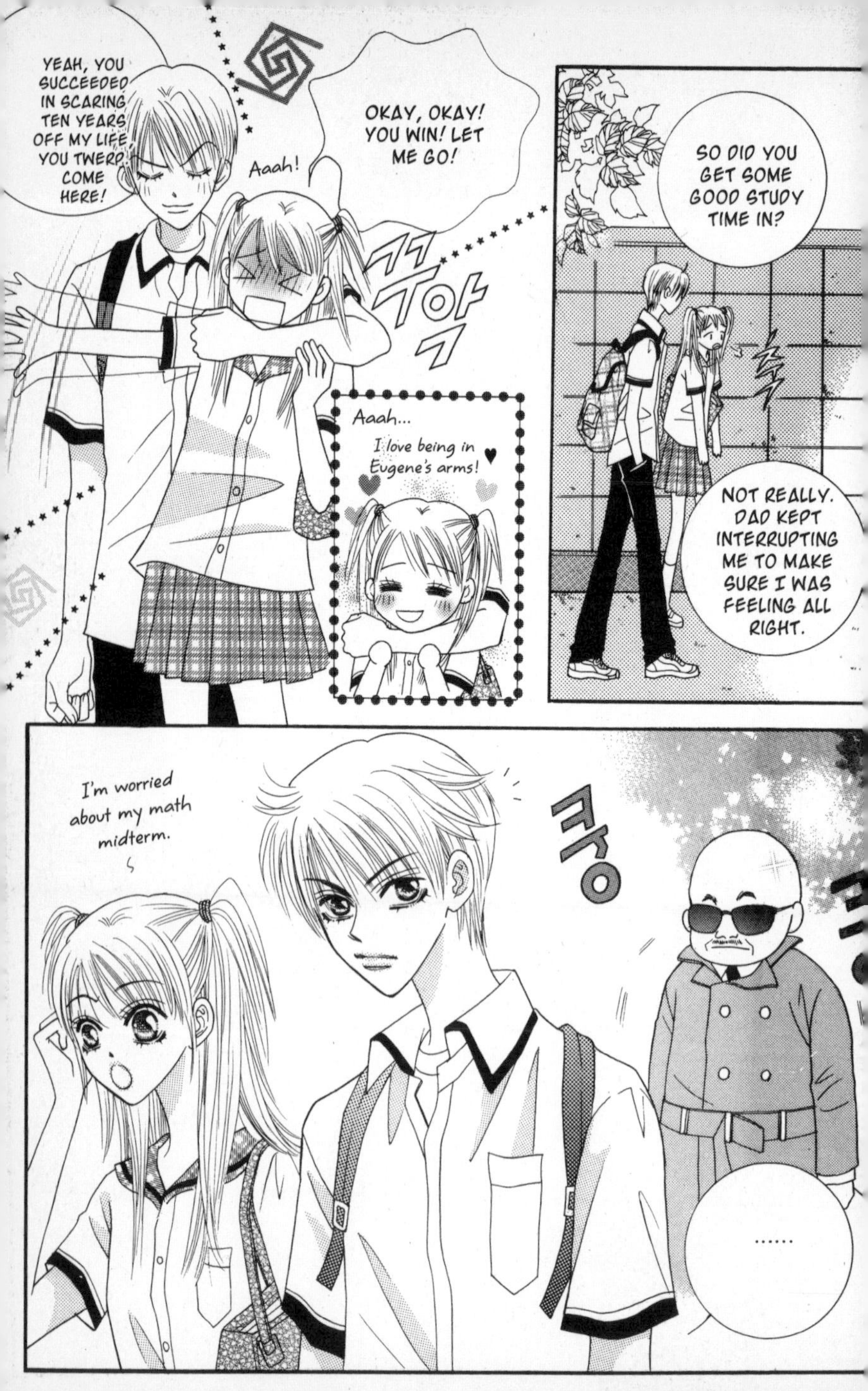
YEAH, YOU SUCCEEDED IN SCARING TEN YEARS OFF MY LIFE, YOU TWERP. COME HERE!
Aaah!
OKAY, OKAY! YOU WIN! LET ME GO!
Aaah...
I love being in Eugene's arms!
SO DID YOU GET SOME GOOD STUDY TIME IN?
NOT REALLY. DAD KEPT INTERRUPTING ME TO MAKE SURE I WAS FEELING ALL RIGHT.
I'm worried about my math midterm.
......

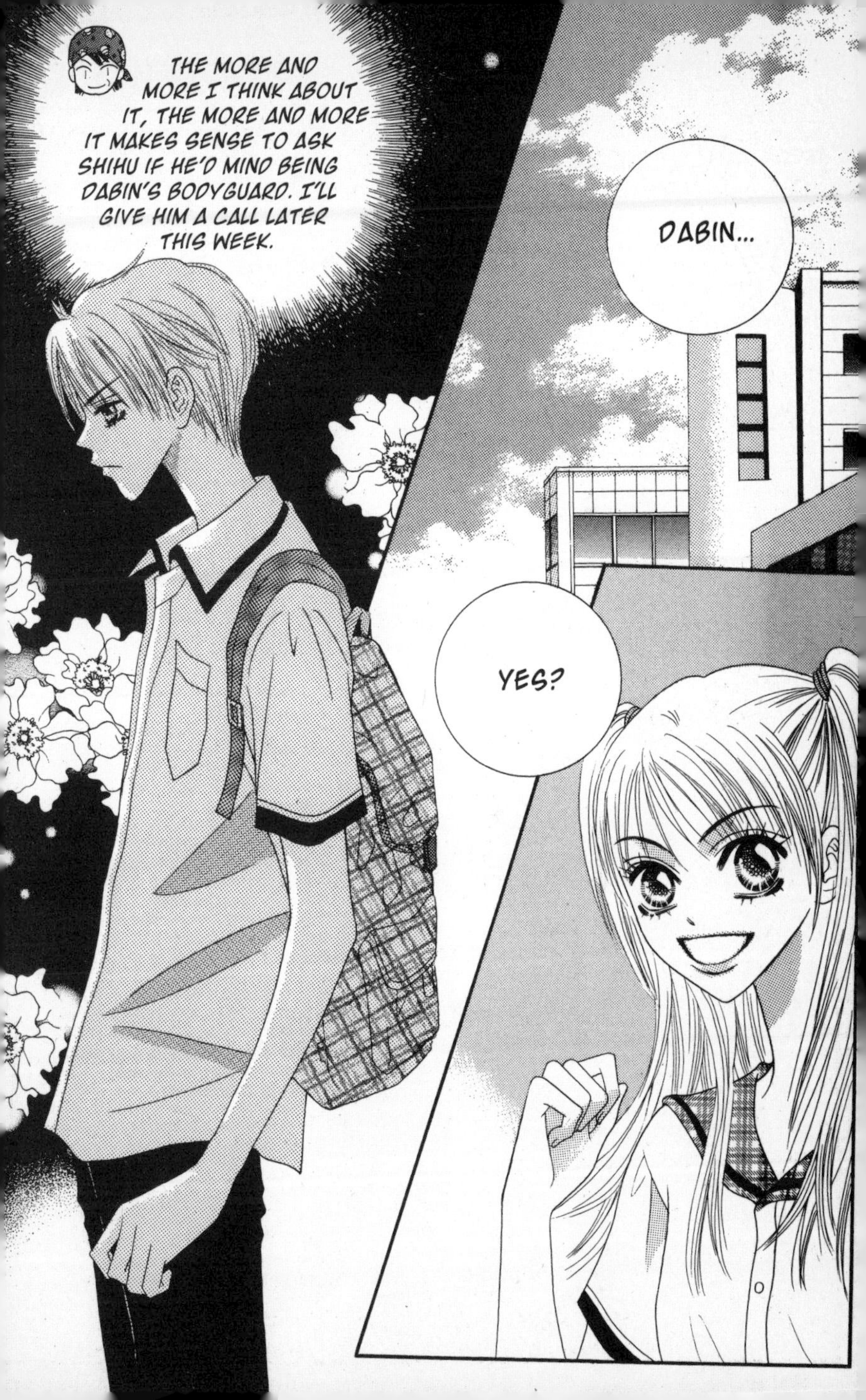
THE MORE AND MORE I THINK ABOUT IT, THE MORE AND MORE IT MAKES SENSE TO ASK SHIHU IF HE'D MIND BEING DABIN'S BODYGUARD. I'LL GIVE HIM A CALL LATER THIS WEEK.
DABIN...
YES?

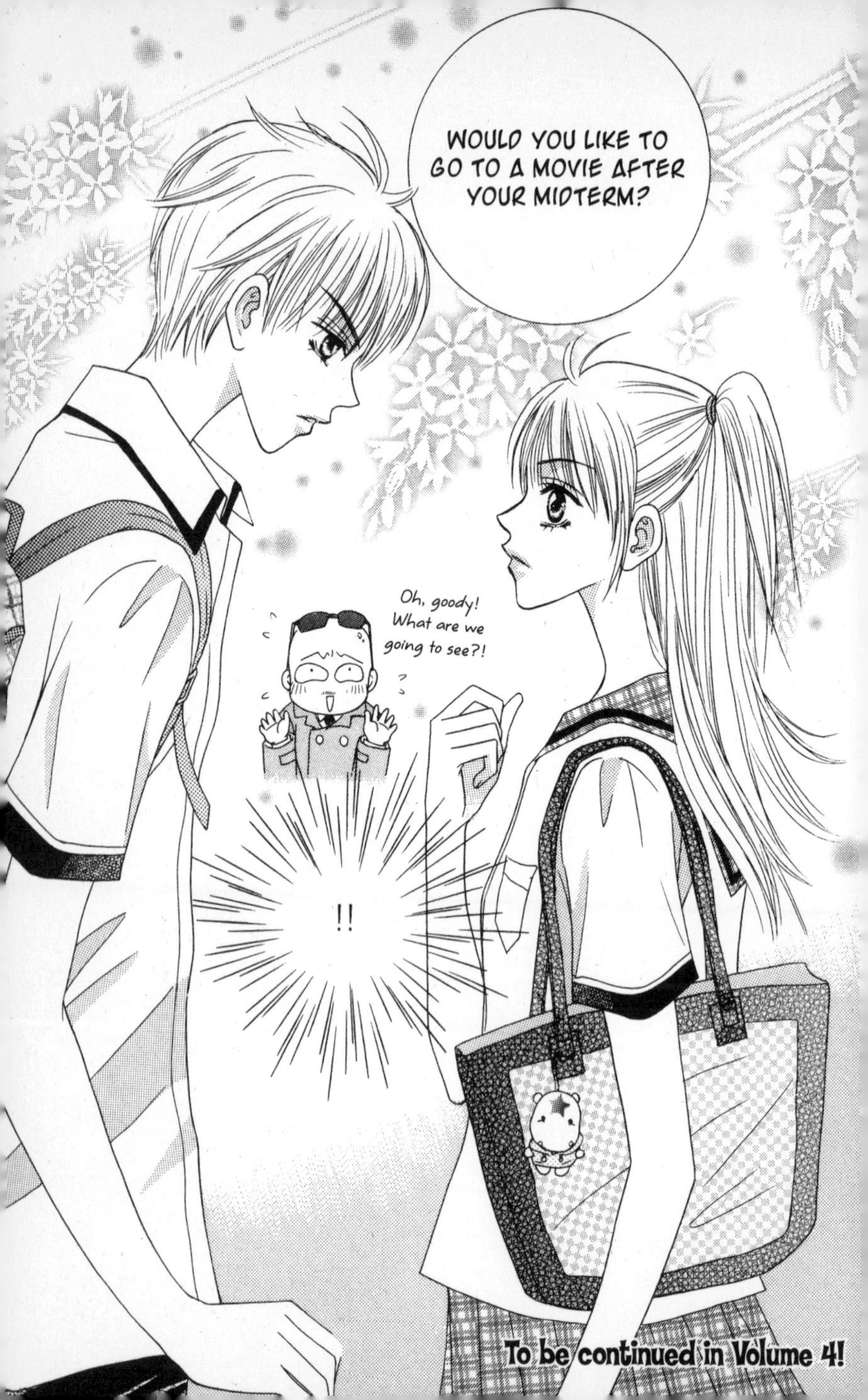
WOULD YOU LIKE TO GO TO A MOVIE AFTER YOUR MIDTERM?
Oh, goody! What are we going to see?!
!!
To be continued in Volume 4!

| Cute | Sweet | Bright | Fresh |

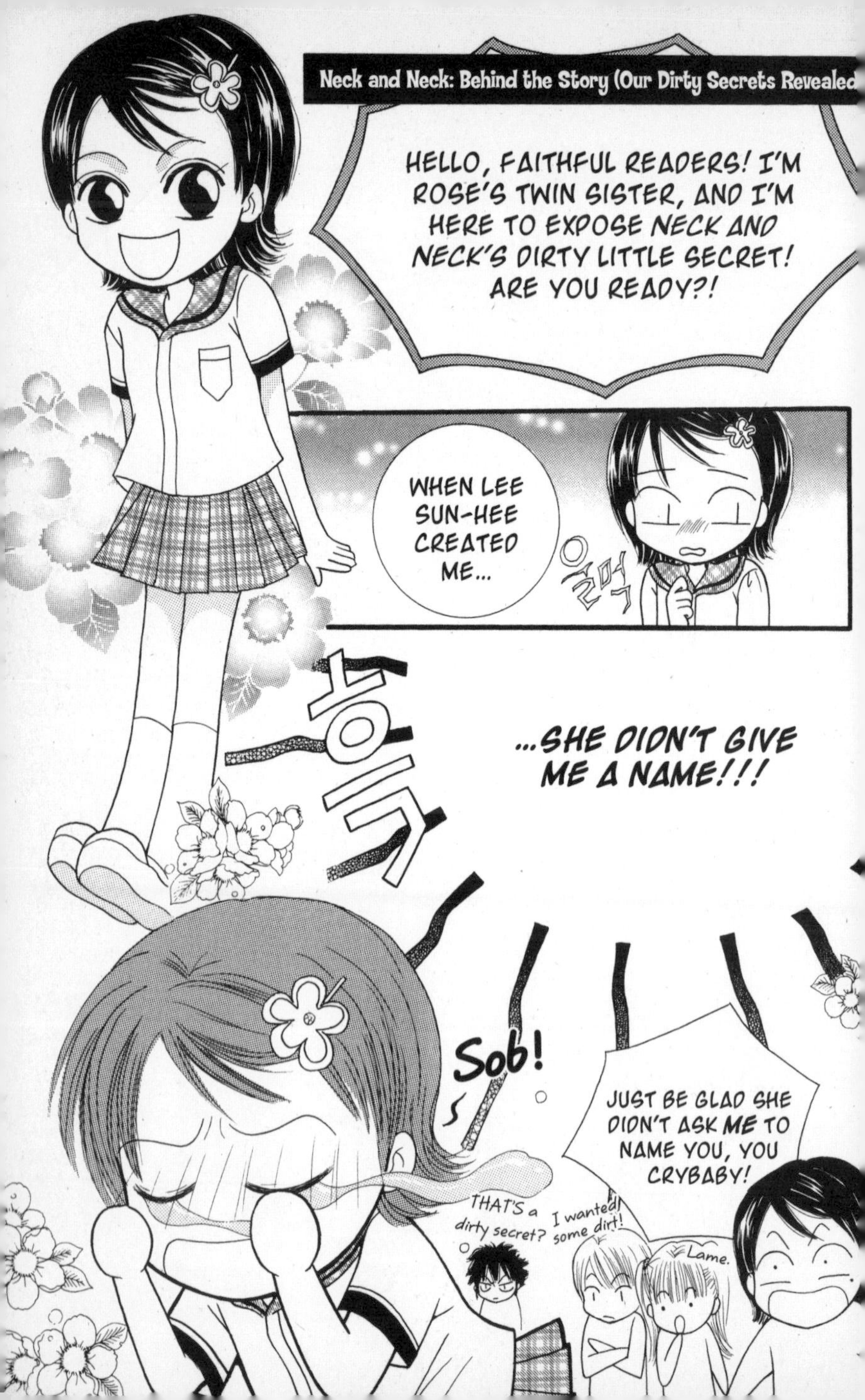
Neck and Neck: Behind the Story (Our Dirty Secrets Revealed
HELLO, FAITHFUL READERS! I'M ROSE'S TWIN SISTER, AND I'M HERE TO EXPOSE NECK AND NECK'S DIRTY LITTLE SECRET! ARE YOU READY?!
WHEN LEE SUN-HEE CREATED ME...
울먹
...SHE DIDN'T GIVE ME A NAME!!!
Sob!
JUST BE GLAD SHE DIDN'T ASK ME TO NAME YOU, YOU CRYBABY!
THAT'S a dirty secret?
I wanted some dirt!
Lame.

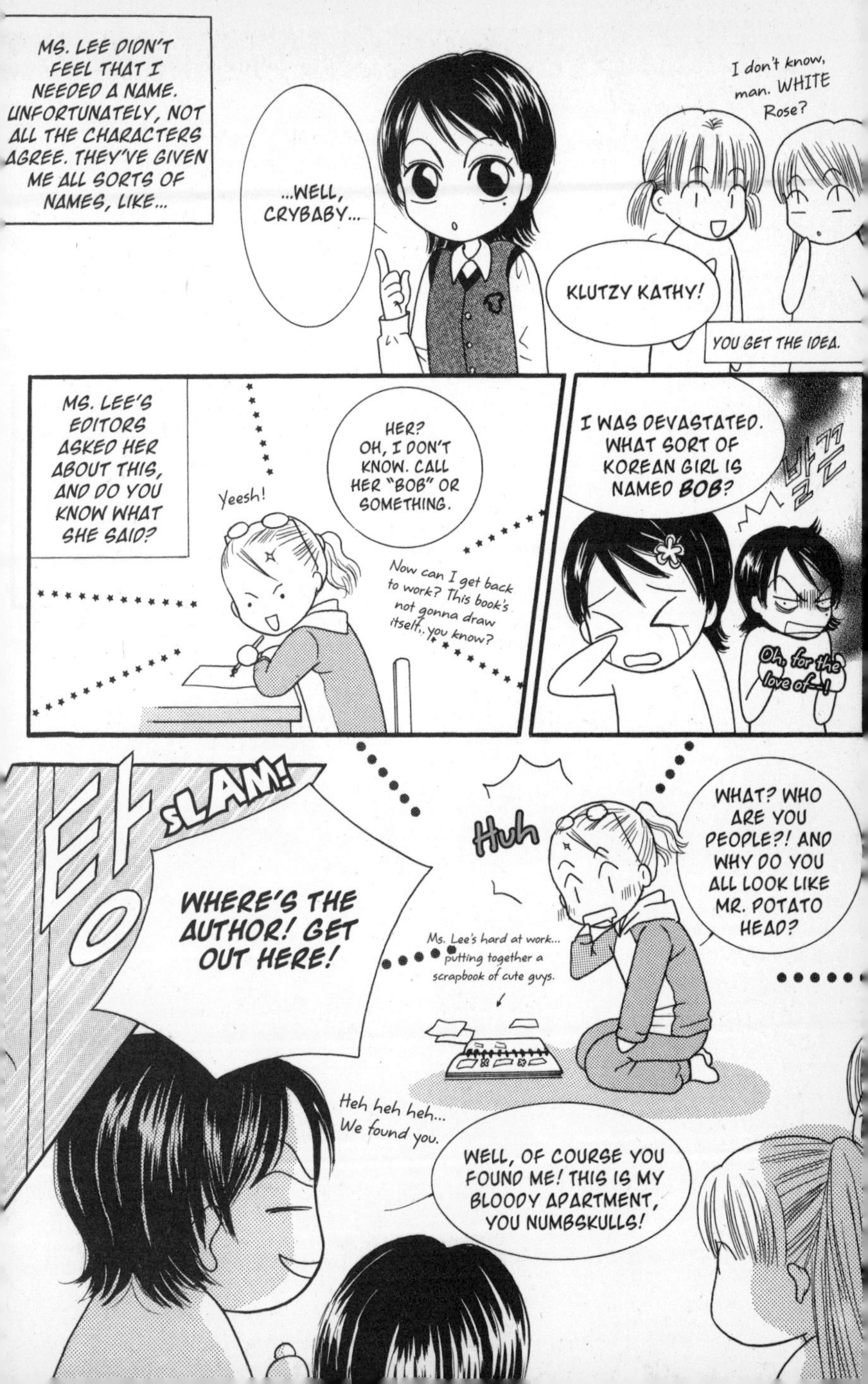

MS. LEE DIDN'T FEEL THAT I NEEDED A NAME. UNFORTUNATELY, NOT ALL THE CHARACTERS AGREE. THEY'VE GIVEN ME ALL SORTS OF NAMES, LIKE...
...WELL, CRYBABY...
I don't know, man. WHITE Rose?
KLUTZY KATHY!
YOU GET THE IDEA.
MS. LEE'S EDITORS ASKED HER ABOUT THIS, AND DO YOU KNOW WHAT SHE SAID?
HER? OH, I DON'T KNOW. CALL HER "BOB" OR SOMETHING.
Yeesh!
Now can I get back to work? This book's not gonna draw itself, you know?
I WAS DEVASTATED. WHAT SORT OF KOREAN GIRL IS NAMED BOB?
발끈
Oh, for the love of—!
탕
SLAM!
WHERE'S THE AUTHOR! GET OUT HERE!
Huh
WHAT? WHO ARE YOU PEOPLE?! AND WHY DO YOU ALL LOOK LIKE MR. POTATO HEAD?
Ms. Lee's hard at work... putting together a scrapbook of cute guys.
Heh heh heh... We found you.
WELL, OF COURSE YOU FOUND ME! THIS IS MY BLOODY APARTMENT, YOU NUMBSKULLS!

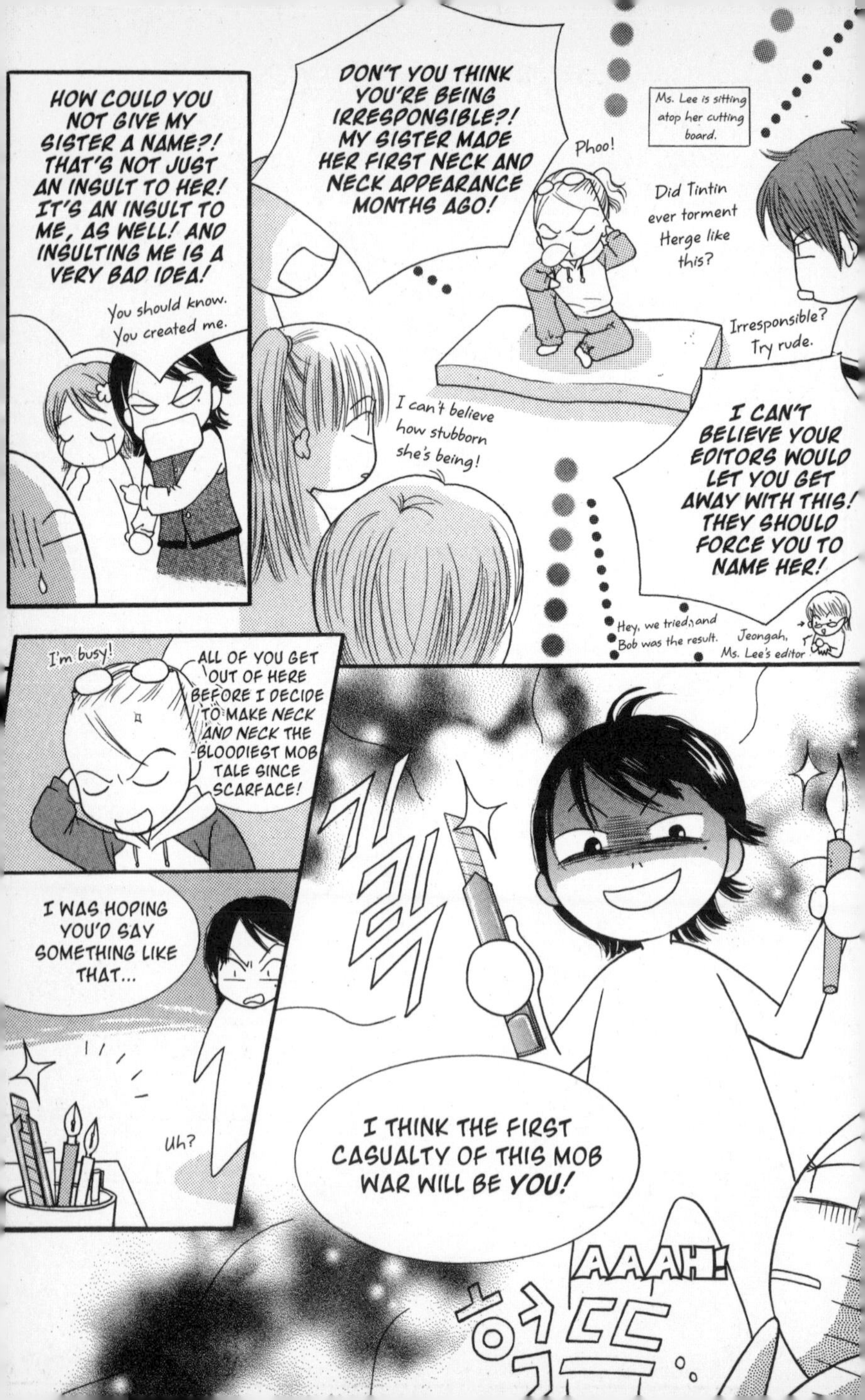
HOW COULD YOU NOT GIVE MY SISTER A NAME?! THAT'S NOT JUST AN INSULT TO HER! IT'S AN INSULT TO ME, AS WELL! AND INSULTING ME IS A VERY BAD IDEA!
You should know. You created me.
DON'T YOU THINK YOU'RE BEING IRRESPONSIBLE?! MY SISTER MADE HER FIRST NECK AND NECK APPEARANCE MONTHS AGO!
Phoo!
Ms. Lee is sitting atop her cutting board.
Did Tintin ever torment Herge like this?
Irresponsible? Try rude.
I can't believe how stubborn she's being!
I CAN'T BELIEVE YOUR EDITORS WOULD LET YOU GET AWAY WITH THIS! THEY SHOULD FORCE YOU TO NAME HER!
Hey, we tried, and Bob was the result.
Jeongah, Ms. Lee's editor
I'm busy!
ALL OF YOU GET OUT OF HERE BEFORE I DECIDE TO MAKE NECK AND NECK THE BLOODIEST MOB TALE SINCE SCARFACE!
I WAS HOPING YOU'D SAY SOMETHING LIKE THAT...
Uh?
I THINK THE FIRST CASUALTY OF THIS MOB WAR WILL BE YOU!
AAAH!

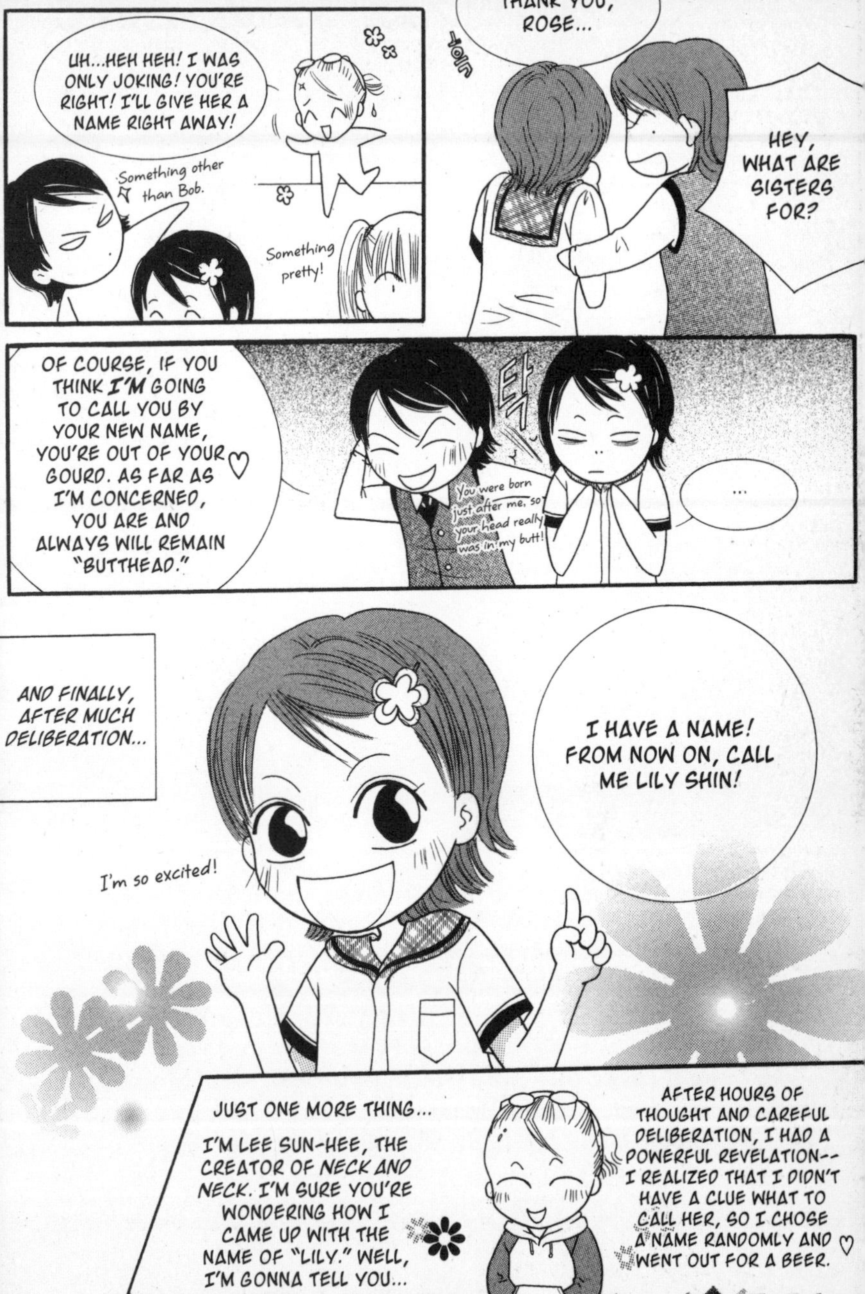
UH...HEH HEH! I WAS ONLY JOKING! YOU'RE RIGHT! I'LL GIVE HER A NAME RIGHT AWAY!
Something other than Bob.
Something pretty!
THANK YOU, ROSE...
HEY, WHAT ARE SISTERS FOR?
OF COURSE, IF YOU THINK *I'M* GOING TO CALL YOU BY YOUR NEW NAME, YOU'RE OUT OF YOUR GOURD. AS FAR AS I'M CONCERNED, YOU ARE AND ALWAYS WILL REMAIN "BUTTHEAD." ♡
탁
You were born just after me, so your head really was in my butt!
...
AND FINALLY, AFTER MUCH DELIBERATION...
I'm so excited!
I HAVE A NAME! FROM NOW ON, CALL ME LILY SHIN!
JUST ONE MORE THING...
I'M LEE SUN-HEE, THE CREATOR OF *NECK AND NECK*. I'M SURE YOU'RE WONDERING HOW I CAME UP WITH THE NAME OF "LILY." WELL, I'M GONNA TELL YOU...
AFTER HOURS OF THOUGHT AND CAREFUL DELIBERATION, I HAD A POWERFUL REVELATION--I REALIZED THAT I DIDN'T HAVE A CLUE WHAT TO CALL HER, SO I CHOSE A NAME RANDOMLY AND WENT OUT FOR A BEER. ♡
The End

Who Wants My First Kiss?!

Author's Comment

I began Who Wants My First Kiss?! shortly after completing Happy Girl vs. Money Boy. Perceptive readers will notice that by this point, I was really starting to develop my style. I really like the character of Doyle a lot. He's not spectacularly good-looking or exceptionally talented, but he's friendly and warm. I think he'd make a wonderful boyfriend (if you were a cartoon character, of course). The female character, Jean, is very much a "girl next door" type. I'm sure many of you know people just like her. I hope you enjoy reading about how their friendship develops into something much deeper.

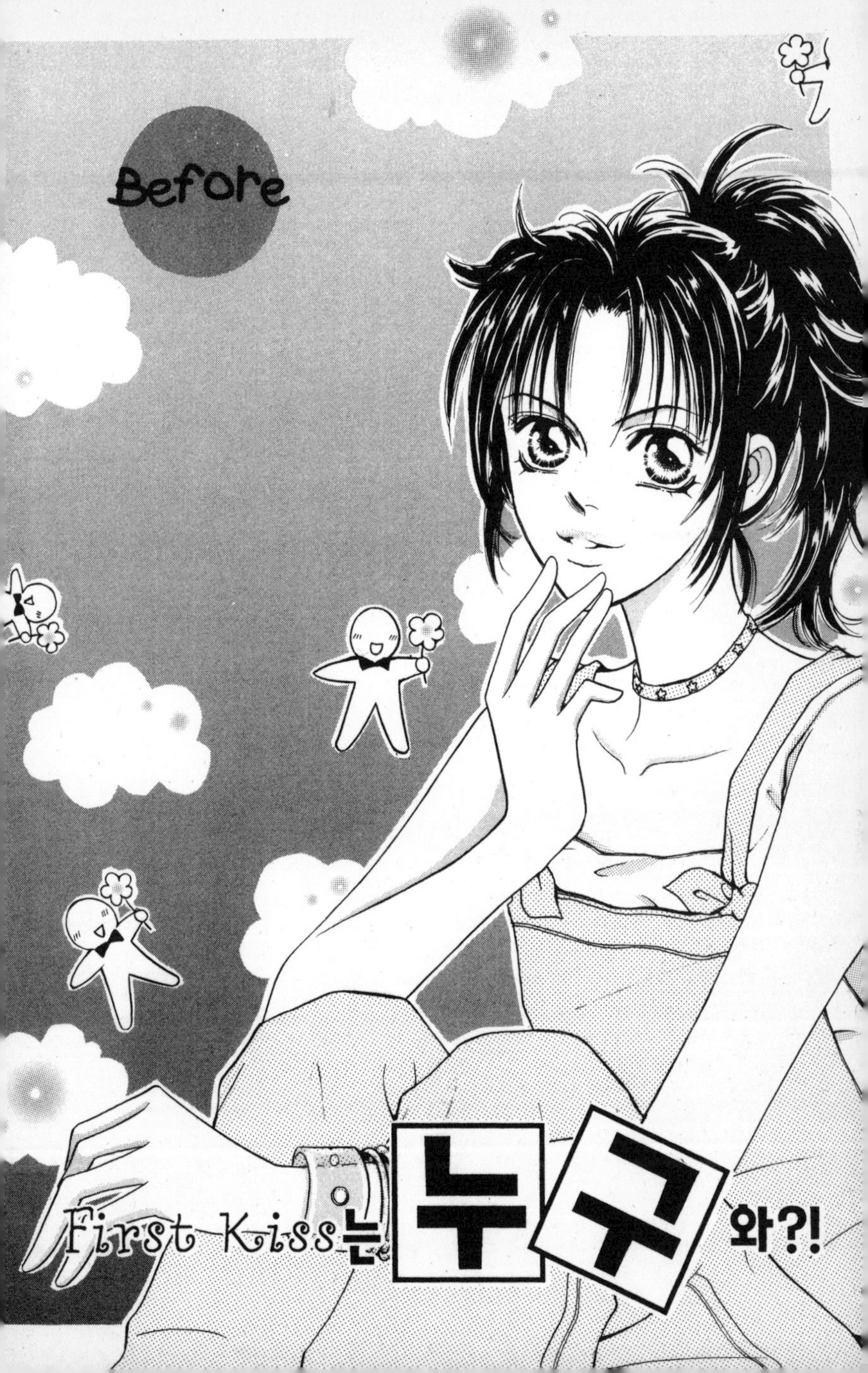
Before
First Kiss는 누구와?!

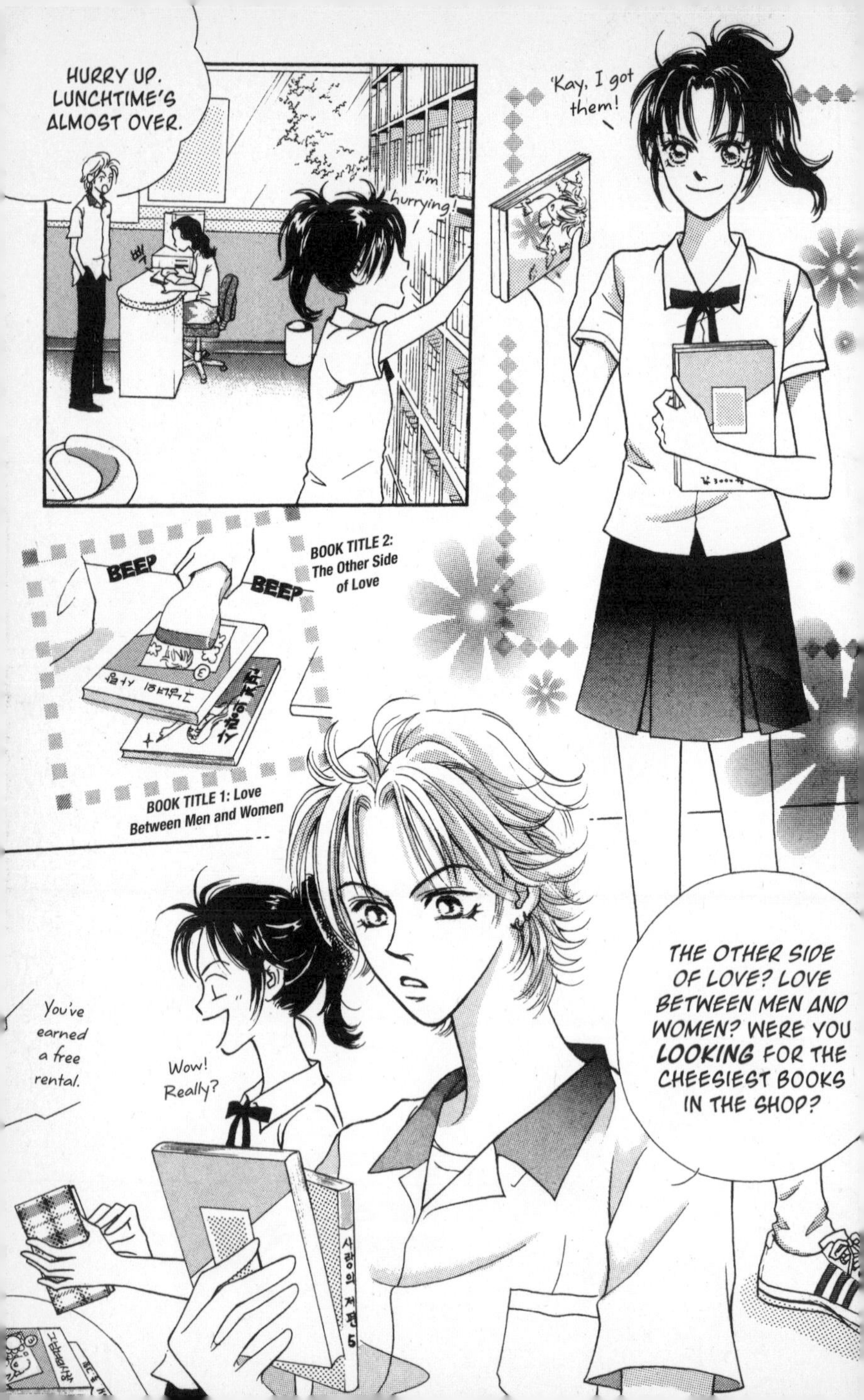
HURRY UP. LUNCHTIME'S ALMOST OVER.
I'm hurrying!
'Kay, I got them!
BEEP
BEEP
BOOK TITLE 2: The Other Side of Love
BOOK TITLE 1: Love Between Men and Women
You've earned a free rental.
Wow! Really?
THE OTHER SIDE OF LOVE? LOVE BETWEEN MEN AND WOMEN? WERE YOU **LOOKING** FOR THE CHEESIEST BOOKS IN THE SHOP?
사랑의 저편 5

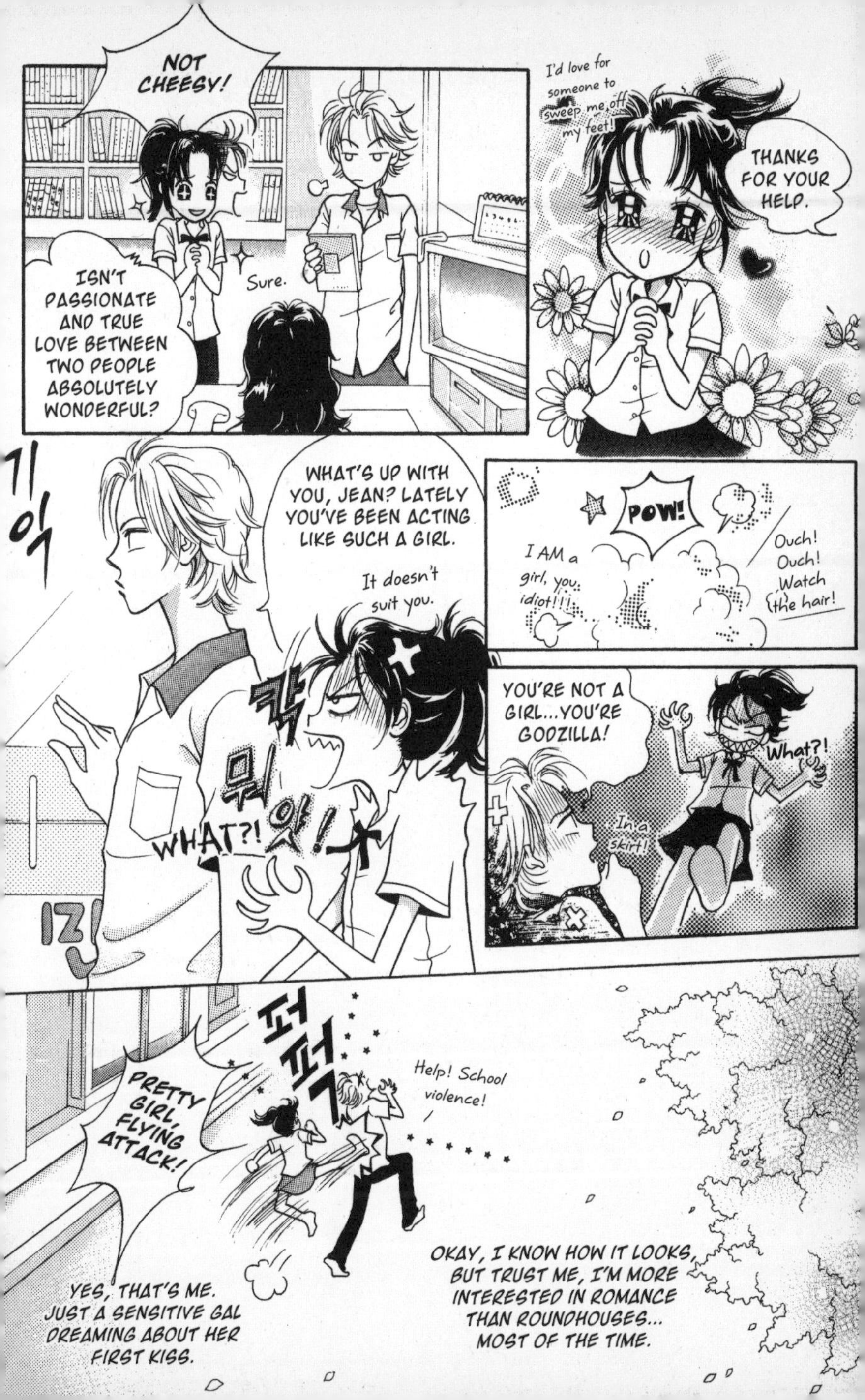
NOT CHEESY!
ISN'T PASSIONATE AND TRUE LOVE BETWEEN TWO PEOPLE ABSOLUTELY WONDERFUL?
Sure.
I'd love for someone to sweep me off my feet!
THANKS FOR YOUR HELP.
WHAT'S UP WITH YOU, JEAN? LATELY YOU'VE BEEN ACTING LIKE SUCH A GIRL.
It doesn't suit you.
WHAT?!
POW!
I AM a girl, you idiot!!!
Ouch! Ouch! Watch the hair!
YOU'RE NOT A GIRL...YOU'RE GODZILLA!
What?!
In a skirt!
PRETTY GIRL, FLYING ATTACK!
Help! School violence!
YES, THAT'S ME. JUST A SENSITIVE GAL DREAMING ABOUT HER FIRST KISS.
OKAY, I KNOW HOW IT LOOKS, BUT TRUST ME, I'M MORE INTERESTED IN ROMANCE THAN ROUNDHOUSES... MOST OF THE TIME.

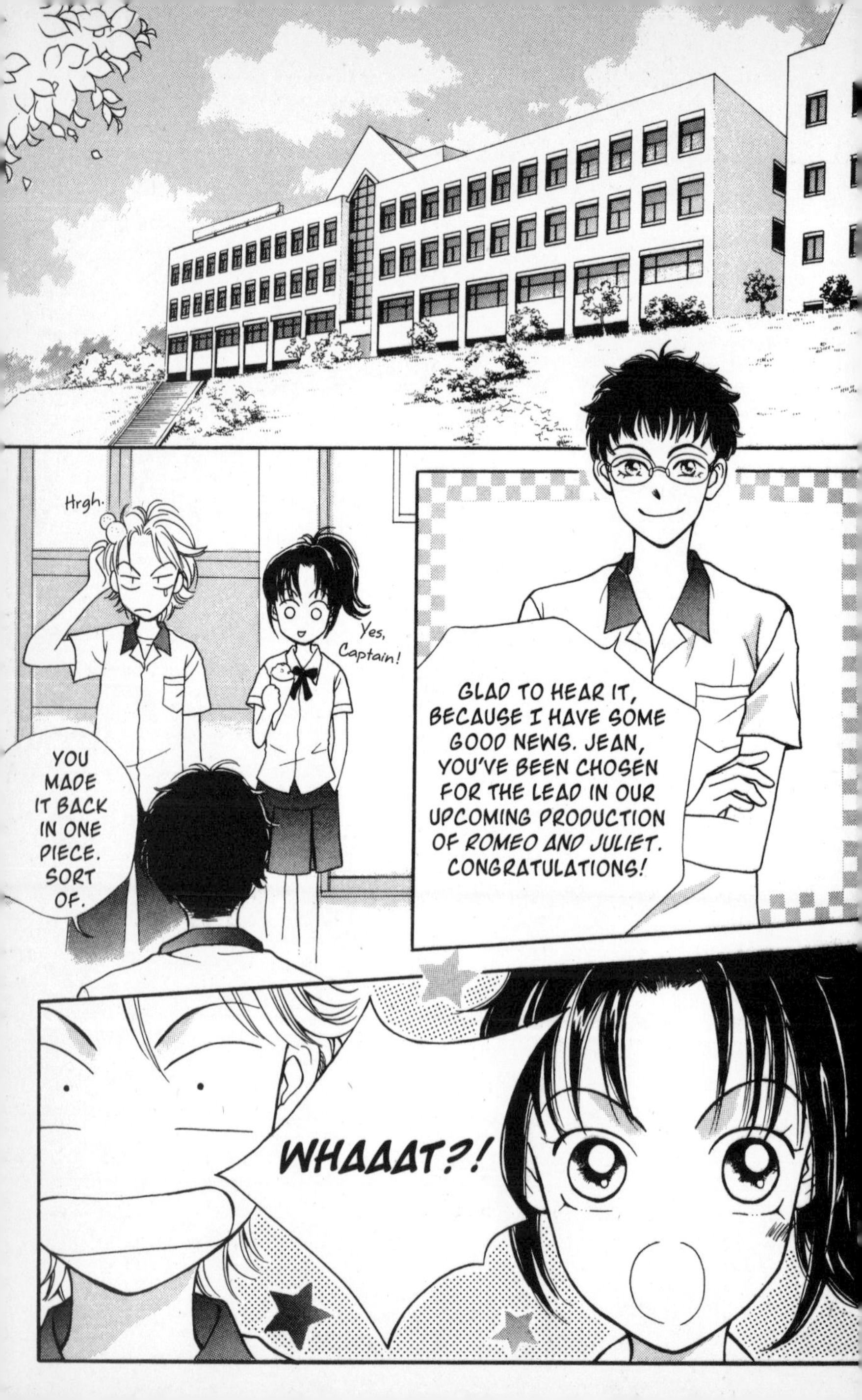
Hrgh.
Yes, Captain!
YOU MADE IT BACK IN ONE PIECE. SORT OF.
GLAD TO HEAR IT, BECAUSE I HAVE SOME GOOD NEWS. JEAN, YOU'VE BEEN CHOSEN FOR THE LEAD IN OUR UPCOMING PRODUCTION OF *ROMEO AND JULIET*. CONGRATULATIONS!
WHAAAT?!

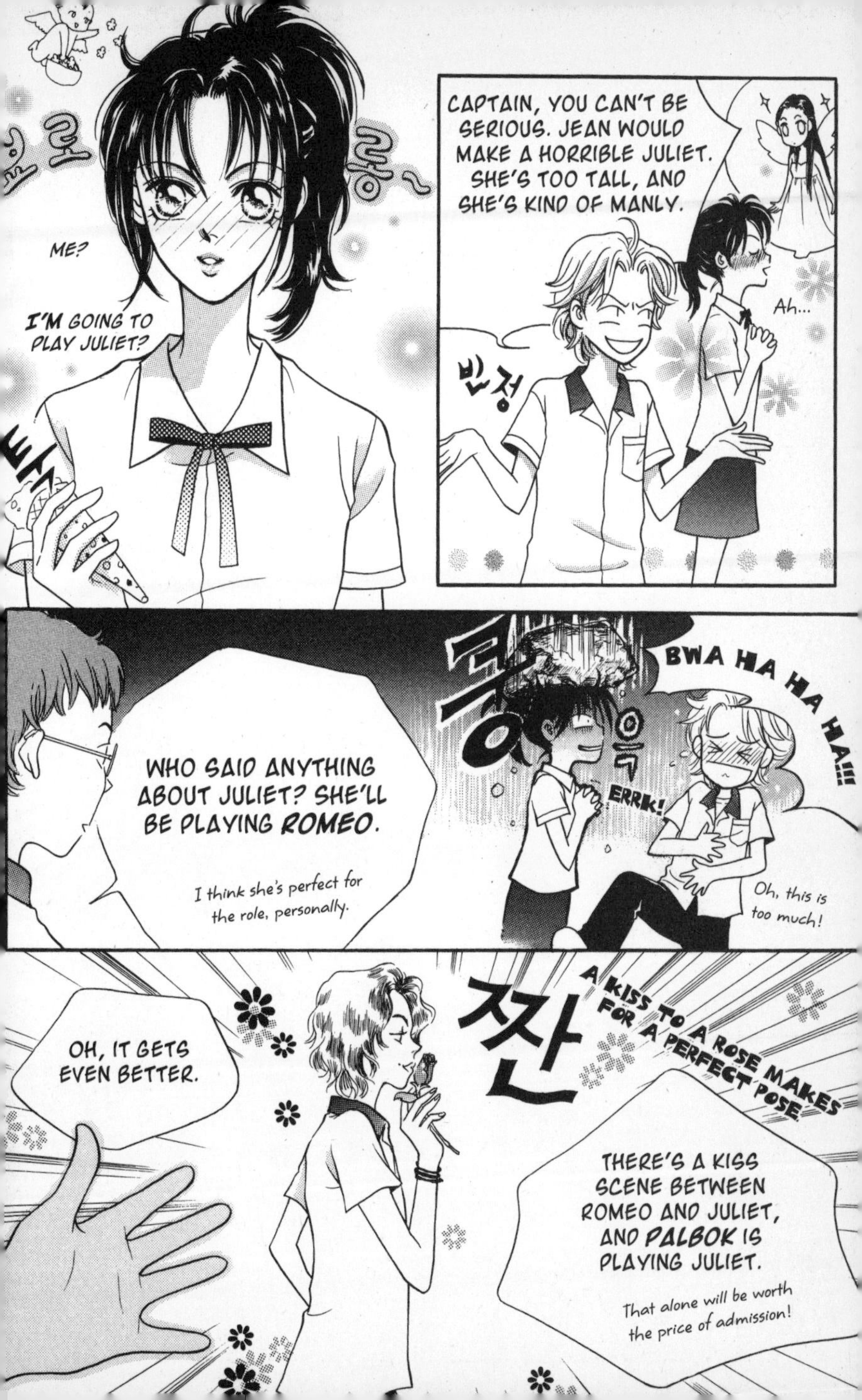
ME?
I'M GOING TO PLAY JULIET?
CAPTAIN, YOU CAN'T BE SERIOUS. JEAN WOULD MAKE A HORRIBLE JULIET. SHE'S TOO TALL, AND SHE'S KIND OF MANLY.
반정
Ah...
WHO SAID ANYTHING ABOUT JULIET? SHE'LL BE PLAYING ROMEO.
I think she's perfect for the role, personally.
쿵
BWA HA HA HA HA!!!
욱
ERRK!
Oh, this is too much!
OH, IT GETS EVEN BETTER.
짠
A KISS TO A ROSE MAKES FOR A PERFECT POSE
THERE'S A KISS SCENE BETWEEN ROMEO AND JULIET, AND PALBOK IS PLAYING JULIET.
That alone will be worth the price of admission!

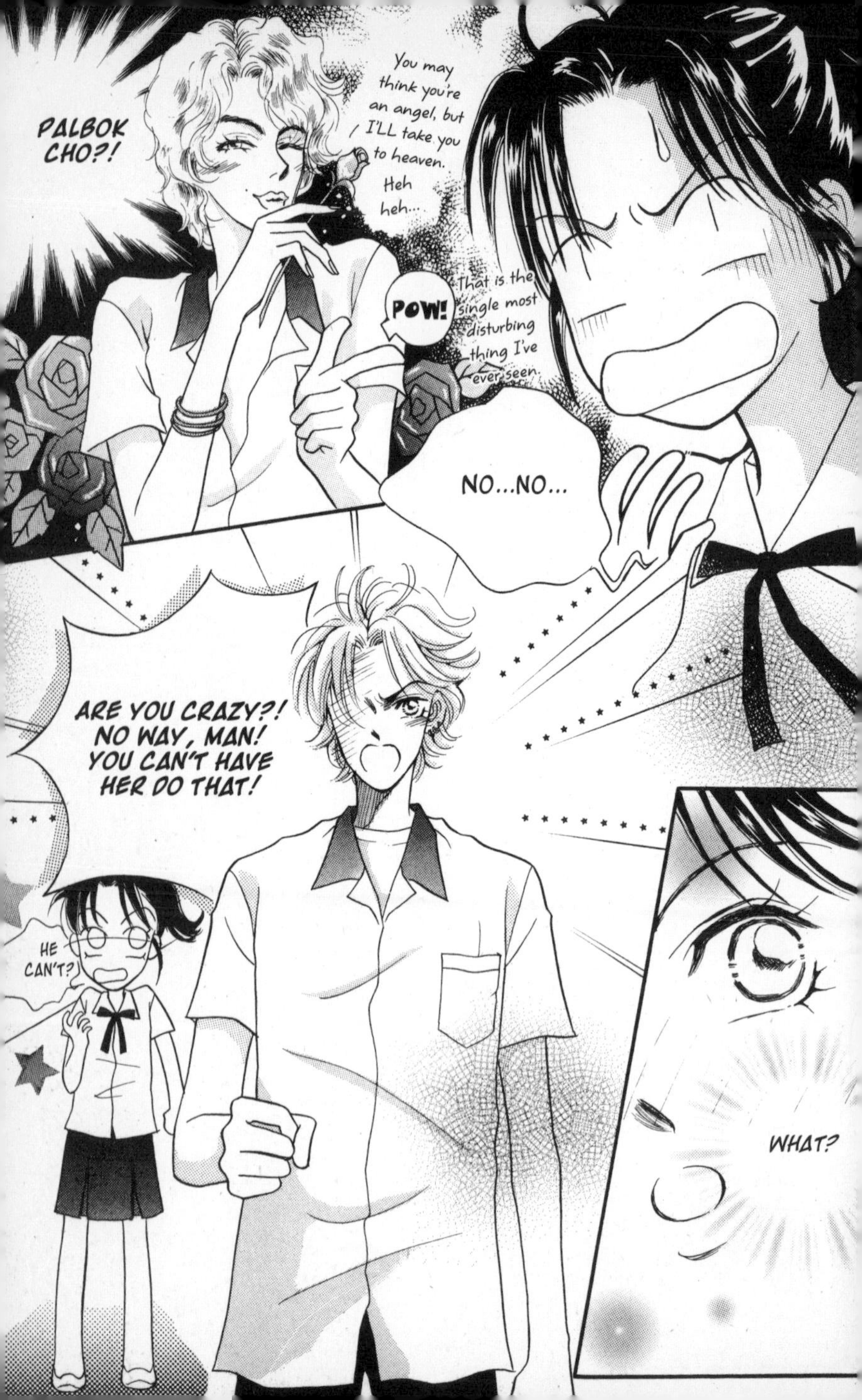
PALBOK CHO?!
You may think you're an angel, but I'LL take you to heaven.
Heh heh...
POW!
That is the single most disturbing thing I've ever seen.
NO...NO...
ARE YOU CRAZY?! NO WAY, MAN! YOU CAN'T HAVE HER DO THAT!
HE CAN'T?
WHAT?

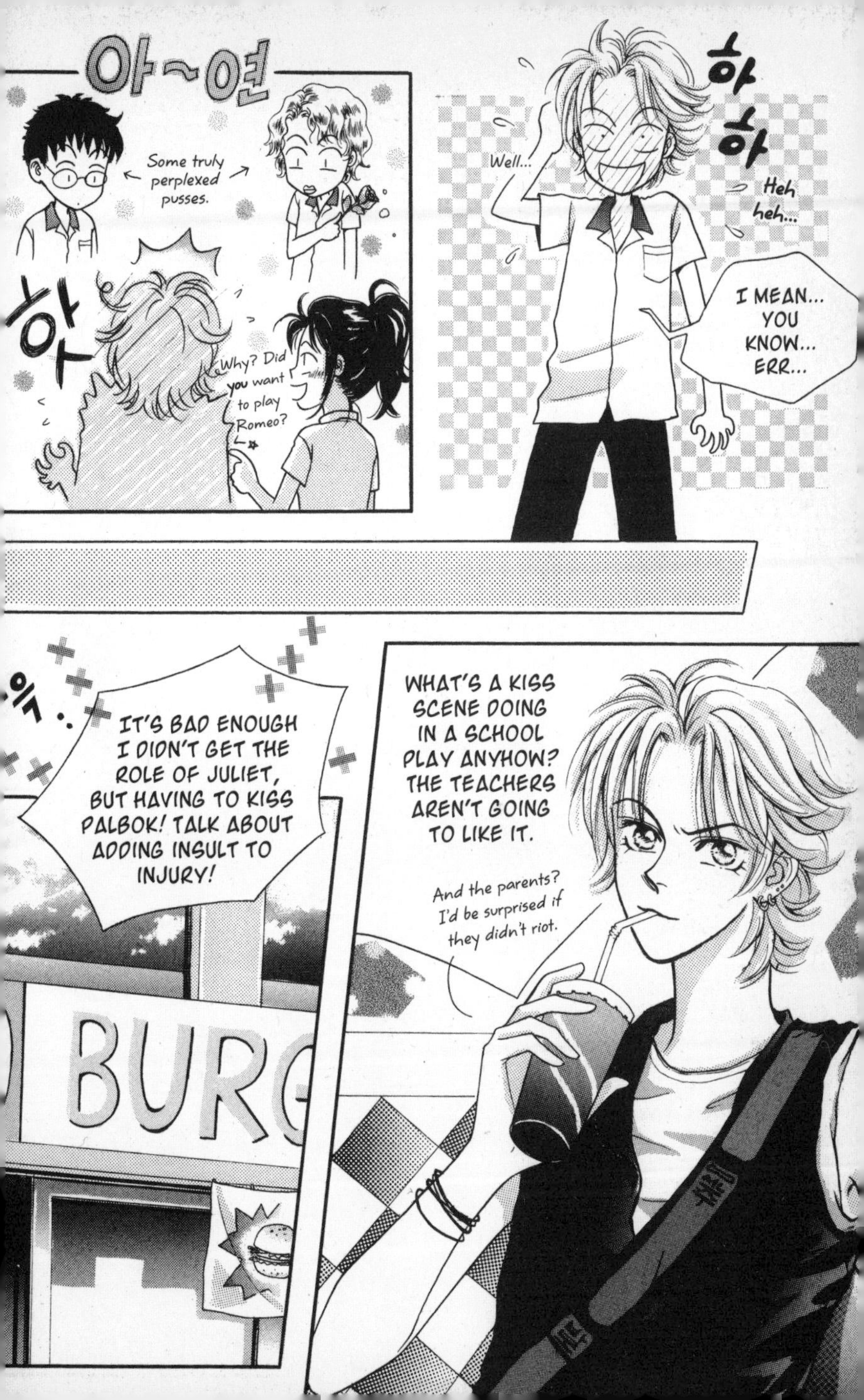
아~연
Some truly perplexed pusses.
Why? Did you want to play Romeo?
하 하
Well...
Heh heh...
I MEAN... YOU KNOW... ERR...
IT'S BAD ENOUGH I DIDN'T GET THE ROLE OF JULIET, BUT HAVING TO KISS PALBOK! TALK ABOUT ADDING INSULT TO INJURY!
BURG
WHAT'S A KISS SCENE DOING IN A SCHOOL PLAY ANYHOW? THE TEACHERS AREN'T GOING TO LIKE IT.
And the parents? I'd be surprised if they didn't riot.

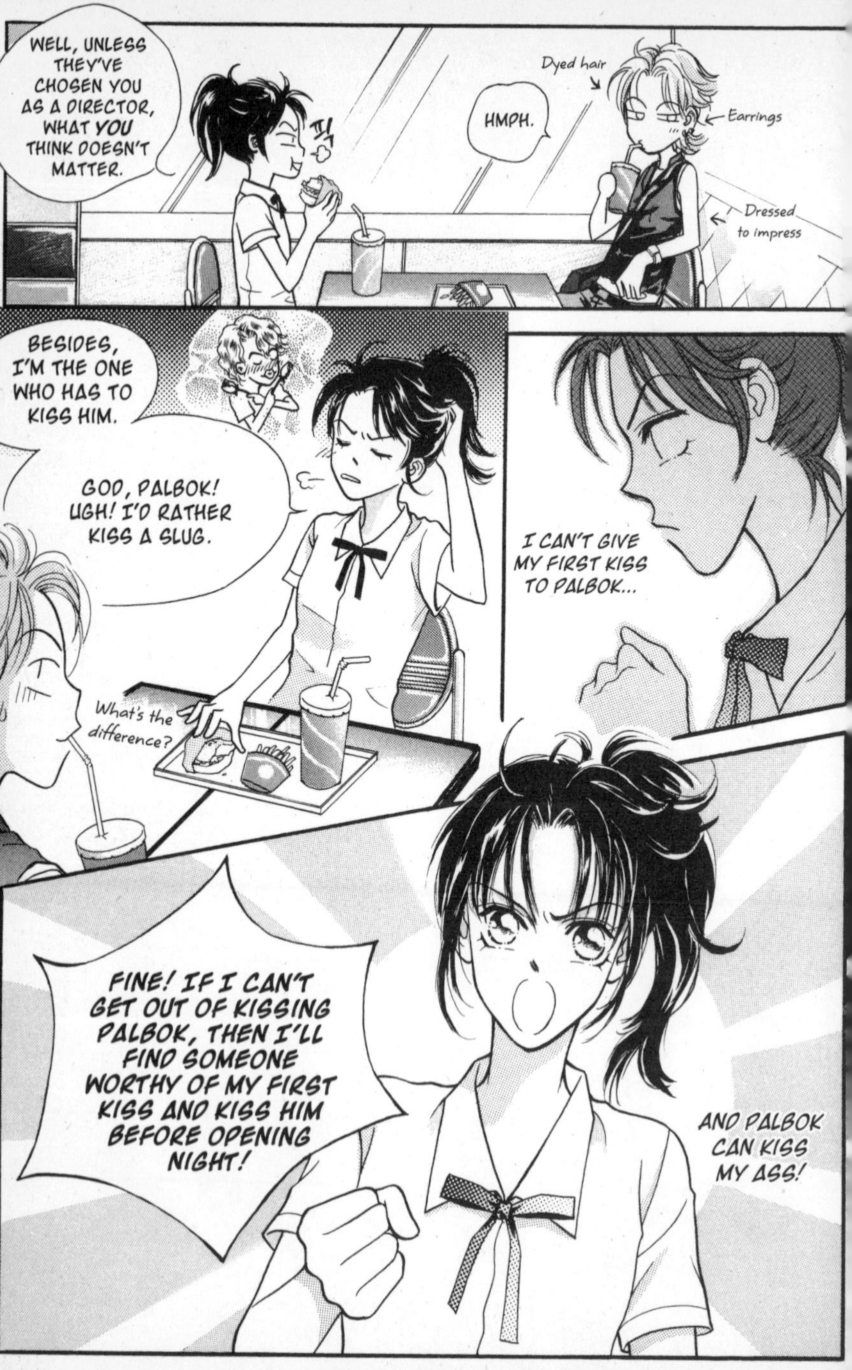
WELL, UNLESS THEY'VE CHOSEN YOU AS A DIRECTOR, WHAT YOU THINK DOESN'T MATTER.
HMPH.
Dyed hair
Earrings
Dressed to impress
BESIDES, I'M THE ONE WHO HAS TO KISS HIM.
GOD, PALBOK! UGH! I'D RATHER KISS A SLUG.
What's the difference?
I CAN'T GIVE MY FIRST KISS TO PALBOK...
FINE! IF I CAN'T GET OUT OF KISSING PALBOK, THEN I'LL FIND SOMEONE WORTHY OF MY FIRST KISS AND KISS HIM BEFORE OPENING NIGHT!
AND PALBOK CAN KISS MY ASS!

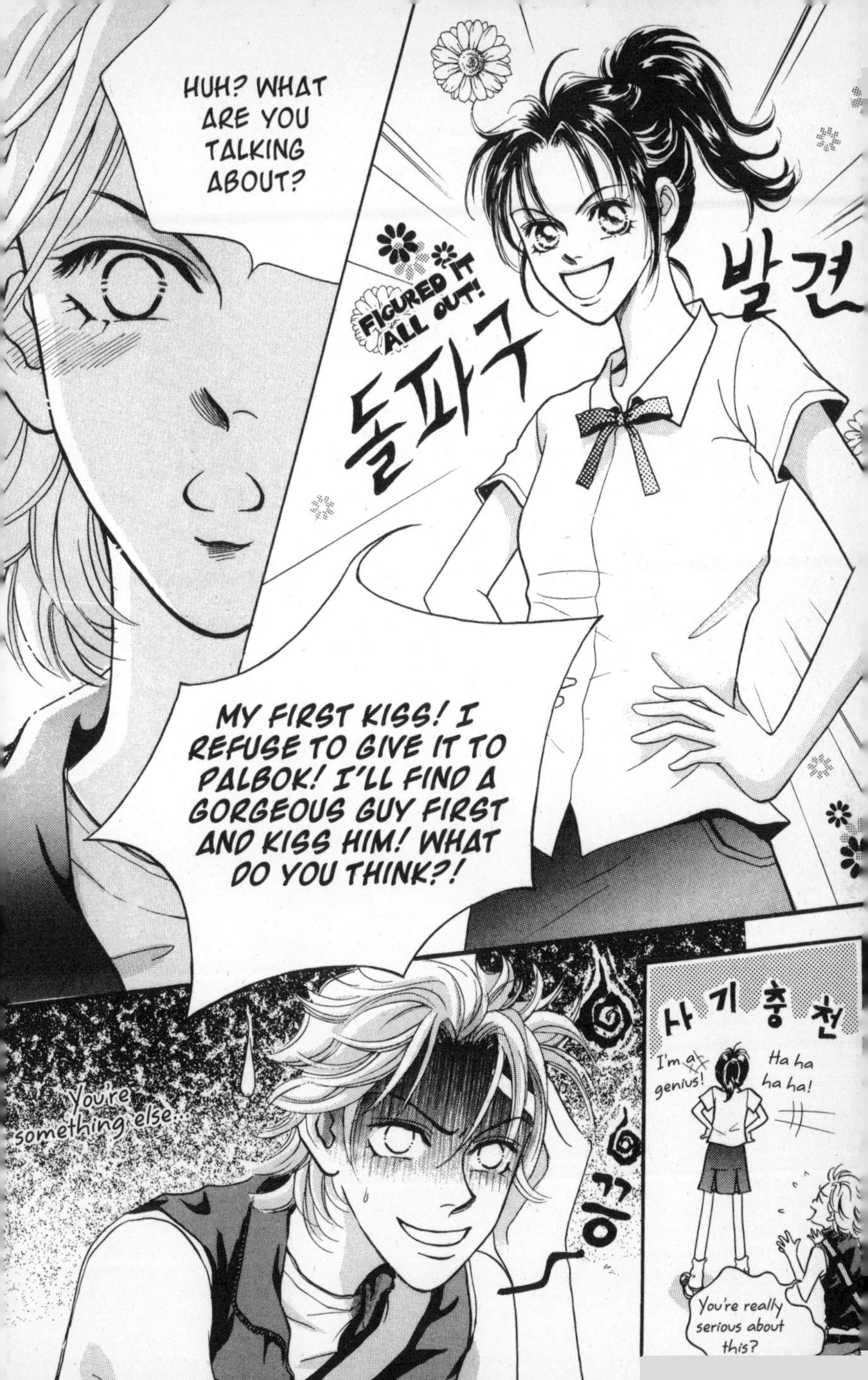
HUH? WHAT ARE YOU TALKING ABOUT?
FIGURED IT ALL OUT!
발견
돌파구
MY FIRST KISS! I REFUSE TO GIVE IT TO PALBOK! I'LL FIND A GORGEOUS GUY FIRST AND KISS HIM! WHAT DO YOU THINK?!
You're something else...
끙
사기충천
I'm a genius!
Ha ha ha ha!
You're really serious about this?

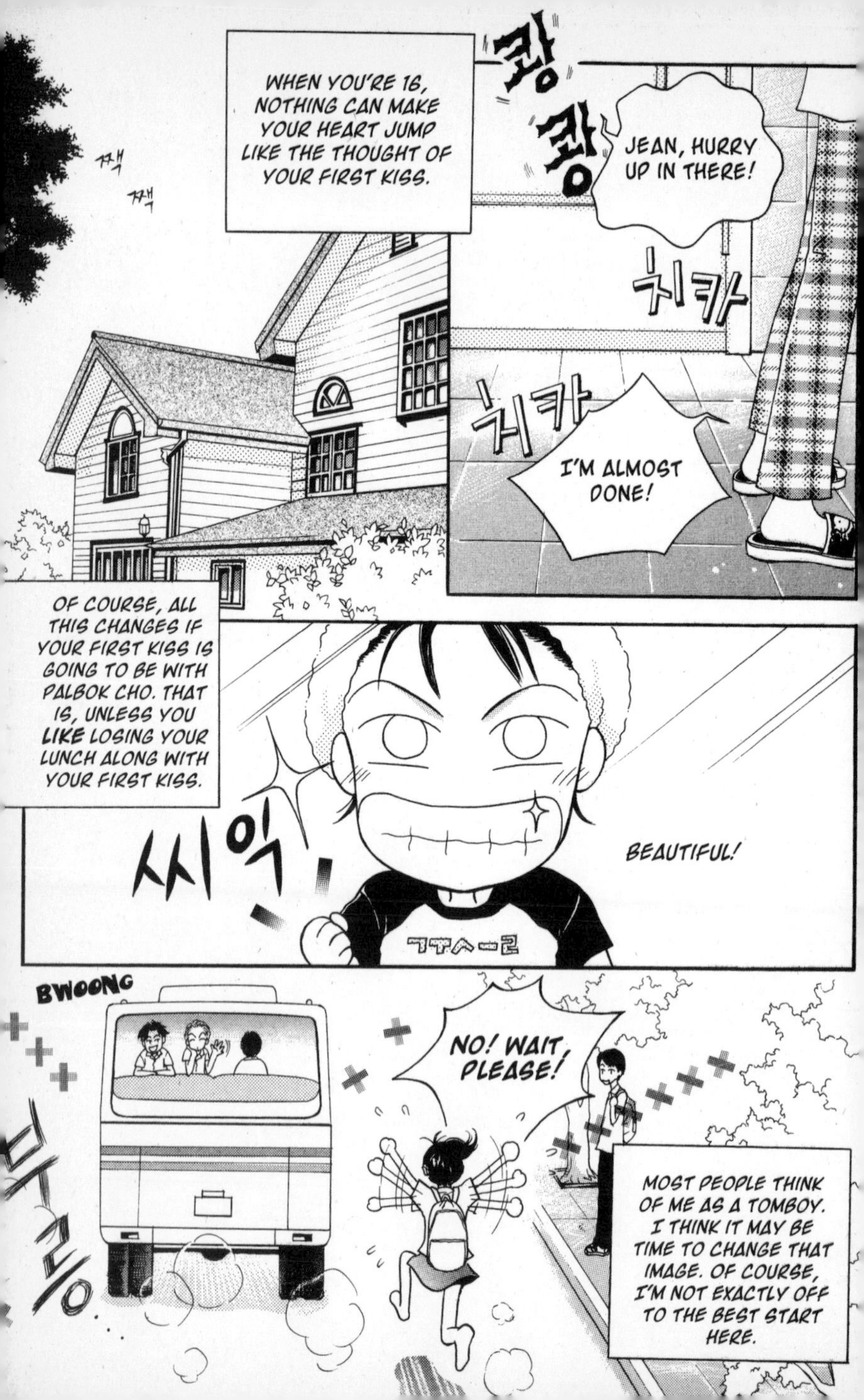
WHEN YOU'RE 16, NOTHING CAN MAKE YOUR HEART JUMP LIKE THE THOUGHT OF YOUR FIRST KISS.
짹
짹
쾅
쾅
JEAN, HURRY UP IN THERE!
치카
치카
I'M ALMOST DONE!
OF COURSE, ALL THIS CHANGES IF YOUR FIRST KISS IS GOING TO BE WITH PALBOK CHO. THAT IS, UNLESS YOU LIKE LOSING YOUR LUNCH ALONG WITH YOUR FIRST KISS.
씨익
BEAUTIFUL!
BWOONG
NO! WAIT, PLEASE!
MOST PEOPLE THINK OF ME AS A TOMBOY. I THINK IT MAY BE TIME TO CHANGE THAT IMAGE. OF COURSE, I'M NOT EXACTLY OFF TO THE BEST START HERE.

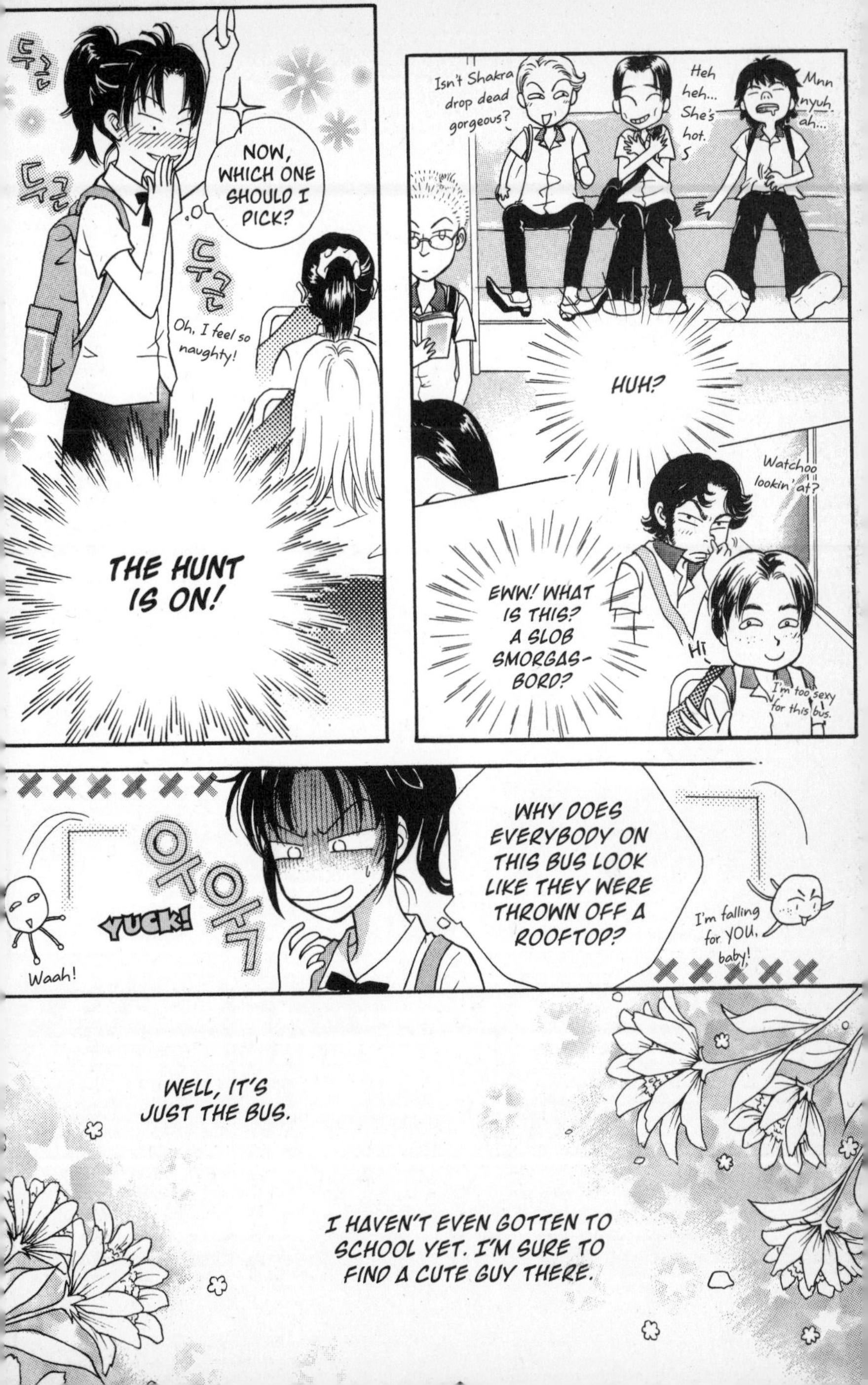

두근
두근
NOW, WHICH ONE SHOULD I PICK?
두근
Oh, I feel so naughty!
THE HUNT IS ON!
Isn't Shakra drop dead gorgeous?
Heh heh... She's hot.
Mnn nyuh ah...
HUH?
Watchoo lookin' at?
EWW! WHAT IS THIS? A SLOB SMORGASBORD?
Hi
I'm too sexy for this bus.
Waah!
YUCK!
WHY DOES EVERYBODY ON THIS BUS LOOK LIKE THEY WERE THROWN OFF A ROOFTOP?
I'm falling for YOU, baby!
WELL, IT'S JUST THE BUS.
I HAVEN'T EVEN GOTTEN TO SCHOOL YET. I'M SURE TO FIND A CUTE GUY THERE.

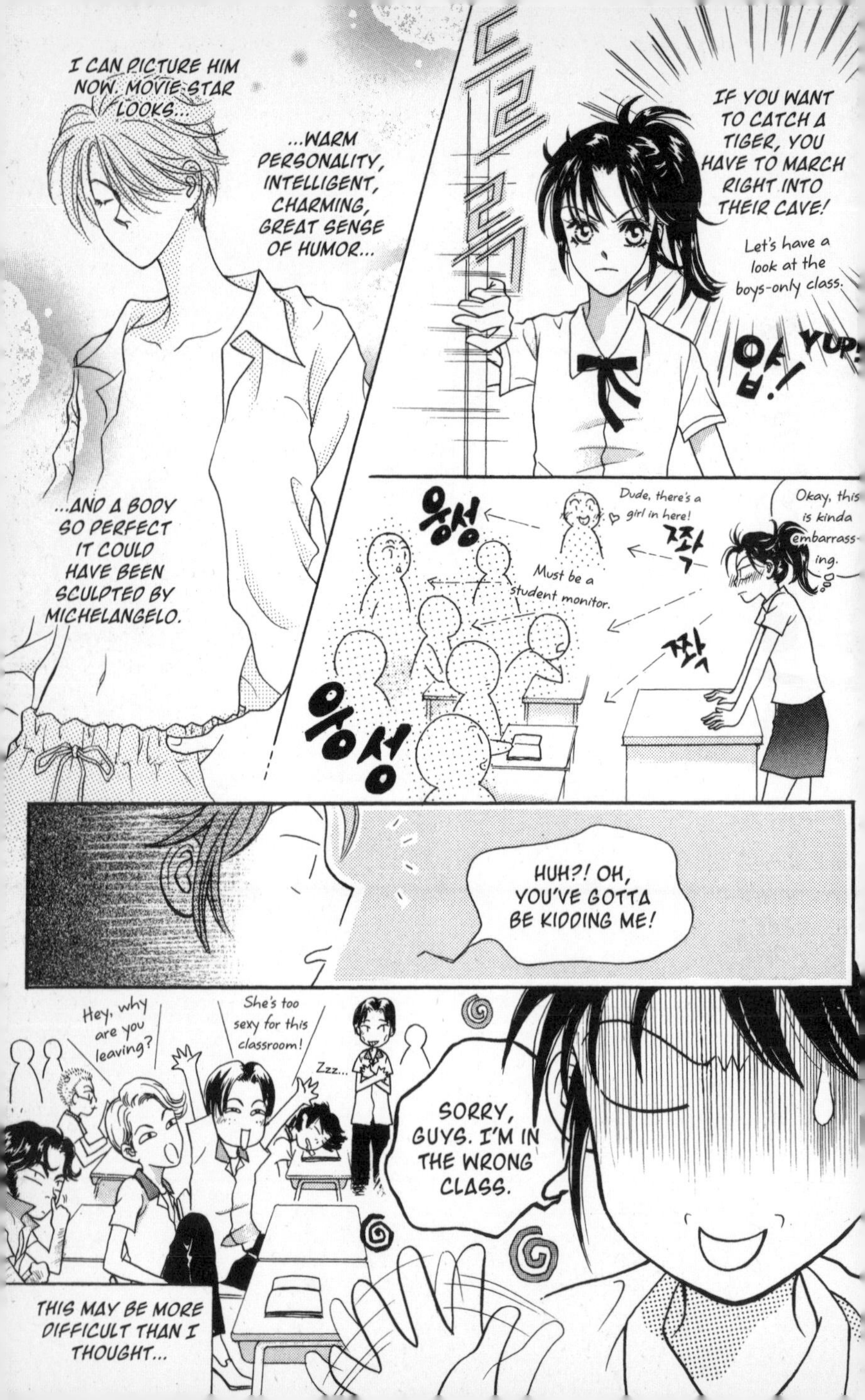
I CAN PICTURE HIM NOW. MOVIE STAR LOOKS...
...WARM PERSONALITY, INTELLIGENT, CHARMING, GREAT SENSE OF HUMOR...
...AND A BODY SO PERFECT IT COULD HAVE BEEN SCULPTED BY MICHELANGELO.
드르륵
IF YOU WANT TO CATCH A TIGER, YOU HAVE TO MARCH RIGHT INTO THEIR CAVE!
Let's have a look at the boys-only class.
업!
YUP!
웅성
Dude, there's a girl in here!
짝
Okay, this is kinda embarrass-ing.
Must be a student monitor.
짝
웅성
HUH?! OH, YOU'VE GOTTA BE KIDDING ME!
Hey, why are you leaving?
She's too sexy for this classroom!
Zzz...
SORRY, GUYS. I'M IN THE WRONG CLASS.
THIS MAY BE MORE DIFFICULT THAN I THOUGHT...

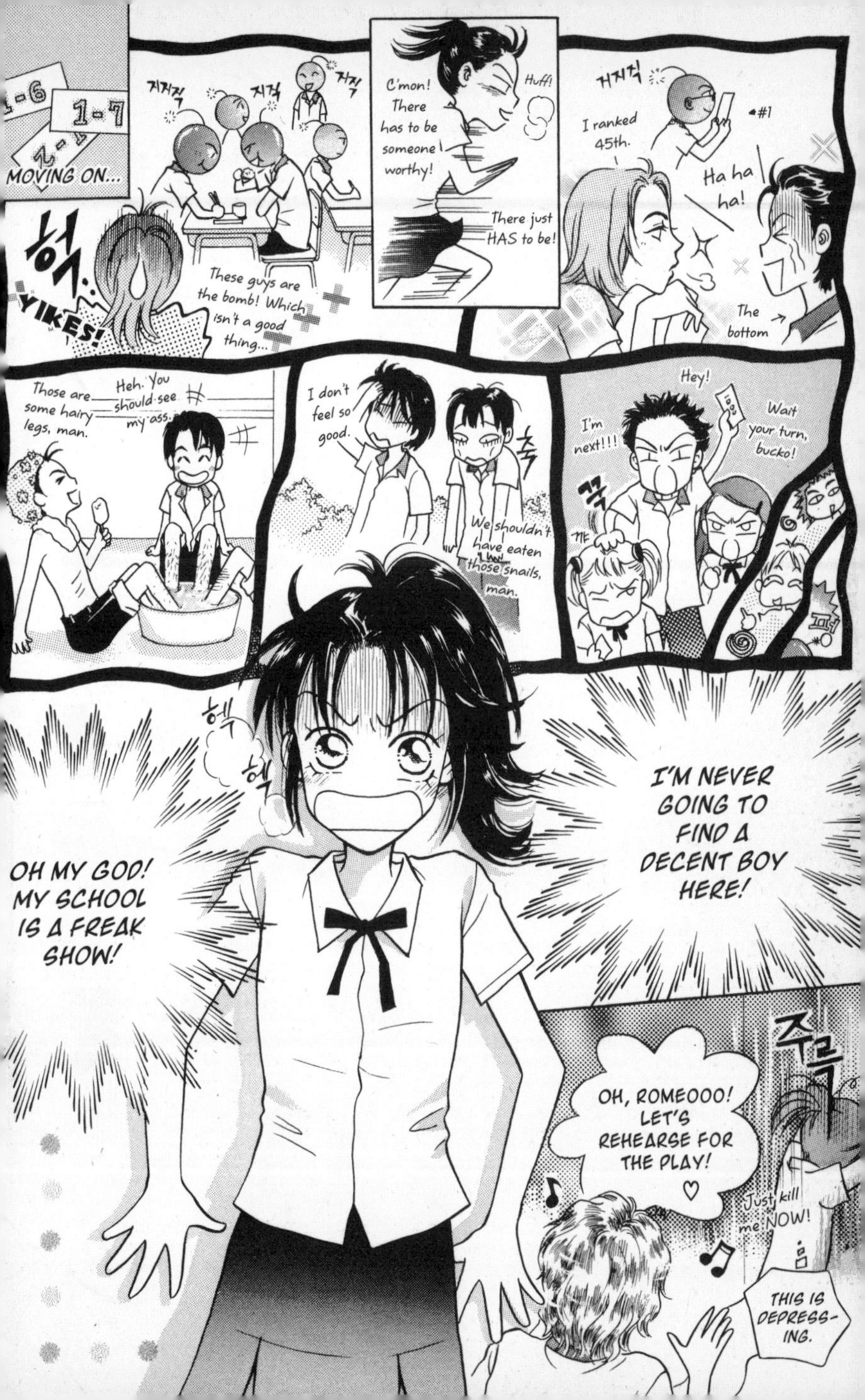
1-6
1-7
2-1
MOVING ON...
지지직
지직
지직
헉
YIKES!
These guys are the bomb! Which isn't a good thing...
C'mon! There has to be someone worthy!
Huff!
There just HAS to be!
거지직
I ranked 45th.
#1
Ha ha ha!
The bottom
Those are some hairy legs, man.
Heh. You should see my ass.
I don't feel so good.
We shouldn't have eaten those snails, man.
Hey!
I'm next!!!
Wait your turn, bucko!
꾹
꺄
퍽
헉
헉
OH MY GOD! MY SCHOOL IS A FREAK SHOW!
I'M NEVER GOING TO FIND A DECENT BOY HERE!
주륵
OH, ROMEOOO! LET'S REHEARSE FOR THE PLAY! ♡
Just kill me NOW!
THIS IS DEPRESS-ING.

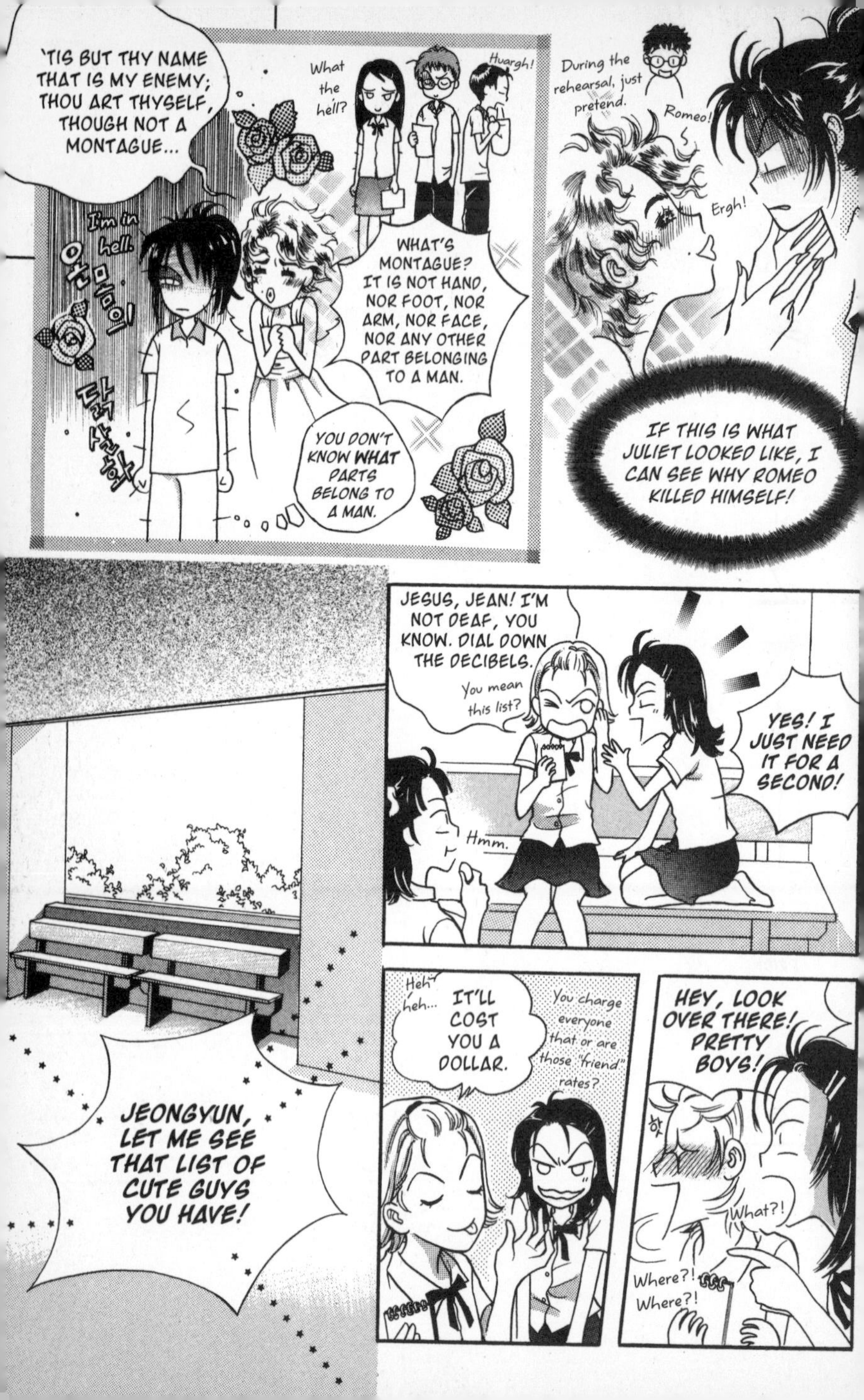
'TIS BUT THY NAME THAT IS MY ENEMY; THOU ART THYSELF, THOUGH NOT A MONTAGUE...
What the hell?
Huargh!
I'm in hell.
WHAT'S MONTAGUE? IT IS NOT HAND, NOR FOOT, NOR ARM, NOR FACE, NOR ANY OTHER PART BELONGING TO A MAN.
YOU DON'T KNOW WHAT PARTS BELONG TO A MAN.
During the rehearsal, just pretend.
Romeo!
Ergh!
IF THIS IS WHAT JULIET LOOKED LIKE, I CAN SEE WHY ROMEO KILLED HIMSELF!
JEONGYUN, LET ME SEE THAT LIST OF CUTE GUYS YOU HAVE!
JESUS, JEAN! I'M NOT DEAF, YOU KNOW. DIAL DOWN THE DECIBELS.
You mean this list?
YES! I JUST NEED IT FOR A SECOND!
Hmm.
Heh heh...
IT'LL COST YOU A DOLLAR.
You charge everyone that or are those "friend" rates?
HEY, LOOK OVER THERE! PRETTY BOYS!
What?!
Where?! Where?!

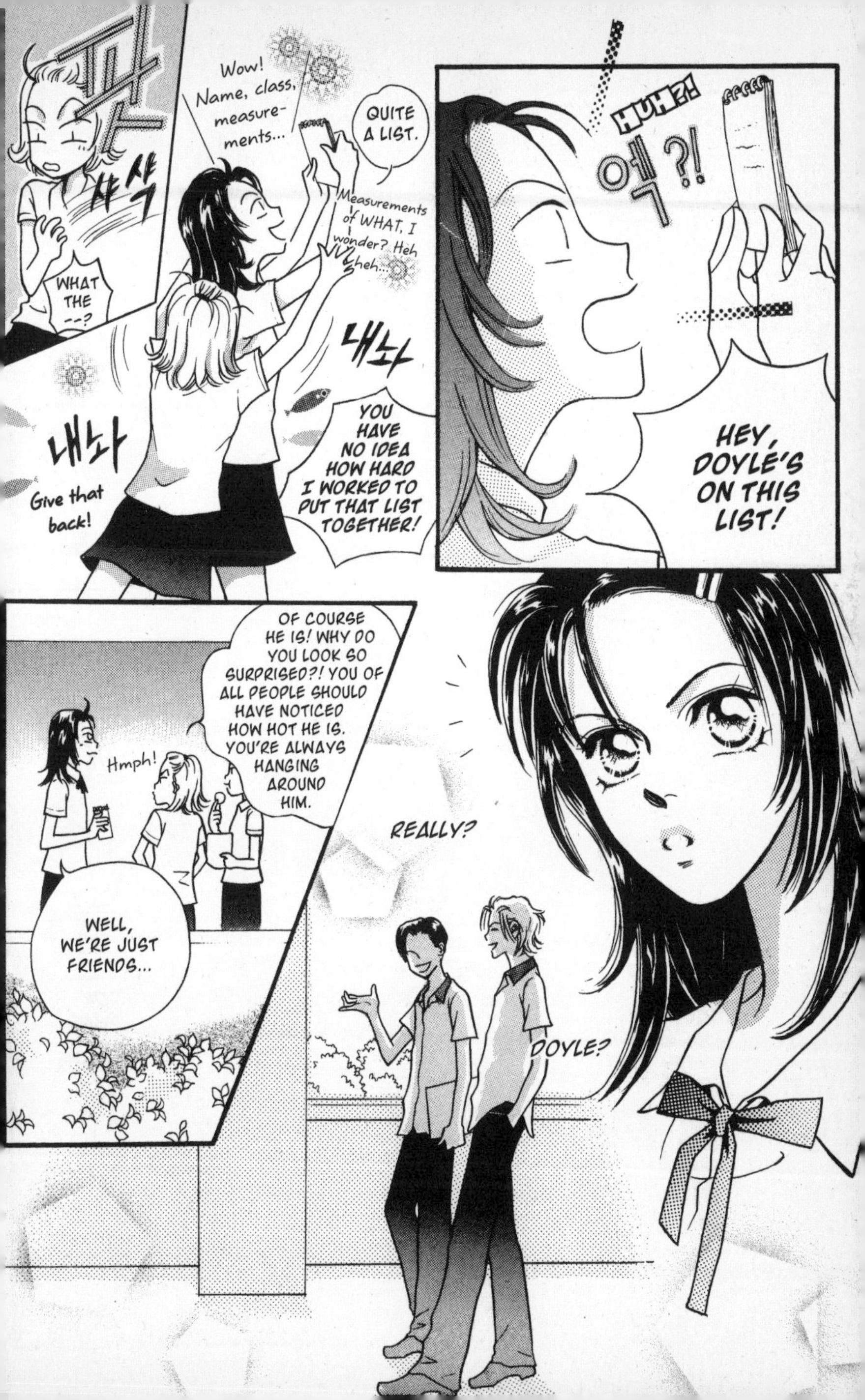
WHAT THE --?
Wow! Name, class, measurements...
QUITE A LIST.
Measurements of WHAT, I wonder? Heh heh...
내놔
내놔
Give that back!
YOU HAVE NO IDEA HOW HARD I WORKED TO PUT THAT LIST TOGETHER!
HUH?!
엑?!
HEY, DOYLE'S ON THIS LIST!
OF COURSE HE IS! WHY DO YOU LOOK SO SURPRISED?! YOU OF ALL PEOPLE SHOULD HAVE NOTICED HOW HOT HE IS. YOU'RE ALWAYS HANGING AROUND HIM.
Hmph!
WELL, WE'RE JUST FRIENDS...
REALLY?
DOYLE?

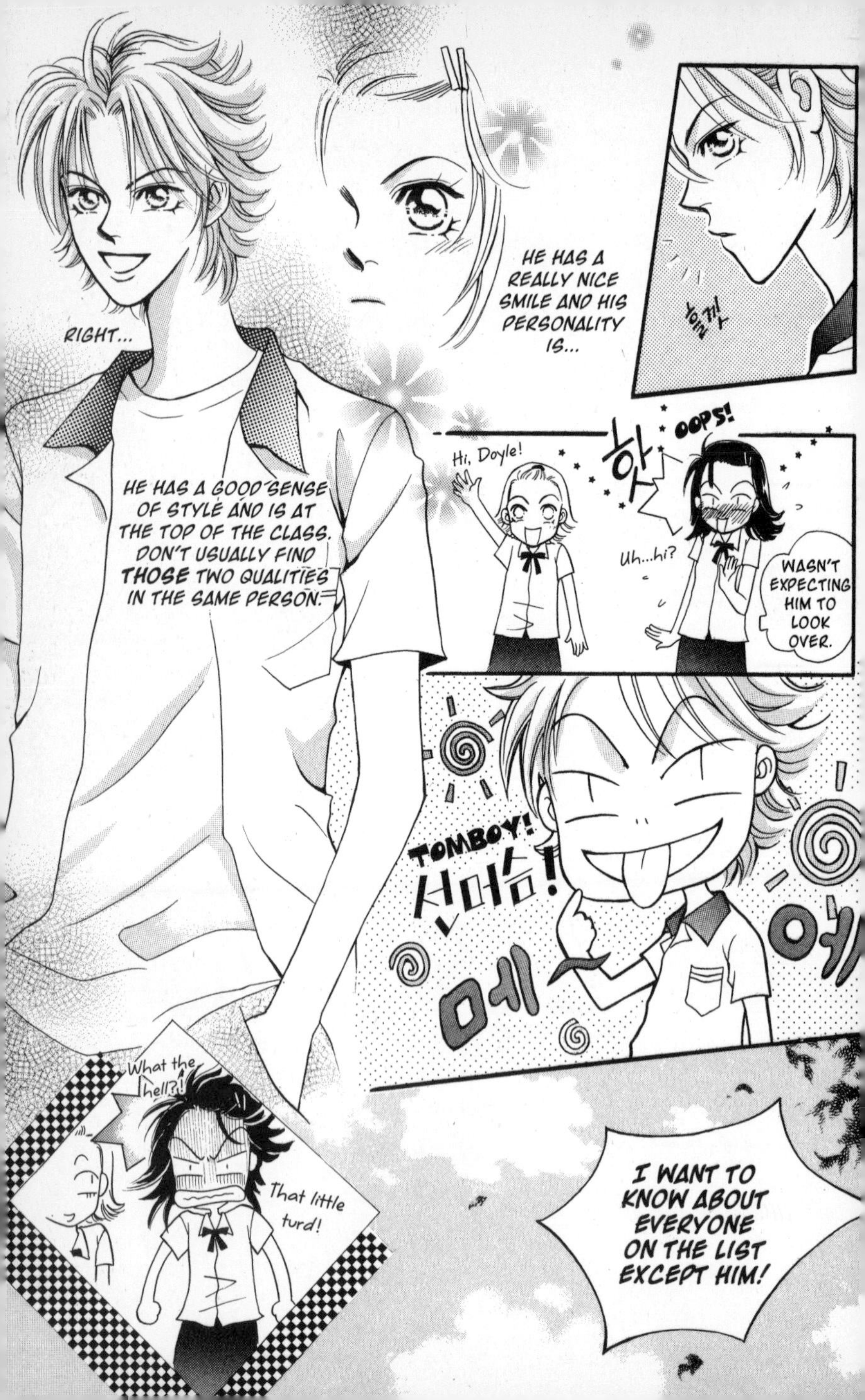
RIGHT...
HE HAS A GOOD SENSE OF STYLE AND IS AT THE TOP OF THE CLASS. DON'T USUALLY FIND **THOSE** TWO QUALITIES IN THE SAME PERSON.
HE HAS A REALLY NICE SMILE AND HIS PERSONALITY IS...
Hi, Doyle!
핫
OOPS!
Uh...hi?
WASN'T EXPECTING HIM TO LOOK OVER.
TOMBOY!
선머슴!
메
에
What the hell?!
That little turd!
I WANT TO KNOW ABOUT EVERYONE ON THE LIST EXCEPT HIM!

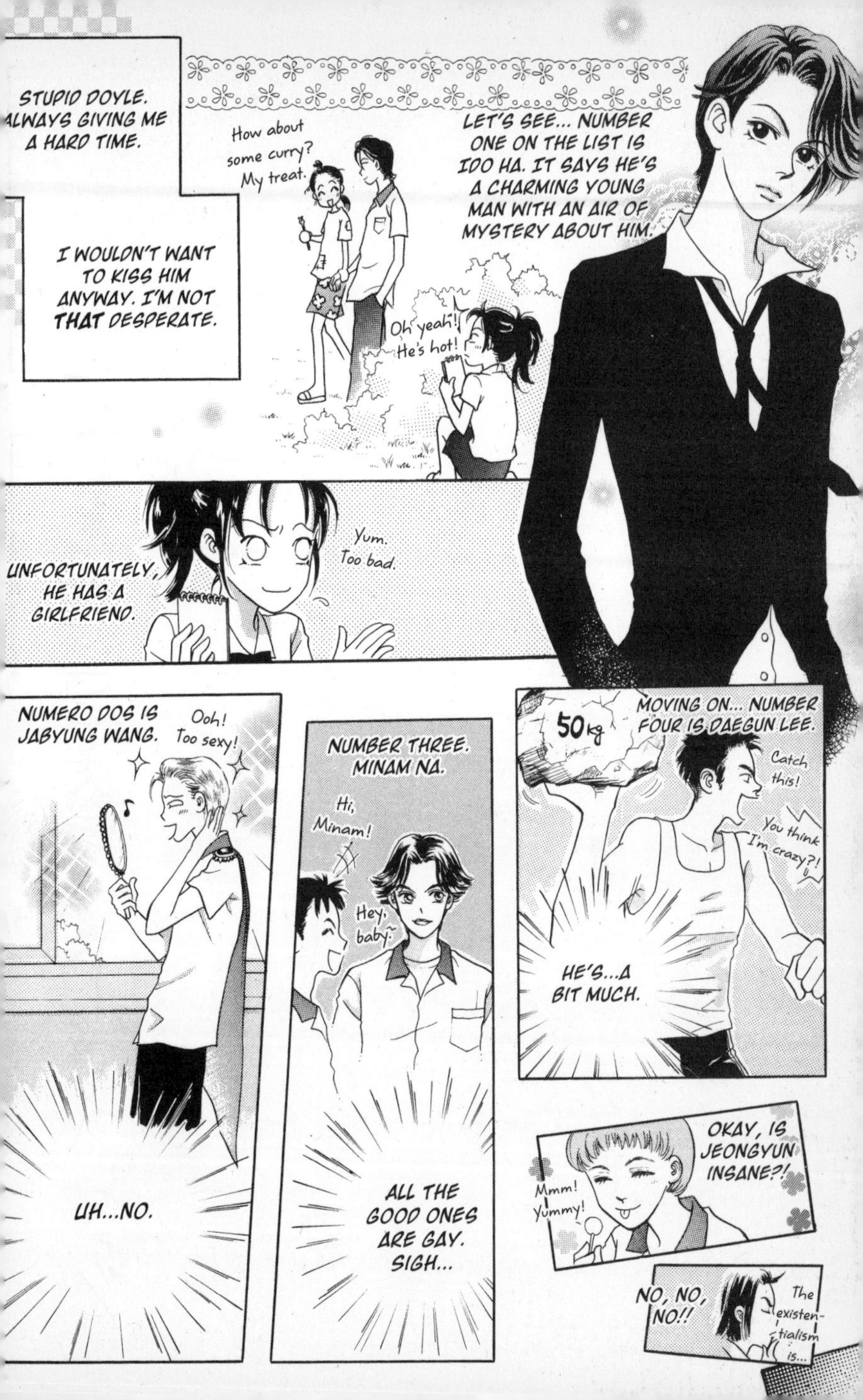

STUPID DOYLE. ALWAYS GIVING ME A HARD TIME.
I WOULDN'T WANT TO KISS HIM ANYWAY. I'M NOT **THAT** DESPERATE.
How about some curry? My treat.
LET'S SEE... NUMBER ONE ON THE LIST IS IDO HA. IT SAYS HE'S A CHARMING YOUNG MAN WITH AN AIR OF MYSTERY ABOUT HIM.
Oh yeah! He's hot!
UNFORTUNATELY, HE HAS A GIRLFRIEND.
Yum. Too bad.
NUMERO DOS IS JABYUNG WANG.
Ooh! Too sexy!
UH...NO.
NUMBER THREE. MINAM NA.
Hi, Minam!
Hey, baby.
ALL THE GOOD ONES ARE GAY. SIGH...
50kg
MOVING ON... NUMBER FOUR IS DAEGUN LEE.
Catch this!
You think I'm crazy?!
HE'S...A BIT MUCH.
OKAY, IS JEONGYUN INSANE?!
Mmm! Yummy!
NO, NO, NO!!
The existentialism is...

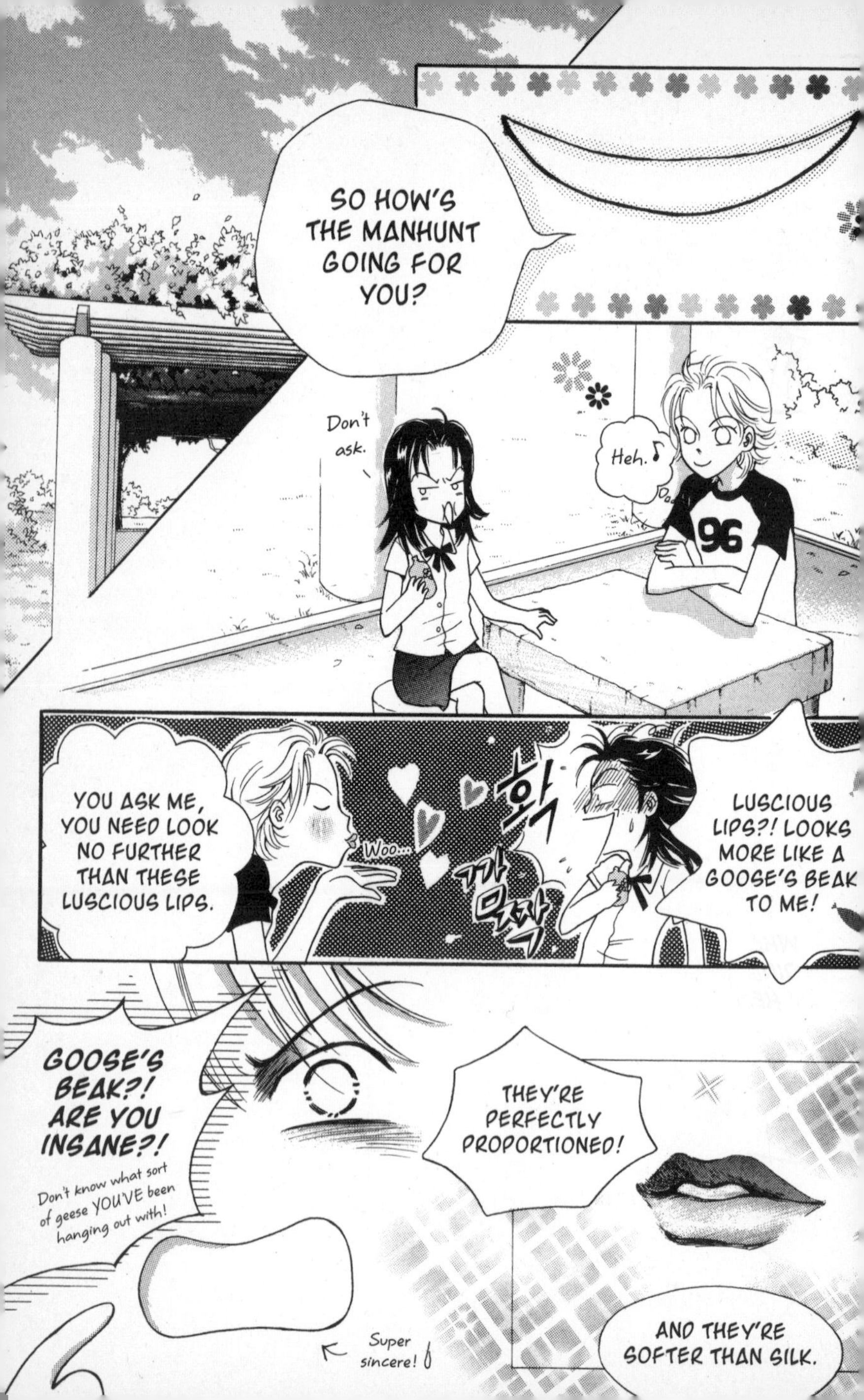
SO HOW'S THE MANHUNT GOING FOR YOU?
Don't ask.
Heh. ♪
YOU ASK ME, YOU NEED LOOK NO FURTHER THAN THESE LUSCIOUS LIPS.
Woo...
확
LUSCIOUS LIPS?! LOOKS MORE LIKE A GOOSE'S BEAK TO ME!
GOOSE'S BEAK?! ARE YOU INSANE?!
Don't know what sort of geese YOU'VE been hanging out with!
THEY'RE PERFECTLY PROPORTIONED!
Super sincere!
AND THEY'RE SOFTER THAN SILK.

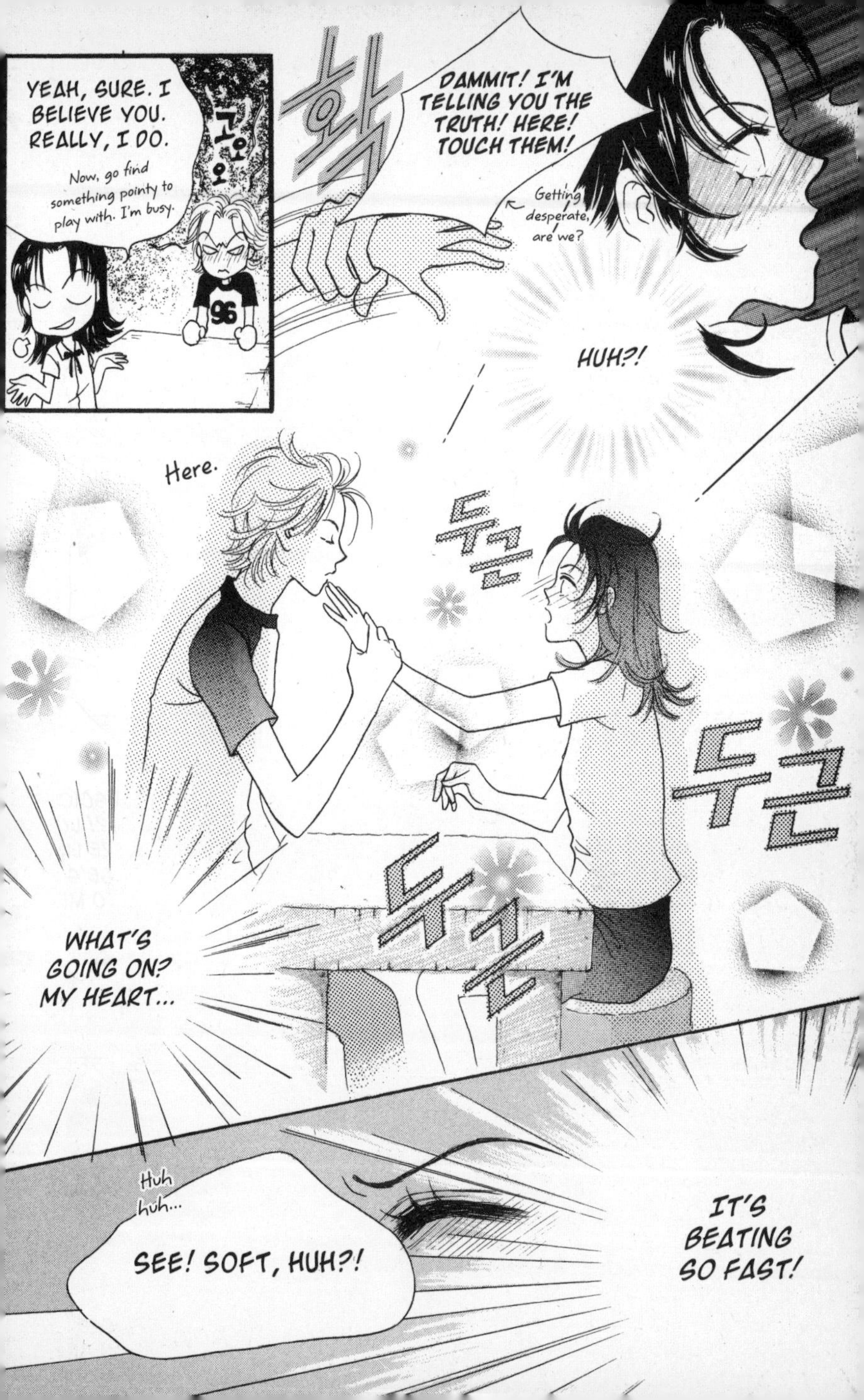
YEAH, SURE. I BELIEVE YOU. REALLY, I DO.
Now, go find something pointy to play with. I'm busy.
고오오
DAMMIT! I'M TELLING YOU THE TRUTH! HERE! TOUCH THEM!
Getting desperate, are we?
HUH?!
Here.
두근
두근
두근
WHAT'S GOING ON? MY HEART...
Huh huh...
SEE! SOFT, HUH?!
IT'S BEATING SO FAST!

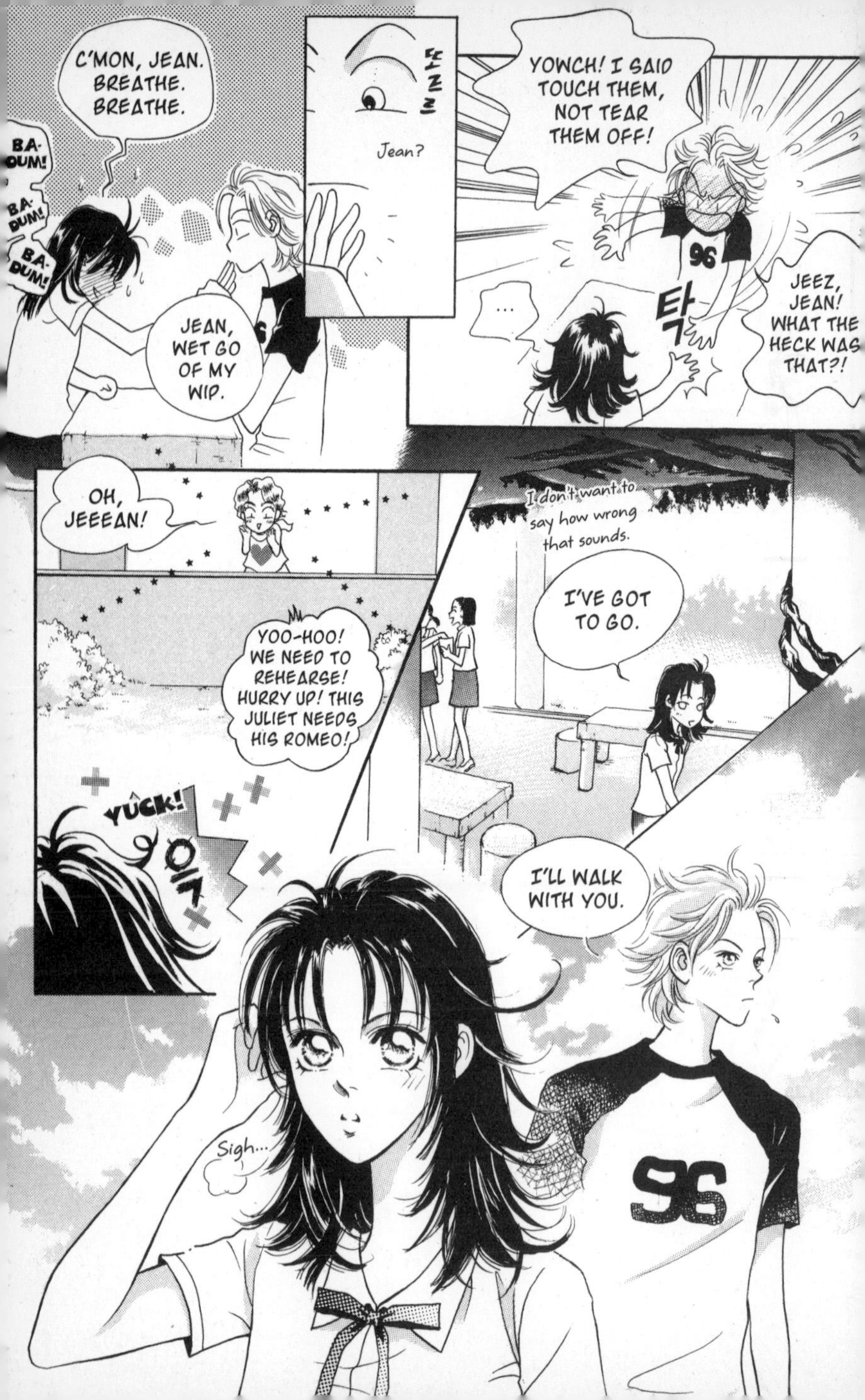
C'MON, JEAN. BREATHE. BREATHE.
BA-DUM!
BA-DUM!
BA-DUM!
JEAN, WET GO OF MY WIP.
Jean?
YOWCH! I SAID TOUCH THEM, NOT TEAR THEM OFF!
...
탁
JEEZ, JEAN! WHAT THE HECK WAS THAT?!
OH, JEEEAN!
YOO-HOO! WE NEED TO REHEARSE! HURRY UP! THIS JULIET NEEDS HIS ROMEO!
YUCK!
I don't want to say how wrong that sounds.
I'VE GOT TO GO.
I'LL WALK WITH YOU.
Sigh...

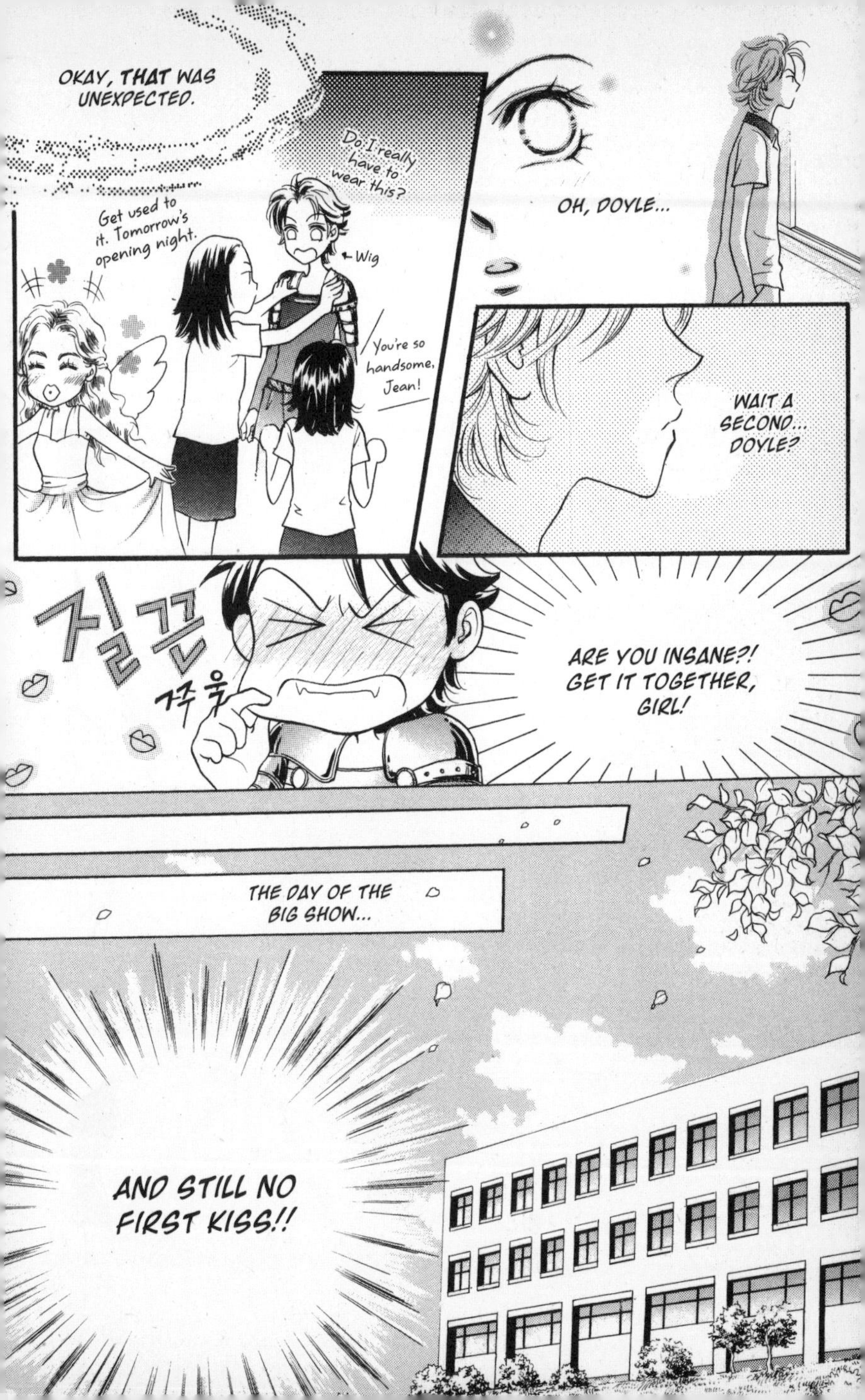
OKAY, THAT WAS UNEXPECTED.
Do I really have to wear this?
Get used to it. Tomorrow's opening night.
Wig
You're so handsome, Jean!
OH, DOYLE...
WAIT A SECOND... DOYLE?
질끈
ARE YOU INSANE?! GET IT TOGETHER, GIRL!
THE DAY OF THE BIG SHOW...
AND STILL NO FIRST KISS!!

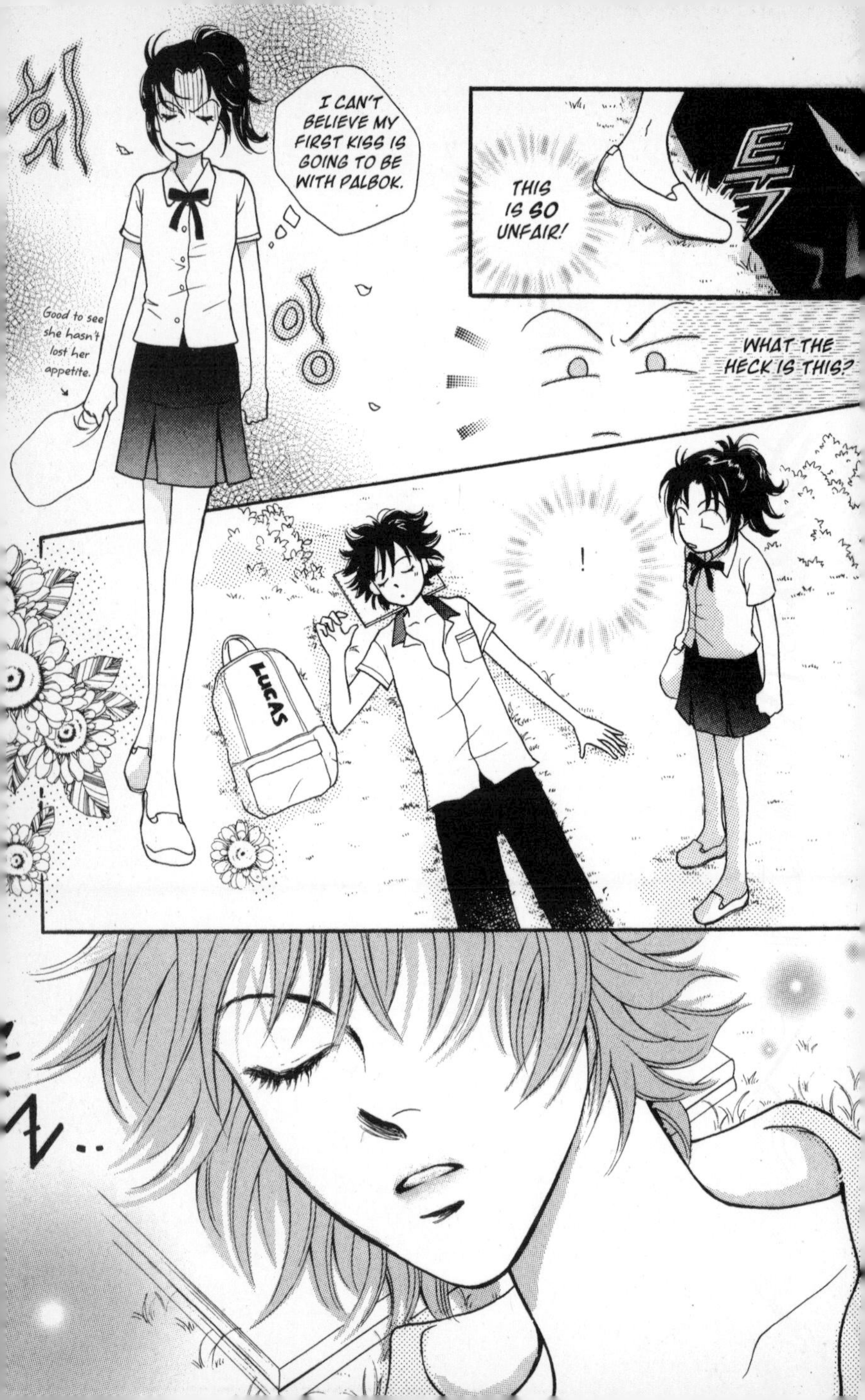
I CAN'T BELIEVE MY FIRST KISS IS GOING TO BE WITH PALBOK.
Good to see she hasn't lost her appetite.
THIS IS SO UNFAIR!
WHAT THE HECK IS THIS?
!
LUCAS
Z..

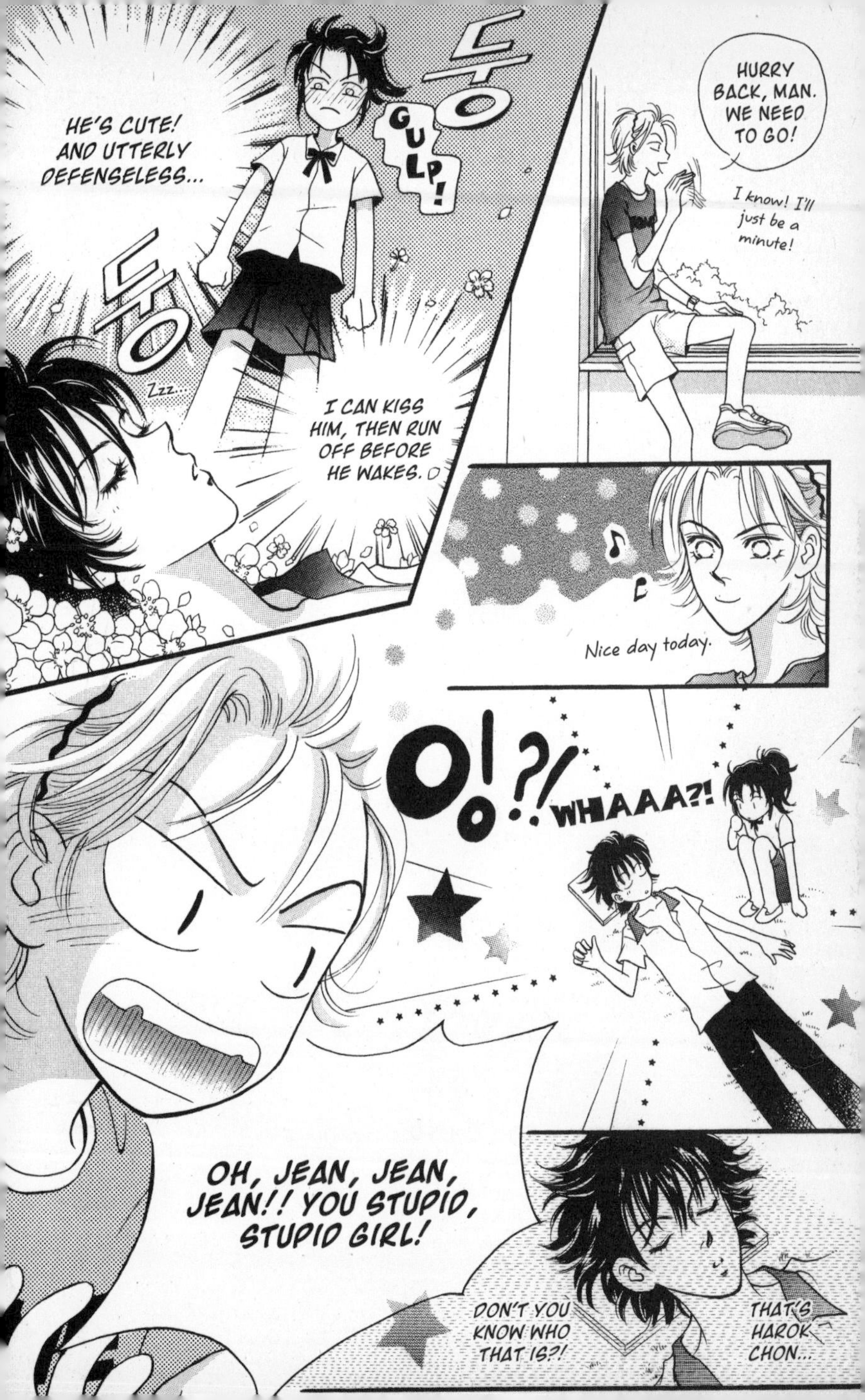

HE'S CUTE! AND UTTERLY DEFENSELESS...
GULP!
Zzz...
I CAN KISS HIM, THEN RUN OFF BEFORE HE WAKES.
HURRY BACK, MAN. WE NEED TO GO!
I know! I'll just be a minute!
Nice day today.
O!?!
WHAAA?!
OH, JEAN, JEAN, JEAN!! YOU STUPID, STUPID GIRL!
DON'T YOU KNOW WHO THAT IS?!
THAT'S HAROK CHON...

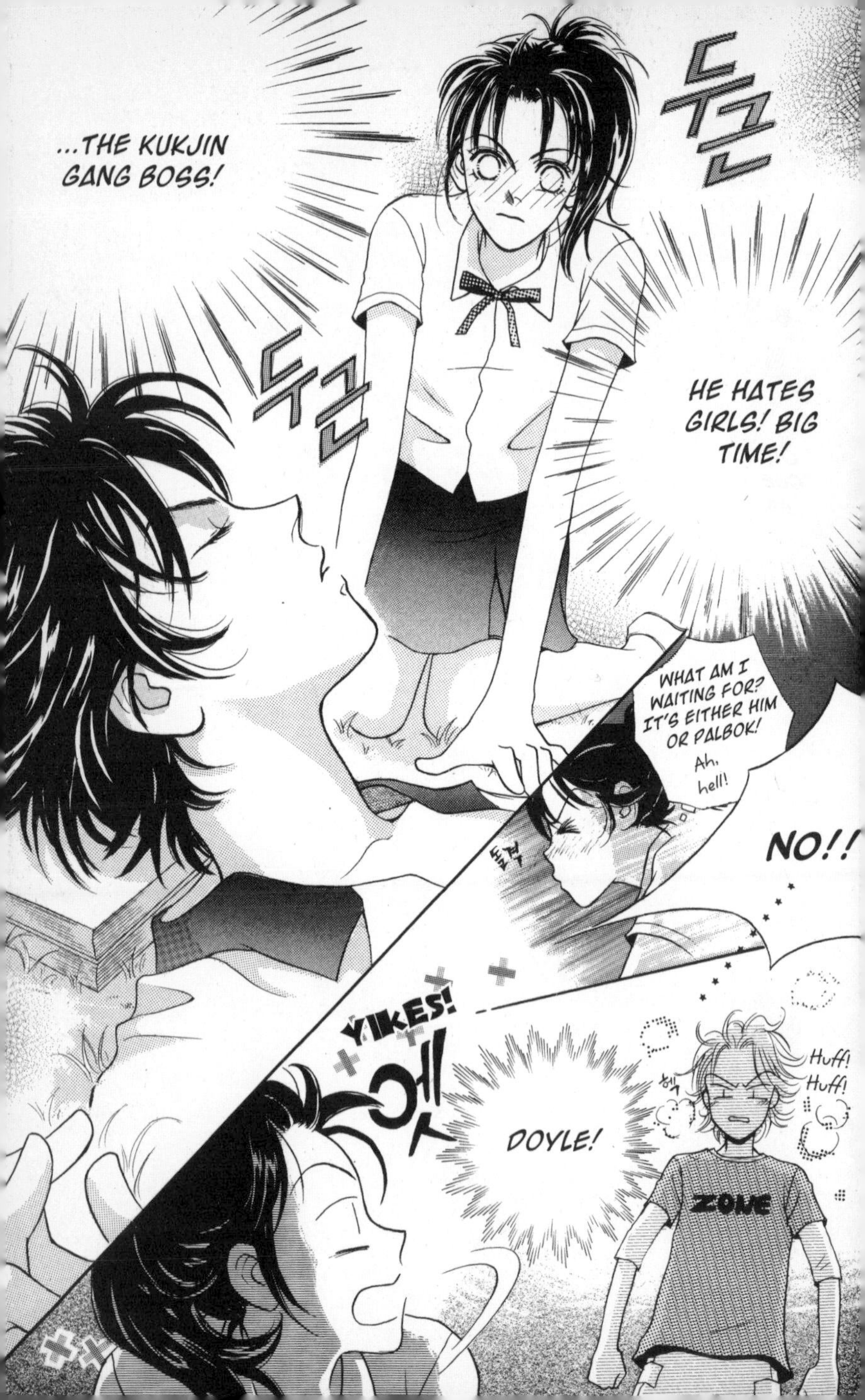
...THE KUKJIN GANG BOSS!
두근
두근
HE HATES GIRLS! BIG TIME!
WHAT AM I WAITING FOR? IT'S EITHER HIM OR PALBOK!
Ah, hell!
NO!!
YIKES!
DOYLE!
Huff! Huff!
ZONE

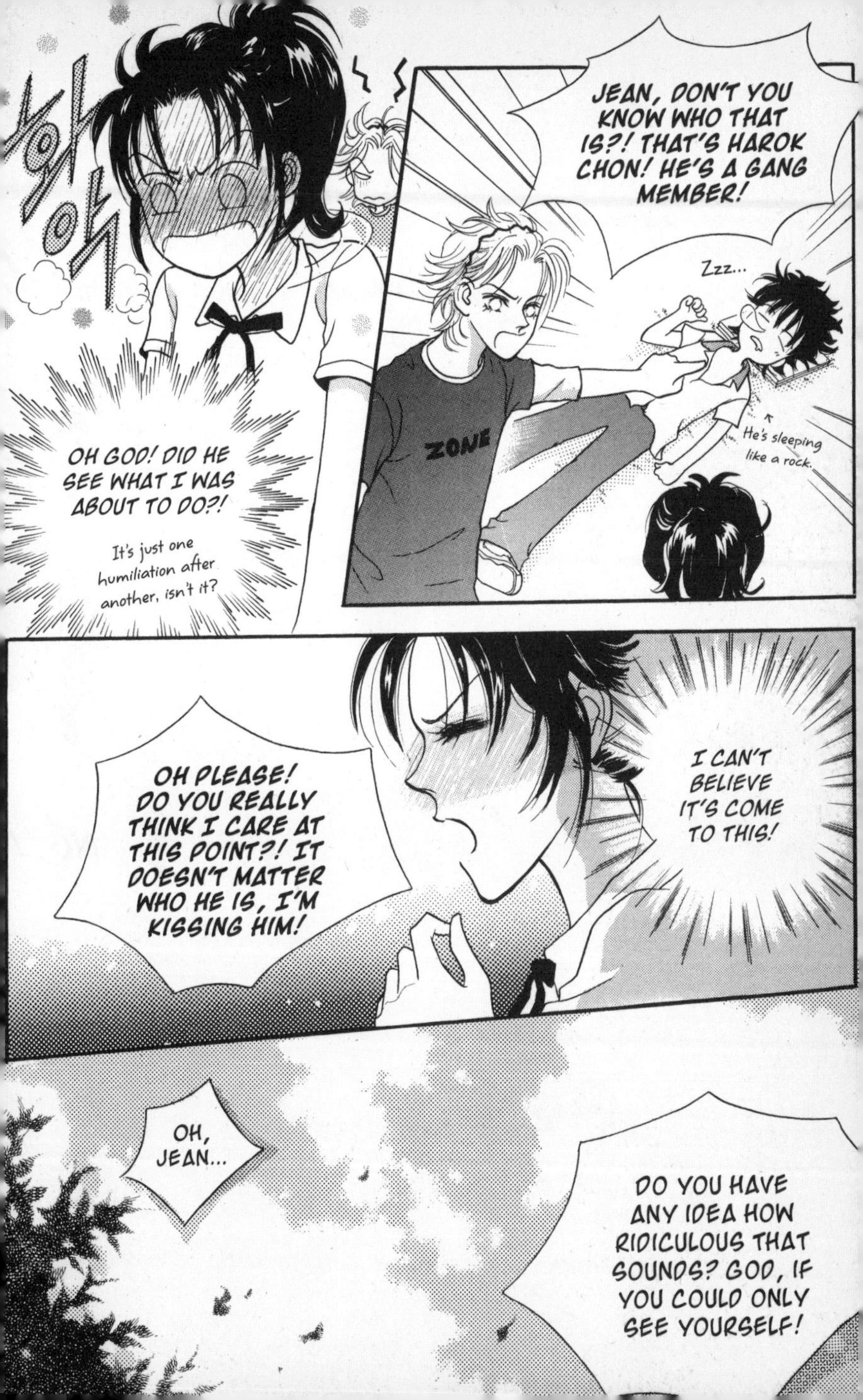
OH GOD! DID HE SEE WHAT I WAS ABOUT TO DO?!
It's just one humiliation after another, isn't it?
JEAN, DON'T YOU KNOW WHO THAT IS?! THAT'S HAROK CHON! HE'S A GANG MEMBER!
Zzz...
He's sleeping like a rock.
ZONE
OH PLEASE! DO YOU REALLY THINK I CARE AT THIS POINT?! IT DOESN'T MATTER WHO HE IS, I'M KISSING HIM!
I CAN'T BELIEVE IT'S COME TO THIS!
OH, JEAN...
DO YOU HAVE ANY IDEA HOW RIDICULOUS THAT SOUNDS? GOD, IF YOU COULD ONLY SEE YOURSELF!

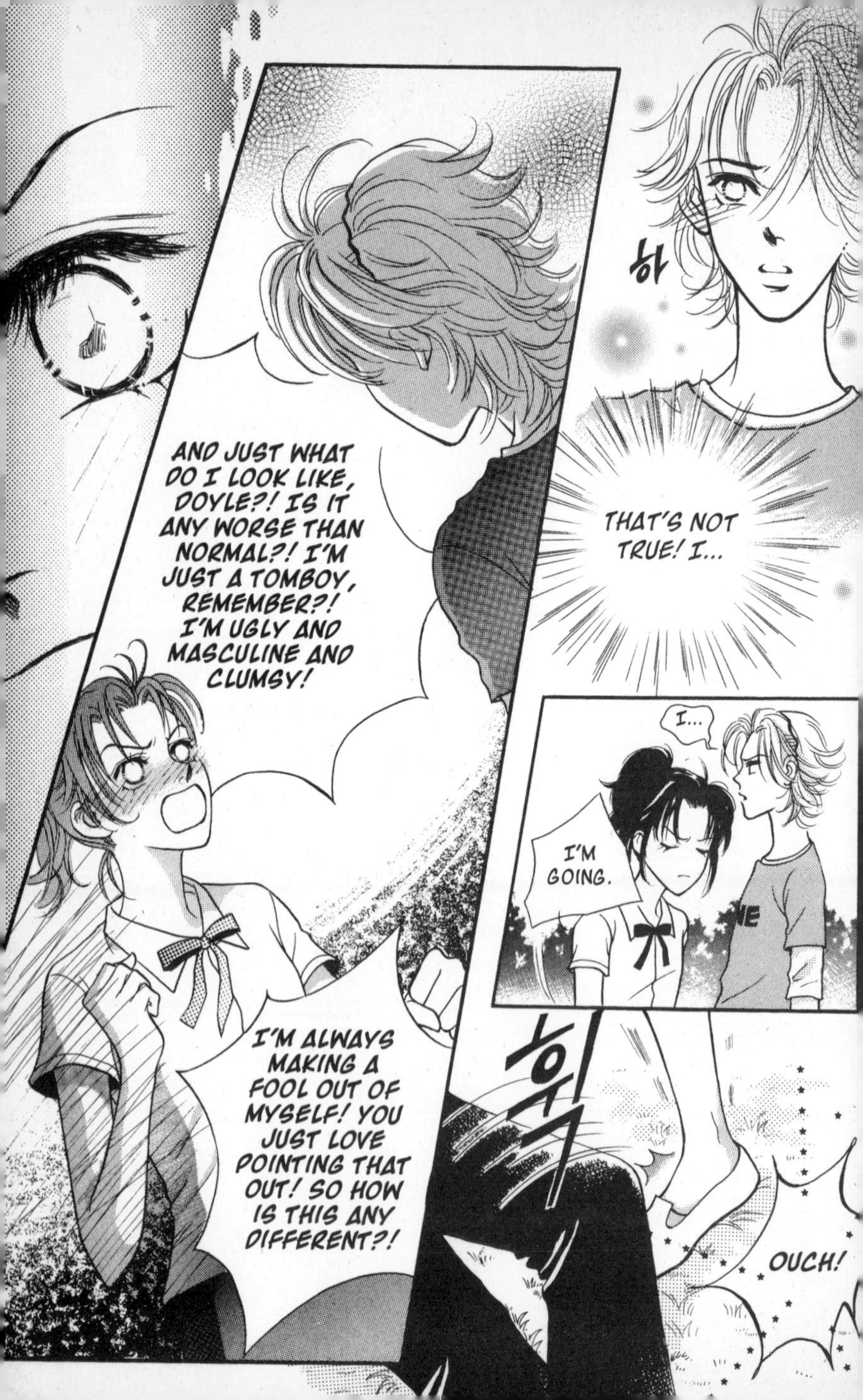
AND JUST WHAT DO I LOOK LIKE, DOYLE?! IS IT ANY WORSE THAN NORMAL?! I'M JUST A TOMBOY, REMEMBER?! I'M UGLY AND MASCULINE AND CLUMSY!
I'M ALWAYS MAKING A FOOL OUT OF MYSELF! YOU JUST LOVE POINTING THAT OUT! SO HOW IS THIS ANY DIFFERENT?!
하
THAT'S NOT TRUE! I...
I...
I'M GOING.
OUCH!

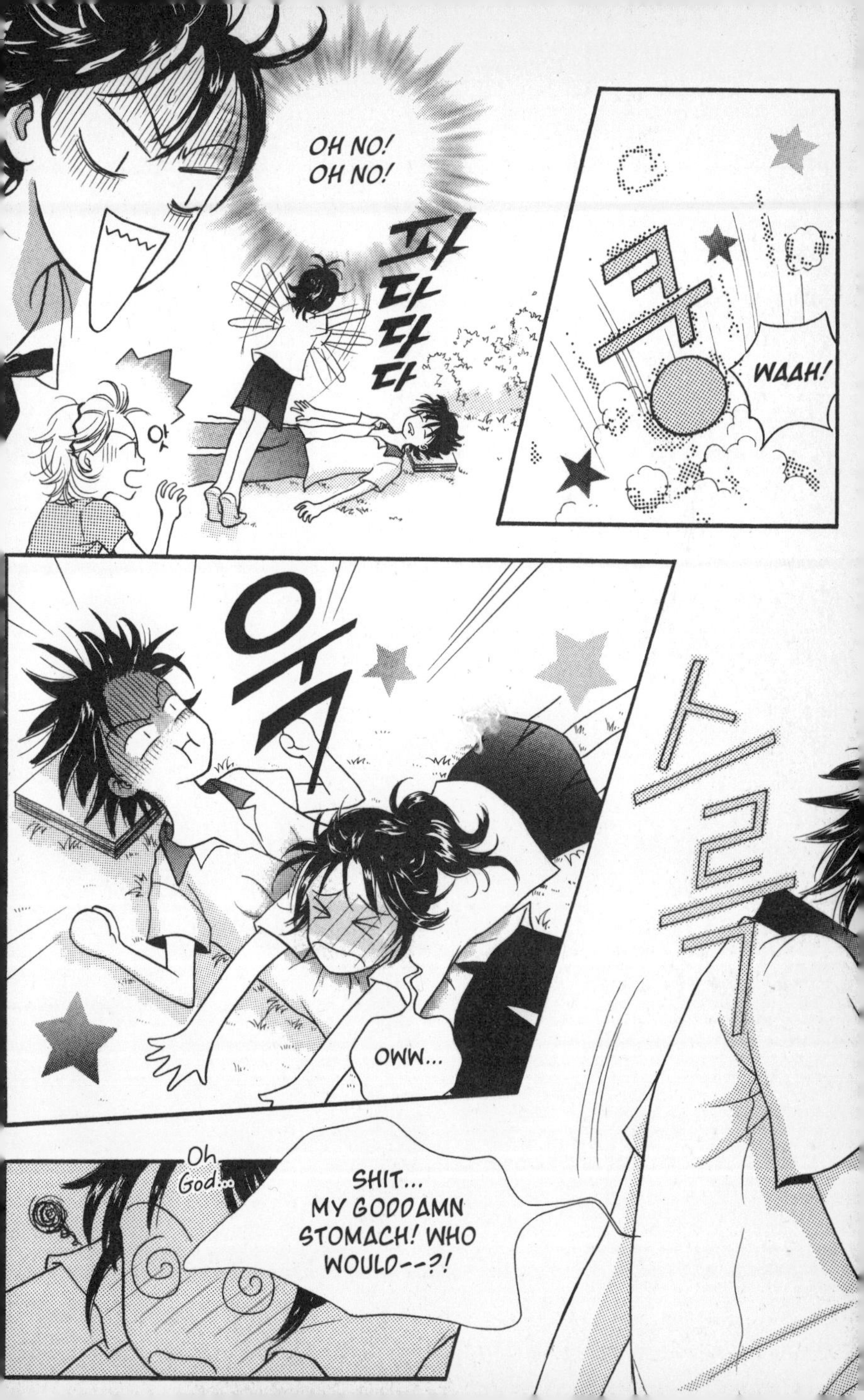
OH NO!
OH NO!
파다다다
악
WAAH!
OWW...
Oh. God...
SHIT... MY GODDAMN STOMACH! WHO WOULD--?!

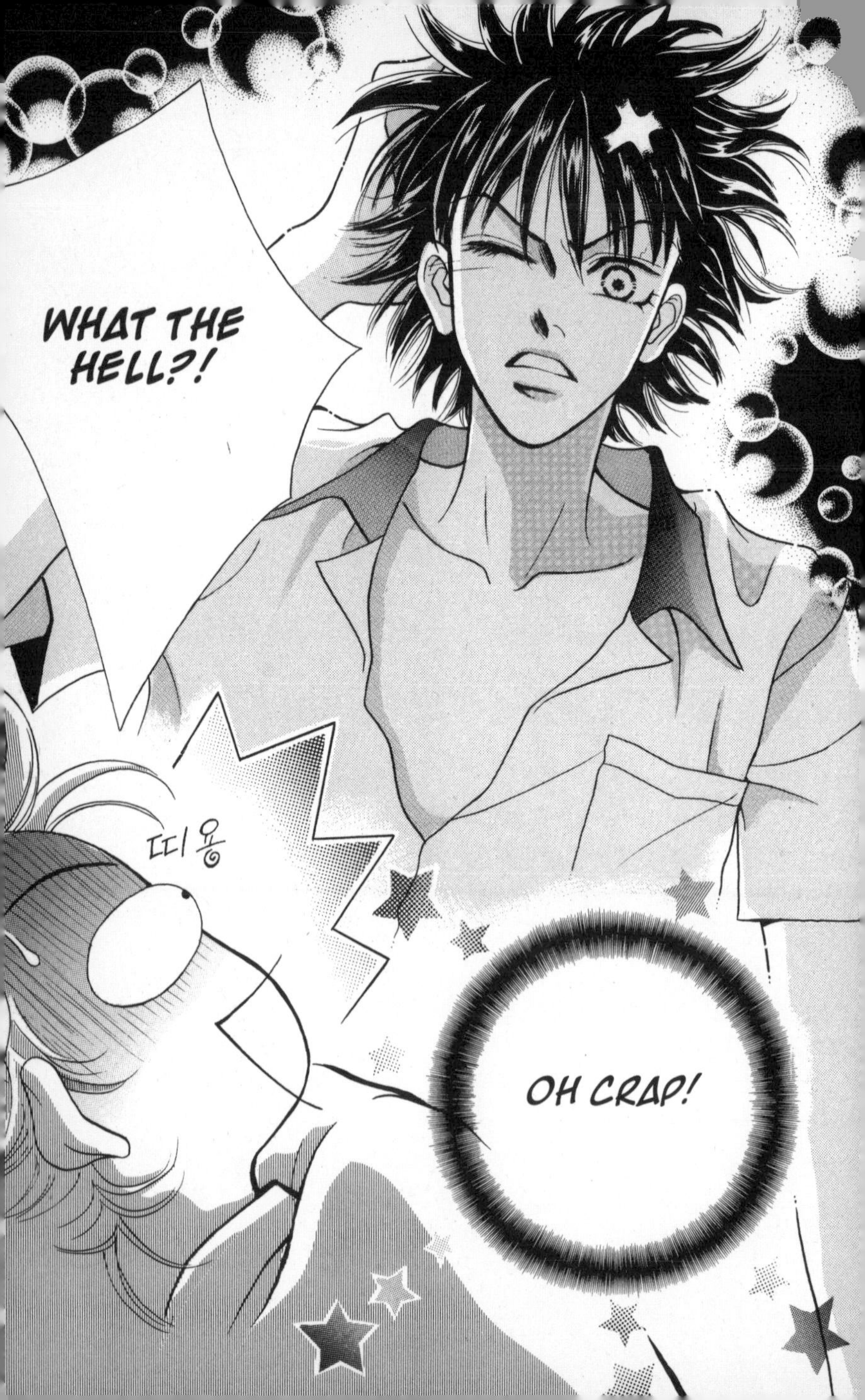
WHAT THE HELL?!
띠옹
OH CRAP!

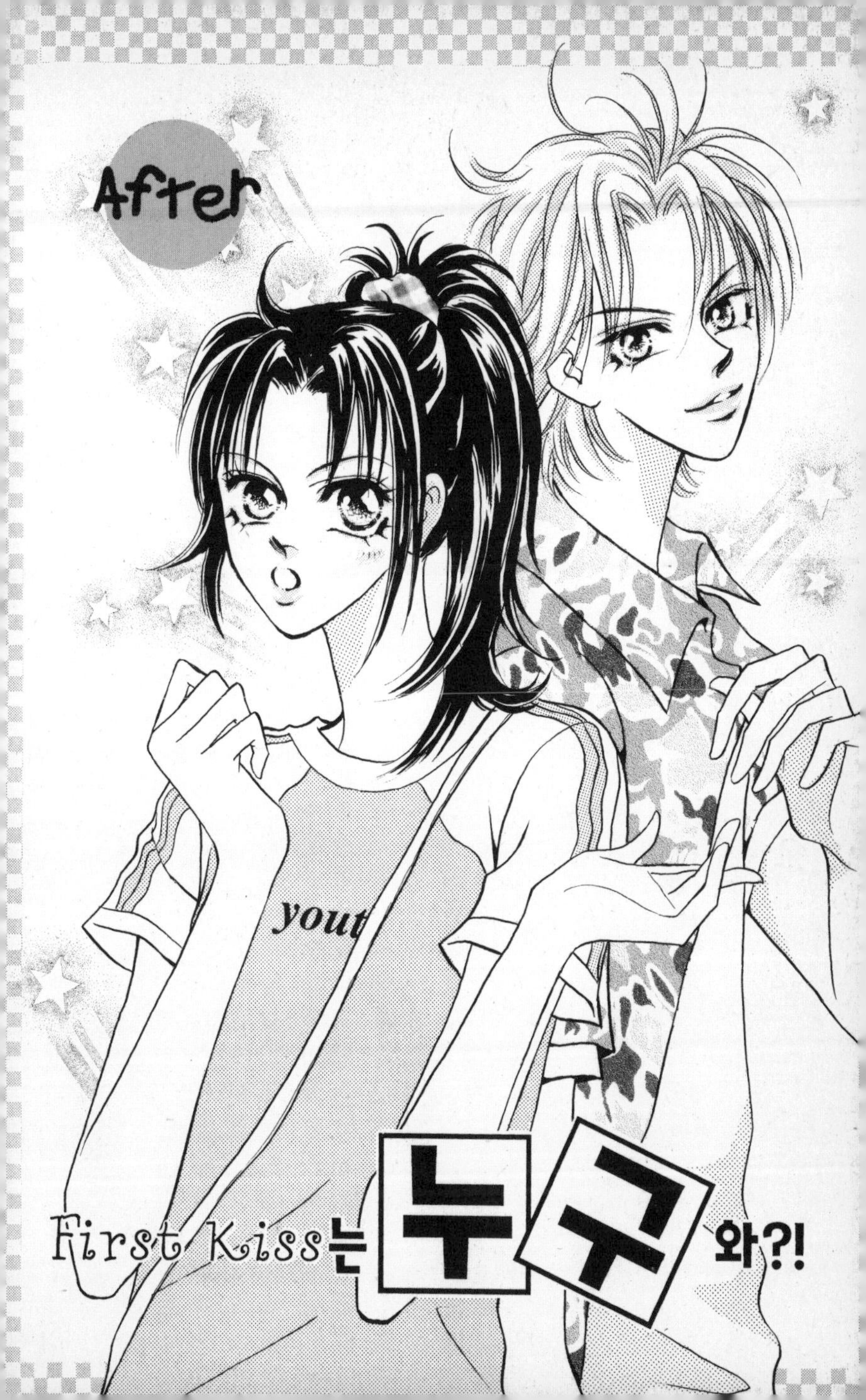
After
yout
First Kiss는 누구와?!

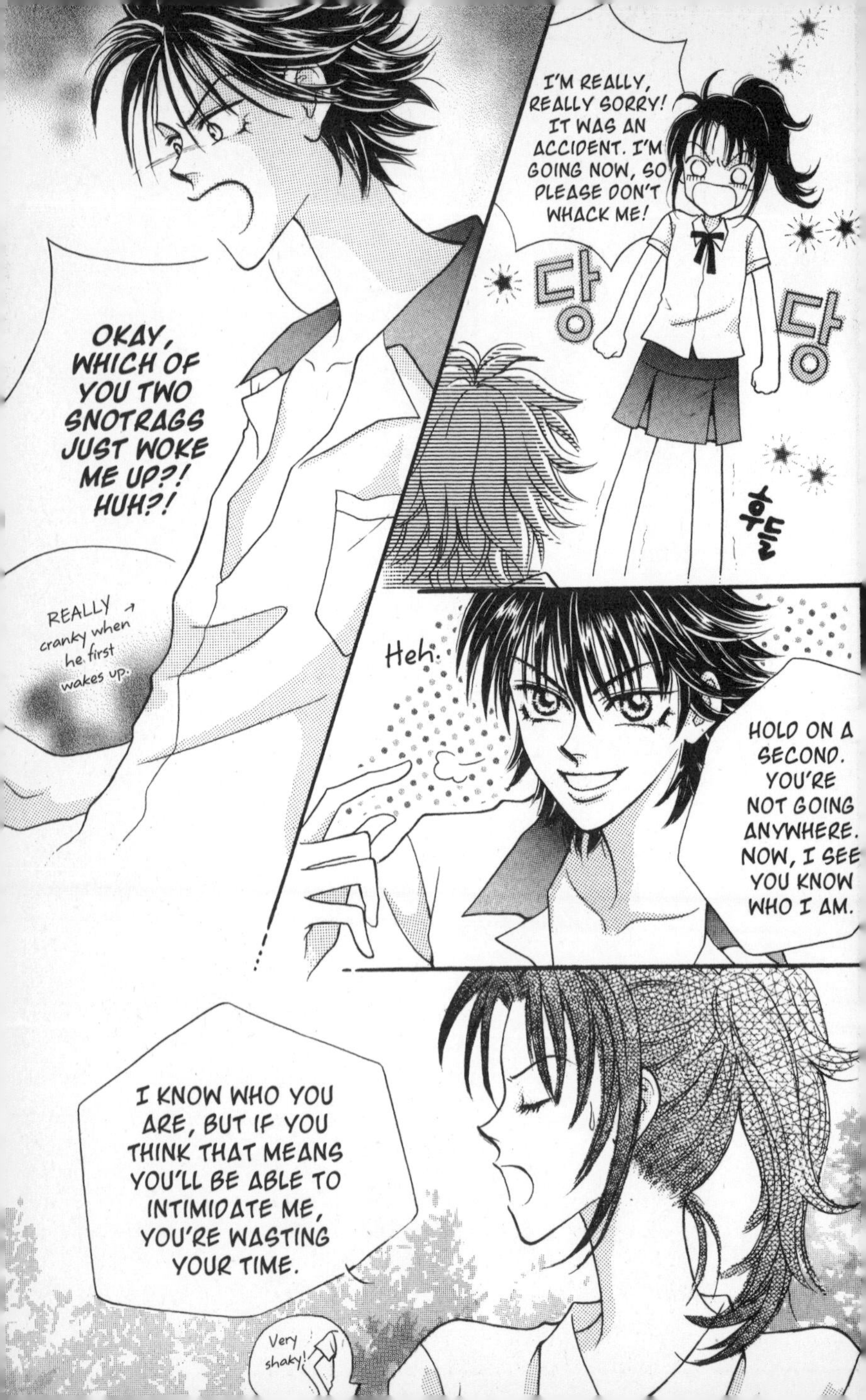

OKAY, WHICH OF YOU TWO SNOTRAGS JUST WOKE ME UP?! HUH?!
REALLY cranky when he first wakes up.
I'M REALLY, REALLY SORRY! IT WAS AN ACCIDENT. I'M GOING NOW, SO PLEASE DON'T WHACK ME!
당
당
Heh.
HOLD ON A SECOND. YOU'RE NOT GOING ANYWHERE. NOW, I SEE YOU KNOW WHO I AM.
I KNOW WHO YOU ARE, BUT IF YOU THINK THAT MEANS YOU'LL BE ABLE TO INTIMIDATE ME, YOU'RE WASTING YOUR TIME.
Very shaky!

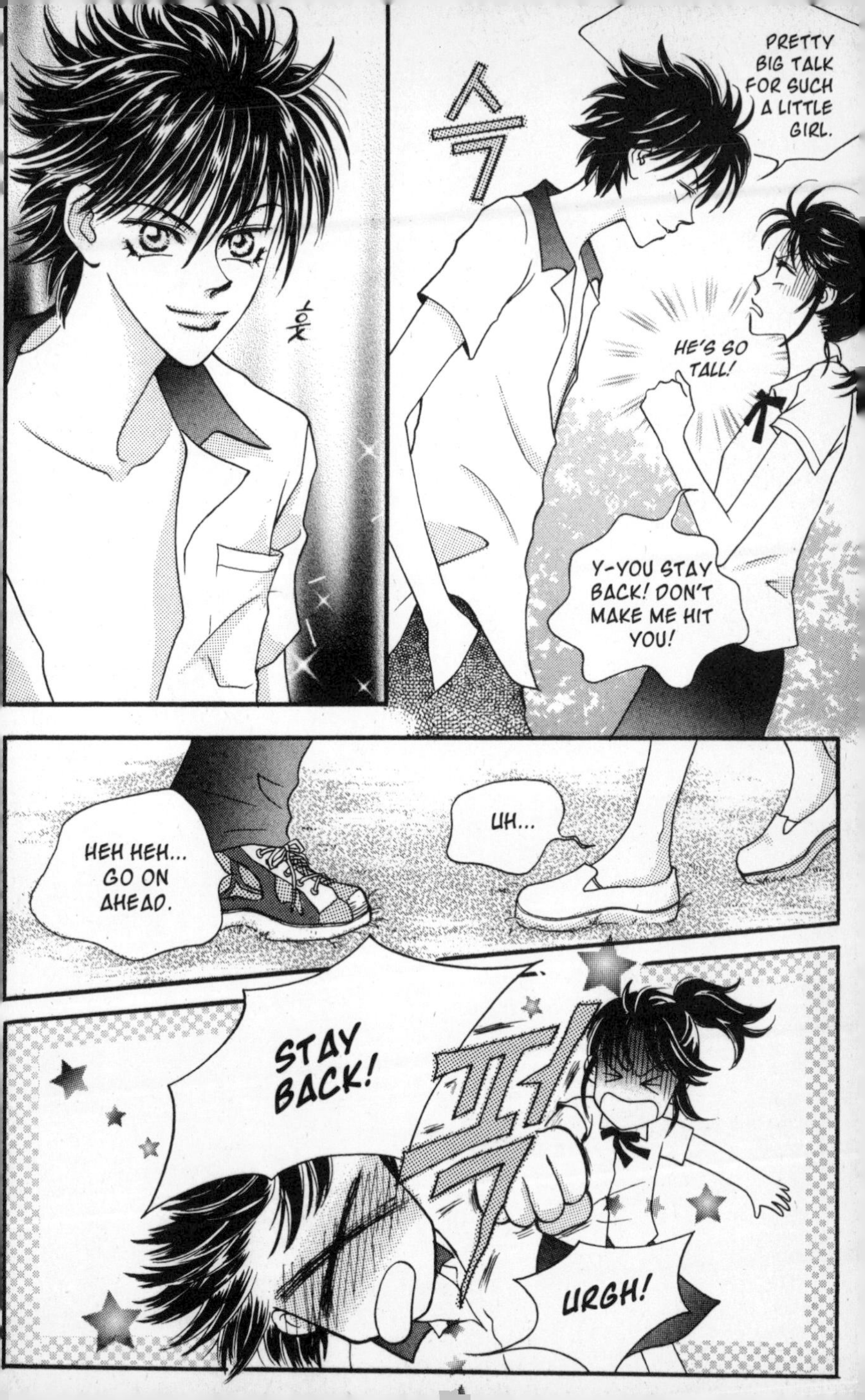
PRETTY BIG TALK FOR SUCH A LITTLE GIRL.
HE'S SO TALL!
Y-YOU STAY BACK! DON'T MAKE ME HIT YOU!
HEH HEH... GO ON AHEAD.
UH...
STAY BACK!
URGH!

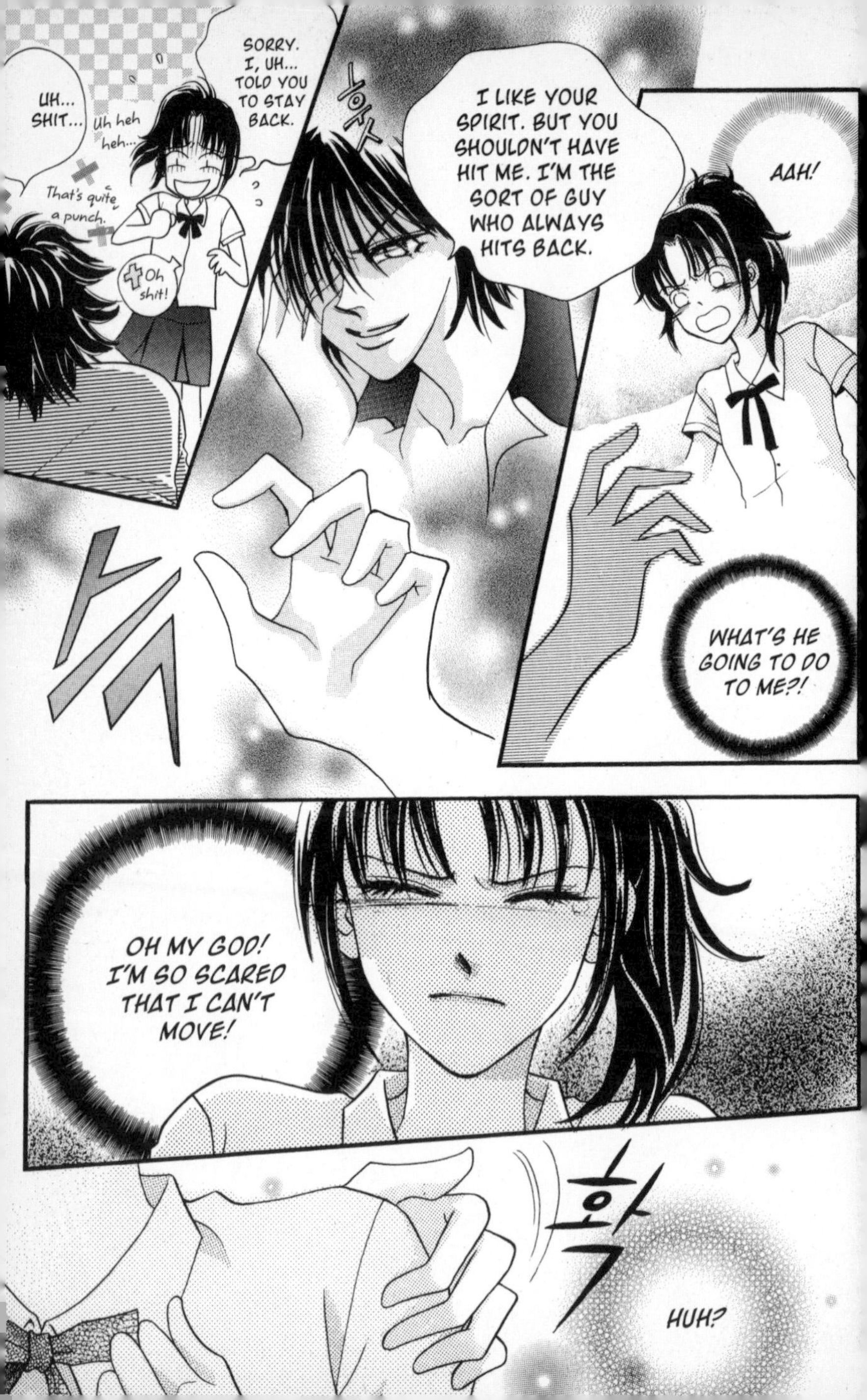
UH... SHIT...
Uh heh heh...
SORRY. I, UH... TOLD YOU TO STAY BACK.
That's quite a punch.
Oh shit!
I LIKE YOUR SPIRIT. BUT YOU SHOULDN'T HAVE HIT ME. I'M THE SORT OF GUY WHO ALWAYS HITS BACK.
AAH!
WHAT'S HE GOING TO DO TO ME?!
OH MY GOD! I'M SO SCARED THAT I CAN'T MOVE!
HUH?

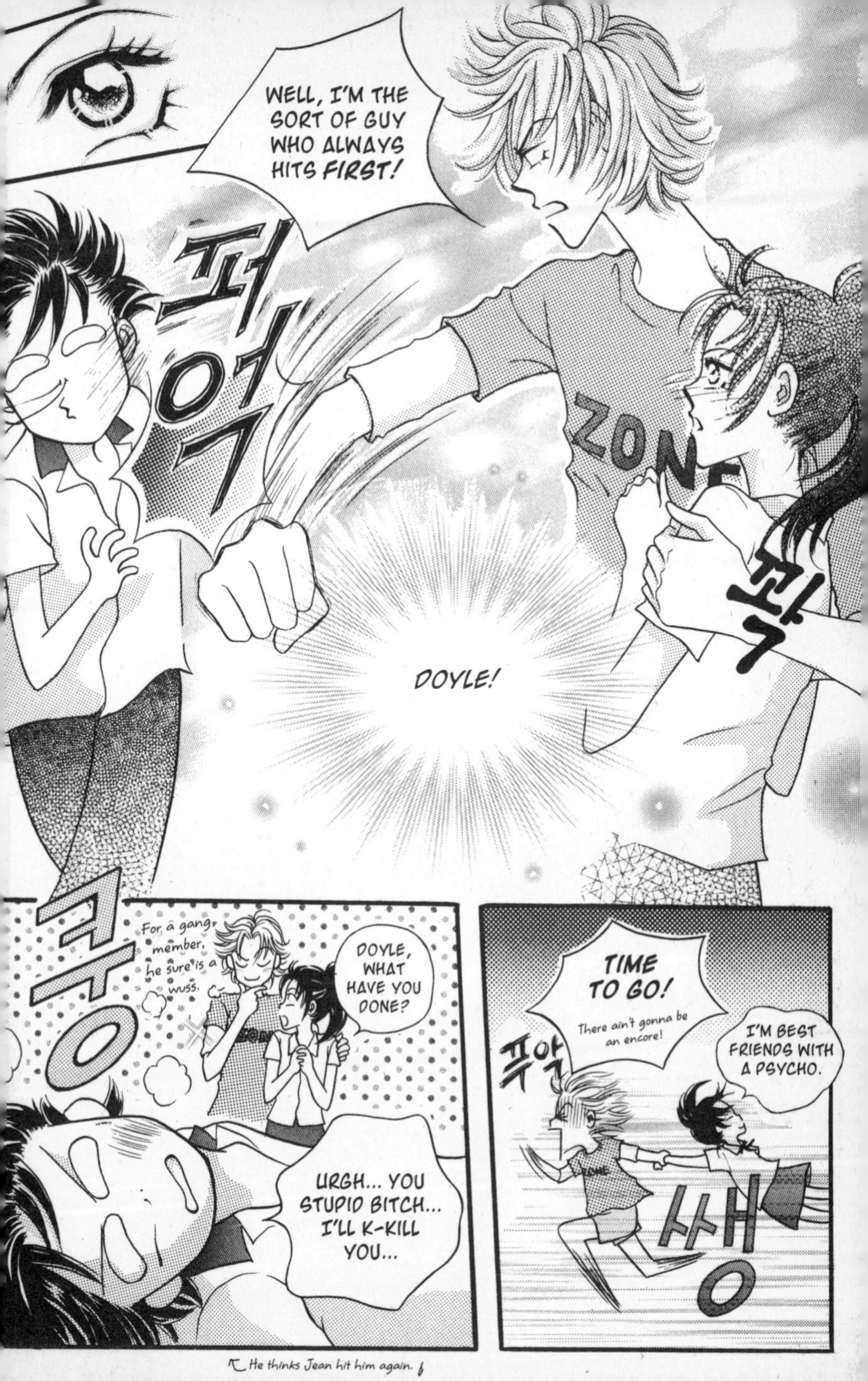
WELL, I'M THE SORT OF GUY WHO ALWAYS HITS FIRST!
DOYLE!
For a gang member, he sure is a wuss.
DOYLE, WHAT HAVE YOU DONE?
URGH... YOU STUPID BITCH... I'LL K-KILL YOU...
TIME TO GO!
There ain't gonna be an encore!
I'M BEST FRIENDS WITH A PSYCHO.

He thinks Jean hit him again.

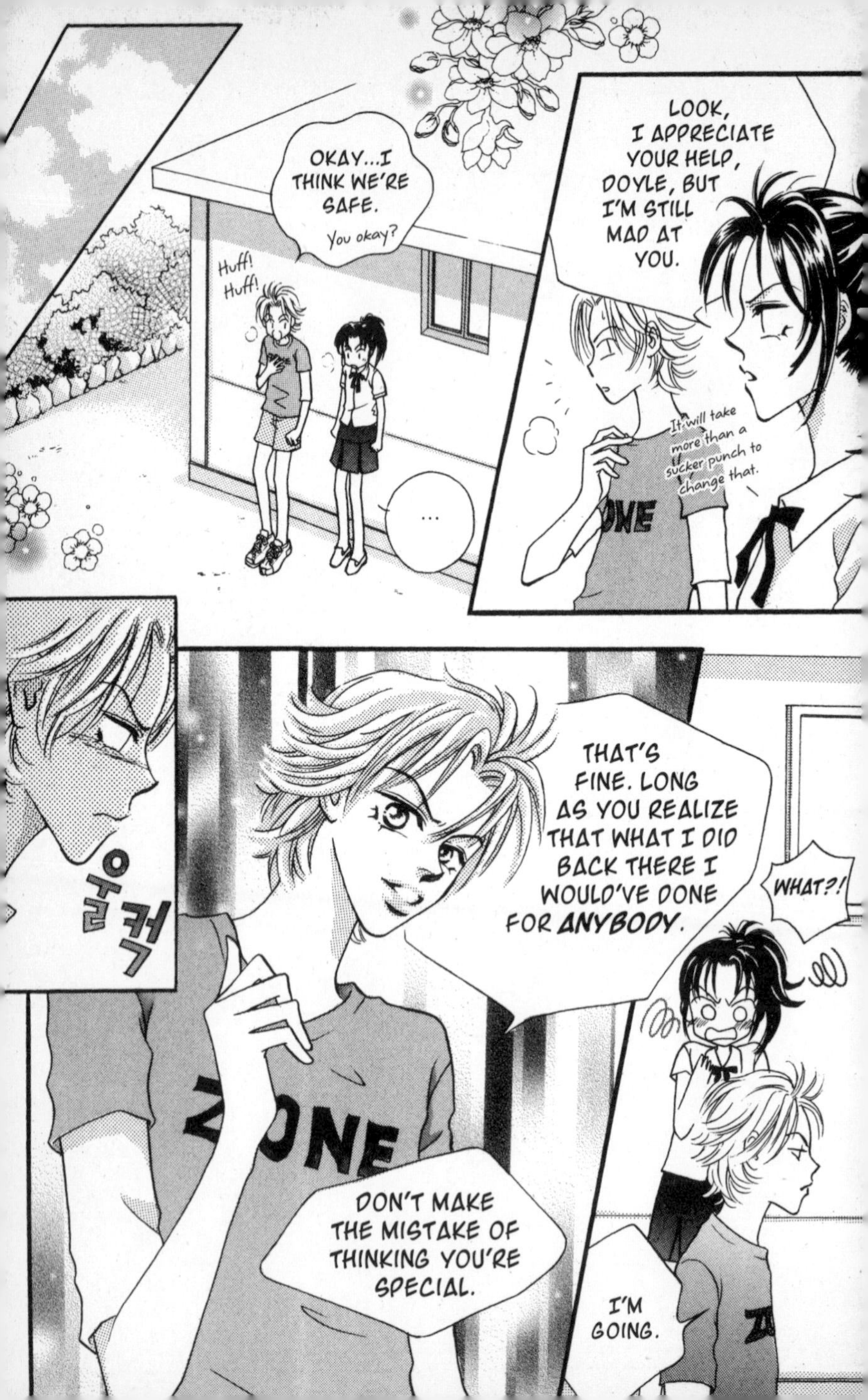
Huff! Huff!
OKAY...I THINK WE'RE SAFE.
You okay?
...
LOOK, I APPRECIATE YOUR HELP, DOYLE, BUT I'M STILL MAD AT YOU.
It will take more than a sucker punch to change that.
울컥
THAT'S FINE. LONG AS YOU REALIZE THAT WHAT I DID BACK THERE I WOULD'VE DONE FOR ANYBODY.
DON'T MAKE THE MISTAKE OF THINKING YOU'RE SPECIAL.
WHAT?!
I'M GOING.

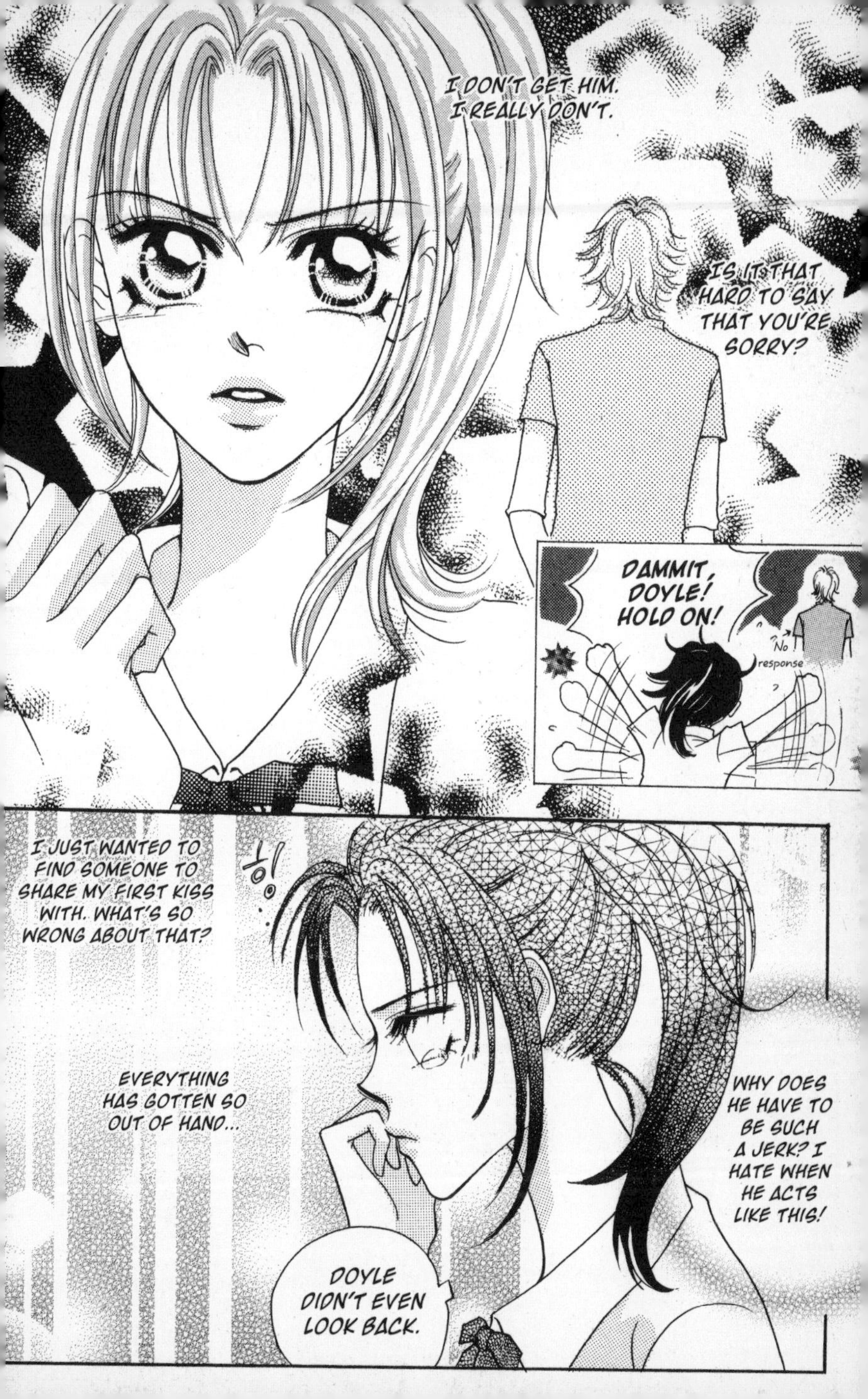
I DON'T GET HIM. I REALLY DON'T.
IS IT THAT HARD TO SAY THAT YOU'RE SORRY?
DAMMIT, DOYLE! HOLD ON!
No response
I JUST WANTED TO FIND SOMEONE TO SHARE MY FIRST KISS WITH. WHAT'S SO WRONG ABOUT THAT?
EVERYTHING HAS GOTTEN SO OUT OF HAND...
DOYLE DIDN'T EVEN LOOK BACK.
WHY DOES HE HAVE TO BE SUCH A JERK? I HATE WHEN HE ACTS LIKE THIS!

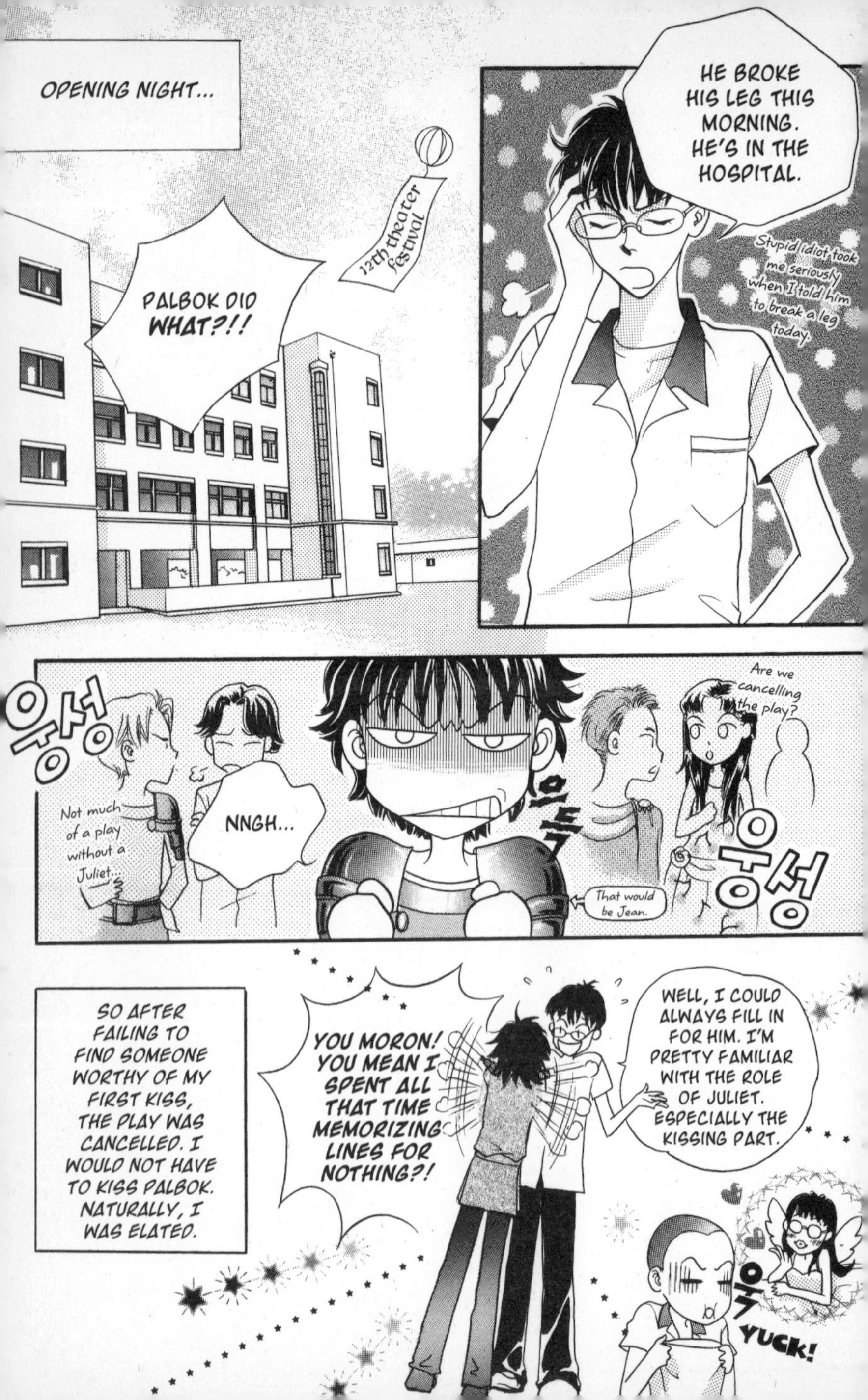
OPENING NIGHT...
12th theater festival
PALBOK DID WHAT?!!
HE BROKE HIS LEG THIS MORNING. HE'S IN THE HOSPITAL.
Stupid idiot took me seriously when I told him to break a leg today.
Not much of a play without a Juliet...
NNGH...
Are we cancelling the play?
That would be Jean.
SO AFTER FAILING TO FIND SOMEONE WORTHY OF MY FIRST KISS, THE PLAY WAS CANCELLED. I WOULD NOT HAVE TO KISS PALBOK. NATURALLY, I WAS ELATED.
YOU MORON! YOU MEAN I SPENT ALL THAT TIME MEMORIZING LINES FOR NOTHING?!
WELL, I COULD ALWAYS FILL IN FOR HIM. I'M PRETTY FAMILIAR WITH THE ROLE OF JULIET. ESPECIALLY THE KISSING PART.
YUCK!

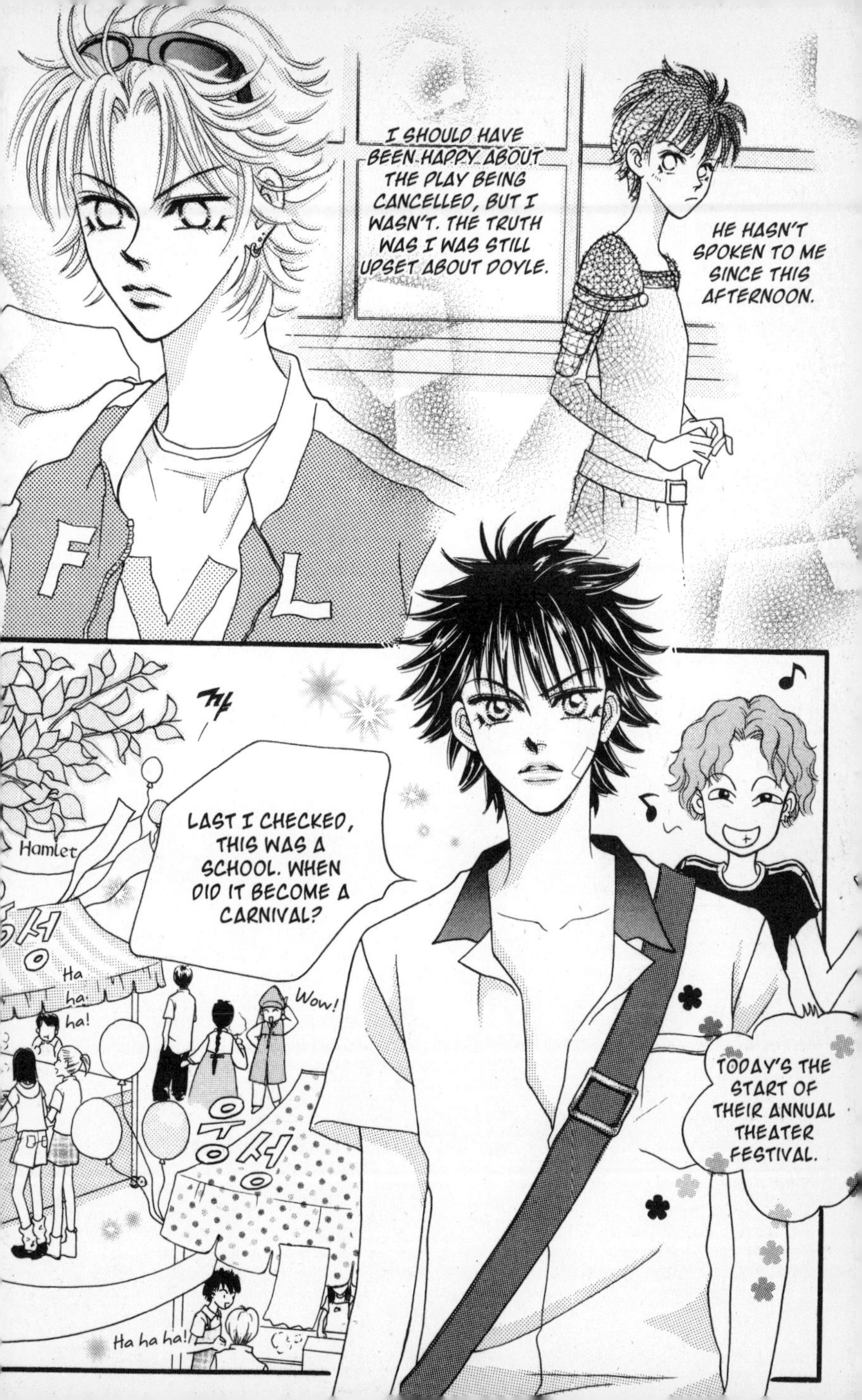
I SHOULD HAVE BEEN HAPPY ABOUT THE PLAY BEING CANCELLED, BUT I WASN'T. THE TRUTH WAS I WAS STILL UPSET ABOUT DOYLE.
HE HASN'T SPOKEN TO ME SINCE THIS AFTERNOON.
Hamlet
Ha ha ha!
Wow!
Ha ha ha!
LAST I CHECKED, THIS WAS A SCHOOL. WHEN DID IT BECOME A CARNIVAL?
TODAY'S THE START OF THEIR ANNUAL THEATER FESTIVAL.

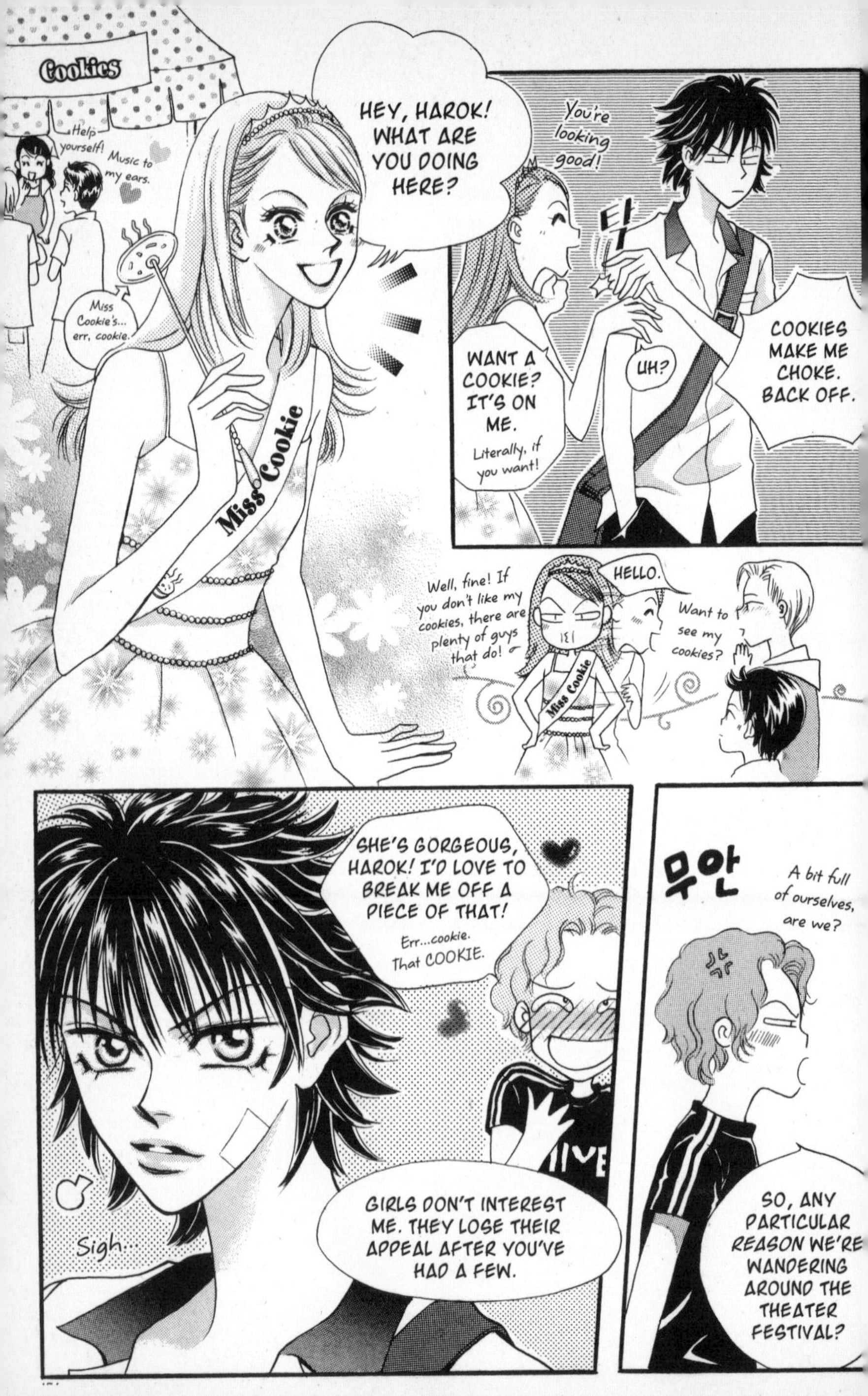
Cookies
Help yourself!
Music to my ears.
Miss Cookie's... err, cookie.
HEY, HAROK! WHAT ARE YOU DOING HERE?
Miss Cookie
You're looking good!
WANT A COOKIE? IT'S ON ME.
Literally, if you want!
UH?
COOKIES MAKE ME CHOKE. BACK OFF.
Well, fine! If you don't like my cookies, there are plenty of guys that do!
Miss Cookie
HELLO.
Want to see my cookies?
SHE'S GORGEOUS, HAROK! I'D LOVE TO BREAK ME OFF A PIECE OF THAT!
Err...cookie. That COOKIE.
Sigh.
GIRLS DON'T INTEREST ME. THEY LOSE THEIR APPEAL AFTER YOU'VE HAD A FEW.
무안
A bit full of ourselves, are we?
SO, ANY PARTICULAR REASON WE'RE WANDERING AROUND THE THEATER FESTIVAL?

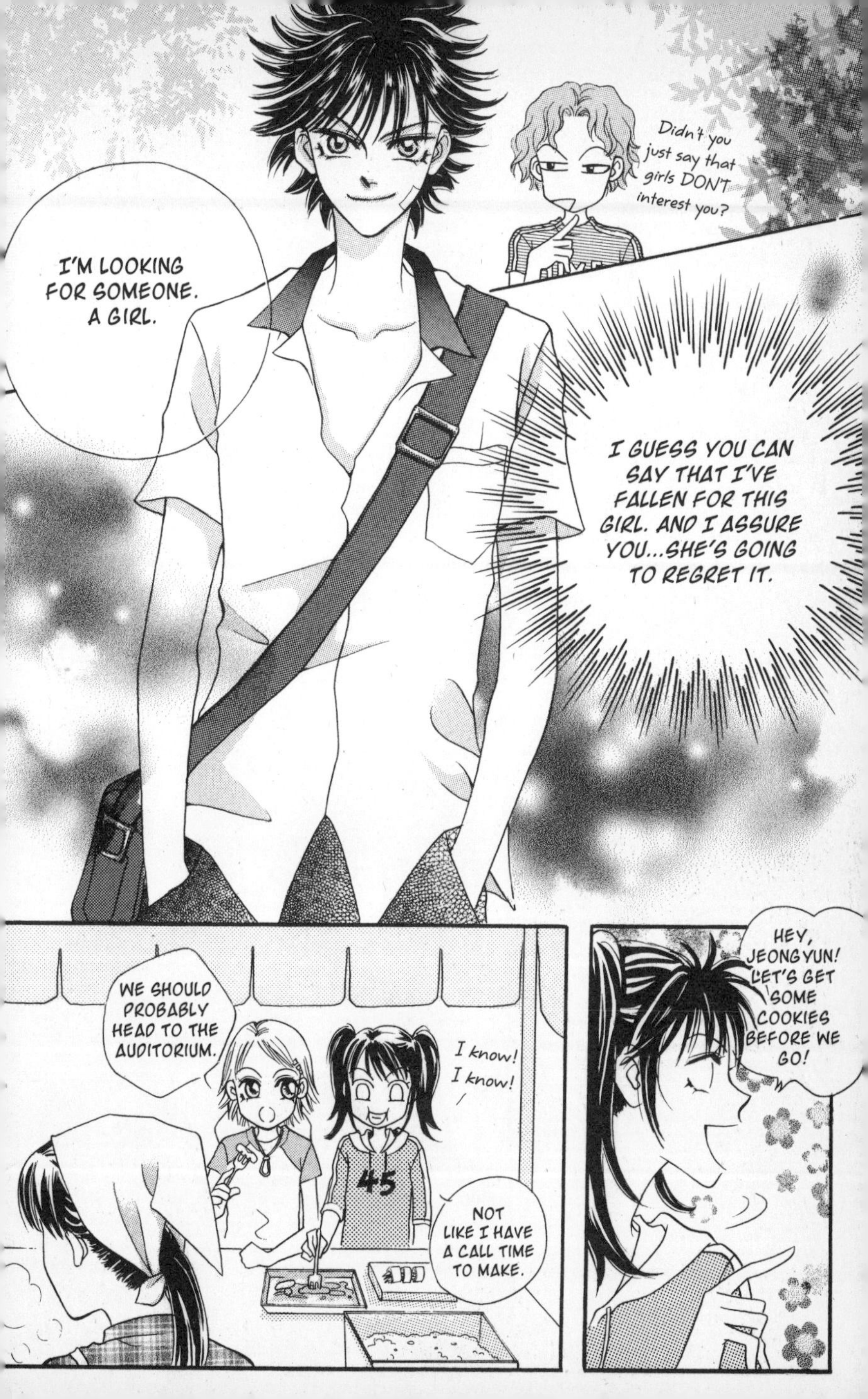
I'M LOOKING FOR SOMEONE. A GIRL.
Didn't you just say that girls DON'T interest you?
I GUESS YOU CAN SAY THAT I'VE FALLEN FOR THIS GIRL. AND I ASSURE YOU...SHE'S GOING TO REGRET IT.
WE SHOULD PROBABLY HEAD TO THE AUDITORIUM.
I know! I know!
NOT LIKE I HAVE A CALL TIME TO MAKE.
HEY, JEONGYUN! LET'S GET SOME COOKIES BEFORE WE GO!

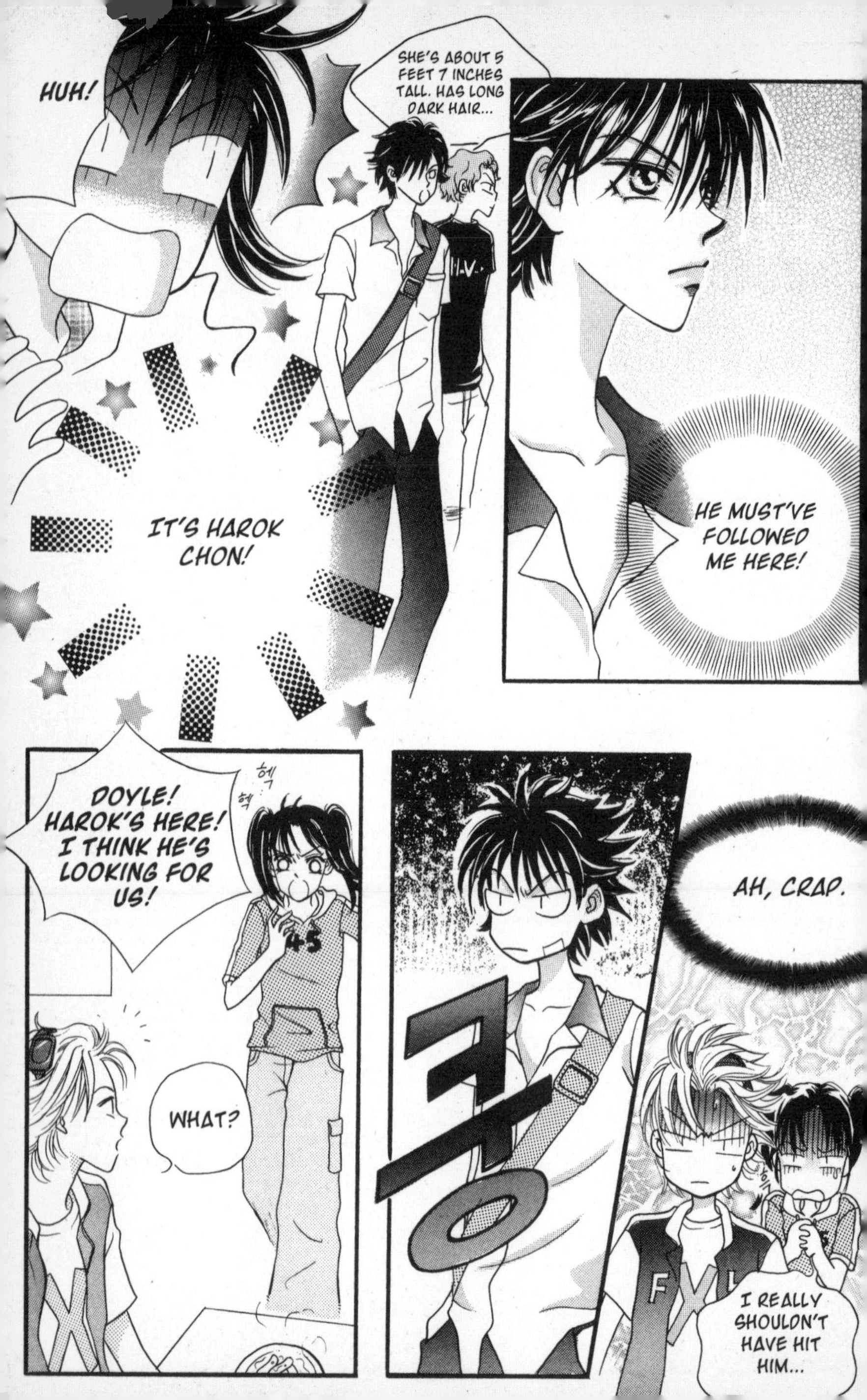
HUH!
SHE'S ABOUT 5 FEET 7 INCHES TALL. HAS LONG DARK HAIR...
IT'S HAROK CHON!
HE MUST'VE FOLLOWED ME HERE!
헥
헉
DOYLE! HAROK'S HERE! I THINK HE'S LOOKING FOR US!
WHAT?
AH, CRAP.
I REALLY SHOULDN'T HAVE HIT HIM...

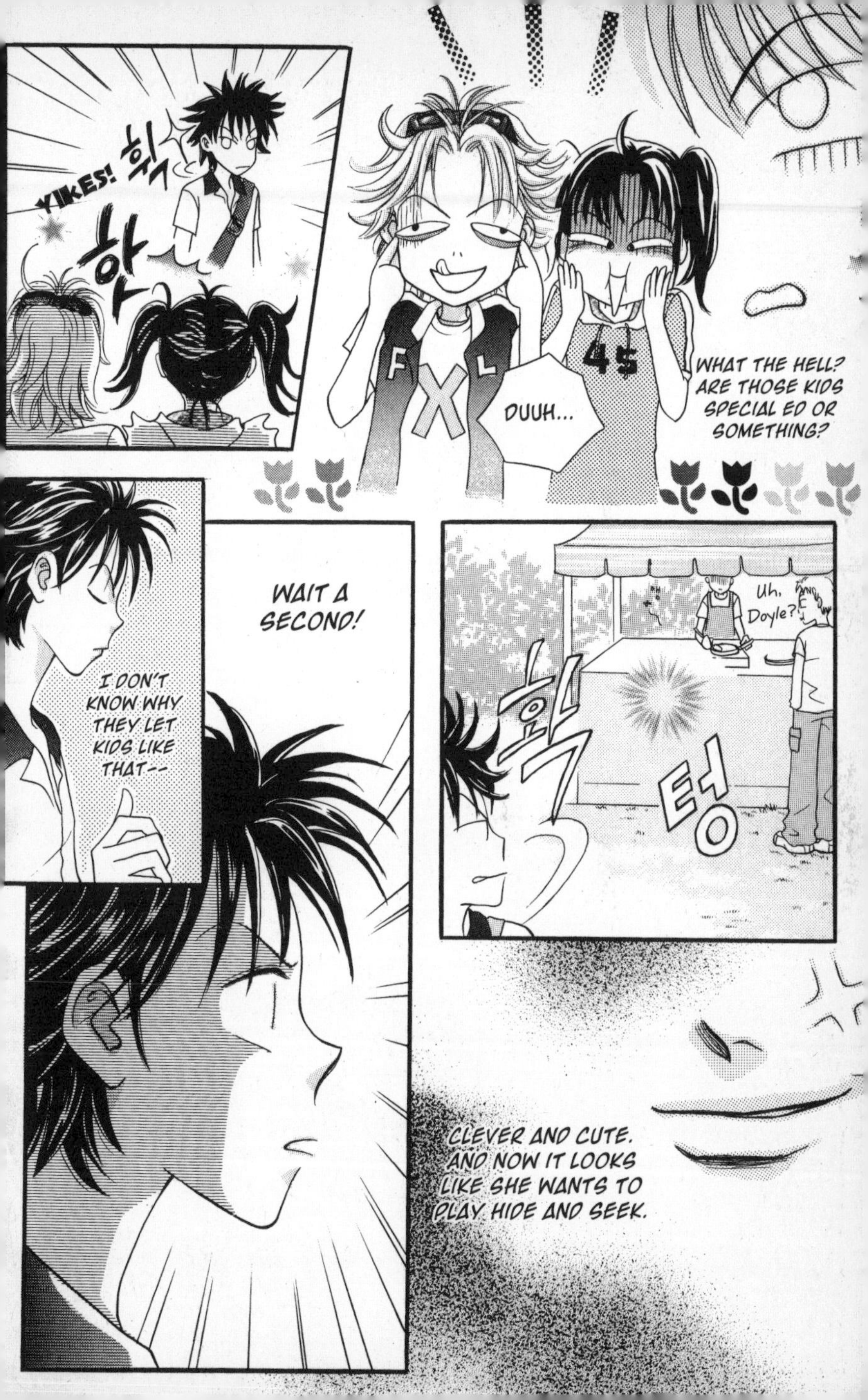
YIKES! 휙
핫
DUUH...
WHAT THE HELL? ARE THOSE KIDS SPECIAL ED OR SOMETHING?
I DON'T KNOW WHY THEY LET KIDS LIKE THAT--
WAIT A SECOND!
Uh, Doyle?
휙
텅
CLEVER AND CUTE. AND NOW IT LOOKS LIKE SHE WANTS TO PLAY HIDE AND SEEK.

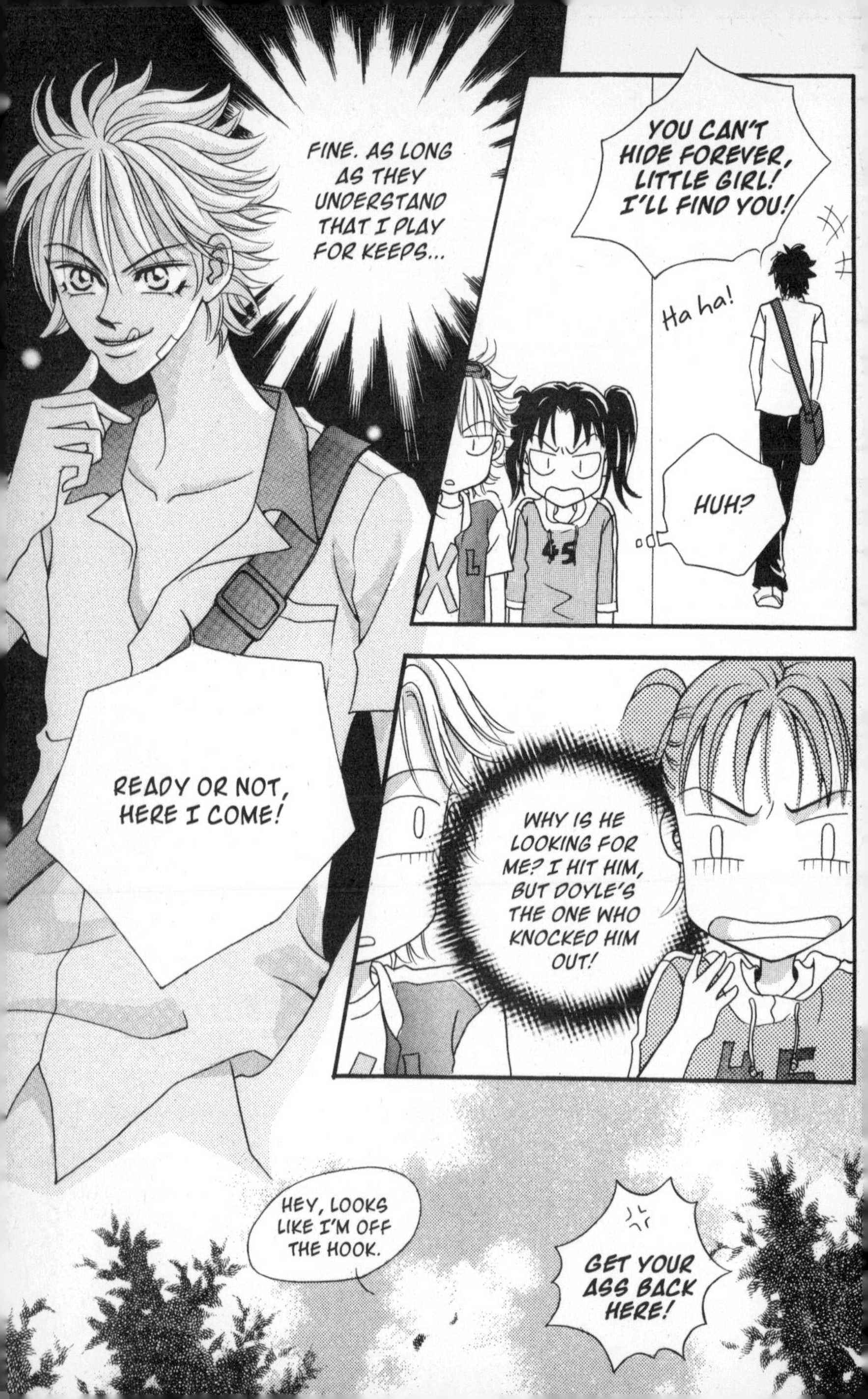
FINE. AS LONG AS THEY UNDERSTAND THAT I PLAY FOR KEEPS...
READY OR NOT, HERE I COME!
YOU CAN'T HIDE FOREVER, LITTLE GIRL! I'LL FIND YOU!
Ha ha!
HUH?
WHY IS HE LOOKING FOR ME? I HIT HIM, BUT DOYLE'S THE ONE WHO KNOCKED HIM OUT!
HEY, LOOKS LIKE I'M OFF THE HOOK.
GET YOUR ASS BACK HERE!

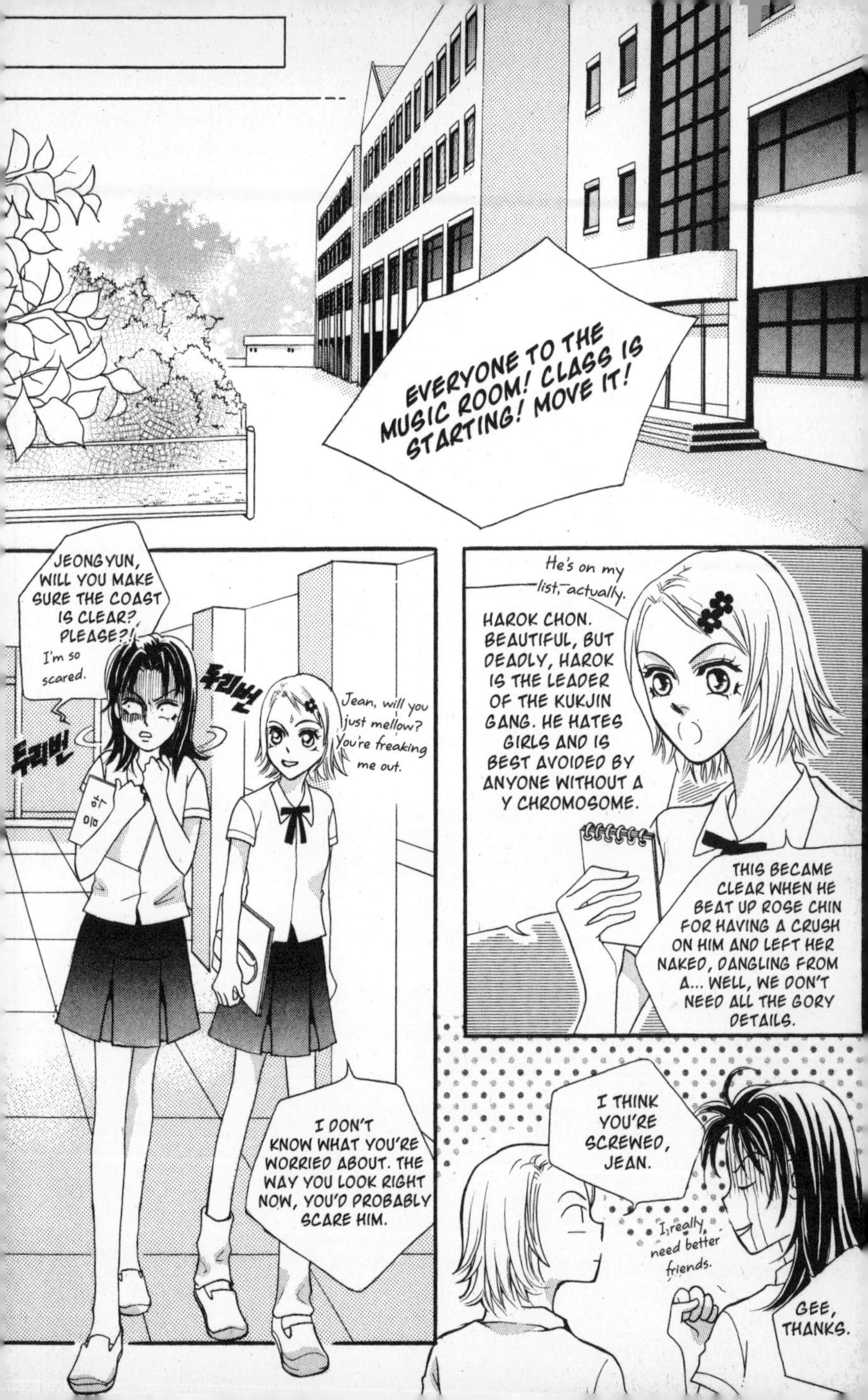
EVERYONE TO THE MUSIC ROOM! CLASS IS STARTING! MOVE IT!
JEONGYUN, WILL YOU MAKE SURE THE COAST IS CLEAR? PLEASE?!
I'm so scared.
두리번
두리번
Jean, will you just mellow? You're freaking me out.
I DON'T KNOW WHAT YOU'RE WORRIED ABOUT. THE WAY YOU LOOK RIGHT NOW, YOU'D PROBABLY SCARE HIM.
He's on my list, actually.
HAROK CHON. BEAUTIFUL, BUT DEADLY, HAROK IS THE LEADER OF THE KUKJIN GANG. HE HATES GIRLS AND IS BEST AVOIDED BY ANYONE WITHOUT A Y CHROMOSOME.
THIS BECAME CLEAR WHEN HE BEAT UP ROSE CHIN FOR HAVING A CRUSH ON HIM AND LEFT HER NAKED, DANGLING FROM A... WELL, WE DON'T NEED ALL THE GORY DETAILS.
I THINK YOU'RE SCREWED, JEAN.
I really need better friends.
GEE, THANKS.

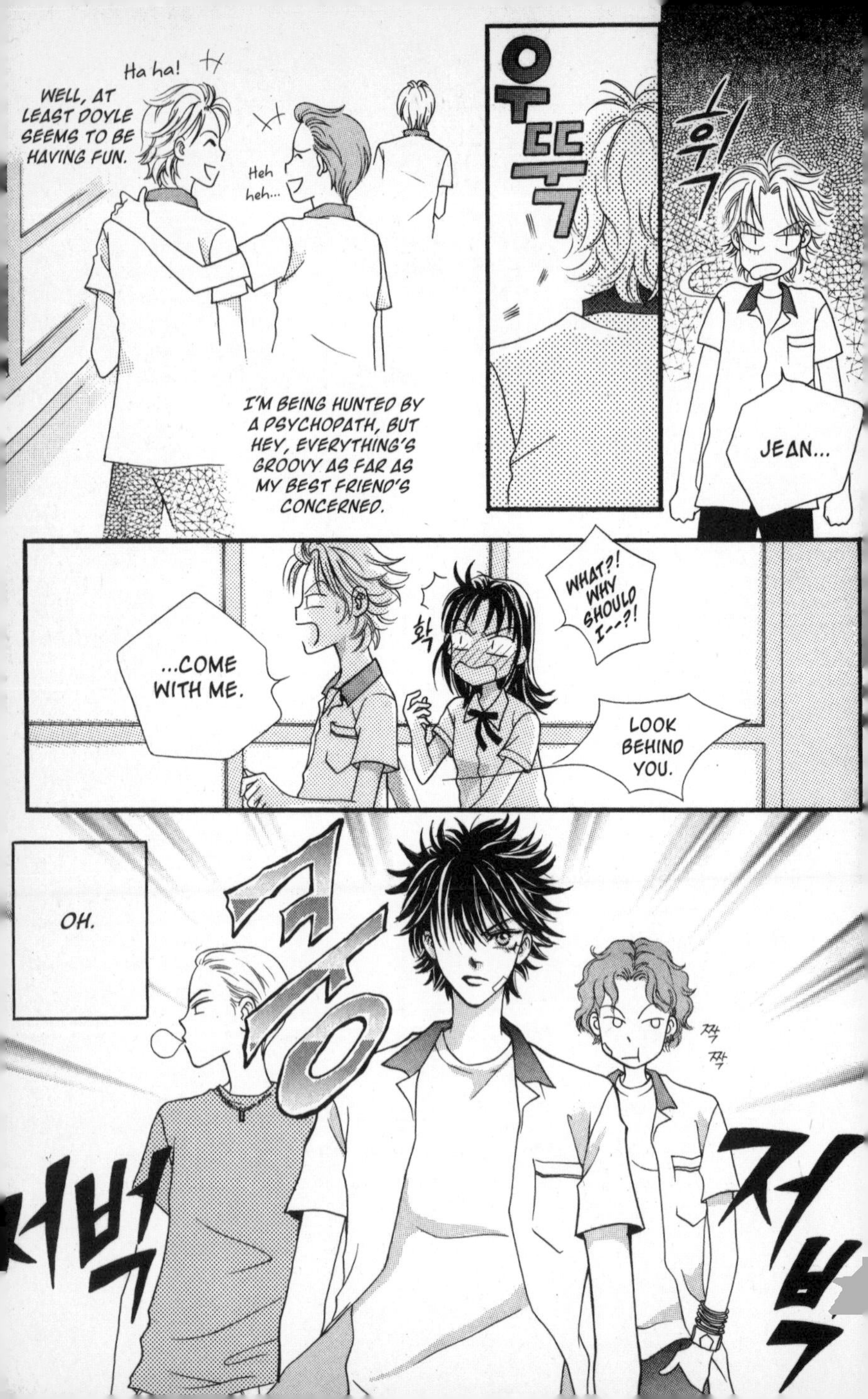

Ha ha!
WELL, AT LEAST DOYLE SEEMS TO BE HAVING FUN.
Heh heh...
I'M BEING HUNTED BY A PSYCHOPATH, BUT HEY, EVERYTHING'S GROOVY AS FAR AS MY BEST FRIEND'S CONCERNED.
우뚝
휙
JEAN...
...COME WITH ME.
확
WHAT?! WHY SHOULD I--?!
LOOK BEHIND YOU.
OH.
궁
저벅
짝 짝
저벅

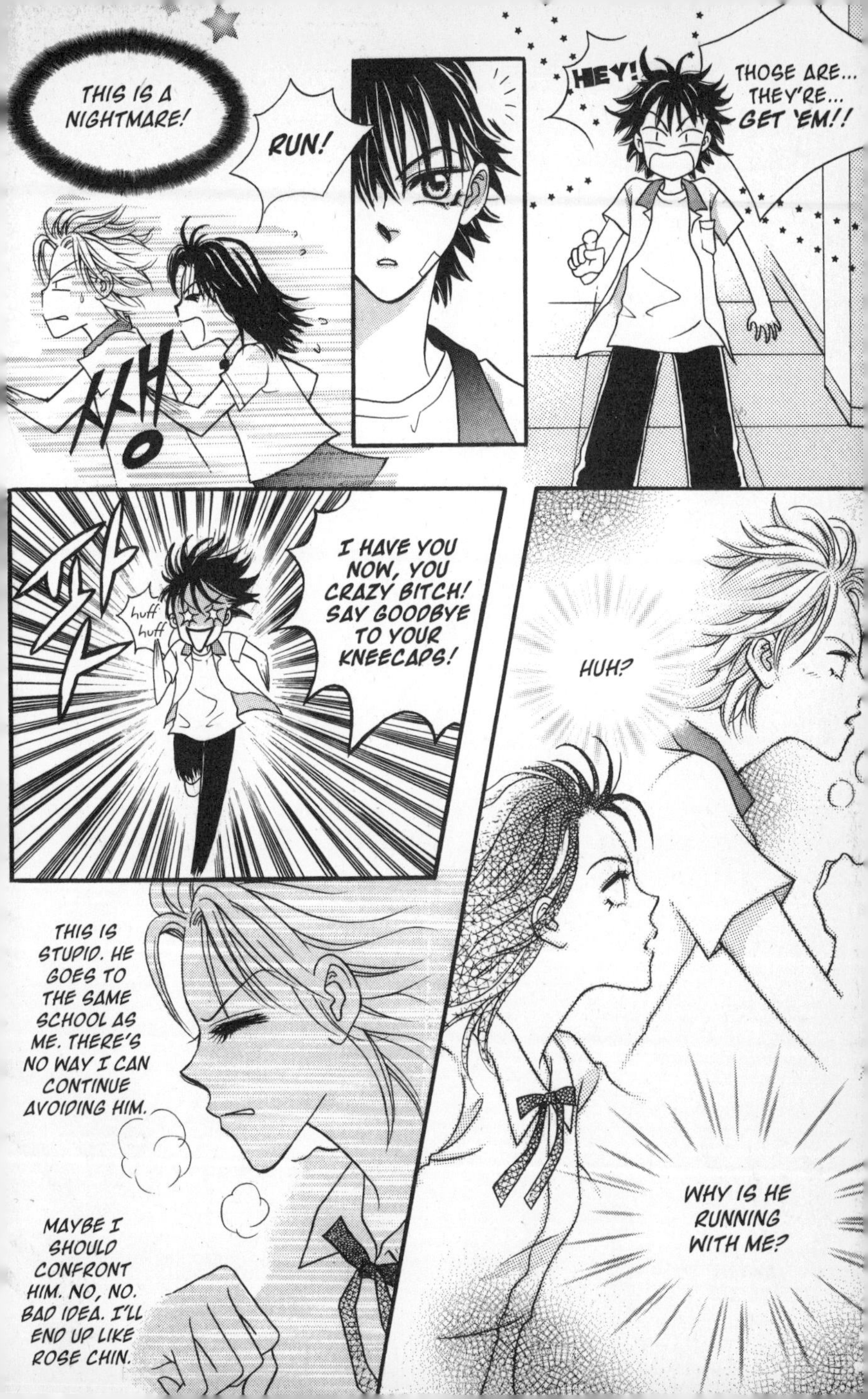
THIS IS A NIGHTMARE!
RUN!
HEY!
THOSE ARE... THEY'RE... GET 'EM!!
I HAVE YOU NOW, YOU CRAZY BITCH! SAY GOODBYE TO YOUR KNEECAPS!
huff huff
THIS IS STUPID. HE GOES TO THE SAME SCHOOL AS ME. THERE'S NO WAY I CAN CONTINUE AVOIDING HIM.
MAYBE I SHOULD CONFRONT HIM. NO, NO. BAD IDEA. I'LL END UP LIKE ROSE CHIN.
HUH?
WHY IS HE RUNNING WITH ME?

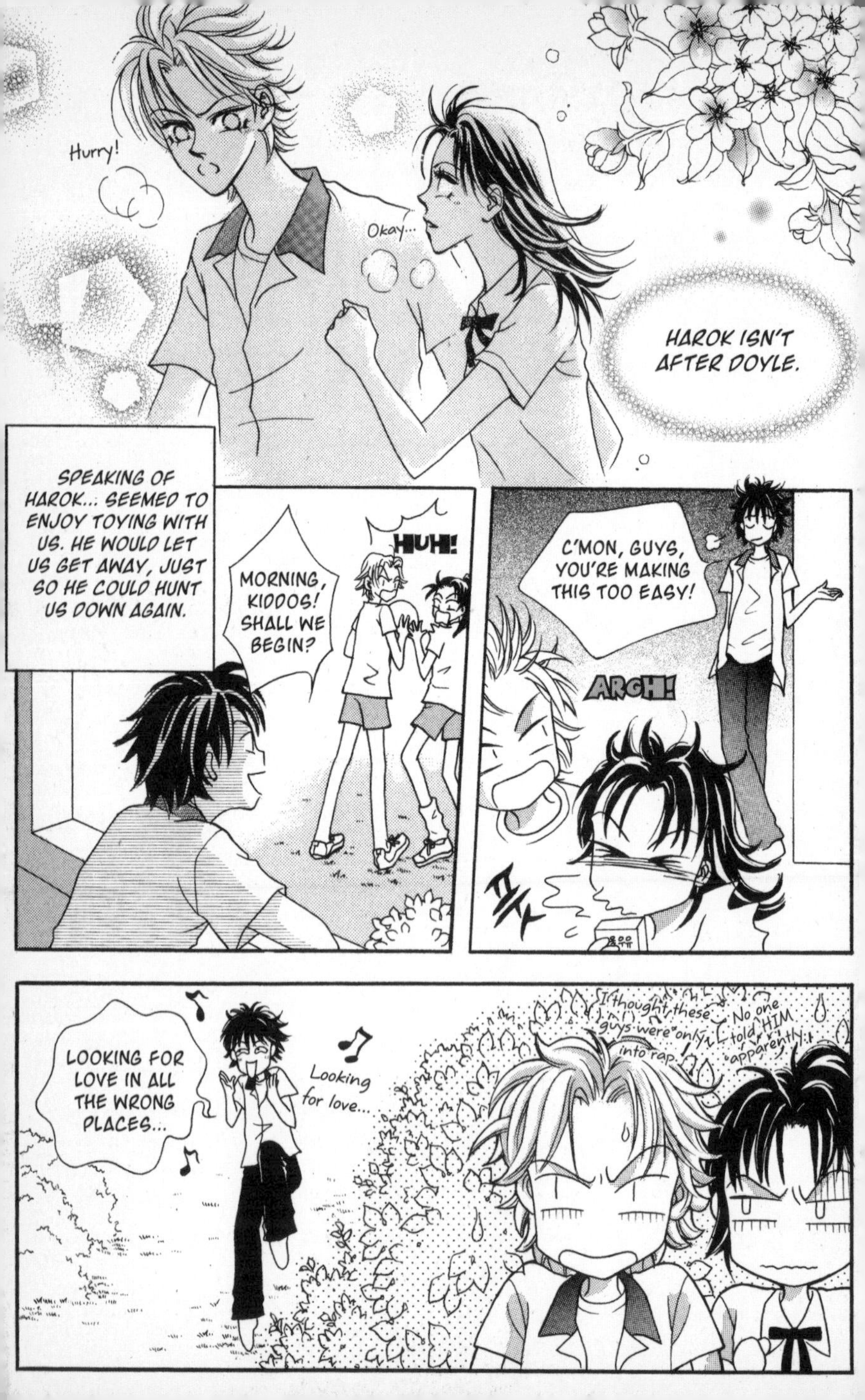
Hurry!
Okay...
HAROK ISN'T AFTER DOYLE.
SPEAKING OF HAROK... SEEMED TO ENJOY TOYING WITH US. HE WOULD LET US GET AWAY, JUST SO HE COULD HUNT US DOWN AGAIN.
MORNING, KIDDOS! SHALL WE BEGIN?
HUH!
C'MON, GUYS, YOU'RE MAKING THIS TOO EASY!
ARGH!
LOOKING FOR LOVE IN ALL THE WRONG PLACES...
Looking for love...
I thought these guys were only into rap.
No one told HIM apparently.

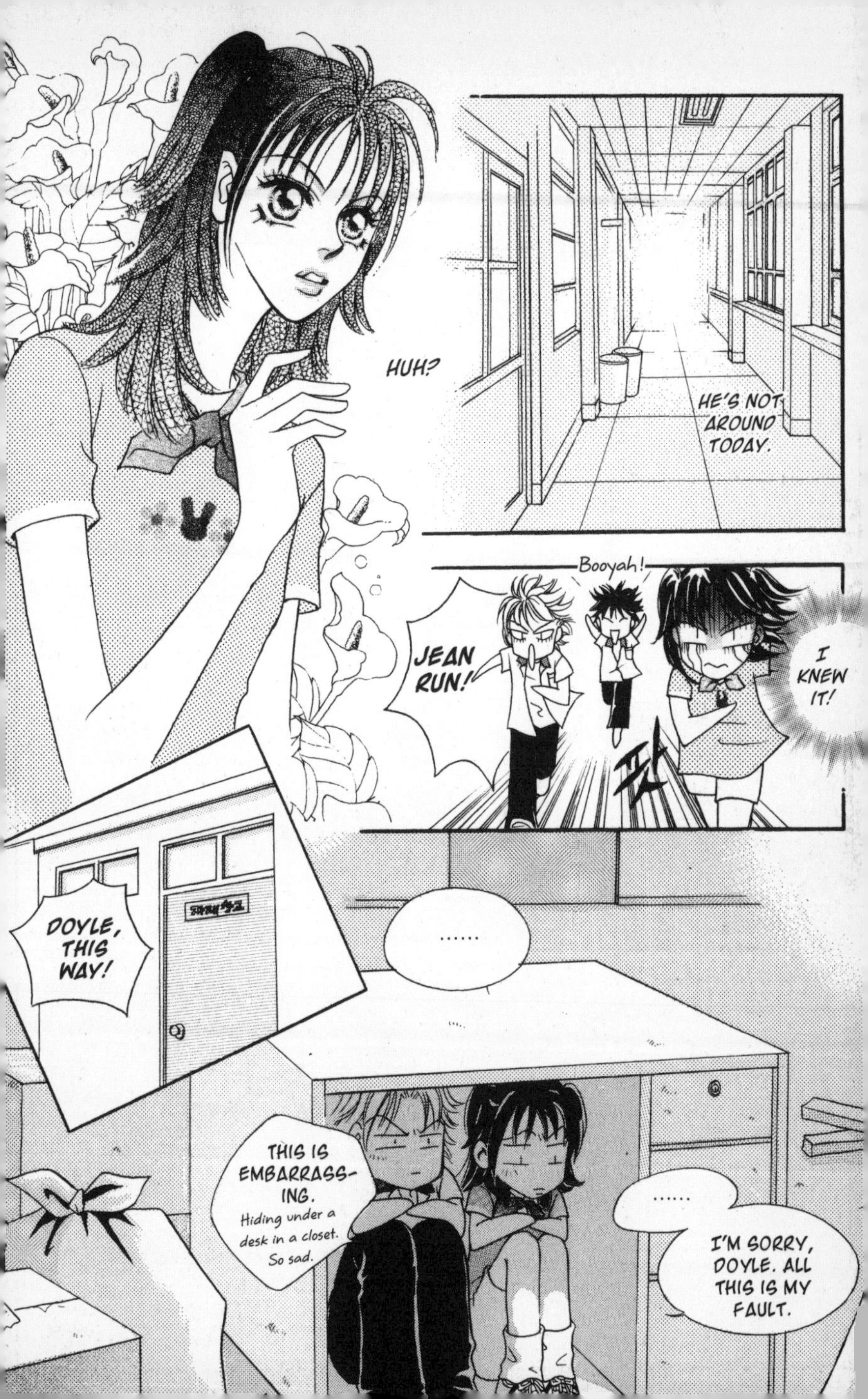
HUH?
HE'S NOT AROUND TODAY.
JEAN RUN!
Booyah!
I KNEW IT!
DOYLE, THIS WAY!
......
THIS IS EMBARRASS-ING.
Hiding under a desk in a closet. So sad.
......
I'M SORRY, DOYLE. ALL THIS IS MY FAULT.

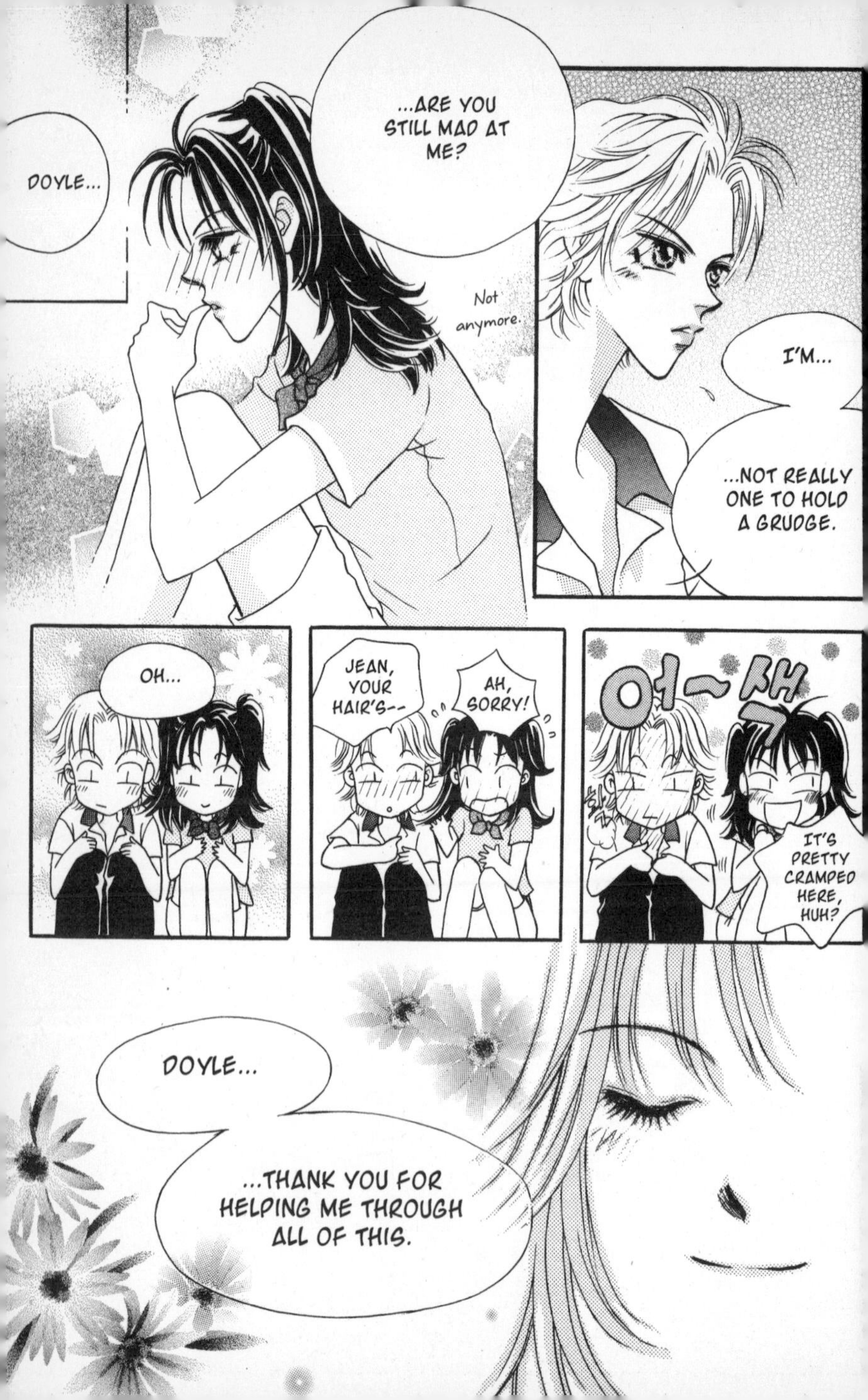
DOYLE...
...ARE YOU STILL MAD AT ME?
Not anymore.
I'M...
...NOT REALLY ONE TO HOLD A GRUDGE.
OH...
JEAN, YOUR HAIR'S--
AH, SORRY!
IT'S PRETTY CRAMPED HERE, HUH?
DOYLE...
...THANK YOU FOR HELPING ME THROUGH ALL OF THIS.

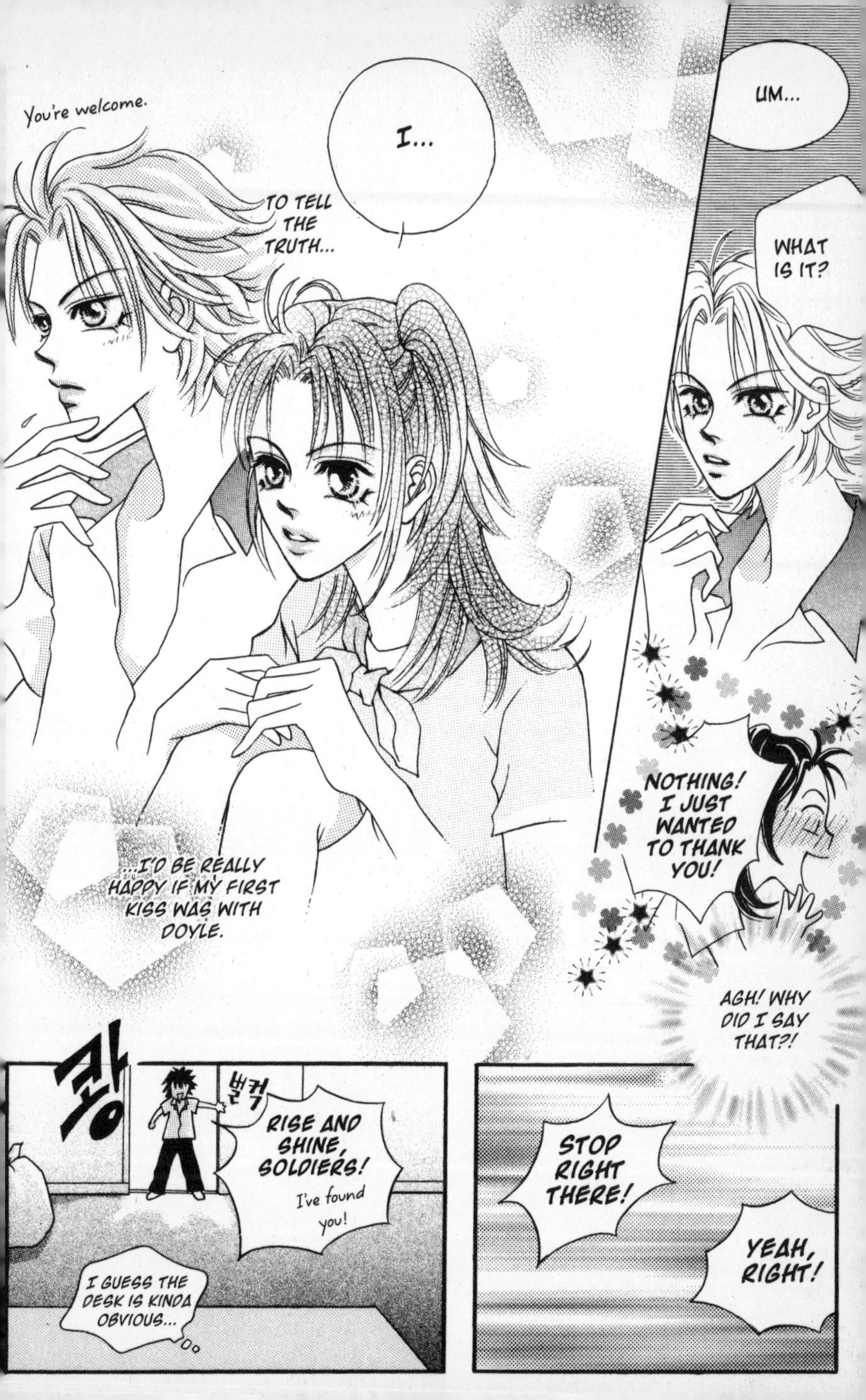
You're welcome.
TO TELL THE TRUTH...
I...
...I'D BE REALLY HAPPY IF MY FIRST KISS WAS WITH DOYLE.
UM...
WHAT IS IT?
NOTHING! I JUST WANTED TO THANK YOU!
AGH! WHY DID I SAY THAT?!
쾅
벌컥
RISE AND SHINE, SOLDIERS!
I've found you!
I GUESS THE DESK IS KINDA OBVIOUS...
STOP RIGHT THERE!
YEAH, RIGHT!

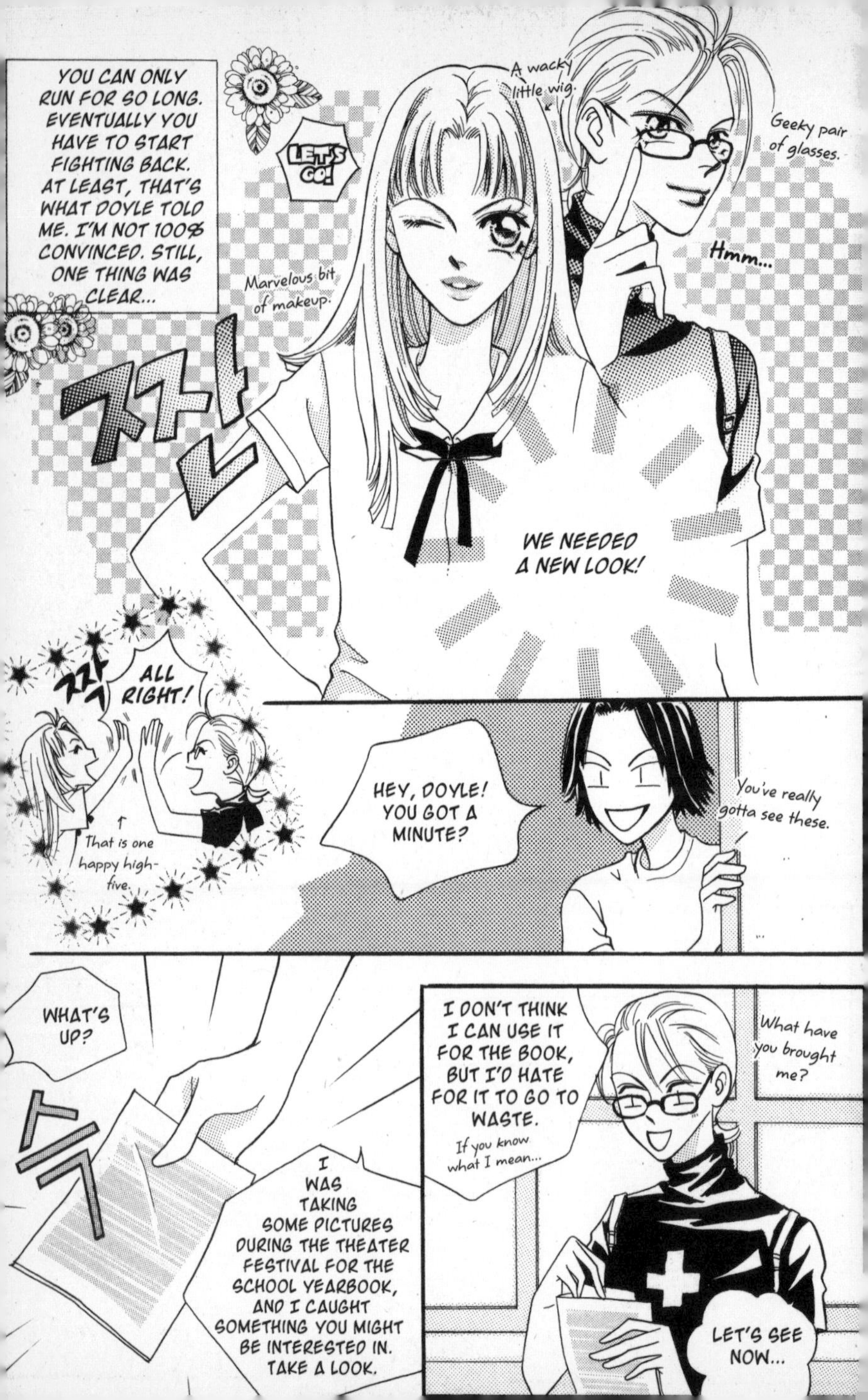
YOU CAN ONLY RUN FOR SO LONG. EVENTUALLY YOU HAVE TO START FIGHTING BACK. AT LEAST, THAT'S WHAT DOYLE TOLD ME. I'M NOT 100% CONVINCED. STILL, ONE THING WAS CLEAR...
LET'S GO!
A wacky little wig.
Geeky pair of glasses.
Hmm...
Marvelous bit of makeup.
WE NEEDED A NEW LOOK!
ALL RIGHT!
That is one happy high-five.
HEY, DOYLE! YOU GOT A MINUTE?
You've really gotta see these.
WHAT'S UP?
I WAS TAKING SOME PICTURES DURING THE THEATER FESTIVAL FOR THE SCHOOL YEARBOOK, AND I CAUGHT SOMETHING YOU MIGHT BE INTERESTED IN. TAKE A LOOK.
I DON'T THINK I CAN USE IT FOR THE BOOK, BUT I'D HATE FOR IT TO GO TO WASTE.
If you know what I mean...
What have you brought me?
LET'S SEE NOW...

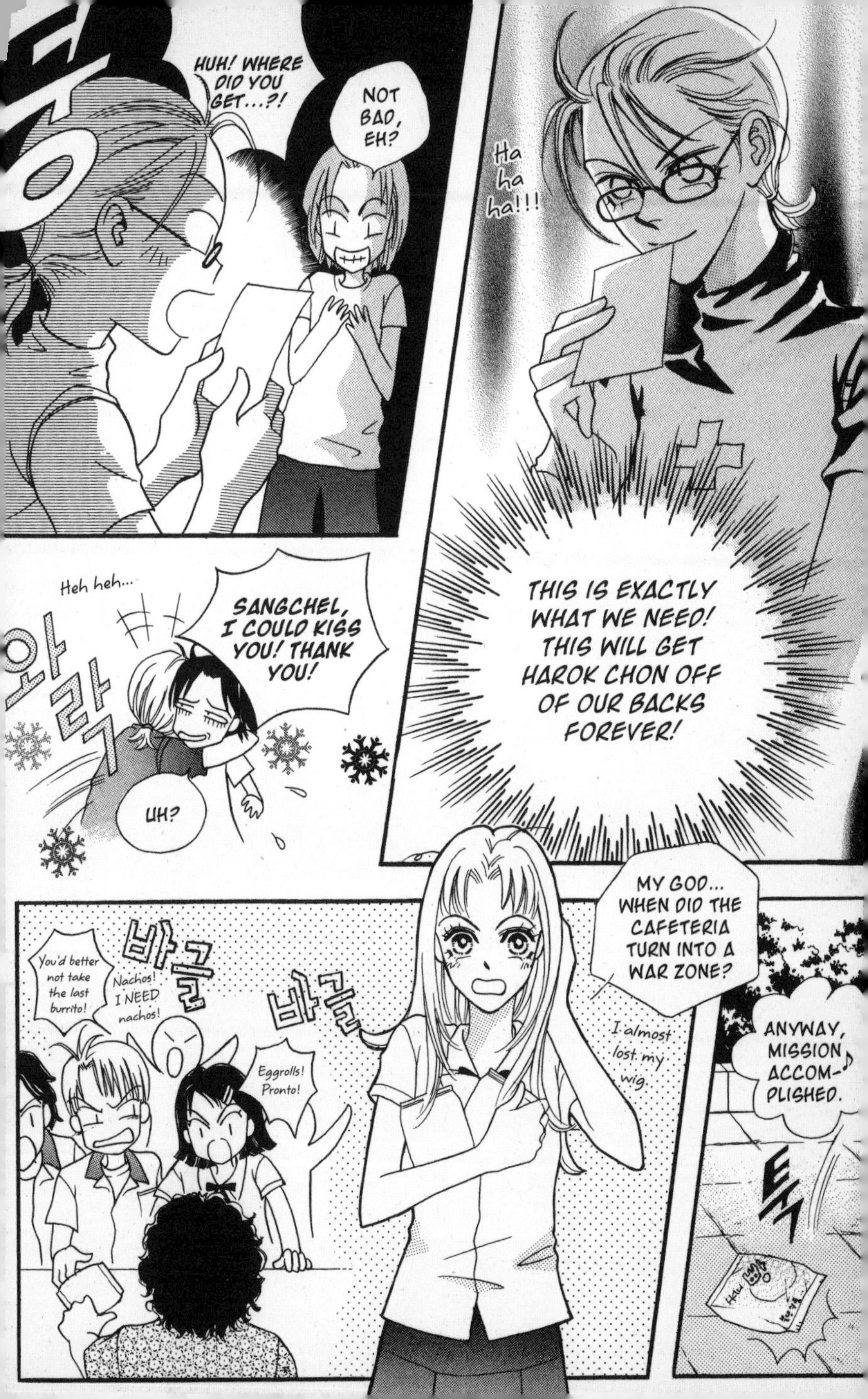
HUH! WHERE DID YOU GET...?!
NOT BAD, EH?
Heh heh...
SANGCHEL, I COULD KISS YOU! THANK YOU!
와락
UH?
Ha ha ha!!!
THIS IS EXACTLY WHAT WE NEED! THIS WILL GET HAROK CHON OFF OF OUR BACKS FOREVER!
You'd better not take the last burrito!
Nachos! I NEED nachos!
바글
바글
Eggrolls! Pronto!
MY GOD... WHEN DID THE CAFETERIA TURN INTO A WAR ZONE?
I almost lost my wig.
ANYWAY, MISSION ACCOM-PLISHED.

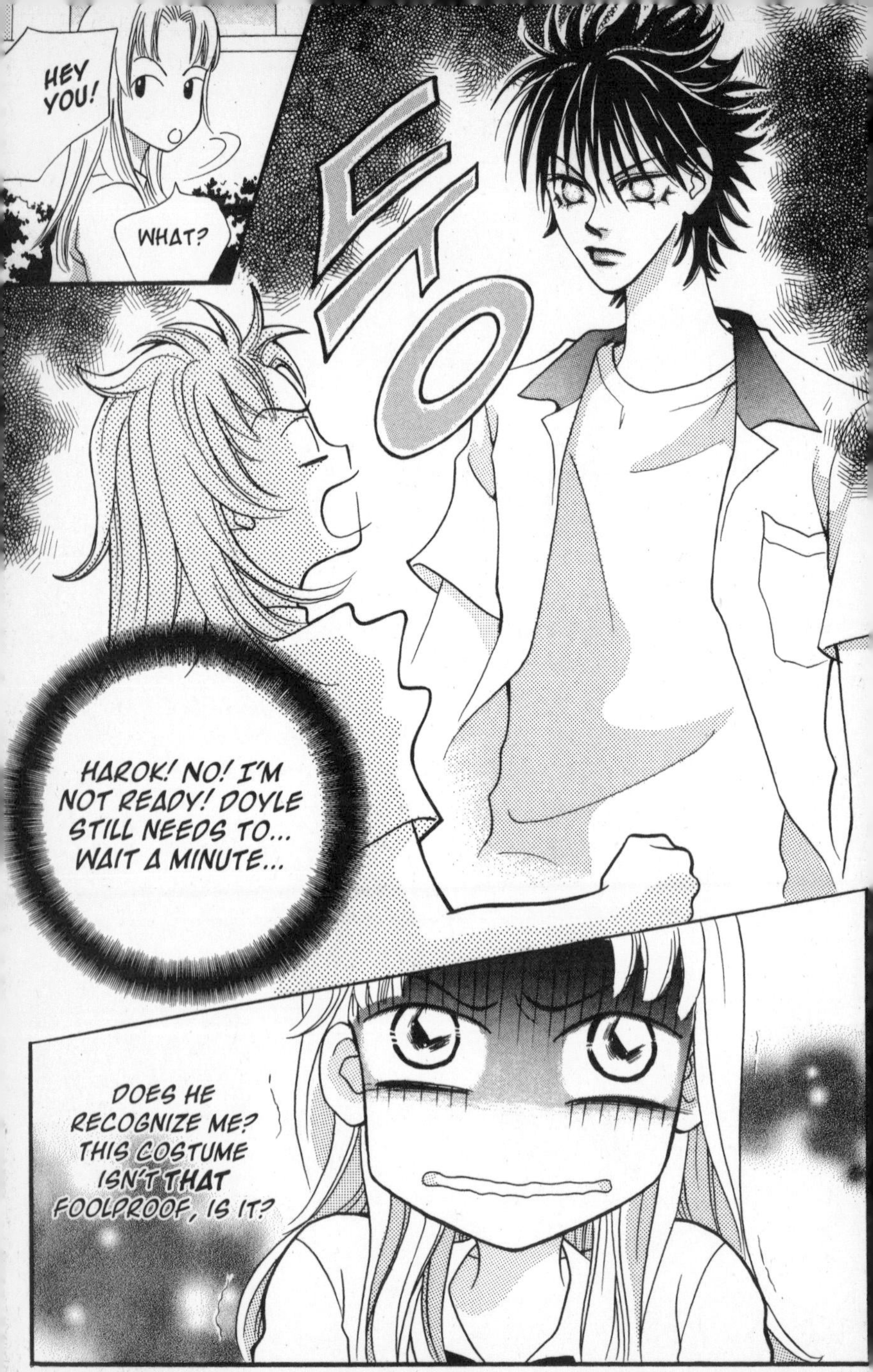
HEY YOU!
WHAT?
HAROK! NO! I'M NOT READY! DOYLE STILL NEEDS TO... WAIT A MINUTE...
DOES HE RECOGNIZE ME? THIS COSTUME ISN'T THAT FOOLPROOF, IS IT?

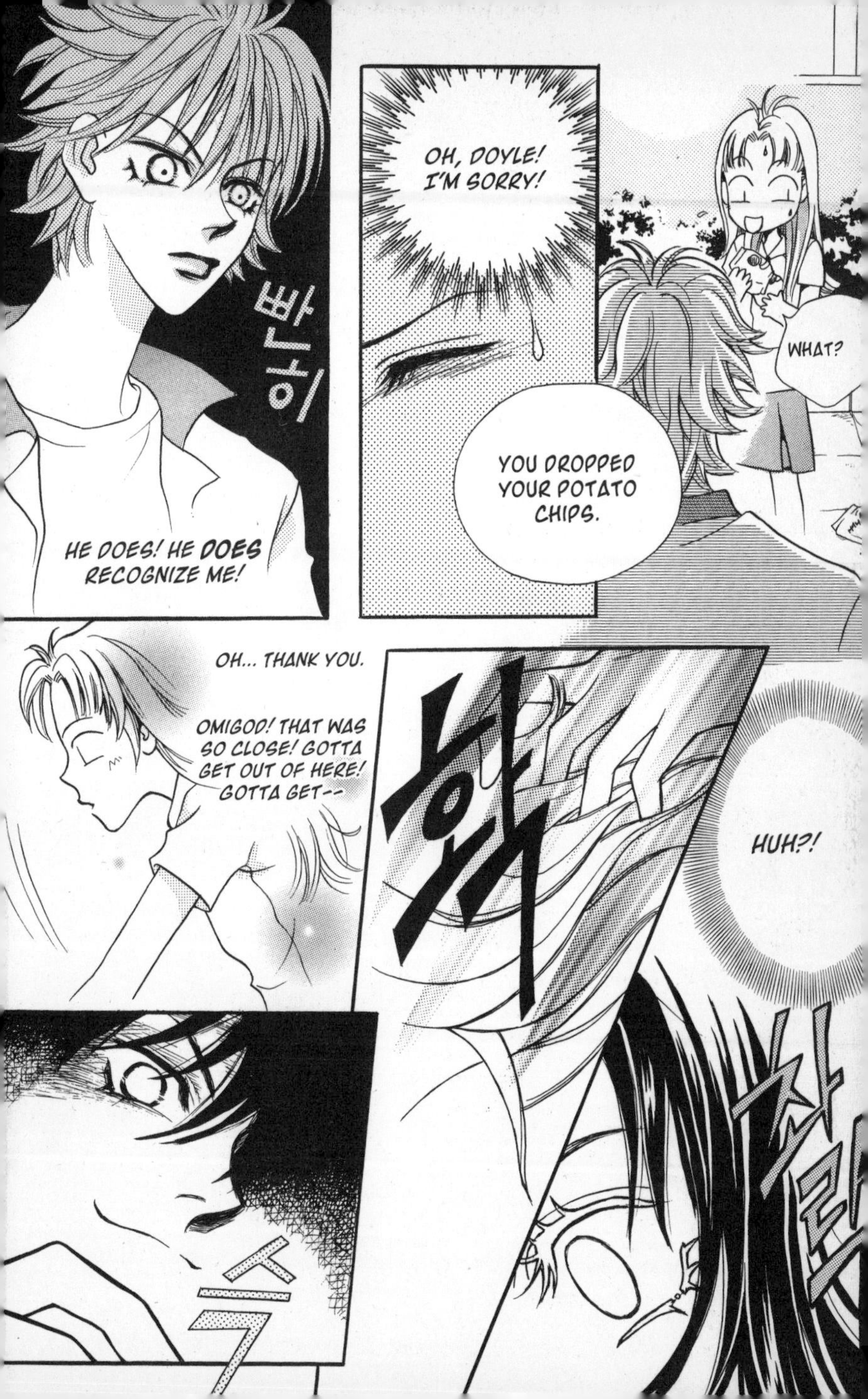
빤히
HE DOES! HE **DOES** RECOGNIZE ME!
OH, DOYLE! I'M SORRY!
WHAT?
YOU DROPPED YOUR POTATO CHIPS.
OH... THANK YOU.
OMIGOD! THAT WAS SO CLOSE! GOTTA GET OUT OF HERE! GOTTA GET--
헉
HUH?!

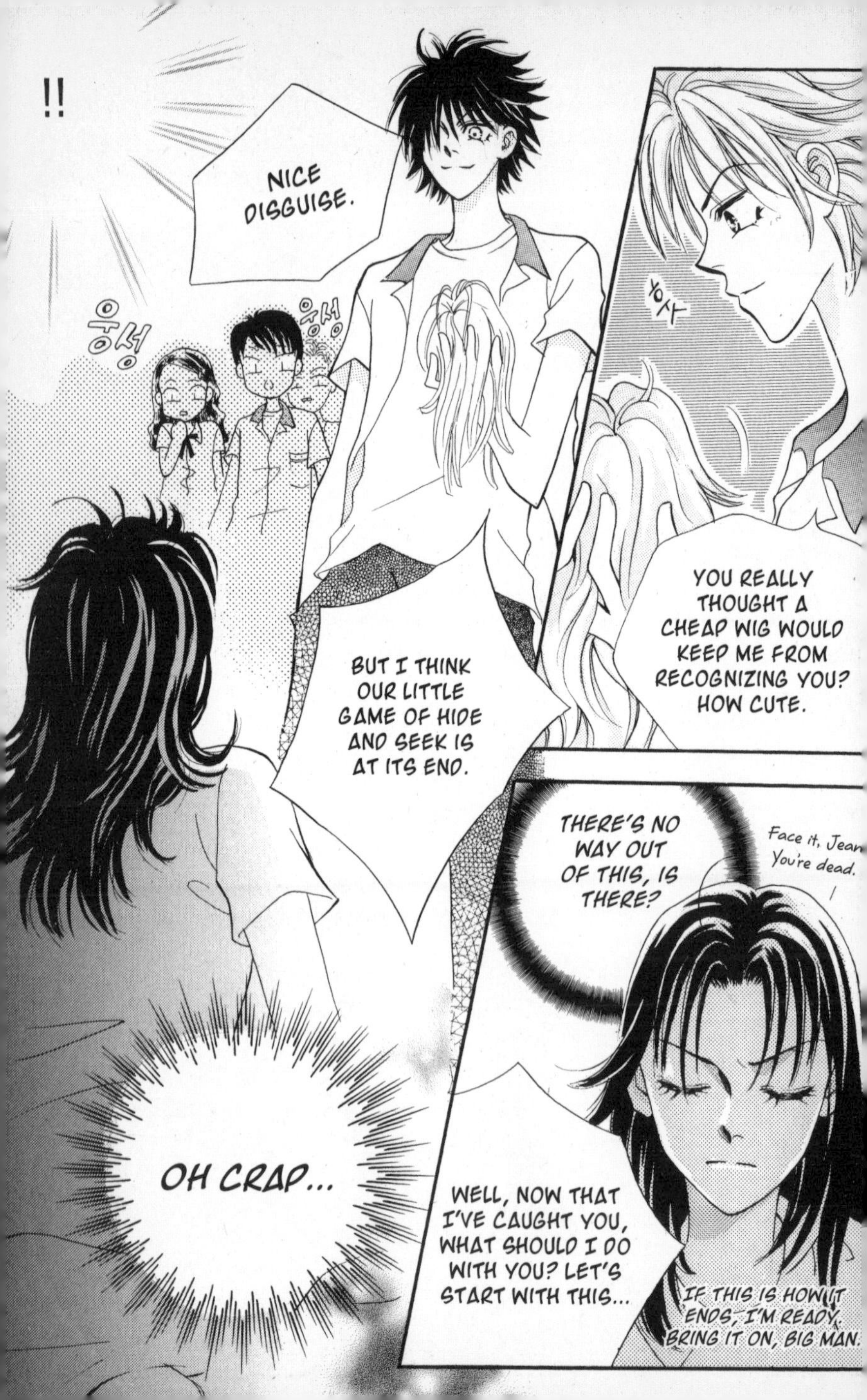
!!
NICE DISGUISE.
웅성
웅성
BUT I THINK OUR LITTLE GAME OF HIDE AND SEEK IS AT ITS END.
OH CRAP...
YOU REALLY THOUGHT A CHEAP WIG WOULD KEEP ME FROM RECOGNIZING YOU? HOW CUTE.
THERE'S NO WAY OUT OF THIS, IS THERE?
Face it, Jean You're dead.
WELL, NOW THAT I'VE CAUGHT YOU, WHAT SHOULD I DO WITH YOU? LET'S START WITH THIS...
IF THIS IS HOW IT ENDS, I'M READY. BRING IT ON, BIG MAN.

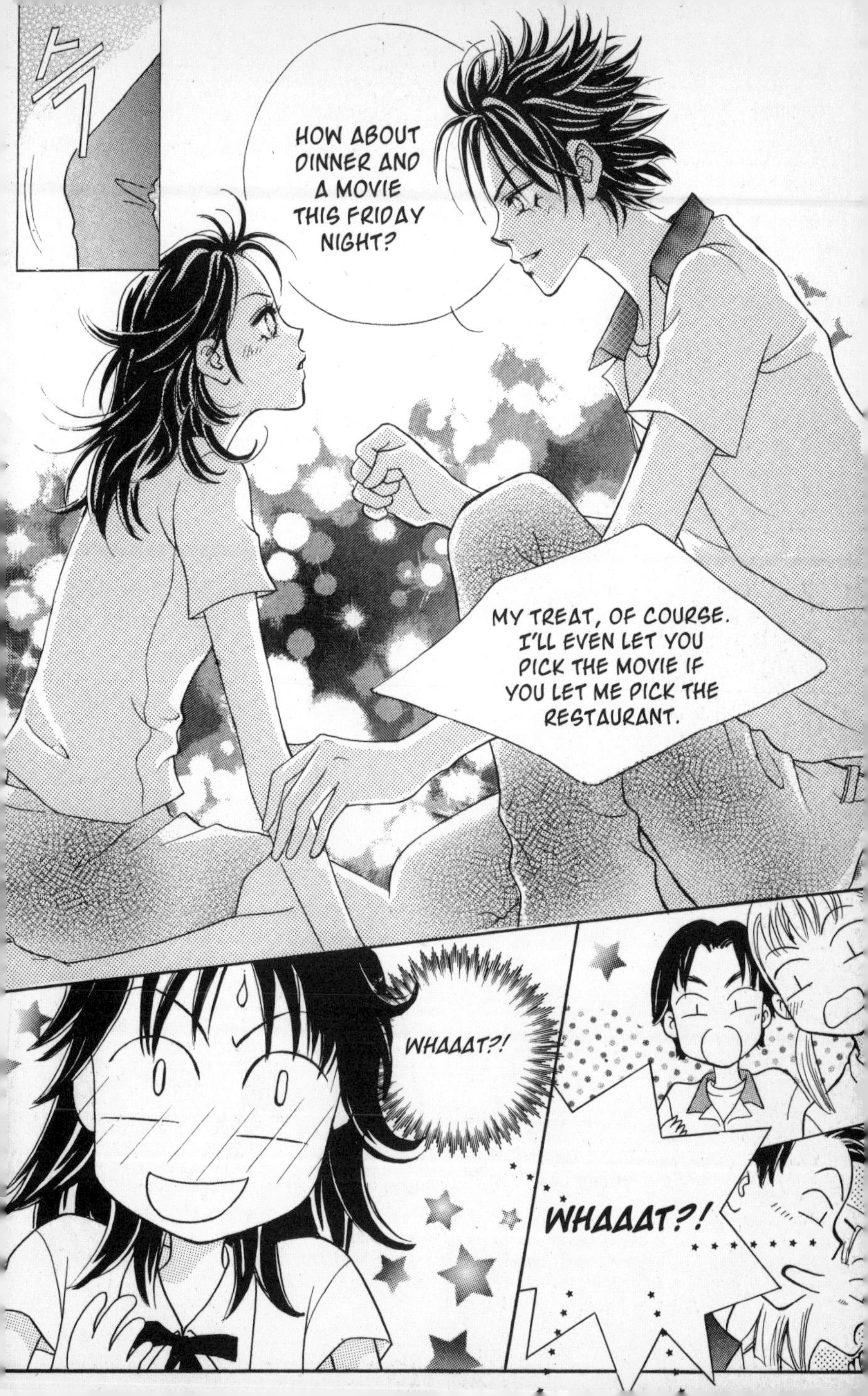
HOW ABOUT DINNER AND A MOVIE THIS FRIDAY NIGHT?
MY TREAT, OF COURSE. I'LL EVEN LET YOU PICK THE MOVIE IF YOU LET ME PICK THE RESTAURANT.
WHAAAT?!
WHAAAT?!

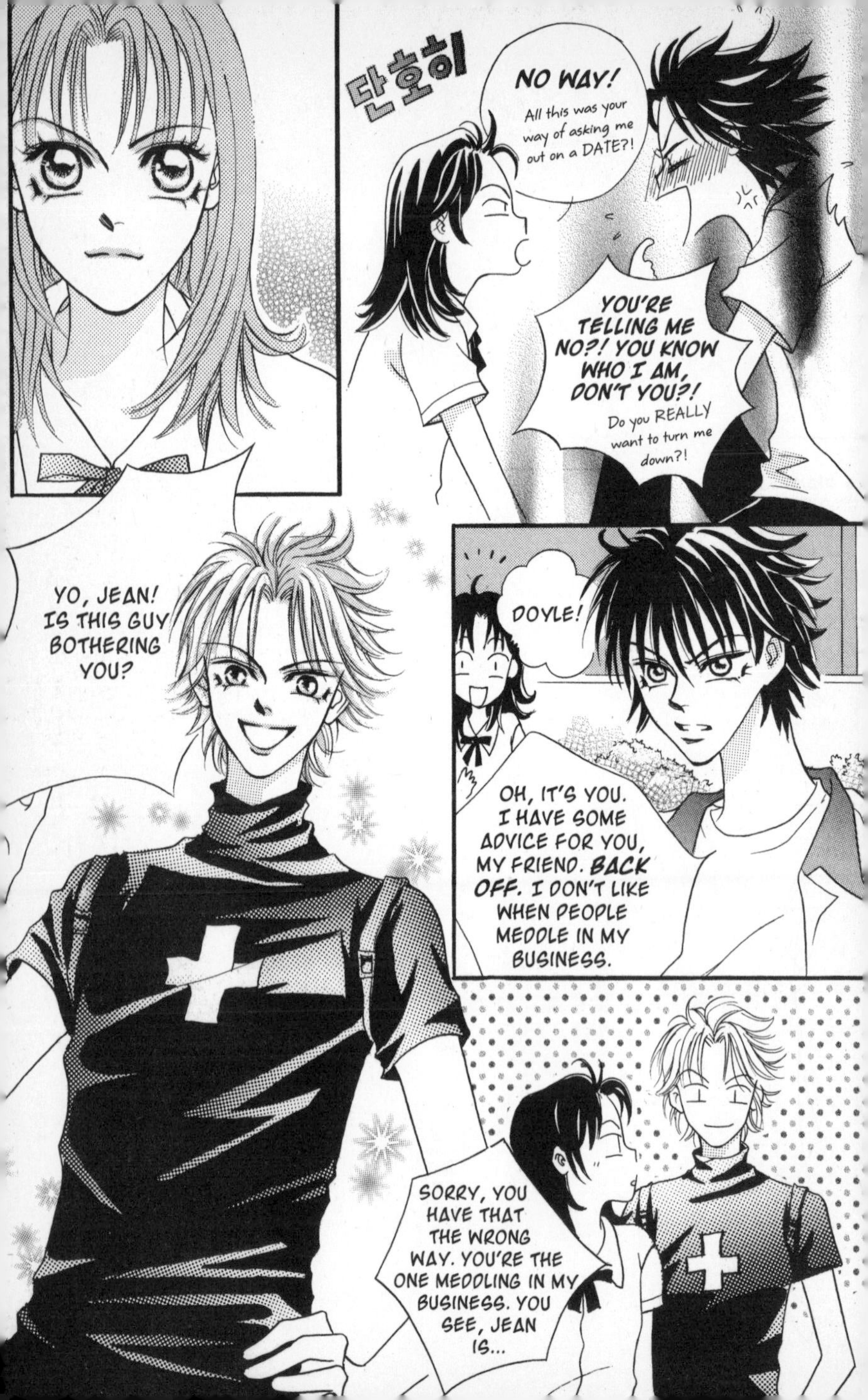

단호히
NO WAY!
All this was your way of asking me out on a DATE?!
YOU'RE TELLING ME NO?! YOU KNOW WHO I AM, DON'T YOU?!
Do you REALLY want to turn me down?!
YO, JEAN! IS THIS GUY BOTHERING YOU?
DOYLE!
OH, IT'S YOU. I HAVE SOME ADVICE FOR YOU, MY FRIEND. BACK OFF. I DON'T LIKE WHEN PEOPLE MEDDLE IN MY BUSINESS.
SORRY, YOU HAVE THAT THE WRONG WAY. YOU'RE THE ONE MEDDLING IN MY BUSINESS. YOU SEE, JEAN IS...

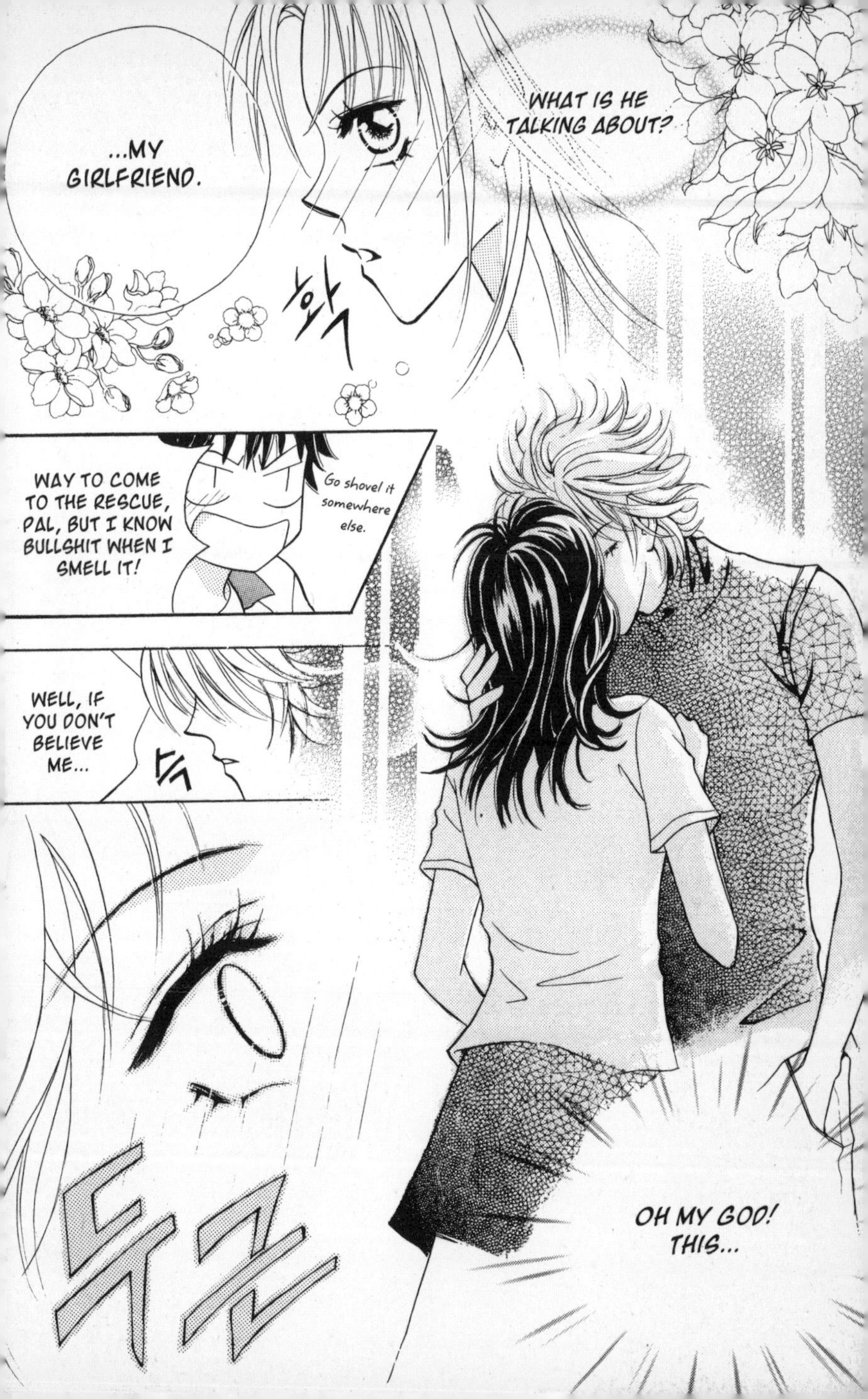
...MY GIRLFRIEND.
WHAT IS HE TALKING ABOUT?
WAY TO COME TO THE RESCUE, PAL, BUT I KNOW BULLSHIT WHEN I SMELL IT!
Go shovel it somewhere else.
WELL, IF YOU DON'T BELIEVE ME...
OH MY GOD! THIS...

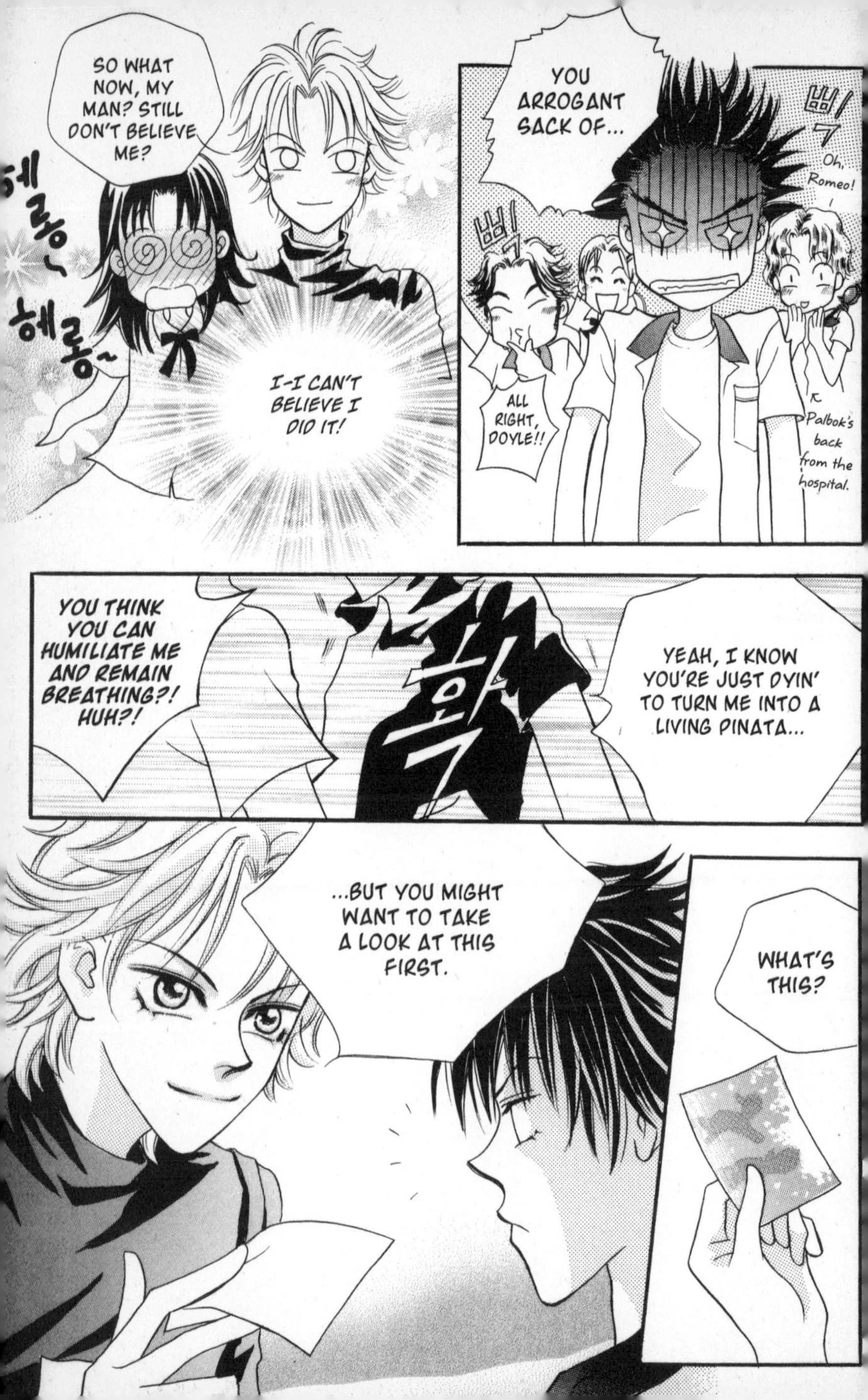
SO WHAT NOW, MY MAN? STILL DON'T BELIEVE ME?
헤롱~
헤롱~
I-I CAN'T BELIEVE I DID IT!
YOU ARROGANT SACK OF...
Oh, Romeo!
ALL RIGHT, DOYLE!!
Palbok's back from the hospital.
YOU THINK YOU CAN HUMILIATE ME AND REMAIN BREATHING?! HUH?!
확
YEAH, I KNOW YOU'RE JUST DYIN' TO TURN ME INTO A LIVING PINATA...
...BUT YOU MIGHT WANT TO TAKE A LOOK AT THIS FIRST.
WHAT'S THIS?

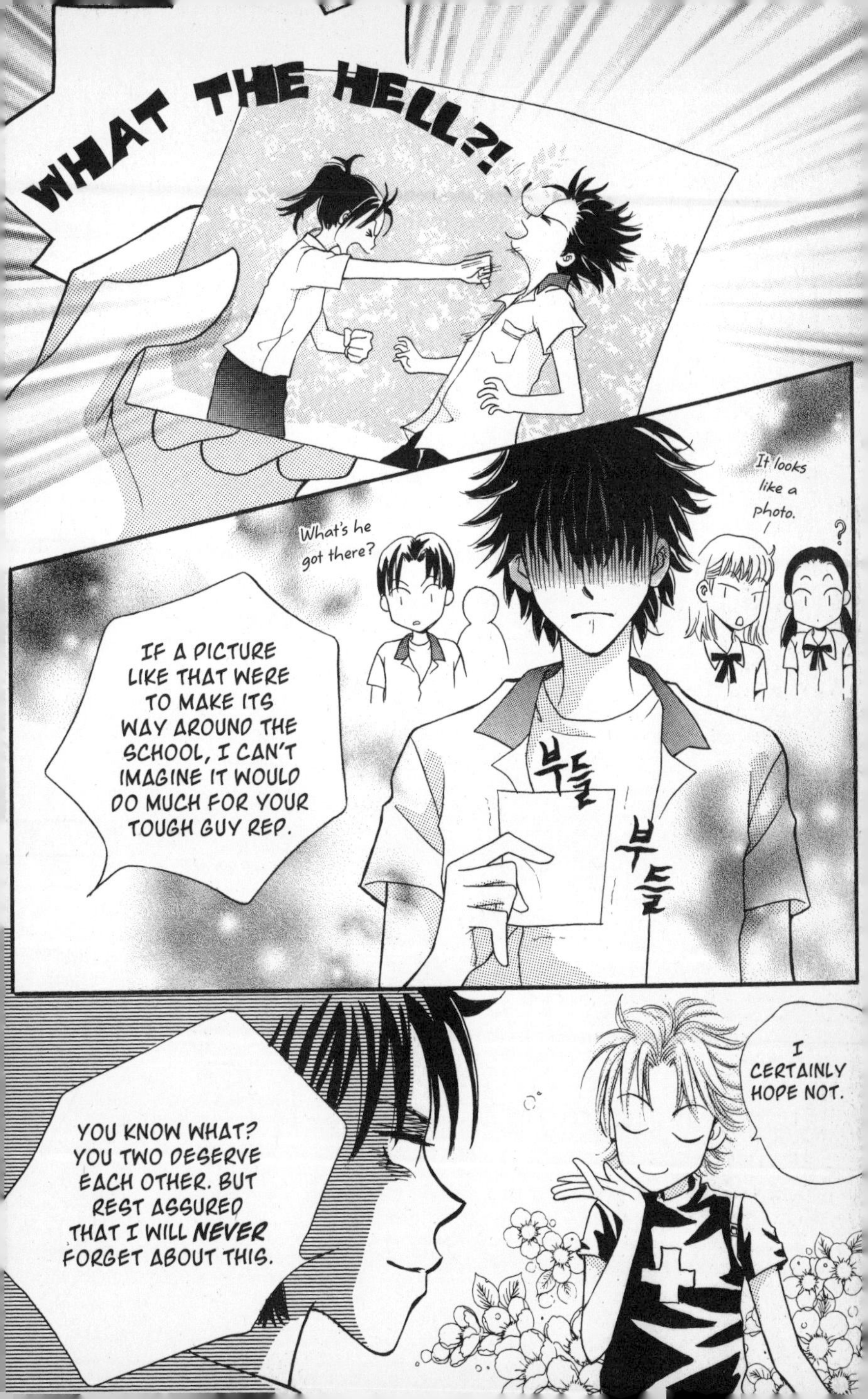
WHAT THE HELL?!
What's he got there?
IF A PICTURE LIKE THAT WERE TO MAKE ITS WAY AROUND THE SCHOOL, I CAN'T IMAGINE IT WOULD DO MUCH FOR YOUR TOUGH GUY REP.
부들
부들
It looks like a photo.
?
YOU KNOW WHAT? YOU TWO DESERVE EACH OTHER. BUT REST ASSURED THAT I WILL *NEVER* FORGET ABOUT THIS.
I CERTAINLY HOPE NOT.

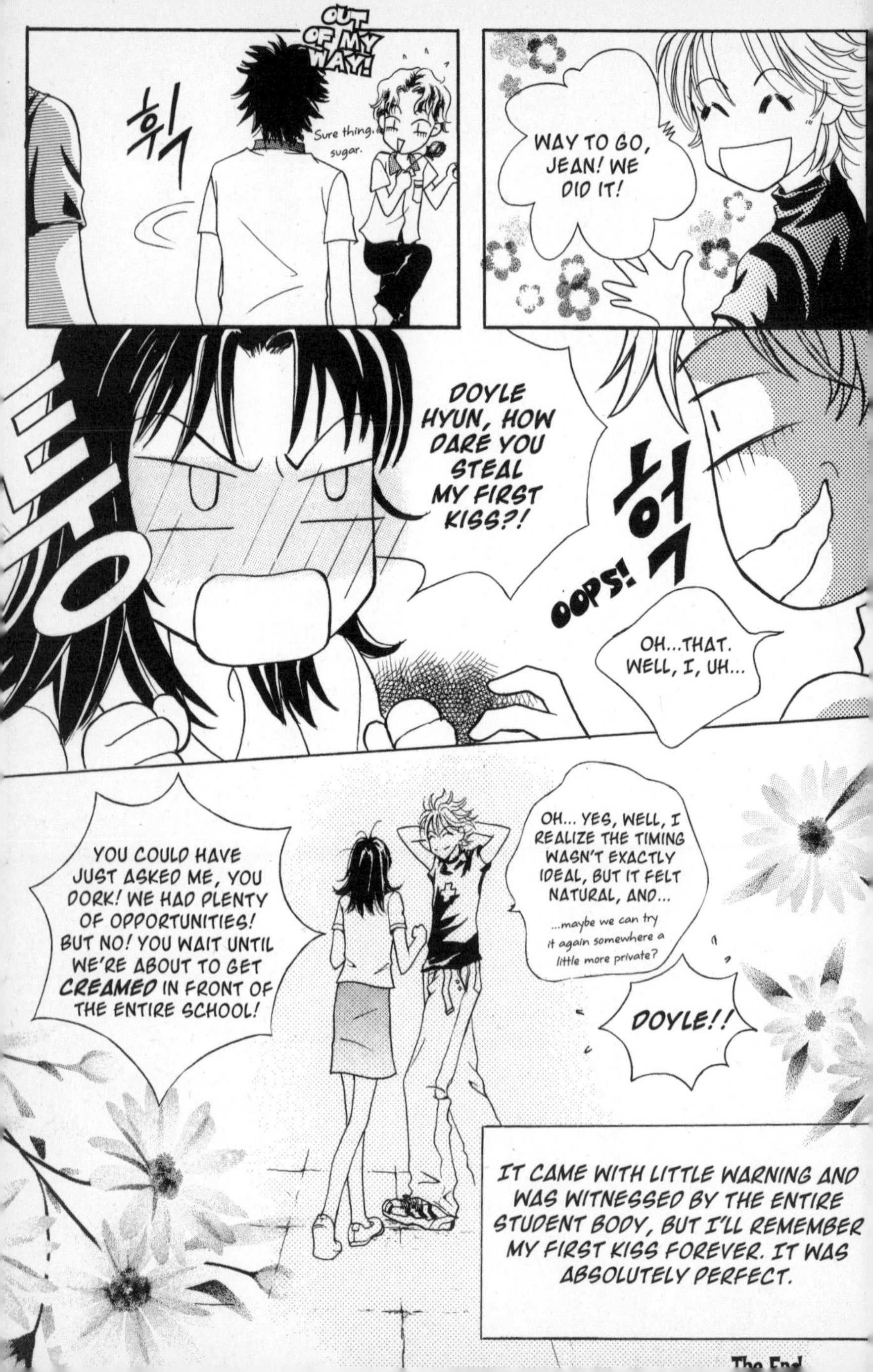
OUT OF MY WAY!
휙
Sure thing, sugar.
WAY TO GO, JEAN! WE DID IT!
DOYLE HYUN, HOW DARE YOU STEAL MY FIRST KISS?!
헉
OOPS!
OH...THAT. WELL, I, UH...
YOU COULD HAVE JUST ASKED ME, YOU DORK! WE HAD PLENTY OF OPPORTUNITIES! BUT NO! YOU WAIT UNTIL WE'RE ABOUT TO GET CREAMED IN FRONT OF THE ENTIRE SCHOOL!
OH... YES, WELL, I REALIZE THE TIMING WASN'T EXACTLY IDEAL, BUT IT FELT NATURAL, AND...
...maybe we can try it again somewhere a little more private?
DOYLE!!
IT CAME WITH LITTLE WARNING AND WAS WITNESSED BY THE ENTIRE STUDENT BODY, BUT I'LL REMEMBER MY FIRST KISS FOREVER. IT WAS ABSOLUTELY PERFECT.
The End

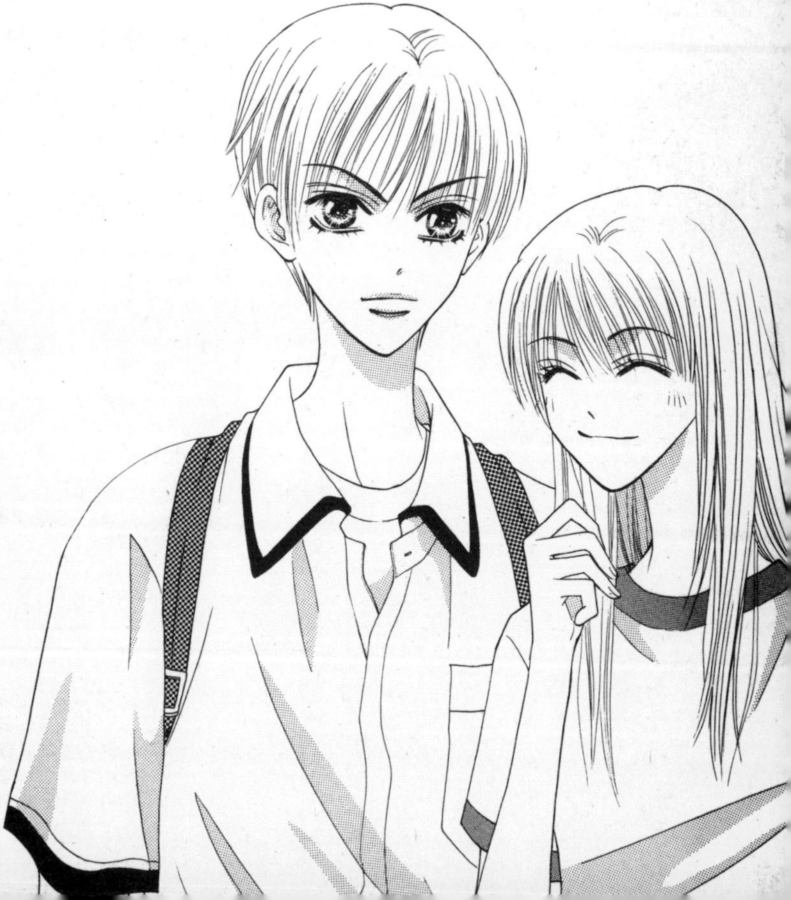

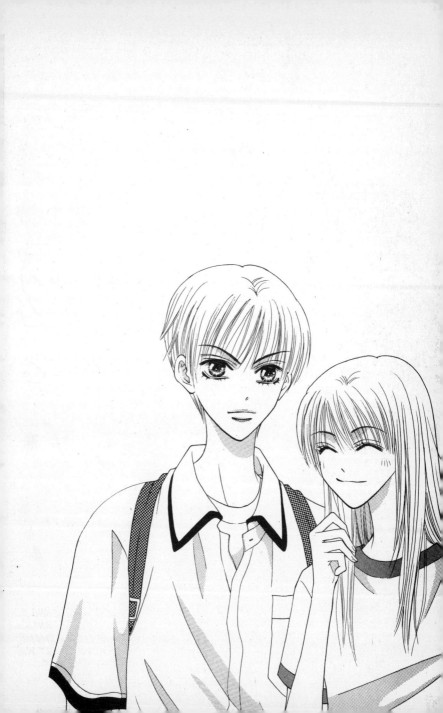

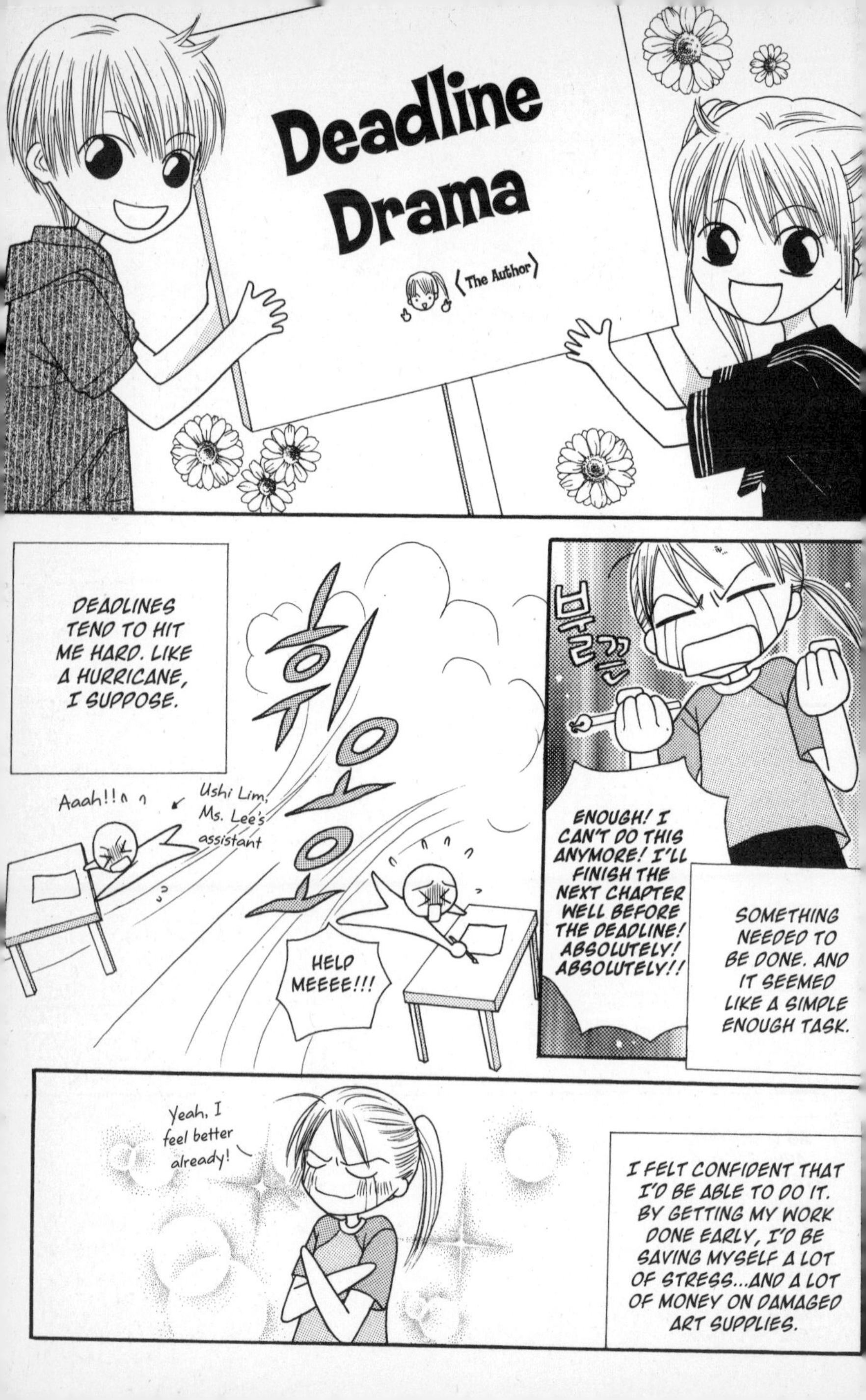
Deadline Drama
〈The Author〉
DEADLINES TEND TO HIT ME HARD. LIKE A HURRICANE, I SUPPOSE.
Aaah!!
Ushi Lim, Ms. Lee's assistant
HELP MEEEE!!!
ENOUGH! I CAN'T DO THIS ANYMORE! I'LL FINISH THE NEXT CHAPTER WELL BEFORE THE DEADLINE! ABSOLUTELY! ABSOLUTELY!!
SOMETHING NEEDED TO BE DONE. AND IT SEEMED LIKE A SIMPLE ENOUGH TASK.
Yeah, I feel better already!
I FELT CONFIDENT THAT I'D BE ABLE TO DO IT. BY GETTING MY WORK DONE EARLY, I'D BE SAVING MYSELF A LOT OF STRESS...AND A LOT OF MONEY ON DAMAGED ART SUPPLIES.

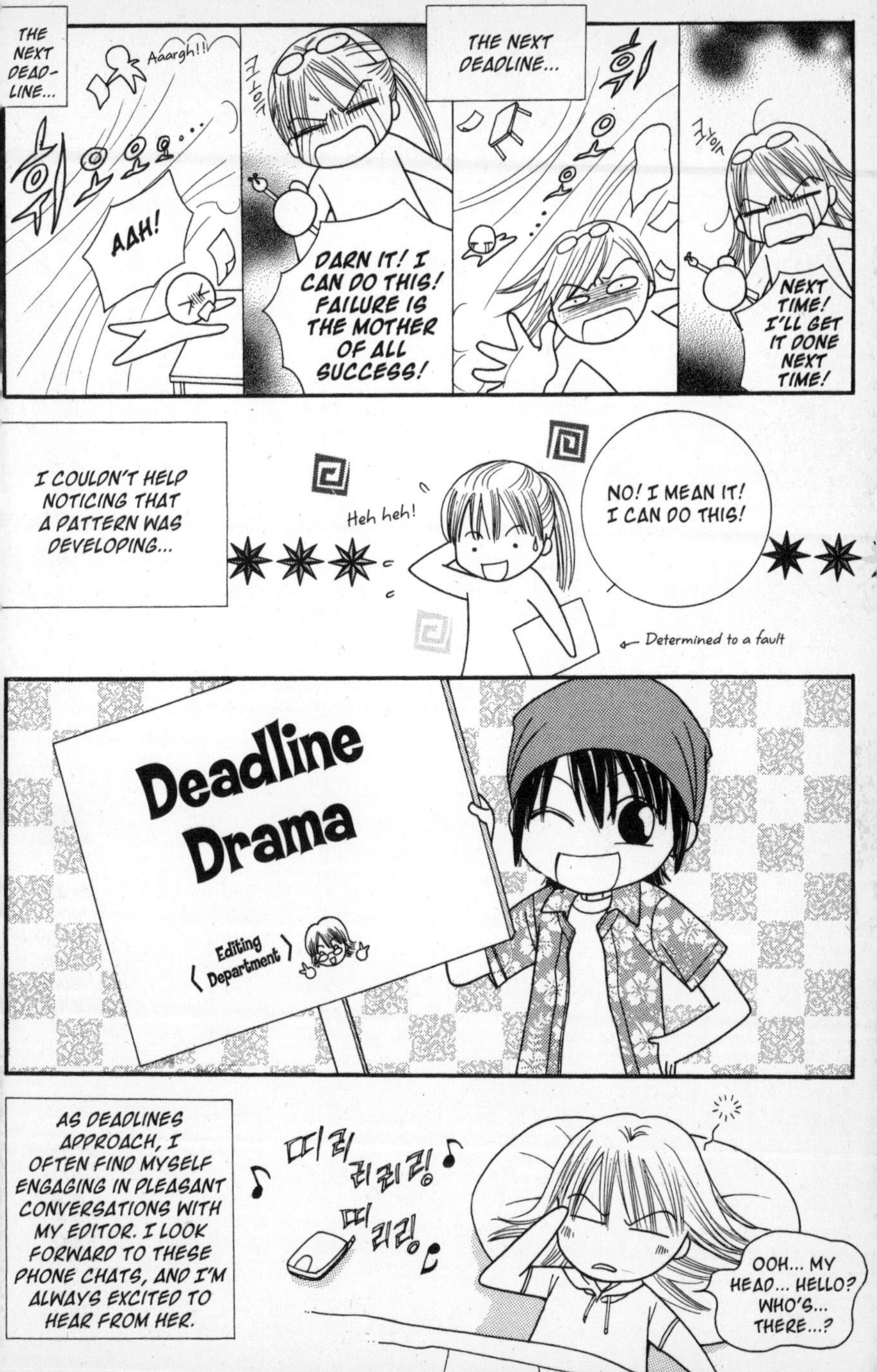

THE NEXT DEADLINE...
Aaargh!!
AAH!
DARN IT! I CAN DO THIS! FAILURE IS THE MOTHER OF ALL SUCCESS!
THE NEXT DEADLINE...
NEXT TIME! I'LL GET IT DONE NEXT TIME!
I COULDN'T HELP NOTICING THAT A PATTERN WAS DEVELOPING...
Heh heh!
NO! I MEAN IT! I CAN DO THIS!
Determined to a fault
Deadline Drama
Editing Department
AS DEADLINES APPROACH, I OFTEN FIND MYSELF ENGAGING IN PLEASANT CONVERSATIONS WITH MY EDITOR. I LOOK FORWARD TO THESE PHONE CHATS, AND I'M ALWAYS EXCITED TO HEAR FROM HER.
띠리리리링
띠리링
OOH... MY HEAD... HELLO? WHO'S... THERE...?

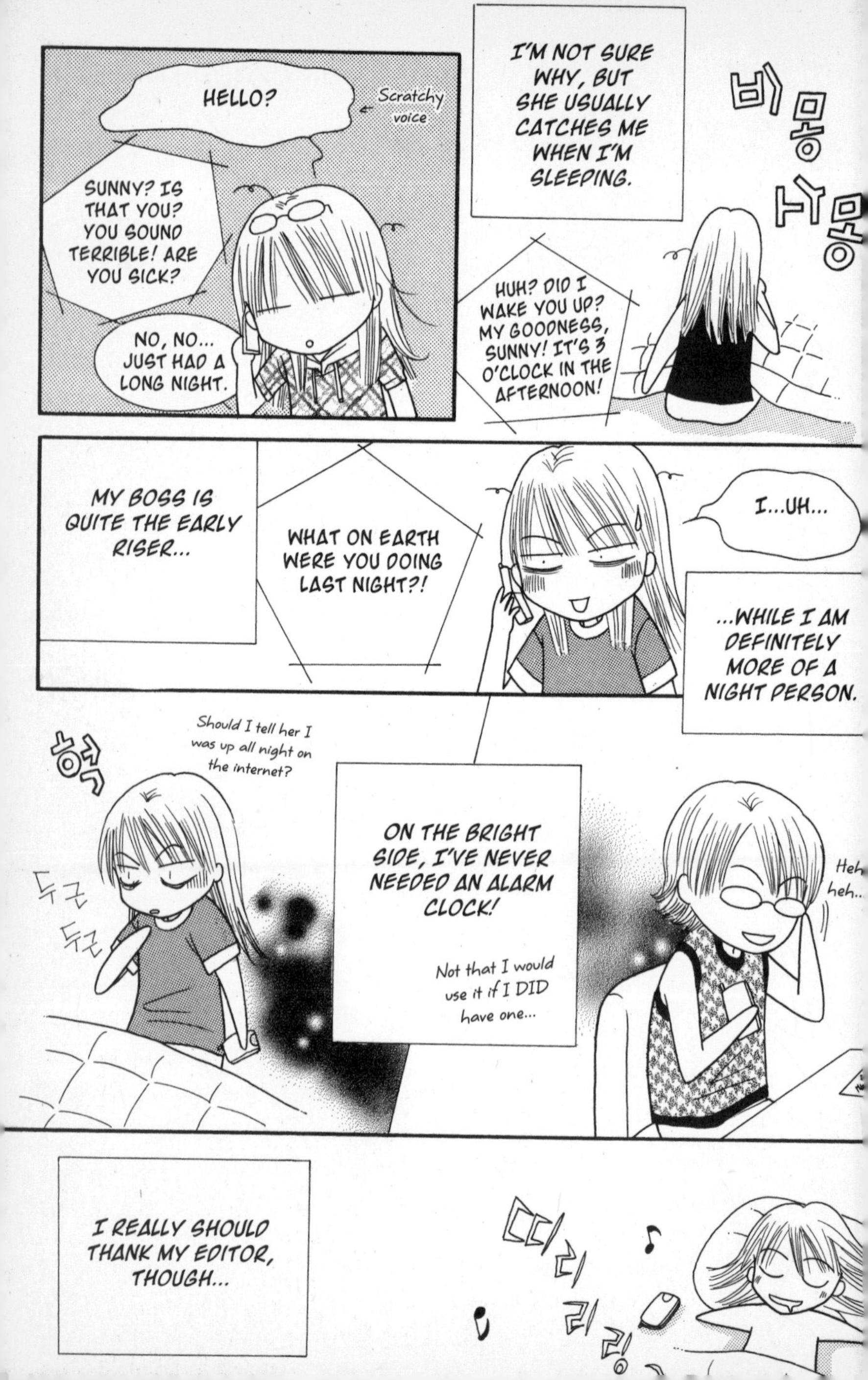
HELLO?
Scratchy voice
SUNNY? IS THAT YOU? YOU SOUND TERRIBLE! ARE YOU SICK?
NO, NO... JUST HAD A LONG NIGHT.
I'M NOT SURE WHY, BUT SHE USUALLY CATCHES ME WHEN I'M SLEEPING.
비몽사몽
HUH? DID I WAKE YOU UP? MY GOODNESS, SUNNY! IT'S 3 O'CLOCK IN THE AFTERNOON!
MY BOSS IS QUITE THE EARLY RISER...
WHAT ON EARTH WERE YOU DOING LAST NIGHT?!
I...UH...
...WHILE I AM DEFINITELY MORE OF A NIGHT PERSON.
Should I tell her I was up all night on the internet?
헉
두근 두근
ON THE BRIGHT SIDE, I'VE NEVER NEEDED AN ALARM CLOCK!
Not that I would use it if I DID have one...
Heh heh...
I REALLY SHOULD THANK MY EDITOR, THOUGH...
띠리리링

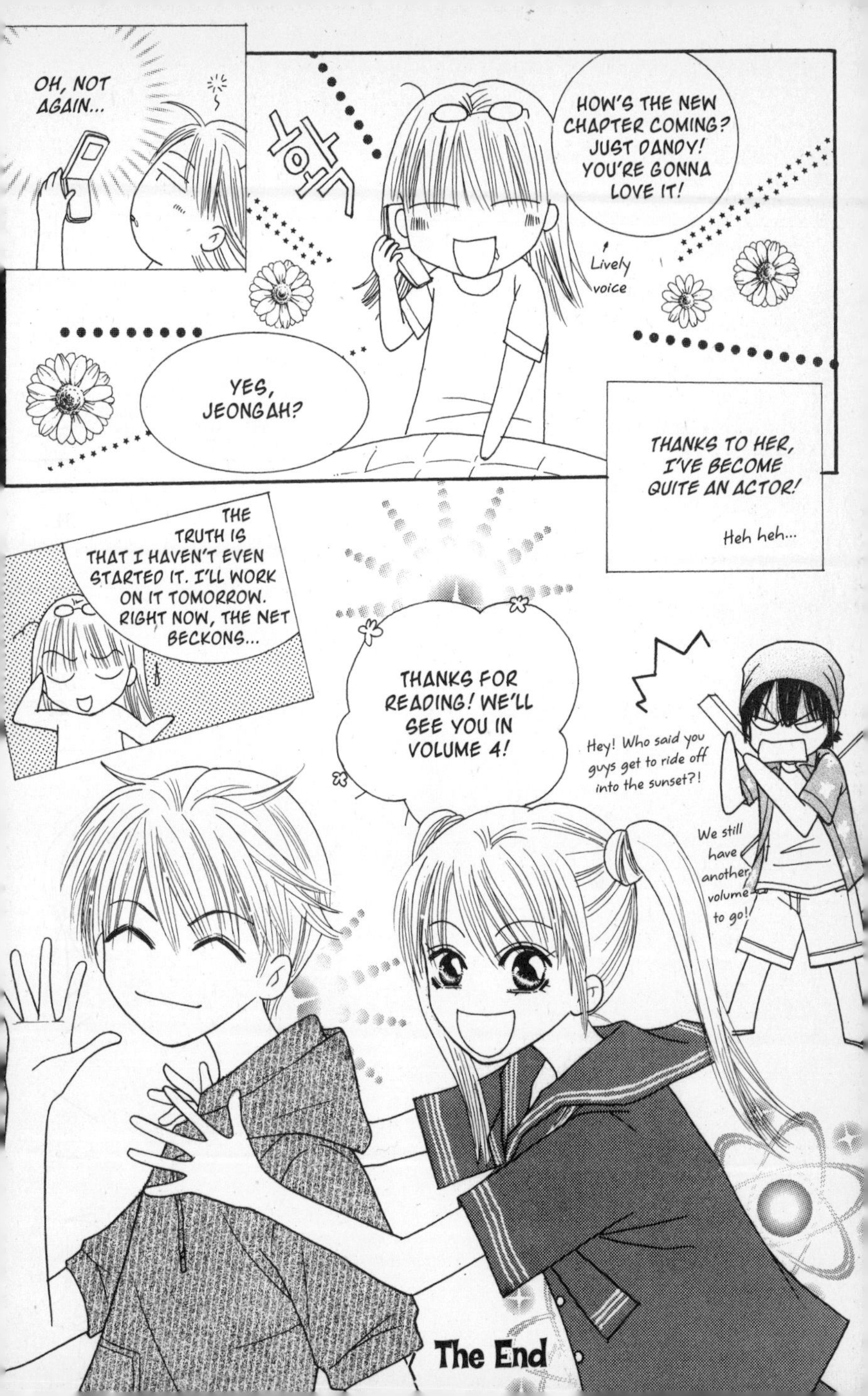
OH, NOT AGAIN...
YES, JEONGAH?
HOW'S THE NEW CHAPTER COMING? JUST DANDY! YOU'RE GONNA LOVE IT!
Lively voice
THANKS TO HER, I'VE BECOME QUITE AN ACTOR!
Heh heh...
THE TRUTH IS THAT I HAVEN'T EVEN STARTED IT. I'LL WORK ON IT TOMORROW. RIGHT NOW, THE NET BECKONS...
THANKS FOR READING! WE'LL SEE YOU IN VOLUME 4!
Hey! Who said you guys get to ride off into the sunset?!
We still have another volume to go!
The End

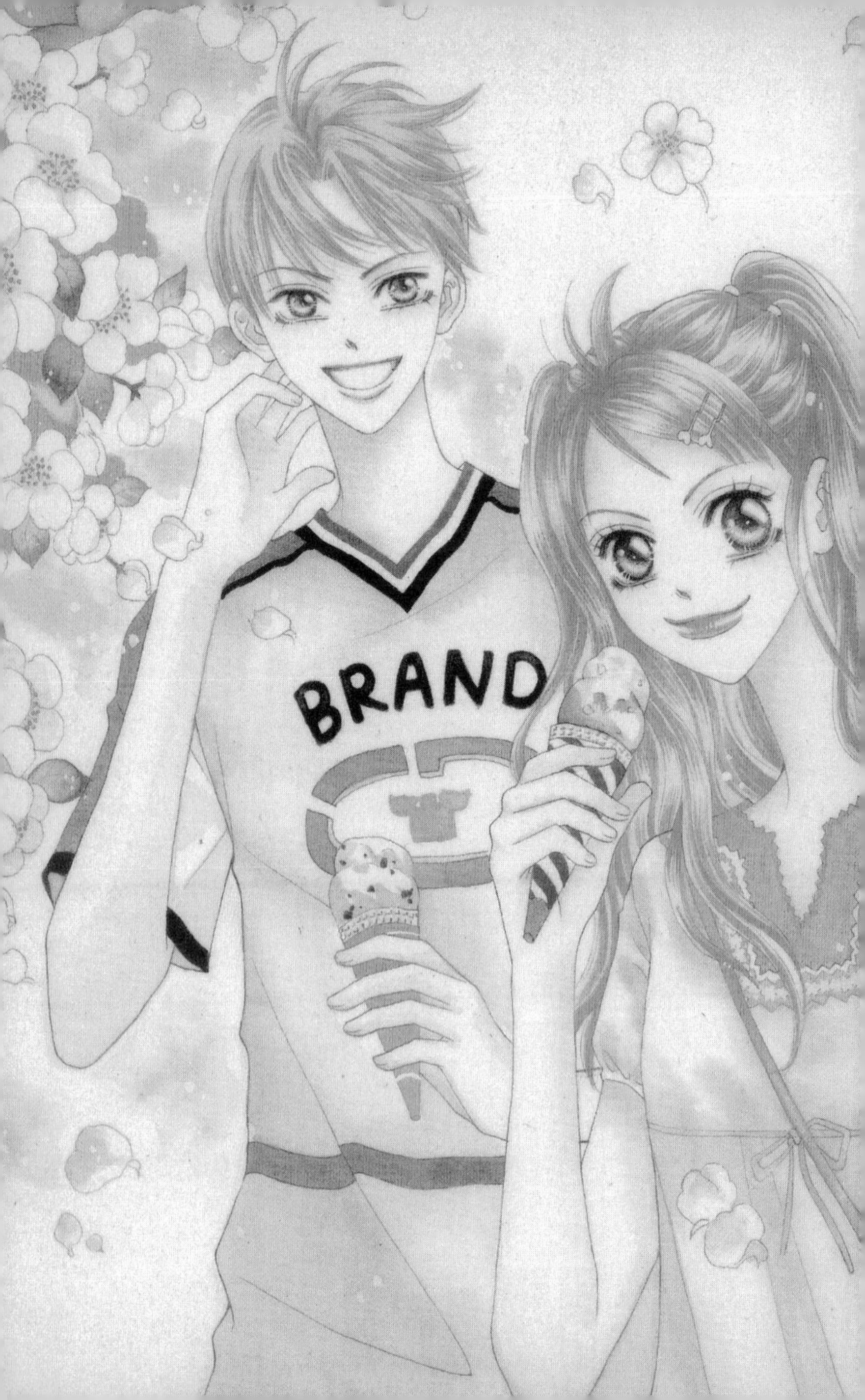
BRAND

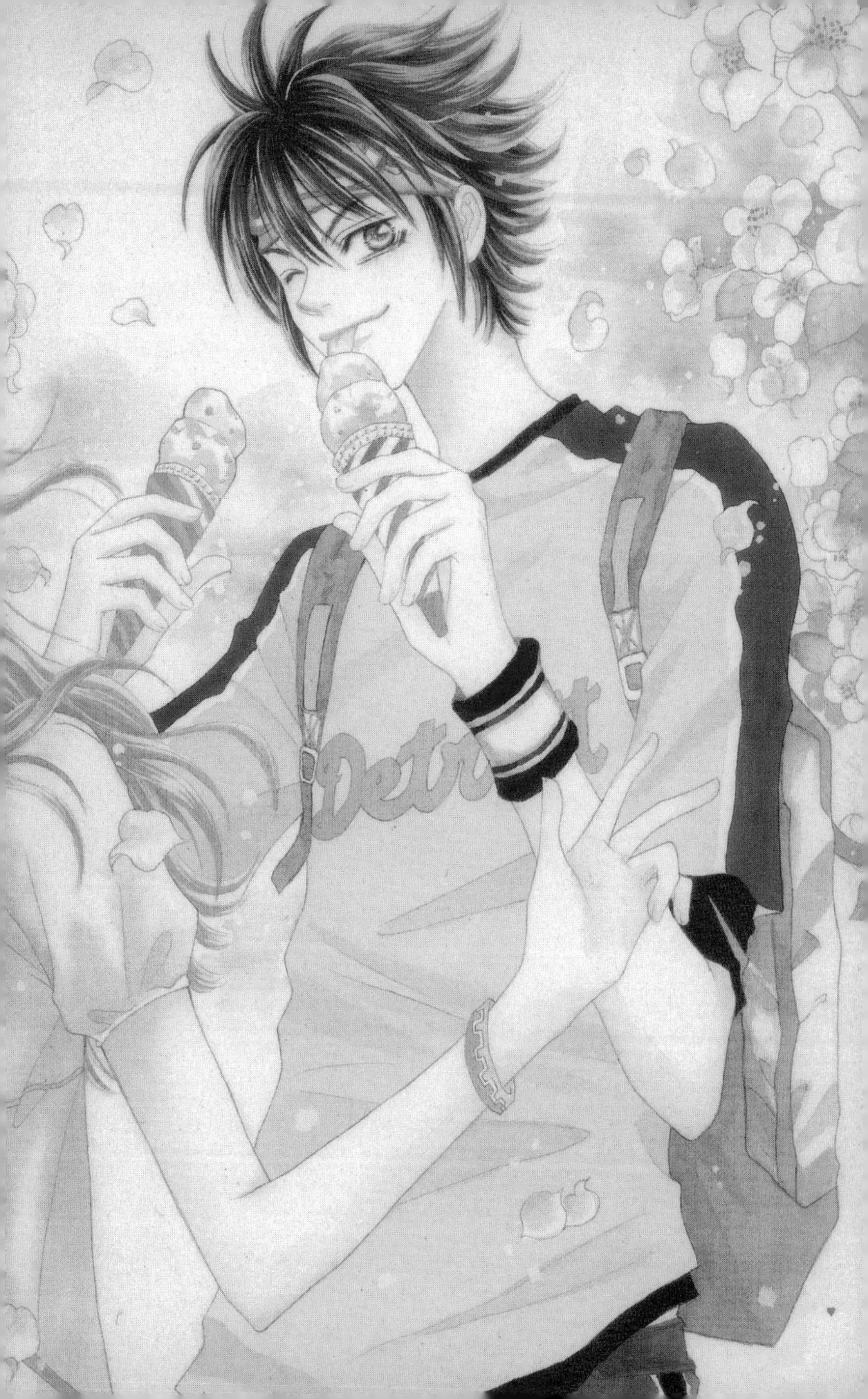

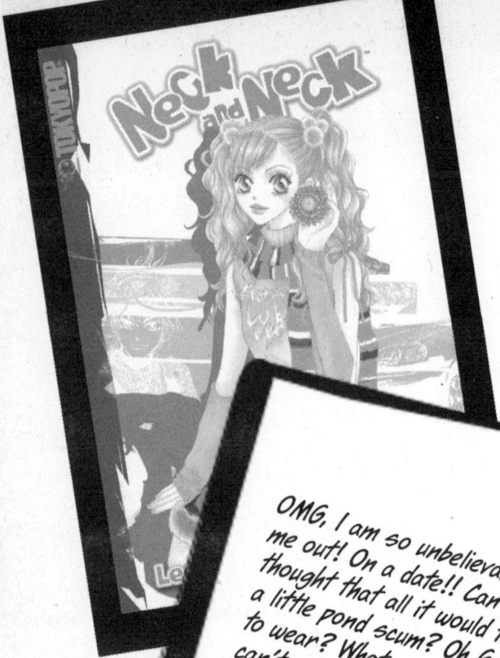
TOKYOPOP
Neck and Neck

Neck and Neck Volume 4 Coming in September 2005

OMG, I am so unbelievably happy!!! Eugene asked me out! On a date!! Can you believe it?! Who'd have thought that all it would take to bring us together was a little pond scum? Oh God, oh God! What am I going to wear? What are we going to see? I'm so excited, I can't even think straight!

Heh, stupid Shihu. He thought he could screw things up for us. I really don't know what that guy's damage is. I wouldn't be surprised to find out that he was somehow responsible for my afternoon swim. He probably paid some girl to push me into the pond. (I'd imagine Shihu would have to pay a girl to do anything!)

He shouldn't have done it. Dad's really angry, and people get hurt when Dad gets angry. And I don't want people to get hurt here. Not even Shihu.

Huh... Why should I care what happens to Shihu? His little stunts have landed me in the infirmary. He probably deserves a little pain. I should be eager to see him suffer...but I'm not. In fact, I'm actually a little worried.

That's weird.

TOKYOPOP SHOP

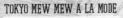

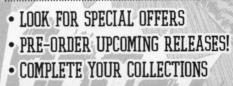

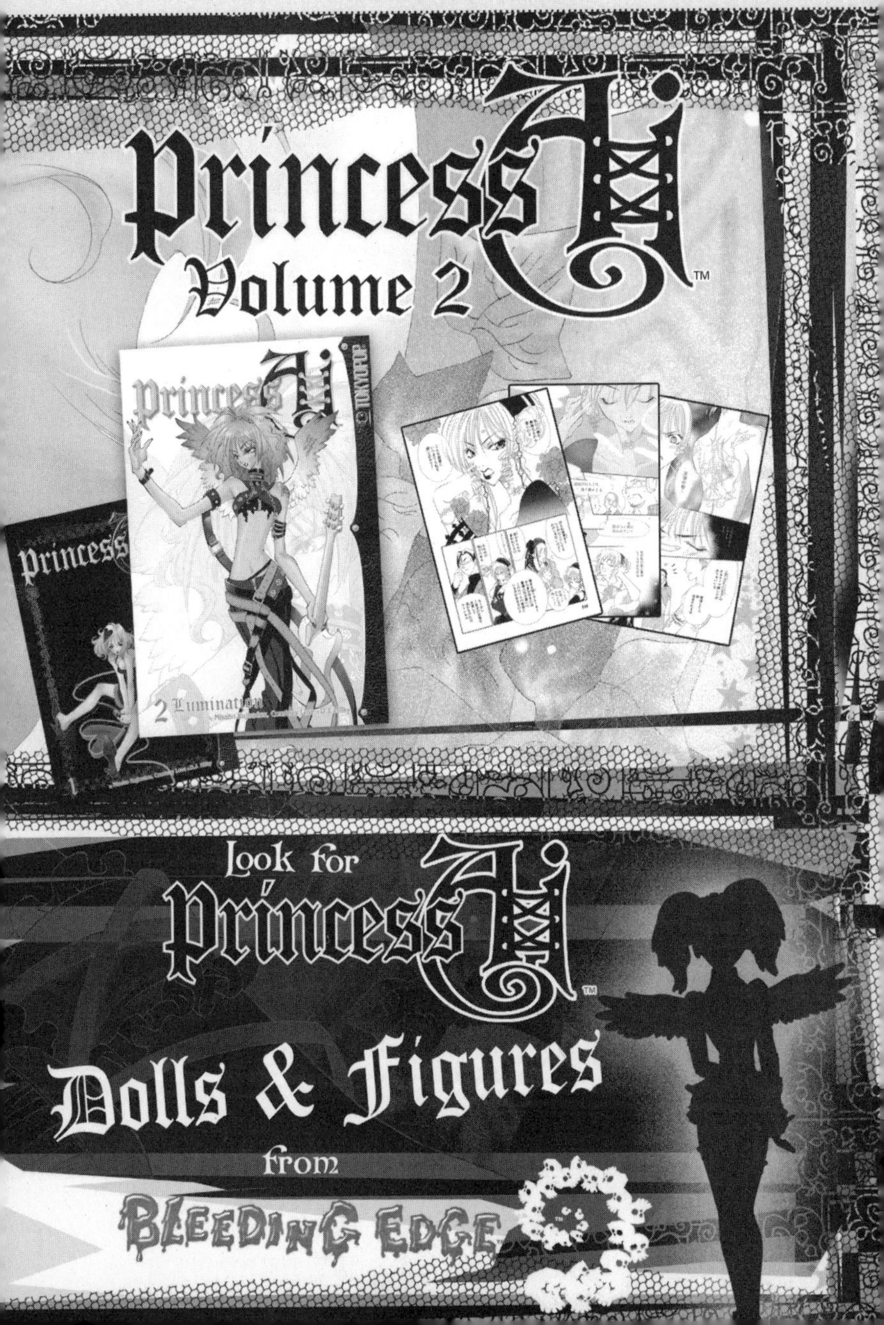
Princess Ai™
Volume 2
Princess Ai
TOKYOPOP
2 Lumination
Look for Princess Ai™
Dolls & Figures
from
BLEEDING EDGE

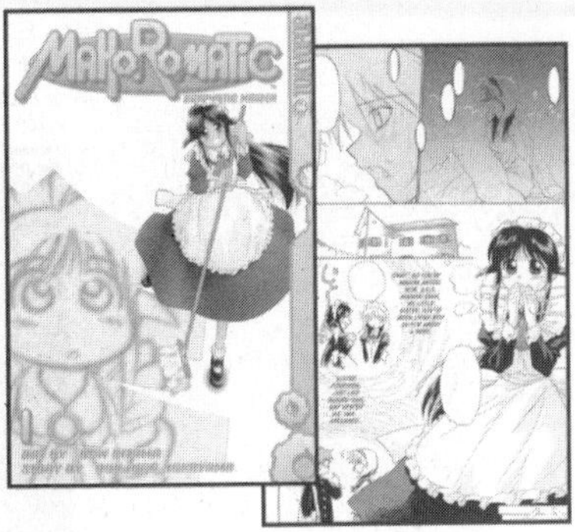

BY BUNJURO NAKAYAMA AND BOW DITAMA

MAHOROMATIC: AUTOMATIC MAIDEN

Mahoro is a sweet, cute, female battle android who decides to go from mopping up alien invaders to mopping up after Suguru Misato, a teenaged orphan boy... and hilarity most definitely ensues. This series has great art and a slick story that easily switches from truly funny to downright heartwarming...but always with a large shadow looming over it. You see, only Mahoro knows that her days are quite literally numbered, and the end of each chapter lets you know exactly how much—or how little—time she has left!

~Rob Tokar, Sr. Editor

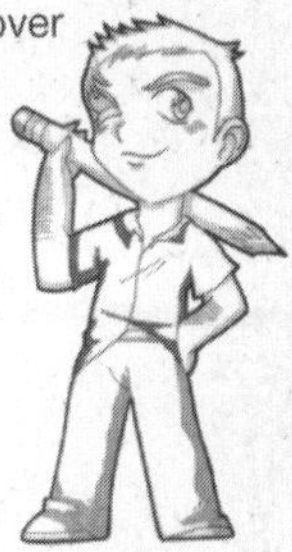

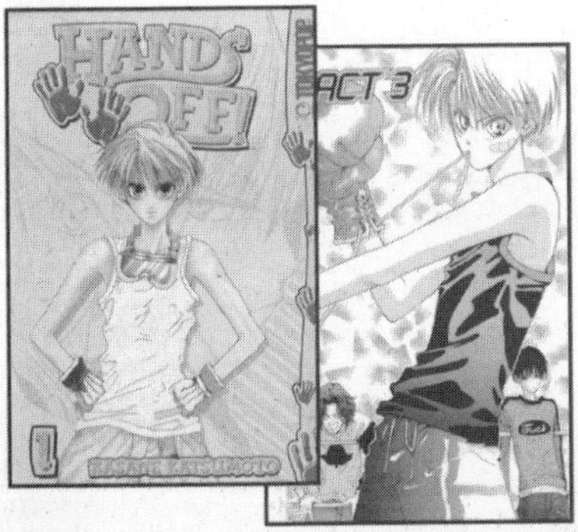
ACT 3

BY KASANE KATSUMOTO

HANDS OFF!

Cute boys with ESP who share a special bond... If you think this is familiar (e.g. *Legal Drug*), well, you're wrong. *Hands Off!* totally stands alone as a unique and thoroughly enjoyable series. Kotarou and Tatsuki's (platonic!) relationship is complex, fascinating and heart-wrenching. Throw in Yuuto, the playboy who can read auras, and you've got a fantastic setup for drama and comedy, with incredible themes of friendship running throughout. Don't be put off by Kotarou's danger-magnet status, either. The episodic stuff gradually changes, and the full arc of the characters' development is well worth waiting for.

~Lillian Diaz-Przybyl, Jr. Editor

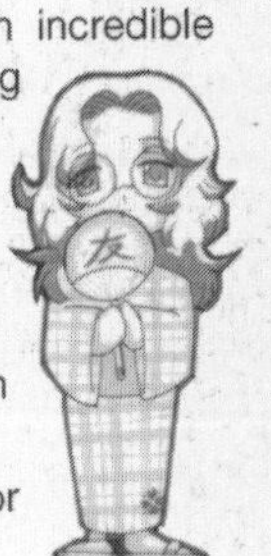

EDITORS' PICKS

TOKYOPOP MANGA SUPPLEMENT

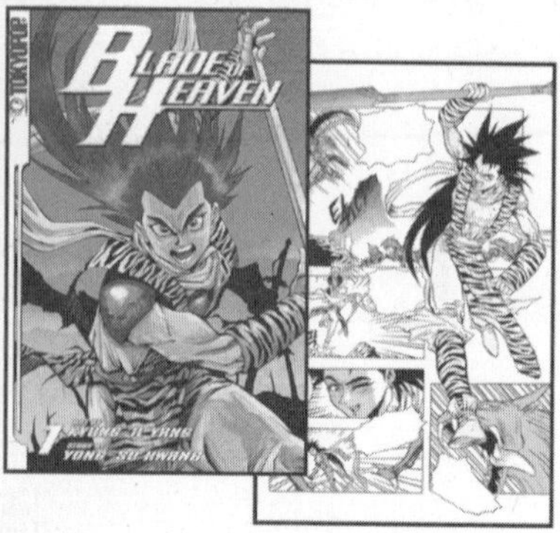

BY YONG-SU HWANG
AND KYUNG-IL YANG

BLADE OF HEAVEN

Wildly popular in its homeland of Korea, *Blade of Heaven* enjoys the rare distinction of not only being a hit in its own country, but in Japan and several other countries, as well. On the surface, Yong-Su Hwang and Kyung-Il Yang's fantasy-adventure may look like yet another "Heaven vs. Demons" sword opera, but the story of the mischievous Soma, a pawn caught in a struggle of mythic proportions, is filled with so much humor, pathos, imagination—and yes, action, that it's easy to see why *Blade of Heaven* has been so popular worldwide.

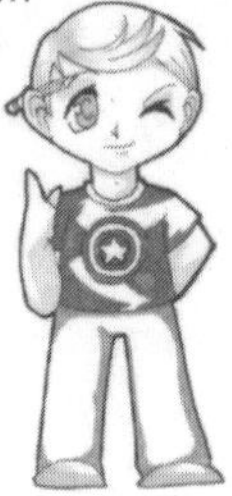

~Bryce P. Coleman, Editor

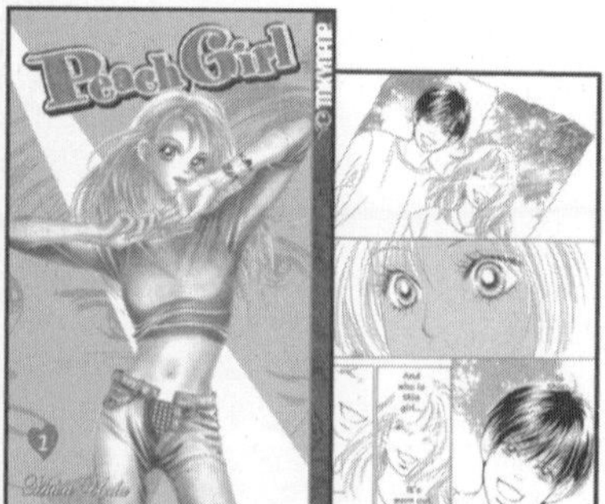
Peach Girl

BY MIWA UEDA

PEACH GIRL

Am I the only person who thinks that *Peach Girl* is just like *The O.C.*? Just imagine Ryan as Toji, Seth as Kiley, Marissa as Momo and Summer as Sae. (The similarities are almost spooky!) Plus, Seth is way into comics and manga—and I'm sure he'd love *Peach Girl*. It has everything that my favorite TV show has and then some—drama, intrigue, romance and lots of will-they-or-won't-they suspense. I love it! *Peach Girl* rules, seriously. If you haven't read it, do so. Now.

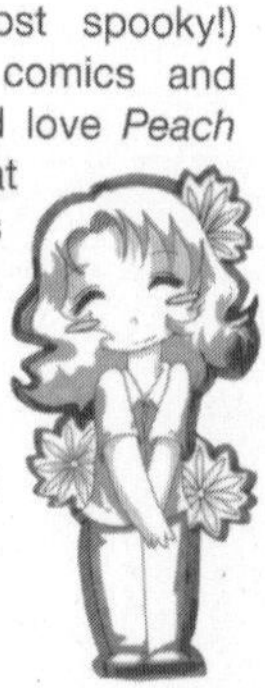

~Julie Taylor, Sr. Editor